Post-editing of Machine Translation

Post-editing of Machine Translation: Processes and Applications

Edited by

Sharon O'Brien, Laura Winther Balling,
Michael Carl, Michel Simard and Lucia Specia

CAMBRIDGE
SCHOLARS

PUBLISHING

Post-editing of Machine Translation: Processes and Applications,
Edited by Sharon O'Brien, Laura Winther Balling, Michael Carl,
Michel Simard and Lucia Specia

This book first published 2014

Cambridge Scholars Publishing

12 Back Chapman Street, Newcastle upon Tyne, NE6 2XX, UK

British Library Cataloguing in Publication Data
A catalogue record for this book is available from the British Library

ISBN (10): 1-4438-5476-X, ISBN (13): 978-1-4438-5476-4

TABLE OF CONTENTS

FOREWORD

Post-editing is possibly the oldest form of human-machine cooperation for translation, having been a common practice for just about as long as operational machine translation systems have existed. Recently however, there has been a surge of interest in post-editing among the wider user community, partly due to the increasing quality of machine translation output, but also to the availability of free, high-quality software for both machine translation and post-editing.

Technology and the challenges of integrating post-editing software and processes into a traditional translation workflow are at the core of research in post-editing. However, this topic involves many other important factors, such as studies on productivity gains, cognitive effort, pricing models, training and quality. This volume aims at covering many of these aspects by bringing together accounts from researchers, developers and practitioners on the topic. These are a compilation of invited chapters from work presented at two recent events on post-editing:

1. The first Workshop on Post-editing Technology and Practice (WPTP), organised by Sharon O'Brien (DCU/CNGL), Michel Simard (CNRC) and Lucia Specia (University of Sheffield) and held in conjunction with the AMTA Conference in San Diego, October 28, 2012; and
2. The International Workshop on Expertise in Translation and Post-editing Research and Application (ETP), organised by Michael Carl, Laura Winther Balling and Arnt Lykke Jakobsen from the Center for Research and Innovation in Translation and Translation Technology and held at the Copenhagen Business School, August 17-18, 2012.

The goals of the two workshops were different, and so was their format. ETP[1] had two related purposes: The first was to explore the process of post-editing machine translation compared with from-scratch translation, and the role of expertise in both processes. The second was to discuss to what extent knowledge of the processes involved in human translation and post-editing might shape advanced machine translation and computer-assisted translation technologies. It invited short summaries to be submitted, with oral presentation slots given to all participants with accepted summaries.

WPTP[2], on the other hand, issued an open call for papers to be published in the workshop proceedings and presented either orally or as posters, and offered slots for post-editing software demonstrations. It focused on research assessing the weaknesses and strengths of existing technology to measure post-editing effectiveness, establish better practices, and propose tools and technological PE solutions that are built around the real needs of users. Despite the wide range of topics in both workshops, most of the actual work submitted and presented at ETP concentrated on studies of the post-editing process, while work at the WPTP workshop focused on technology for post-editing and their impact on productivity.

This volume aims at bringing these two perspectives together in one book. It compiles contributions of 28 authors into 13 chapters, which are structured in three parts: (I) macrolevel processes, (II) microlevel processes and (III) guidelines and evaluation. We hope that this compilation will contribute to the discussion of the various aspects involving post-editing processes and applications and lead to a better understanding of its technological and cognitive challenges. Finally, we would like to thank all authors and reviewers for their committed work

The editors

Notes

[1] http://bridge.cbs.dk/platform/?q=ETP2012

[2] https://sites.google.com/site/wptp2012/

INTRODUCTION

MIKE DILLINGER

These are very exciting times for translation research

As global communication and commerce increase, the importance and scale of translation have skyrocketed. As technology becomes more complex and competition leads to accelerating innovation, exponentially more content has to be translated not only much more quickly but also much more cheaply than ever before. Consequently, it has become crucial to understand how to make the translation process as quick, accurate, and effective as possible – both with and without software tools. In this context, the role of machine translation and post-editing MT output have taken on new importance.

In an equally significant shift, translation researchers have shifted away from studies of conceptual and pedagogical issues to a new focus on systematic empirical data about real-world translation tasks – data about industrial and cognitive translation *processes*. As a result, there are more researchers, more numerous and more sophisticated tools for research, and more and more detailed data than were available only ten years ago.

Where is translation research going?

Translation research is quickly moving toward building detailed process models. These are step-by-step descriptions of exactly what happens in individual translators as they translate source texts or post-edit source text/draft translation pairs. For each step, we will soon be able to identify the text, task, and translator characteristics that have the biggest impact on performance. As we generalise across translators and texts, we can identify optimal practices – based on reliable data rather than only on intuition – that will have a significant impact on the translation industry.

What would a processing model of post-editing look like?

It would start with a framework of steps that make up text comprehension in L1 and L2. We know already that monolingual text comprehension plays a key role in post-editing. Fortunately, both theory and research in this field are very rich and detailed. However, post-editing raises new questions for research. For example, do the post-editor's comprehension strategies change when reading about an unfamiliar topic specifically for post-editing or for translation? Do the specific characteristics of MT output change reading strategies or performance significantly? Do post-editors need more or different topic or linguistic knowledge than readers do? Recall that one common use case for post-editing MT deals with technical information that most translators are not very familiar with. Comprehension clearly varies based on source-text characteristics, as well as on the post-editor's language skills and topic knowledge. Future studies will measure post-editors' comprehension in L1 and L2 more directly and explore which source-text characteristics affect which steps of the post-editing process.

Another step (and a defining core competence) of post-editing and translation is the ability to judge the equivalence of two sentences in different languages after they have been understood. However, there is limited research even in how monolinguals detect similarities and differences across sentences in the same language (the vast research into how people perceive similarities and differences of *words* seems not to have continued with sentences). Which sentence characteristics or typological differences make it easier or harder to judge equivalence across languages? Do post-editors pay more (or less) attention to some sentence characteristics than do translators? Post-editors also have to switch often between L1 reading and L2 reading – does this switch slow them down or affect accuracy? The research literature on monolingual revising is definitely a good place to start, at the very least as a detailed process model to start from. Judging equivalence across languages seems to be a new area of study and may become a defining area of translation research.

In yet another step, post-editors have to produce sentences and texts – or edit existing options. Again, there is a rich existing research literature on sentence production – not as well developed as the comprehension literature, but it focuses on normal, monolingual writing tasks that usually start from conceptual plans rather than from other texts. Are the production processes during post-editing (or during translation) different from normal, monolingual writing-from-ideas? *How* are they different? Do the post-editors' *writing* skills in L1 and L2 affect how (and how well) this happens? Is post-editing easier or harder than monolingual revising, and why? Are some kinds of edits easier or harder than others, and why?

One likely possibility is that both text comprehension and text production will be very similar in monolingual tasks and in bilingual tasks such as post-editing and translation. The key novelty – and crucial difference – for bilingual tasks, then, may turn out to be the ability to compare sentences (and texts) across languages, in terms of both literal meaning and the culturally determined patterns of inference and connotation that different phrasings will entail. Moving forward, translation researchers will check these possibilities much more carefully then identify and focus on the abilities that make post-editing and translation so special.

This discussion shows that there are many factors to consider each time we study post-editing. Too many factors, in fact. Methodologically, we have three basic ways to deal with the factors that we know about: *ignore* the influence of these factors, *control* the effects of these factors, or *focus* on their influence. Standard experimental practice is to focus on a couple of factors, control the effects of as many known factors as practically possible, and ignore the rest – then change them in subsequent studies. To provide more detailed results, future studies will control more and more relevant factors.

Where is the field now?

The present volume shows that the study of translation processes is full of promise – there is much more to come. There is a clear emphasis in these chapters on developing and testing the wide range of methods, tools, and datasets that we need to start building the kinds of process models sketched above. There are great examples of how to apply sophisticated statistical methods to post-editing data, such as principal components analysis and multiple regression. There are exciting new tools for collecting (and integrating) data about keystrokes, eye movements, and pauses as post-editors work in real time. There are reports on growing and increasingly detailed datasets that have been built with these tools (and with others) – and that can be analysed in very many different ways.

Note that the studies in this volume are all very difficult to do because they require skills and detailed understanding of concepts from multiple disciplines: translation, linguistics, cognitive psychology, applied statistics, process engineering, management, software engineering, computational linguistics, and many others. Since there are very, very few researchers today with all of this background, interdisciplinary collaboration is essential. For the reader, this means that each chapter will have a surprising and different mix of interdisciplinary perspectives, methods, and data.

Unavoidably, in beginning stages of interdisciplinary research, there are methodological errors. Don't let them distract you from the fact that the questions that these studies pose and the tools and datasets that they have succeeded in building constitute significant progress and a sign of more progress to come – even in the cases where the analyses are weak and the conclusions are not so reliable. This is normal for new areas of research – it simply reinforces the need and opportunity for intense interdisciplinary collaboration.

The contributions to this volume seem to fall naturally into three parts: (I) studies of macro-level translation processes, (II) studies of micro-level translation processes and (III) theoretical studies.

Studies of macro-level translation processes

These studies focus on the industrial translation process from receiving the client's source text to delivering the client's target text. In these studies, the individual translator plays a crucial role but is not the focus of research. Instead, the chapters seek to establish reliable baselines for the whole translation process, with and without the introduction of specific tools, training, management techniques, etc. They generally focus on overall, after-the-fact measures such as productivity or speed. The time frame for these processes is days or weeks.

1. **Zhechev** describes in detail how productivity in very mature post-editing processes varies across language pairs and across source documents for different products.
2. **Silva** insightfully describes how rolling out new post-editing processes can affect a translation company as a whole and provides valuable lessons learned.
3. **Guerberof** focuses on how different translator characteristics may affect overall productivity.

Studies of micro-level translation processes

These studies focus on the individual translator's behaviours, preferences, and cognitive processes – often monitoring the translator in near-real time by measuring eye movements, keystrokes, pauses, etc. as the translator is working. These chapters seek to establish reliable information about how and how much a wide range of factors affects the individual translator during the translation task itself. The time frame for these processes is milliseconds or seconds.

4. **Depraetere, De Sutter & Tezcan** measure post-editing effort as the similarity between MT output and the final post-edited translation and find that (i) MT enhances the translator's productivity, even if translators are in the initial stages of their careers, (ii) MT does not have a negative impact on the quality of the final translation, and (iii) post-editing distance is more stable across informants than are human evaluation scores, so distance is a potentially more objective measure.
5. **Teixeira** explores the hypothesis that translation metadata might be useful for translators. While too many translation options would be a time drain in hectic localisation projects, the GUI should account for personalisation/customisation, so that it can be adapted to different work styles.
6. **Moran, Lewis & Saam** describe an exciting new tool (iOmegaT) for collecting detailed online data in an ecologically valid translation environment – and some preliminary data gathered with it. They enhanced an open-source translation environment – that is very similar to the industry-standard Trados environment – with a range of logging and reporting functions. Their detailed measurements suggest that post-editing is about twice as fast as translating from scratch (across several languages, with similar content) and they alert us to the fact that translators often go back and review their translations so measures of first-pass translation speed may be misleading.
7. **Elming, Winther Balling & Carl** describe the CASMACAT workbench in detail and show how useful expertly done regression analysis can be with a first dataset that they collected. They showed that post-editing keystroke ratio is a better predictor of post-editing time divided by translation time than edit distance is.
8. **Aziz, Koponen, & Specia** show very clearly how detailed attention to source-text characteristics, sub-sentence post-editing time, and a fruitful mix of qualitative and quantitative analysis lead to insightful and precise results. This is an interesting example of one effective way to use the Principal Components Analysis. Careful readers will notice that they generalised about different kinds of post-editing units because there was not enough data to generalise about translator similarities or differences.

9. **Čulo, Guermuth, Hasen-Schirra & Nitzke** give interesting examples of qualitative differences in strategies that are used to edit, post-edit, and translate the same texts, extracted from a new multilingual dataset built using the CASMACAT workbench. Their key idea is to compare post-editing with both monolingual revising and with translation, so we can be sure that further generalisations from their analyses will provide unique insights about how these processes compare.
10. **Mesa-Lao** correlated source-text complexity with an interesting range of on-line measures during both translation and post-editing tasks. His attention to the details of the source texts means that as more of this kind of data becomes available, it will be possible to make more detailed generalisations about the effects of the source text.
11. **Lacruz & Shreve** focus on patterns of pausing during post-editing, extending early studies of selective attention during shadowing and interpreting done by Anne Treisman in the 1970s. Their finding that more cognitive effort seems to be associated with fewer pauses raises interesting questions when compared to earlier research that concluded the opposite.

Theoretical studies

These studies step back from detailed data to identify the concepts that we need to understand in more detail.

12. **Melby, Fields & Housely** provide detailed specifications for describing post-editing tasks by specifying all of the relevant parameters of this kind of translation job, including different notions of translation quality. They make the very important point that studies of translation processes will lead to inconsistent results if researchers do not define and measure the quality of the output translation in explicit and similar ways.
13. **Rico & Ariano** define detailed and insightful guidelines for post-editing based on their experience rolling out new post-editing processes at a company.

These three types of studies are all equally necessary for the progress of the field. Studying macro-level translation processes provides context, relevance, and crucial practical motivation for the other two types of studies. Without the link to economic consequences that these macro-level studies contribute, the other studies run the risk of becoming academic exercises that are ignored in practice. Studying micro-level translation processes adds support and more detailed understanding to macro-level studies and suggests directions for specific improvements in practice. These micro-level studies explain just why (and in more detail), for example, some tools or procedures work better than others do in a macro-level setting. In addition, theoretical studies keep everyone honest by checking key concepts in detail and integrating results to check for consistency – so that everyone's results are more reliable.

Mike Dillinger
California, USA
June, 2013

Part I:

Macro-level Translation Processes

CHAPTER ONE

ANALYSING THE POST-EDITING OF MACHINE TRANSLATION AT AUTODESK

VENTSISLAV ZHECHEV

Abstract

In this chapter, we provide a quick overview of the machine translation (MT) infrastructure at Autodesk, a company with a very broad range of software products with worldwide distribution. MT is used to facilitate the localisation of software documentation and UI strings from English into thirteen languages. We present a detailed analysis of the post-edited data generated during regular localisation production. Relying on our own edit-distance-based JFS metric (Joint Fuzzy Score), we show that our MT systems perform consistently across the bulk of the data that we localise and that there is an inherent order of language difficulty for translating from English. The languages in the Romance group typically have JFS scores in the 60–80% range, the languages in the Slavic group and German typically have JFS scores in the 50–70% range and Asian languages exhibit scores in the 45–65% range, with some outlying language/product combinations.

Introduction

Autodesk is a company with a very broad range of software products that are distributed worldwide. The high-quality localisation of these products is a major part of our commitment to a great user experience for all our clients. The translation of software documentation and user interface (UI) strings plays a central role in our localisation process and we need to provide a fast turnaround of very large volumes of data. To accomplish this, we use an array of tools—from document- and localisation-management systems to machine translation (MT).

In this chapter, we focus on the detailed analysis of the post-editing of MT during the localisation process. After a quick look at our MT infrastructure, we focus on the productivity test we organised to evaluate the potential benefit of our MT engines to translators. We then turn to the analysis of our current production post-editing data.

MT Infrastructure at Autodesk

In this section, we briefly present the MT infrastructure that we have built to support the localisation effort at Autodesk. For an in-depth discussion, see Zhechev (2012).

We actively employ MT as a productivity tool and we are constantly improving our toolkit to widen our language coverage and achieve higher quality. At the core of this toolkit are the tools developed and distributed with the open-source Moses project (Koehn et al. 2007). Currently, we use MT for translating from US English into twelve languages: Czech, German, Spanish, French, Italian, Japanese, Korean, Polish, Brazilian Portuguese, Russian, Simplified and Traditional Chinese (hereafter, we will use standard short language codes). We recently introduced MT for translating into Hungarian in a pilot project.

Training Data

Of course, no statistical MT training is possible unless a sufficient amount of high-quality parallel data is available. In our case, we create the parallel corpora for training by aggregating data from four internal sources. The smallest sources by far consist of translation memories (TMs) used for the localisation of marketing materials and educational materials. The next source is our repositories for translated User Interface (UI) strings. This data contains many short sentences and partial phrases, as well as some strings that contain UI variables and/or UI-specific formatting. The biggest source of parallel data is our main TMs used for the localisation of the software documentation for all our products.

To ensure broader lexical coverage, as well as to reduce the administrative load, we do not divide the parallel data according to product or domain. Instead, we combine all available data for each language and use them as one single corpus per language. The sizes of the corpora are shown on Figure 1-1, with the average number of tokens in the English source being approximately 13.

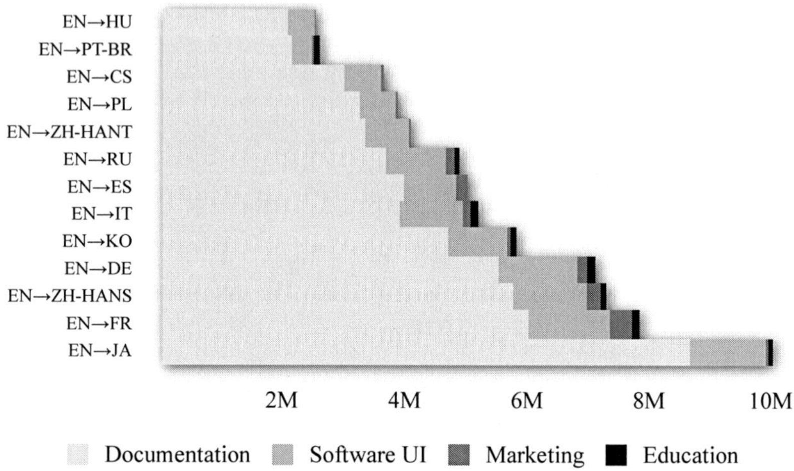

Figure 1-1: Training Corpora Sizes in Millions of Segments

As Figure 1-1 shows, we have the least amount of data for PT-BR and HU, while our biggest corpus by far is for JA. The reader can refer to this chart when we discuss the evaluation of MT performance—it turns out that the difficulty of translating into a particular language from English is a stronger factor there than training data volume.

After we have gathered all available data from the different sources, we are ready to train our MT systems. For this, we have created a dedicated script that handles the complete training workflow. In effect, we simply need to point the script to the corpus for a particular language and—after a certain amount of time—we get a ready-to-deploy MT system. Further information on the training infrastructure can be found in Zhechev (2012).

MT Info Service

We now turn to the MT Info Service that is the centrepiece of our MT infrastructure, handling all MT requests from within Autodesk. This service and all its components are entirely based on the Perl programming language and handle service requests over internal and external network connections over TCP (Transmission Control Protocol).

The first elements of this infrastructure are the MT servers that provide the interface to the available MT engines running in a data centre. At launch time, the server code initiates the Moses translation process. The MT servers receive translation requests for individual segments of text (typically sentences) and output translations as soon as they are available. For each language that we use in production, we currently have up to seven MT engines running simultaneously on different servers to provide higher overall throughput.

The MT Info Service itself acts as a central dispatcher and hides the details of the MT servers' setup, number and location from the clients. It is the single entry point for all MT-related queries, be it requests for translation, for information on the server setup or administrative functions. It has real-time data on the availability of MT servers for all supported languages and performs load balancing for all incoming translation requests to best utilise the available resources. In real-life production, we often see twenty or more concurrent requests for translation that need to be handled by the system—some of them for translation into the same language. We have devised a simple and easy-to-use API that clients can use for communication with the MT Info Service.

Over the course of a year, the MT Info Service may receive over 180,000 translation requests that are split into more than 700,000 jobs for load balancing. These requests include over one million documentation segments and a large volume of UI strings.

Integrating MT in the Localisation Workflow

Once we have our MT infrastructure in place and we have trained all MT engines, we need to make this service available within our localisation workflow so that raw data is machine translated and the output reaches the translators in due course. We use two main localisation tools—SDL Passolo for UI content and SDL WorldServer for localisation of documentation.

Unfortunately, the current version of Passolo that we use does not provide good integration with MT and requires a number of manual steps. First, the data needs to be exported into "Passolo bundles". These are then processed with in-house Python scripts that send any data that has not been matched against previous translations to the MT info service. The processed bundles are then passed on to the translators for post-editing. Due to limitations of Passolo, the MT output is not visibly marked as such and Passolo has no way to distinguish it from human-produced data. We expect this to be addressed in an upcoming version of the tool.

It is much easier to integrate MT within WorldServer. As this is a Java-based tool, it allows us to build Java-based plugins that provide additional functionality. In particular, we have developed an MT adapter for WorldServer that communicates directly with the MT Info Service over

TCP and sends all appropriate segments for machine translation. The MT output is then clearly marked for the convenience of the translators both in the on-line workbench provided by WorldServer and in the files used to transfer data from WorldServer to standalone desktop CAT tools.

WorldServer presents us with its own specific issues to handle, for a discussion of which we would like to refer the reader to Zhechev (2012).

Product-Specific Terminology Processing

To support the spectrum of domains represented by our broad product portfolio, we needed an effective system that would select product-appropriate terminology during machine translation, as terminology lookup is one of the most time consuming and cognitively intense tasks translators have to deal with. This is particularly true for the data typically found in our software manuals—rich in industry-specific terminology from architecture, civil engineering, manufacturing and other domains.

One solution to this problem would be to create product and/or domain specific MT engines that should produce domain-specific output. Unfortunately, as can be seen in Figure 1-14 below, most of the localisation volume is concentrated in a few flagship products, while the rest of the products have fairly low amounts of data. Trying to train MT engines only on product-specific data is thus destined to fail, as out of the approximately 45 products that we currently localise, only about five have sufficient amounts of TM data for training an operational MT engine.

We could, of course, always train on the whole set of data for each language and only perform tuning and/or language model domain adaptation for each specific product/domain group. However, this would result in as much as 585 different product specific engines (13 languages times 45 products) that need to be maintained, with each further language we decide to localise into adding another 45 engines. The engine maintenance would include regular retraining and deployment, as well as the necessary processing power to have that number of engines (plus enough copies for load-balancing) available around the clock—the latter being particularly important as the software industry moves to agile continuous development of software products, rather than yearly (or similar) release cycles.

Our solution allows us to only train one MT engine per target language and use built-in Moses functionality to fix the product-specific terminology during a pre-processing step. As part of our regular localisation process, product-specific glossaries are manually created and maintained for use by human translators. When new data is sent to the MT Info Service for processing, the MT request includes the corresponding product name. This allows the selection of the proper product-specific glossary and annotating any terms found in the source data with XML tags providing the proper translations. Moses is then instructed to only use these translations when processing the data, thus ensuring that the MT output has the proper target-language terminology for the specified product.

One drawback of this approach is that the product glossaries only contain one translation per language per term, which is one particular morphological form. This means that for morphologically rich languages like Czech, the product-specific terminology will often carry the wrong morphological form. However, we estimate that the time needed to fix the morphology of a term is significantly less than the time needed to consult the glossaries in the appropriate tools to make sure the source terms are translated correctly.

Our approach also allows us to eschew the tuning step during MT training. Given our broad product portfolio, selecting a representative tuning set is particularly hard and necessarily biases the MT system towards some products at the cost of others. Considering these factors, as well as the level of performance of our non-tuned MT engines, we have decided to bypass the tuning step. We thus save computing time and resources, without losing too much in MT quality.

So far we had a look at the complex MT infrastructure at Autodesk. The question that arises is if there is any practical benefit to the use of MT for localisation and how to measure this potential benefit. We present our answer in the next sections.

Post-Editing Productivity Test

We now turn to the setup of our last productivity test and analyse the data that we collected. The main purpose of the productivity test was to measure the productivity increase (or decrease) when translators are presented with raw MT output for post-editing, rather than translating from scratch.

We are presenting here the results of the third productivity test that Autodesk has performed. The results of the first test in 2009 are discussed in Plitt and Masselot (2010). Each of the tests has had a specific practical goal in mind. With the first productivity test we simply needed a clear indicator that would help us decide whether to use MT in production or not and it only included DE, ES, FR and IT. The second test focused on a different set of languages, for which we planned to introduce MT into production, like RU and ZH-HANS.

The goal of the productivity test described in this chapter was mainly to confirm our findings from the previous tests, to help us pick among several MT options for some languages and compare MT performance across products. In the following discussion we will only concentrate on the overall outcome of the productivity test and on our analysis of the post-editing performance against automatic, edit-distance-based indicators.

Test Setup

The main challenge for the setup of the productivity test is the data preparation. It is obviously not possible for the same translator to first translate a text from scratch and then post-edit an MT version without any bias—the second time around the text will be too familiar and this will skew the productivity evaluation. Instead, we need to prepare data sets that are similar enough, but not exactly the same, while at the same time taking into account that the translators cannot translate as much text from scratch as they can post-edit—as our experience from previous productivity tests has shown. This is further exacerbated by the fact that we need to find data that has not been processed yet during the production cycle and has not yet been included in the training data for the MT engines.

Due to resource restrictions, we only tested nine out of the twelve production languages: DE, ES, FR, IT, JA, KO, PL, PT-BR and ZH-HANS. For each language, we enrolled four translators—one each from our usual localisation vendors—for two business days, i.e. sixteen working hours. We let our vendors select the translators as per their usual process.

We put together test sets with data from four different products, but most translators only managed to process meaningful amounts of data from two products, as they ran out of time due to various reasons (connectivity issues; picked the wrong data set; etc.). These included three tutorials for AutoCAD users and a user's manual for PhysX (a plug-in for 3ds Max). In all cases about one-third of the data was provided without MT translations—for translation from scratch—while the other two-thirds were presented for post-editing MT. The number of segments the individual translators processed differed significantly based on the productivity of the individual translators. The total number of post-edited MT segments per language is shown below in Figure 1-3.

The translators used a purpose-built online post-editing workbench that we developed in-house. While this workbench lacked a number of features common in traditional CAT tools (e.g. TM and terminology search), it allowed us to calculate the time the translators took to look at and translate/post-edit each individual segment. For future productivity tests we plan to move away from this tool and use, for example, a modified version of Pootle (translate.sourceforge.net) instead, as it is easier to manage and provides typical CAT functionality, or one of the many tools that have been released recently to address this type of testing.

Evaluating Productivity

After gathering the raw productivity data, we automatically removed any outlier segments, for which the translators took unreasonably long time to translate or post-edit. To calculate the average productivity increase resulting from the provision of MT output to translators for post-editing, we needed a baseline metric that would reflect the translator productivity when translating from scratch. Selecting this baseline was a complex task for a number of reasons. We could not have a direct measurement of productivity increase for each individual segment, as translators were not post-editing the same segments they had translated from scratch. Furthermore, the variability in productivity between the different translators for one language, as well as in the individual translator productivity for different products, precluded us from establishing a unified (language-specific) productivity baseline. Instead, we set up separate mean-productivity baselines for each translator-product combination (measured in words per eight-hour business day—WPD), also treating documentation and UI content for the same product as separate sets.

The post-editing productivity for each individual segment within each set was then compared to the corresponding baseline to establish the observed productivity increase (or decrease). The calculated average productivity increase per language is presented in Figure 1-2.

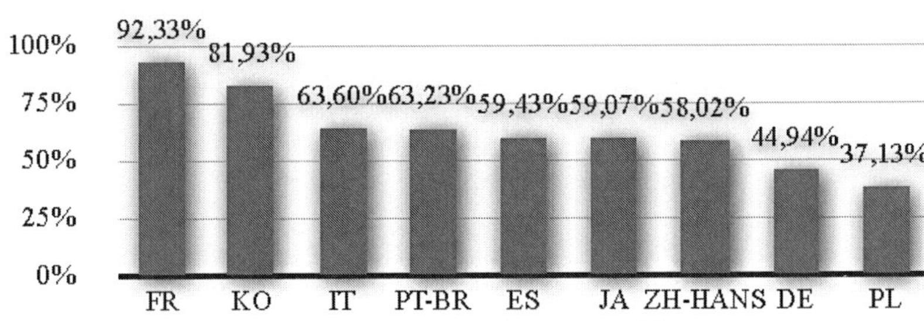

Figure 1-2: Average Productivity Increase when Post-Editing, per Language

A caveat is in order here. Due to the setup of our online workbench, we chose to exclude from the productivity calculation certain translator tasks that are independent of the quality of MT. This includes in particular the time that translators would usually spend looking up terminology and consulting the relevant style guides. The calculation also does not include any pauses taken for rest, coffee, etc.

Analysing the Post-editing Performance

Going deeper, we went on to analyse the post-edited data using a battery of metrics. The metric scores were computed on a per-segment basis so that we could look for a correlation between the amount of post-editing undertaken by the translators and their productivity increase. The goal of this endeavour was to single out a metric (or several metrics) that we could use for the analysis of our production data, where productivity measurements are not available. This would give us tools to quickly diagnose potential issues with our MT pipeline, as well as to rapidly test the viability of potential improvements or new developments without having to resort to full-blown productivity tests.

The metrics we used were the following: METEOR (Banerjee and Lavie 2005) treating punctuation as regular tokens, GTM (Turian, Shen, and Melamed 2003) with exponent set to three, TER (Snover et al. 2006), PER (Position-independent Error Rate—Tillmann et al. 1997) calculated as the inverse of the token-based F-measure, SCFS (Character-based Fuzzy Score, taking whitespace into account), and WFS (Word-based Fuzzy Score, on tokenised content). The Fuzzy Scores are calculated as the inverse of the Levenshtein edit distance (Levenshtein 1965) weighted by the token or character count of the longer segment. They produce similar, but not equal, results to the Fuzzy Match scores familiar from the standard CAT tools. All score calculations took character case into account. *SLength* denotes the number of tokens in the source string after tokenisation, while *TLength* denotes the number of tokens in the MT output after tokenisation.

After calculating the scores for all relevant segments, we obtained an extensive data set that we used to evaluate the correlation between the listed metrics and the measured productivity increase. The correlation calculation was performed for each language individually, as well as combining the data for all languages. We used Spearman's ρ (Spearman 1907) and Kendall's τ (Kendall 1938) as the correlation measures. The results are shown in Table 1-1.

	Productivity Increase	
	ρ	τ
JFS	0,609	0,439
SCFS	0,583	0,416
WFS	0,603	0,436
METEOR	0,541	0,386
GTM	0,577	0,406
TER	-0,594	-0,427
PER	-0,578	-0,415
SLength	-0,128	-0,087
TLength	-0,143	-0,097

Table 1-1: Correlation of Automatic Metrics to Translator Productivity Increase

We see that among the metrics listed above, WFS exhibits the highest correlation with the measured productivity increase, while METEOR shows the least correlation. The results also show that there is no significant correlation between the productivity increase and the length of the source or translation (cf. the *SLength* and *TLength* metrics). This suggests, for example, that a segment-length-based payment model for MT (e.g. adjusting the MT discount based on segment length) may not be a fair option. Also, we do not need to impose strong guidelines for segment length to the technical writers.

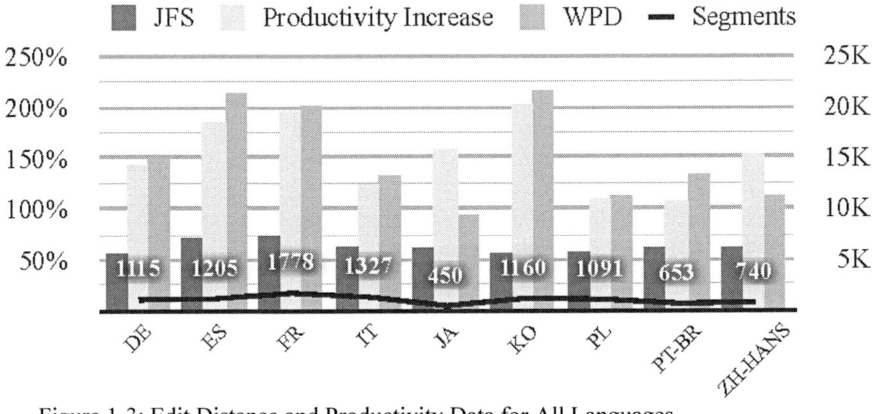

Figure 1-3: Edit Distance and Productivity Data for All Languages

Considering the results, we decided to look for a possibility to create a joint metric that might exhibit an even higher level of correlation. The best available combination turned out to be taking the minimum of SCFS and WFS, which we list in the table as JFS (Joint Fuzzy Score). We also tested using the maximum of SCFS and WFS, as well as other combinations of metrics and different types of means (arithmetic, geometric, etc.). The JFS metric has also an intuitive meaning in that it represents the worst-case editing scenario based on the character and token levels. All other metric combinations we evaluated resulted in lower correlation than WFS. Figure 1-3 presents the JFS scores per language and the corresponding average productivity increase and post-editing speed. It also lists the total number of segments that were post-edited for each language.

In Figures 1-.4–1-11, we investigate the distribution of the JFS scores for the different languages tested. The per-segment data is distributed into categories based on the percentile rank. Due to their particular makeup, we separate the segments that received a score of 0% (worst translations) and those that received a score of 100% (perfect translations) from the rest. For each rank, we show the maximum observed JFS (on the right scale). This gives us the maximum JFS up to which the observed average productivity increase is marked by the lower line on the chart (on the left scale). For all languages, we can observe a sharp rise in the productivity increase for the perfect translations, while otherwise the productivity increase grows mostly monotonically.

Additionally, for each percentile rank, the left bar on the graph shows the percentage of the total number of tokens, while the right bar shows the percentage of the total number of segments.

We do not include a chart for KO, as it does not appear to follow the monotonicity trend and, indeed, our evaluation of the KO data on its own showed a ρ coefficient of only 0,361 for JFS. We suspect that this is due to one of the KO translators ignoring the MT suggestions and translating everything from scratch. Because of this peculiarity of the KO data, we excluded it when calculating the overall results shown in Table 1-1. This also suggests that the productivity increase for KO shown in Figure 1-2 might not be realistic.

It can be argued that we should nonetheless include the KO data in our evaluation, as it represents the real-life scenario of translators being averse to the use of MT. The current trend, however, is for a rise in the level of acceptance of MT, so we expect a decrease in the translator proclivity for ignoring the provided MT output and translating from scratch. Our goal in this test was to discover and analyse the operating parameters of our infrastructure for the case where the MT output is indeed used by the translators.

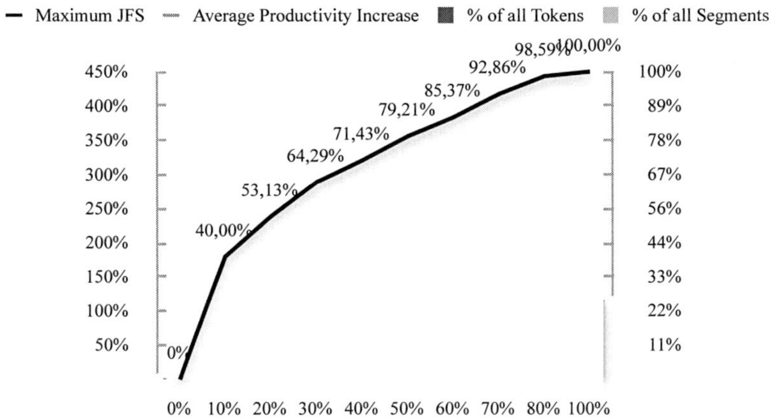

Figure 1-4: JFS to Productivity Correlation FR

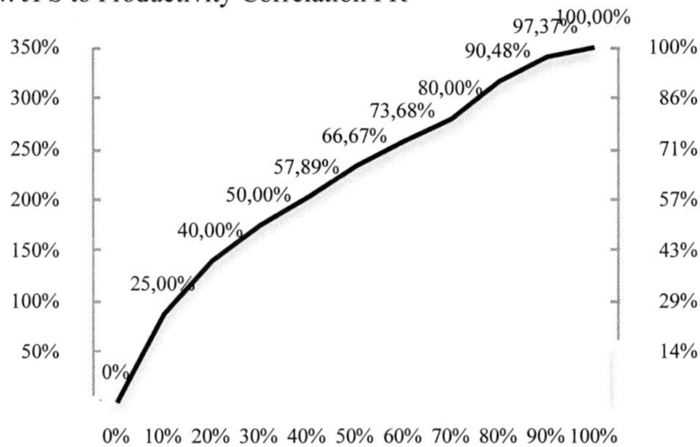

Figure 1-5: JFS to Productivity Correlation IT

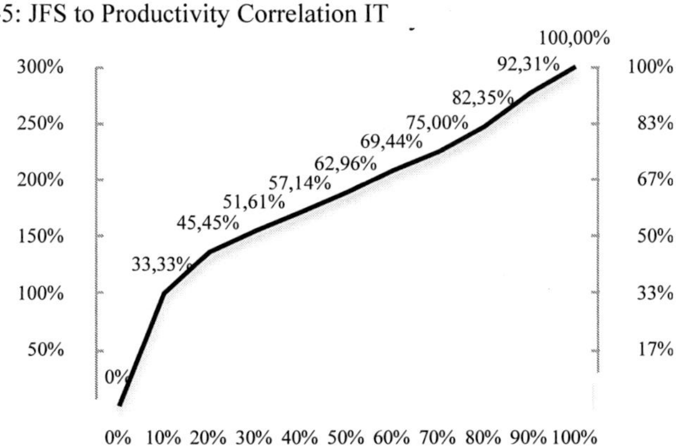

Figure 1-6: JFS to Productivity Correlation PT-BR

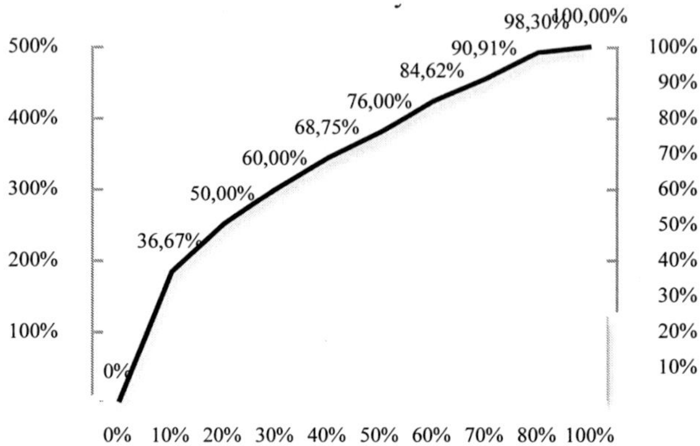

Figure 1-7: JFS to Productivity Correlation ES

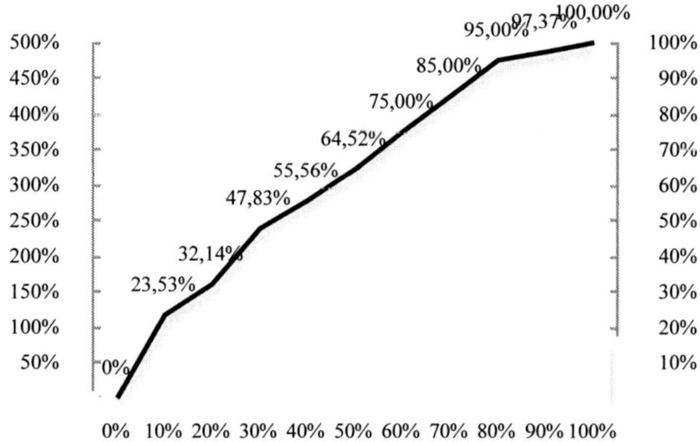

Figure 1-8: JFS to Productivity Correlation JA

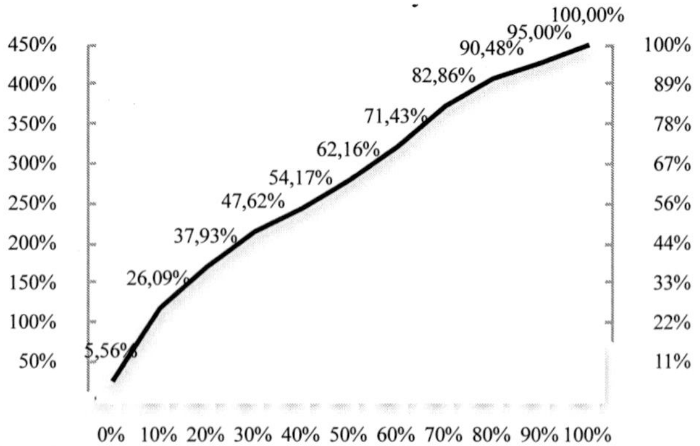

Figure 1-9: JFS to Productivity Correlation ZH-HANS

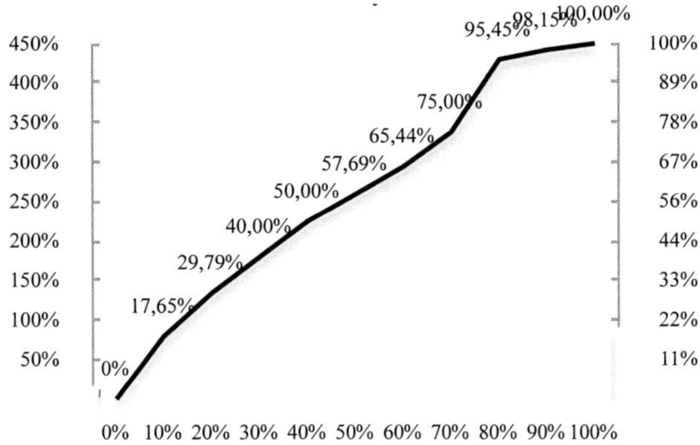

Figure 1-10: JFS to Productivity Correlation DE

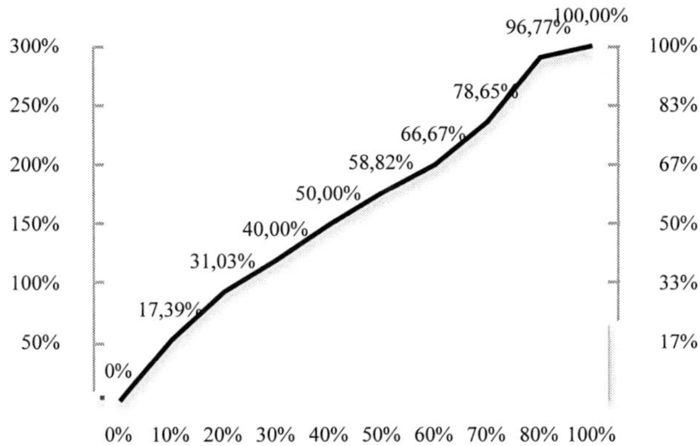

Figure 1-11: JFS to Productivity Correlation PL

A common observation for all languages is that both the worst and the perfect translations are predominantly short segments (relatively large percentage of segments versus relatively low percentage of tokens), which is as expected. First, it is much easier to achieve a perfect translation for a relatively short segment—especially given that JFS takes whitespace into account and our detokeniser is not perfect. Second, a complete rewrite of the MT suggestion usually results from an out-of-context translation of very short segments.

We also see that the JFS scores for the languages with the highest productivity increase (see Figure 1-2) are predominantly in the higher ranges, while for DE and PL there is a larger amount of segments with lower JFS.

In the next section, we try to apply the same evaluation methods to real-life post-editing data.

Evaluating Production Performance

At Autodesk we keep an extended archive of all documentation segments that are post-edited in production and plan to extend this to software segments in the future. For each segment, we store at least the EN source, the TM and MT target and the final target produced by the translators, as well as the original Fuzzy Match score from our TMs and the score Moses produces during decoding.

Of course, we do not have productivity data attached to the production segments, as our production environment does not provide for the aggregation of such data. Nonetheless, this is a wealth of post-editing data that we can analyse using the automatic metrics discussed above.

The first interesting piece of information is the proportion of worst and perfect MT translations, based on the post-editing performed. It is taken as the number of tokens in the worst/perfect translations versus all tokens for each language. Recall that only documentation segments that receive a fuzzy match score below 75% against our TMs are sent to MT. This statistic is presented in Figure 1-12.

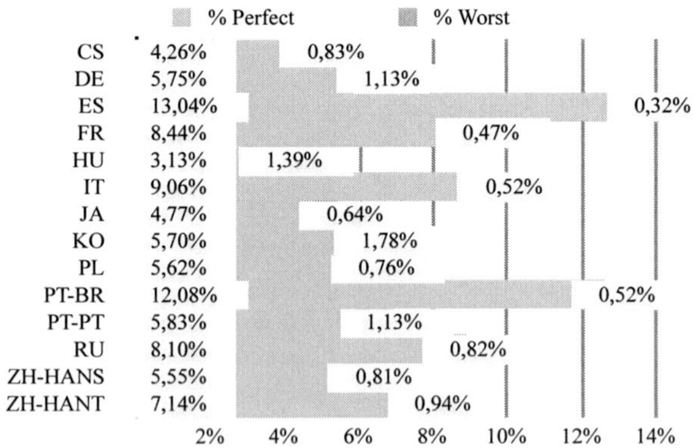

Figure 1-12: Proportion of Worst and Perfect MT

Here a perfect translation is one where the translator accepted the MT output without making any corrections. A worst translation, conversely, is one where the translator changed at least one character in each token of the MT output, which would result in a JFS score of 0%.

The most important takeaway from this figure is that the proportion of worst translations is negligibly low. On the other hand, there are many perfect translations, despite the disadvantage of MT applying to only those source segments that were not found in the TMs the MT engines were originally trained on. (That is, the segments we apply MT on obtain at most a similarity score of 75% when leveraged against the TMs.)

In Figure 1-13, we investigate the performance of our MT engines for different segment lengths, by using the mean JFS across all segments with a particular length, as well as the observed variance in JFS for each particular length. What we can see on the example of CS and ES (the trends are similar for all other languages) is that MT performance is unstable for segments of up to five tokens, exhibiting high variance in JFS. On the other hand, our data does not contain enough segments with length above about 35 tokens for reliable evaluation results. At the same time, the MT performance (based on JFS evaluation) is relatively stable across the bulk of the data we process (accounted by number of processed tokens).

As a further analysis step, we can order the MT engines for the individual languages based on a specific metric per software product. The language order based on the derived JFS metric is presented in Figure 1-14 for the 18 products with the largest translation volume during the period of highest localisation activity at Autodesk.

Although this chart does not include data across all languages for all products, some trends are clearly visible. Namely, we find the Romance languages occupying the top portion of the chart with the best JFS, while Asian languages perform less well on average and are found mostly in the lower portion of the chart. The Slavic languages fill in the middle ranges, with DE performing at or below their level. These results present a much higher correlation of MT performance to the difficulty for MT to translate into a particular language from EN, rather than to the volume of available training data. This is also clearly seen in Figure 1-15.

Results for PT-PT and HU are reported only for one product category each and are not representative. As mentioned earlier, MT for HU is currently in pilot stage and not used consistently across products. As for PT-PT, we do not have a dedicated engine due to lack of sufficient data and requests for PT-PT translations are handled using our PT-BR engine. Nonetheless, the results are promising as they are in line with the overall performance for the product in question, Moldflow. As this product is a relatively recent acquisition by Autodesk, its documentation style still differs from the overall Autodesk style, leading to lower post-editing scores overall.

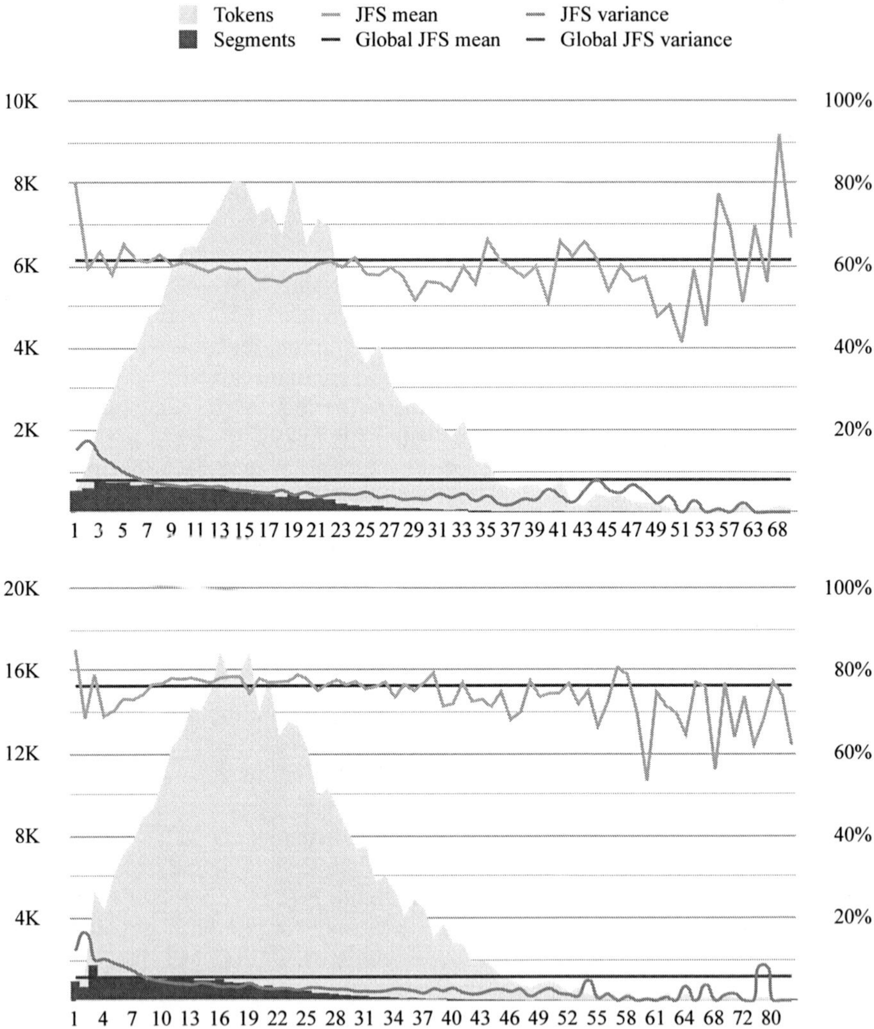

Figure 1-13: JFS Performance per Segment Length for CS (above) and ES (below)

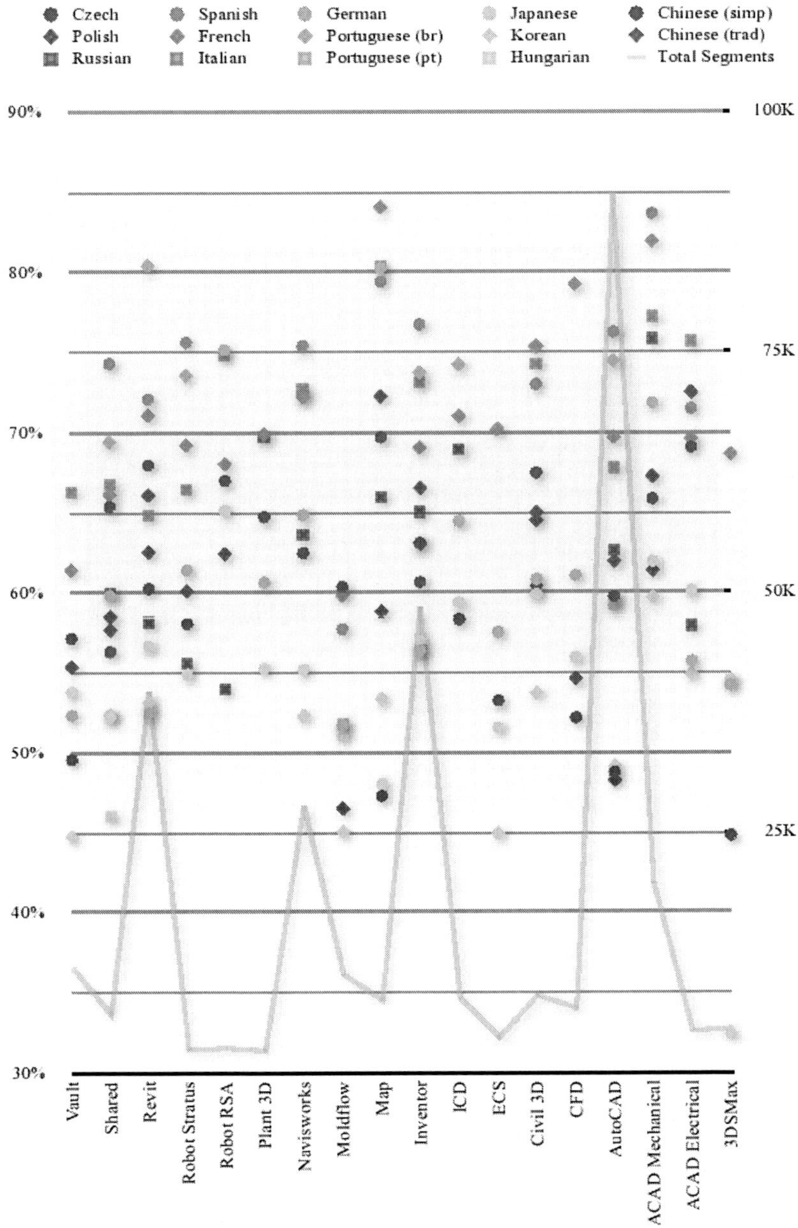

Figure 1-14: Language Order per Product according to JFS

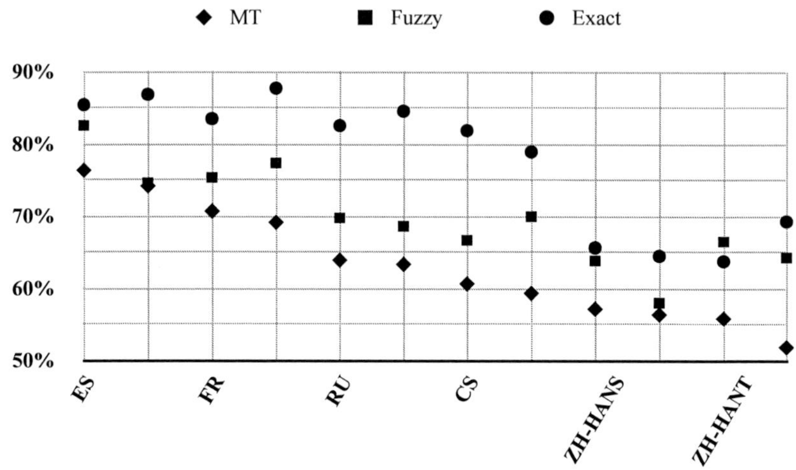

Figure 1-15: Average JFS per Language, by Fuzzy Match Type

Other products with lower-than-average post-editing scores are Vault, ECS and 3ds Max. While the source data for Vault is known to be particularly hard for MT with a specific style and longer-than-average segments, we need to investigate the performance for ECS and particularly 3ds Max. The evaluation results suggest that there might have been content-related issues specific to these two products that negatively affected MT performance.

We need to pay extra attention to the low scores observed for KO MT, even though we have not received any complaints from translators regarding the quality of MT for KO. Most importantly, the observed production results run contrary to the findings of our latest productivity test, which casts further doubt on the validity of the latter. One of the main goals of the productivity test at the time was to check whether the source-reordering scheme we use for JA (cf. Zhechev 2012) can be applied to EN–KO MT, the rationale being that KO and JA have similar surface syntax. The results from the productivity test were inconclusive and we decided not to use source-side reordering for EN–KO MT, as this would greatly simplify the MT training process. We are now revisiting this decision and plan to run new tests on production data to properly evaluate the usability of source-side reordering in this case.

Potentially, we could also develop a similar reordering system for EN-DE MT, as DE is known for its SOV syntax in subordinate clauses. So far, however, the MT quality for DE has been acceptable as is, albeit it tends towards the mid to low parts of Figure 1-14.

We have plans to integrate the type of analysis presented in this section in a dedicated monitoring system, where we will automatically point our teams to potential issues with the localisation process. This will be accomplished by looking for suspicious patterns in the evolution of the JFS metric—a larger number of over- or under-edited segments may often be related to either MT issues or translator under-performance.

For example, we are currently investigating the higher-than-average number of unedited PT-BR segments, given that there we have the smallest training corpus across all languages. We suspect that this could be due to translators erroneously leaving the raw MT output unedited. This suspicion is also supported by the presence of a very large number of unedited Fuzzy matches for PT-BR.

In addition to the findings detailed above, we can examine Figure 1-15, where we compare the MT performance for low fuzzy matches (below 75% fuzzy match score from the TM), for high fuzzy matches (for which the translators post-edited the TM suggestion and not MT) and exact matches. We see that MT performs uniformly better for high fuzzy matches compared to low fuzzy matches, as is to be expected, given that the MT engines are trained on the same data used for fuzzy matching. The gap between the two measures varies significantly across languages, which can to a large extent be explained by the different product mix processed for each language.

The JFS scores for MT output generated for exact matches can to some extent be used as an indicator of a potential quality upper bound for each language. Here, we see the Asian languages obtaining about 20% lower JFS scores compared to the rest of the languages we localise into—a further attestation to the high level of difficulty for automatically translating from English into an Asian language. German is also below average for a similar syntax-related reason, but with a far less noticeable gap.

Curiously, the average JFS for high fuzzy ZH-HANT matches is higher than for exact matches. This is a result that needs to be reviewed more closely, searching for potential issues with our localisation process for ZH-HANT.

Conclusion

In this chapter, we described the MT infrastructure at Autodesk that is used to facilitate the localisation of software documentation and UI strings from English into 13 languages. We saw how MT integrates in our localisation process and how we effectively handle product-specific terminology.

We then investigated the data collected during our last post-editing productivity test and found a strong correlation between the edit distance after post-editing and the productivity increase compared to translating from scratch, developing and further relying on our own JFS metric.

Finally, we presented a detailed analysis of the post-edited data generated during regular localisation production. We showed that our MT systems perform consistently across the bulk of the data that we localise and that there is an inherent order of language difficulty for translating from English. The languages in the Romance group typically have JFS scores in the 60–80% range, the languages in the Slavic group and German typically have JFS scores in the 50–70% range and Asian languages exhibit scores in the 45–65% range, with some outlying language/product combinations.

We plan to use the insights from the presented data analysis to continuously monitor the performance of our MT engines and to assist in the detection of potential issues in the MT process.

Bibliography

Banerjee, Santajeev, and Alon Lavie. 2005. "METEOR: An Automatic Metric for MT Evaluation with Improved Correlation with Human Judgements." *Proceedings of the Workshop on Intrinsic and Extrinsic Evaluation Measures for MT and/or Summarization at the 43rd Annual Meeting of the Association for Computational Linguistics (ACL '05)*, 65–72. Ann Arbor, MI.

Kendall, Maurice G. 1938. "A New Measure of Rank Correlation". *Biometrika* 30(1/2):81–93. doi: 10.1093/biomet/30.1-2.81.

Koehn, Philipp, Hieu Hoang, Alexandra Birch, Chris Callison-Burch, Marcello Federico, Nicola Bertoldi, Brooke Cowan, Wade Shen, Christine Moran, Richard Zens, Chris Dyer, Ondřej Bojar, Alexandra Constantin, and Evan Herbst 2007. "Moses: Open Source Toolkit for Statistical Machine Translation." *Proceedings of the Demo and Poster Sessions of the 45th Annual Meeting of the Association for Computational Linguistics (ACL '07)*, 177–180. Prague, Czech Republic.

Levenshtein, Vladimir. I. 1965. "Двоичные коды с исправлением выпадений, вставок и замещений символов (Binary Codes Capable of Correcting Deletions, Insertions, and Reversals)". *Доклады Академий Наук СССР* 163(4):845–848. [reprinted in: *Soviet Physics Doklady*, 10:707–710.].

Plitt, Mirko, and François Masselot. 2010. “A Productivity Test of Statistical Machine Translation Post-Editing in a Typical Localisation Context”. *The Prague Bulletin of Mathematical Linguistics* 93:7–16.

Snover, Matthew, Bonnie J. Dorr, Richard Schwartz, Linnea Micciulla, and John Makhoul. 2006. “A Study of Translation Edit Rate with Targeted Human Annotation.” *Proceedings of the 7th Conference of the Association for Machine Translation in the Americas (AMTA ’06)*, 223–231. Cambridge, MA.

Spearman, Charles 1907. "Demonstration of Formulæ for True Measurement of Correlation. *The American Journal of Psychology* 18(2):161–169. doi: 10.2307/1412408.

Tillmann, Christoff, Stephan Vogel, Hermann Ney, Alex Zubiaga, and Hasan Sawaf. 1997. “Accelerated DP-Based Search for Statistical Translation.” *Proceedings of the Fifth European Conference on Speech Comunication and Technology (Eurospeech ’97)*, 2667–2670. Rhodos, Greece.

Turian, Joseph P., Luke Shen, and I. Dan Melamed 2003. *Evaluation of Machine Translation and its Evaluation.* Computer Science Department, New York University.

Zhechev, Ventsislav 2012. “Machine Translation Infrastructure and Post-editing Performance at Autodesk.” *Proceedings of the AMTA 2012 Workshop on Post-editing Technology and Practice (WPTP ’12)*, edited by S. O’Brien, M. Simard and L. Specia. San Diego, CA.

CHAPTER TWO

INTEGRATING POST-EDITING MT IN A PROFESSIONAL TRANSLATION WORKFLOW[1]

ROBERTO SILVA

Abstract

This chapter provides an insight in the process of adopting MT and integrating post-editing MT into the workflow of a small sized Language Service Provider[2]. Its main intention is to show the difficulties, the strategies adopted and critical points and issues found along the way in a period that covers more than ten years. It gives an overview of some experiments only as examples. More importantly, it shows key points to improve the translation workflow. The findings show that although this is a complex and time consuming process, it can provide benefits for every player in the translation chain, from the end client to the professional translator, including the translation company.

Introduction

Machine translation (MT) has been around for quite a while, many decades in fact. MT is now available in many forms: as online service or as software, for various platforms and devices, and at many different prices. However, wide and standard adoption by the professional translation community appears to be still missing[3] and transfer from the research community to the language service provider (LSP) sector is not happening at the same speed as research advances. The challenges are numerous, be they technical (integration complexity, information security), managerial (implementation cost, definition and training of new roles and profiles), or ethical (pricing scheme). But more fundamentally, the benefits of post-editing MT are still not well understood by many of the involved parties, in particular translators. Yet, the professional translation industry is slowly adopting post-editing MT and integrating it into its workflows. Recent initiatives, research developments (Koehn et al. 2007) and findings (Koehn 2012), along with today's turbulent financial situation, have surely helped.

Why has MT not been widely adopted by the professional translation industry? There are many reasons and it is likely that opinions differ according to one's role in the process (whether you are a developer, researcher, LSP or end user), knowledge of translation technologies and position in a language company. There are many specialist forums in which extensive and passionate debates can be found around this question. Although MT acceptance has started to change recently (DePalma 2011), in particular within LSPs, many issues remain.

MT has been commercially available at different prices and for different target audiences for many years now. In appropriate domains, for some language combinations and source sentences, MT systems provide translations whose meaning is more or less understandable. However, with early MT ("rule-based") systems, adapting to a specific or new terminology (for instance, that required by a client of an LSP) was typically a long and tedious manual process. This reality, combined with difficulties in customizing the software, and the resulting perception that quality was low have been key factors in its low adoption by the professional translation community. The effort required to manually customize MT to specific needs or to solve issues detected during its use is beyond what most small to medium sized companies can afford. Specially trained personnel are required, and this is expensive. Although there have been recent initiatives (Wolf et al. 2013) aimed at circumventing this weakness, it certainly was an issue when the company tried to implement the technology.

Recent advances and the advent of so-called "statistical" systems have pushed MT into the forefront debate of the translation community, complementing most requirements not covered by earlier technologies. Recent research projects (Koehn 2007) have had a huge impact on all interested parties, and it now seems possible to consider MT as a useful addition in the translator's toolbox. In general, however, LSPs do not have the needed technical skills to implement and integrate MT into their workflow, and the process is expensive. Additionally, easy ways of measuring MT productivity improvements remain to be found, and there is no consensus regarding a pricing scheme post-editing that is fair for translators.

End clients are asking LSPs to lower their rates, and LSPs are turning to MT as a lifesaver, hoping it will allow them to lower their costs. But to what extent are translators involved in this process? How does MT and post-editing impact translation workflow? Is it possible to improve the overall post-editing experience? Answering these questions can help to improve translators' opinion about post-editing MT. LSPs efforts to push MT without taking into account feedback from translators, reviewers and other concerned language professionals are doomed to fail.

This chapter provides an insight into the process of adopting MT and integrating post-editing MT (PEMT) into the workflow of a small sized LSP (which we refer to hereafter as "the company"). After reviewing some key notions and definitions, we describe the original translation workflow in the company before MT was introduced. We then present the initial steps taken in order to blend MT into the existing procedures. Next, a description of the findings is summarized, including the factors identified to have a negative effect on the quality of MT and the changes needed in the existing CAT workflow in order to incorporate post-editing MT. Follows a brief description of some key performance indicators researched with the goal of measuring the benefits of MT on productivity. This chapter finishes with final remarks and conclusions.

Many of the advances, techniques and implementation of machine translation into the workflow of the company would not have been possible without the continuous learning and cooperation with the research community through a series of European funded projects in which the company was involved: MLIS Quartet[4] in 1999 and 2000, TransType2[5] from 2002 to 2005, SMART[6] from 2006 to 2009 and CASMACAT[7] in 2011 and 2012. Each of these projects provided knowledge that was crucial at some stage. Cooperation with the research community continued even after the projects finished.

Key Definitions and Concepts

In translation, the term *post-editing* refers to the act of correcting a translation proposal (from a single word or character to a complete document). If this proposal comes from an MT system, we talk of *post-editing MT* (PEMT); if it comes from human translation, we talk of *human post-editing* (HPE). In general, post-editing itself is performed by (human) translators, but it can also be performed automatically: we then talk of *automatic post-editing* (APE).

MT systems typically fall under two broad categories: *rule-based* (RBMT – e.g. Systran, Apertium, PAHOMT and ProMT) and *statistical*

(SMT – e.g. Moses and Language Weaver). RBMT systems typically rely on large sets of hand-written rules; in contrast, SMT systems "learn" automatically from large collections of existing translations. Recently, hybrid systems have appeared, in which an RBMT system performs a first-pass translation, which is then automatically post-edited by an SMT system. In this chapter, we use the acronym "MTAPE" to refer to such hybrid MT systems.

Many translators nowadays work with *computer-aided translation* (CAT) tools, such as Trados, WordFast, MemoQ or Déjà Vu. A key functionality of these tools is the *translation memory* (TM), which is used to archive existing translations. Given a new segment of text to translate, the CAT tool can offer the translator a number of matching pairs of source/target segments from the TM. The best matching is determined based on the similarity between the new and archived source segments, as estimated by the CAT tool's internal matching algorithm. When a previously stored source segment in the TM and the new source segment to be translated are not identical, it is called a *fuzzy match*. The degree of similarity is expressed as a percentage, which the CAT tool displays alongside the match. The corresponding translation will typically need to be post-edited to adapt to the new segment. But even exact matches (100%) may need human post-editing if the context of the new segment is not identical to the context of the archived segment, or if the previous translation is incorrect or inadequate for any reason.

When translators already use a CAT tool, one way of integrating MT into the translation workflow is to use MT only for segments for which the CAT tool cannot find a good matching in its TM. The resulting machine translated segments are then added to the TM, so that they can later be proposed to the translator by the CAT tool, just as if they were exact matches. In this chapter, unless stated otherwise, the standard translation environment always includes a CAT tool and translation memories, and MT segments are always part of a translation memory and are presented to the translator as part of a CAT tool setup.

The scenarios discussed on this chapter are identical for human and post-editing MT. Translators open a text editor, a CAT tool, and sometimes a terminology databank linked to the CAT tool. Human translations are stored in the TM along with MT proposals. MT proposals are marked in such a way that translators can clearly establish if the proposal is coming from a previous human translation or MTAPE. From the translator's point of view, there is no difference in the translation scenario.

Integrating MT in the Workflow

At the end of the 90s, the company was an SME with offices in Madrid and Barcelona, employed more than 30 in-house workers, several hundred freelancers (translators, reviewers, DTP, etc), and translated several million words per year. Main domains were medical (including pharmaceutical), technical and institutional. Clients ranged from corporations to individuals. The standard translation workflow is illustrated in Figure 2-1. Different projects followed alternative and simpler paths according to their requirements, and certainly the workflow varied at different points in time, but the figure synthesizes the complete set of procedures. Standard industry elements are present, including CAT tools: translation memory, terminology, editors, translators, reviewers, project managers, and guidelines, support documents, quality assessment (QA), project-specific instructions, etc. MT was still not part of the process. Different translation agencies may have different procedures or elements, and localization certainly follow different paths at some stages, but this is a valid example of a translation workflow.

This workflow was used for many years (see Figure 2-2), but the opportunity to test and implement RBMT appeared at the end of 1999. The main goal for integrating MT in the workflow was to reduce cost, by increasing productivity (speed) and reducing the need to fraction tasks among many translators. If translators were able to translate faster, jobs might not need splitting. The reviewer task is much more challenging if a single document/translation is done by more than a single translator. If translators were able to translate faster, many jobs might not need splitting or may be completed by fewer translators.

Initially at least, MT software had to run on Microsoft Windows, given than more than 98% of translators were already using that OS. Because professional translators rarely worked on plain text, and maintaining sometimes complex formatting throughout the process is very important, a pre-processing stage would be necessary.

Figure 2-2 shows the main milestones in integrating translation technologies, including a line representing the percentage of finished projects yearly using MT at some stage. MT adoption was a slow process: it took years and a great deal of effort. SMT and APE greatly helped to push MT coverage, but there were also economical reasons.

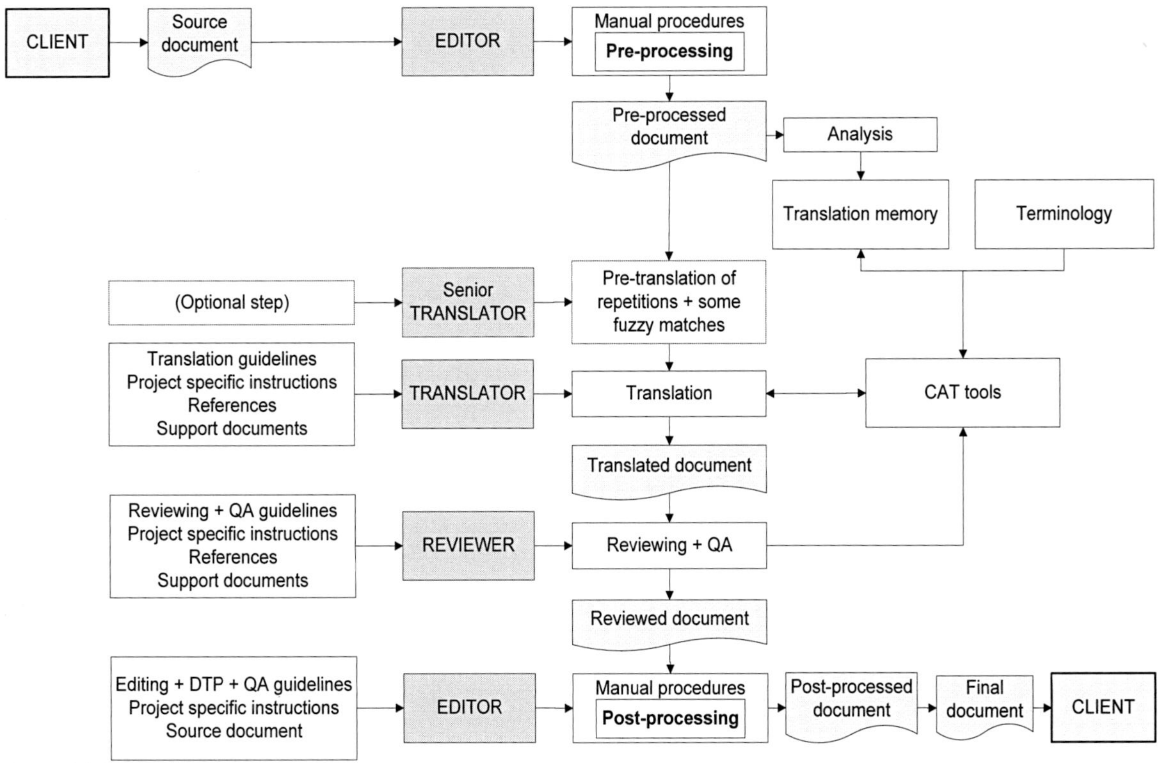

Figure 2-1: Initial workflow

Between 1999 and 2000 the company took part in a European translation research project[8], which helped to incorporate quality metrics and better management procedures. Experiments with RBMT started in 1999. The first step was to select commercially available MT software. Pilot quality tests were carried out for three RBMT systems. Company translators were involved in assessing the quality of these systems. Texts were chosen from Life Sciences, Automotive and Software domains, segmented and translated with each system. Translators were then asked to assign scores to each translation according to their degree of acceptability (on a scale of 1-5), and on the effort required to post-edit them compared to translating from scratch. There were no significant differences between systems, but one stood out as the best overall. It is important to note that the translators were the ones who made the final decision on the best software to use.

Following this experiment, MT was used and tested on a separate environment within the company, aside from real translation projects. Nevertheless, this involved changes in the workflow, which went as far as affecting the management system, code naming of translation memories, projects and folder structure. The traceability of the translation process from quote to invoicing was reviewed and an ERP/CMS/Quality system was developed internally. This program proved to be the critical piece for the perdurability and success of the whole enterprise, providing traceability and management.

In 2001, the author interviewed a representative number of translators who worked routinely for the company. This would serve as a basis for MT implementation. The results showed that most translators had no previous experience with PEMT and most thought that MT would not help them. They were also worried that MT would gradually replace them and that PEMT would negatively affect the "artistic" or "creative" part of their work. There was an almost unanimous opinion among them that the final result would be of lower quality than the standard procedure (HPE). Translators with an excellent command on a specific domain and language pair were the most reluctant to using machine translation. Clearly, the company needed to slowly build a more positive attitude towards PEMT.

Additionally, translators did not know how to tackle the new post-editing task, and this required a specific strategy and proper training. When MT is not used, there are many source segments for which the CAT tool does not propose any translation, depending on source text matching. In the HPE + PEMT task, every sentence can receive a translation proposal, either coming from the TM or from MT. This is quite different to translating from scratch and even to HPE.

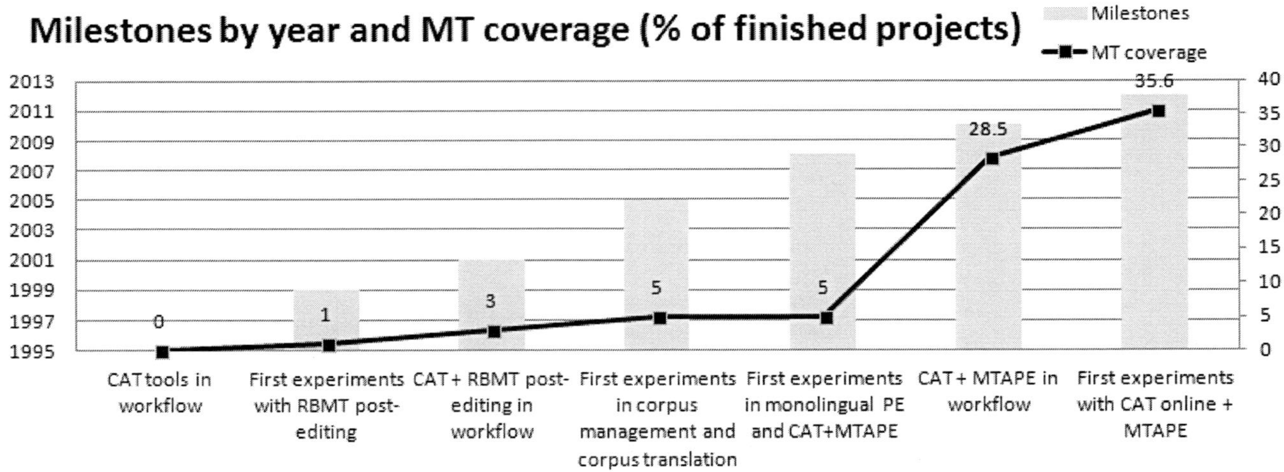

Figure 2-2: Milestones and MT coverage

A pilot group of translators was chosen to take part in the initial integration of MT. English-Spanish was identified as the core language pair. MT software was selected and tested for compatibility with the domains and languages on use. Quality was to be evaluated directly using reviewers and indirectly measuring the number of non-conformities. Manual and automatic post-processing techniques were developed. The whole company needed to be motivated and involved in the process. A basic formal training in PEMT was given. No new pricing scheme was introduced at this point. The internally developed enterprise management system was updated according to the new workflow.

One of the decisions to make was how to select candidate segments for MT. Translators and project managers were consulted to determine the level of fuzzy matching below which CAT tools typically propose translations that require more effort to post-edit than to translate from scratch. Previous experience within the company showed that, depending on the domain and characteristics of the source text, best overall results could be obtained with a flexible 50–90% threshold. Nevertheless, it was unanimously decided that 70% was a reasonable threshold: segments whose fuzzy matching score was below 70% would be submitted to MT. This decision was left to an agreement between translators and project managers depending on the project or document. MT segments were imported to the translation memory and presented to the translators in their usual environment.

There was an additional decision to be made. The order in which translation proposals are presented by CAT tools depends on the fuzzy matching percentage. Penalties can be applied to proposed translations, based on different factors, among which their origin. It was suggested that a 30% penalty would be applied to translation proposals coming from MT. But in the end, translators were free to apply a different penalty if desired to change the visibility of segments, for instance, if they detected a lower than average MT quality.

The first years using RBMT

During the first years of using of MT in the company, MT was used in less than 5% of all projects (2007). It was more a test-bench to give the technology a chance to prove itself. Testing and integrating MT was a real challenge: it was costly and resources were scarce. The goal was to assess its potential in a real translation workflow, while slowly building a positive attitude about the technology. In order to achieve this, MT was mainly used by trusted translators with a long track of projects for the company and good attitude towards new translation tools and workflows. It was applied mainly to large projects (10,000 words or more) from English to Spanish, in particular where not enough translators and reviewers were available to finish on time following the standard routine.

Cost reduction was marginal, given that translator rate scales were not modified. MT proposals were paid as translated from scratch (100% of translator's rate), and there was no specific target price for post-editing. Productivity improvements (translation speed in words per hour) measured for in-house translators were below 20% at best; most of the time, they were below 7%. It has to be mentioned that the effort requested at all stages within the company to introduce MT was very high. Among translators, the perceived quality of MT proposals was considered very low. Low quality of source text and complexity of source format acted against the system. In any event, no practical benefits were perceived from the introduction of MT.

It was observed that the low quality of some MT proposals was linked to the length of source sentences: in some cases longer than 60 words. Splitting some sentences helped to achieve higher quality and also made it easier for translators to understand source and target sub-sentence relationship. The presence in some texts of non-standard tags, such as client specific tags, was also a big problem. Additionally TM quality issues were identified.

The feedback from translators, project managers, operation managers and language technology experts allowed a number of issues to be identified. PEMT was perceived as much more demanding than translating from scratch or post-editing previous human translations. Translators reported that their productivity had decreased, which was confirmed by project managers. Post-editing effort had to be reduced: in a standard CAT translation setting, most translators were comfortable working six to eight hours a day, but they were really tired after a six hour of HPE+PEMT task. Many causes were identified. Better training was needed as most translators were taking a long time to post-edit some MT sentence. Also, even though the quality of some MT sentences was lower than average in some documents, translators did not warn project managers. In order to improve quality, better pre-processing of source documents was required. This was an incidental discovery: higher quality source documents of certain domains were consistently producing better productivity figures from translators. It was observed that some source documents were coming either from an automatically scanned and unedited document (not corrected), or from authors whose mother tongue was not the one in the document. In both cases, source text quality was negatively affecting MT results and making the whole experience much more demanding.

In order to save time, reduce cost and mitigate effort, it was observed that the right combination of translator and reviewer was critical. Reviewers do not translate or post-edit, but instead supervise the work of translators in order to further ensure and enhance quality and compliance. They typically only consult the source text when needed. We already knew that under most circumstances, it is counterproductive to use experienced reviewer to review the translation of an experienced translator; this was confirmed as valid for MT assignments as well.

In general, MT proposals were judged to be understandable, but rated low with regard to style and compliance with domain-specific and client-specific terminology. And correcting the same mistakes over and over again proved to be exasperating for translators. Such details can really have a negative impact on translator's attitude. MT quality of rule-based systems generally required extensive post-editing, and therefore was not acceptable for post-editing purposes. Less than 5% of the translators working for the company were doing PEMT at the time. The company was eager to involve more of them, but also cautious given the problems encountered. The intention was not to impose MT, but to help translators on their way into the transition.

Experiments in Automatic Post-editing

Between 2002 and 2005, the company and the author participated in the Transtype2 EC project, which explored advanced forms of post-editing MT and interactive MT. This action was very useful for testing and understanding some of the potential benefits of more advanced MT technologies, particularly statistical approaches which learned automatically from existing translations. From this point, the company started to consider translation memories as a potentially useful linguistic asset besides their use on CAT translation and terminology extraction.

In parallel to the participation in European projects, the company was starting to test corpus based SMT helped by the ITI and The Pattern Recognition and Human Language Technology (PRHLT) research groups of the Universidad Politécnica de Valencia. While reviewing problematic proposals coming from SMT, it was detected that some of the errors seemed to be a consequence of incorrect translations present in the translation memory. Most of these were not due to translator's errors, but to idiosyncrasies of CAT tools. Quality issues in the source text, that were not relevant before introducing MT, were of critical importance for the

RBMT system in place. In parallel, translation memories were manually reviewed and a document pre-processing stage was introduced in order to identify and correct weak points that might be negatively affecting CAT sentence matching and MT quality in general, mainly due to errors in source text. Improving TMs was an activity that yielded excellent results in the standard translation workflow years before developments in the MT field finally guided the company to introducing statistical MT a few years later and confirmed the great value of the combination TM-MT.

In 2008, after years of using RBMT on a low profile, an experiment was designed to measure how an improvement in the quality of MT proposals could impact the productivity and quality of the whole translation process, as well as exploring the potential benefits of adding an APE step on top of the existing RBMT, all without compromising the current translation workflow and delivery dates. For the purposes of this experiment, MT quality was improved by means of adding a "monolingual post-editing" step: readers were asked to correct the MT proposal without access to the original source text. The resulting improved translations were then handed down to translators as usual; the goal was to measure if the combined monolingual PE + CAT translation could be faster than providing the translators with the original MT proposal. Speed and quality were the key factors; cost was not considered. Quality of final translation delivered by post-editors was required to be up to company standards, but the desire was to improve it.

195,600 English source words coming from European Parliament sessions were translated using the RBMT system currently in place. The resulting translations were handled to three monolingual post-editors. Their task was to try to improve the translated text grammatically and to correct obvious errors, without access to the source text. They worked using just a text editor, no CAT tool was involved. Precise instructions were provided. The reviewed text was then passed over to four translators, whose task was a standard CAT post-editing. They were not aware of the previous monolingual PE step. Both translators and monolingual post-editors worked in-house so that we could measure their productivity rates, and compare them to their previous known speed for this type of documents. A productivity increase of more than 100% was observed for the slowest translator: up to 540.54 words per hour. The productivity for the fastest translator reached 1,325.59 words per hour, an increase of 30%. In short periods of time, some translators were able to achieve a peak productivity rate of more than 2,000 words per hour. For the two medium speed translators, a small performance increase of 14.28% was observed, up to 571.43 words per hour. It was noticed that productivity decreased significantly after a long period (+6 hours) and this was confirmed in personal interviews with the translators. Translators also commented that they were tired after a 6 hour session, but their productivity increase after 6 hours was still noticeable. Monolingual post-editors processed anywhere between 769.23 to 1,868.18 words per hour. The texts were then handled to reviewers for QA as usual; reviewers did not report an increase or a decrease in overall quality. It seemed that quality was not affected.

In the following years, the findings of this experiment and the participation in the EC-funded project SMART lead to the introduction in the company of a hybrid MT system, which incorporates a first stage of RBMT, and a second stage of automatic post-editing, performed by an SMT system trained on relevant post-edited translations. To help in the integration of SMT in the company, between 2008 and 2010 experiments and developments were run in collaboration with the Instituto Tecnológico de Informática (ITI) and The Pattern Recognition and Human Language Technology (PRHLT) groups of the Universidad Politécnica de Valencia (UPV).

While PEMT was and is still perceived as a demanding task under most circumstances, the increased quality of MT proposals has allowed productivity improvements and a change of attitude among the participating translators towards post-editing. This finally resulted in a company widely used hybrid MT platform (RBMT+SMT) for automatic post-editing (APE), which includes semi-automated modules for handling translation memory and corpus management.

Understanding Factors that Affect Quality and Effort

While MT usage was growing within the company, numerous factors were analysed in order to establish what elements were relevant to final quality and overall effort (including but not limited to post-editing). This research continued until 2012 along with the definition of key performance indicators (KPI). The items described below and the associated data correspond to the period 2009–2011.

File format: this remains one of the main factors affecting effort. CAT tools generally include components for handling file format conversion. MT engines are much more limited in this regard, and sometimes do not offer any such mechanisms. If the MT software cannot directly deal with the format received, documents have to go through costly intermediate conversions and processing. This requires effort, may affect quality and induces delays in the lead time. Many file formats are in use at the company, though Microsoft Word, HTML files and PDF files are predominant (Figure 2-3). Most PDF files are not editable, thus requiring an additional OCR and text manipulation stage. Image files, tables and slides present their own challenges.

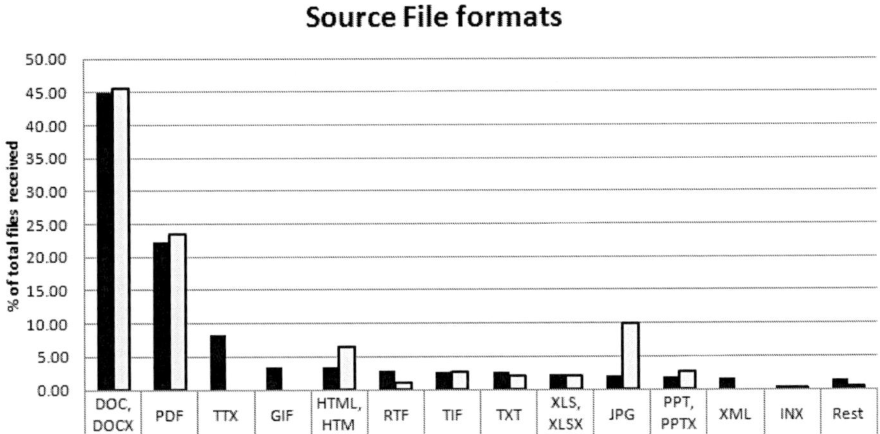

	DOC, DOCX	PDF	TTX	GIF	HTML, HTM	RTF	TIF	TXT	XLS, XLSX	JPG	PPT, PPTX	XML	INX	Rest
■2010	44.92	22.24	8.33	3.49	3.37	2.82	2.68	2.54	2.32	2.04	1.86	1.57	0.46	1.36
□2011	45.62	23.40			6.40	1.10	2.58	2.02	2.10	10.01	2.60		0.26	0.33

Figure 2-3: Source file format

Domain and style of source document: MT software may yield better results in some specific domains and text styles. The number of projects received per domain and the number of corresponding words was measured. Various RBMT and SMT systems were tested on the selected domains using relevant documents. Project managers, translators and reviewers helped in this task. A group of selected translators was chosen to assess MT quality per domain and suitability of domain documents for MT. They were given a spreadsheet with source text and the corresponding translations, as produced by four different RBMT and one SMT systems. They were asked to select the best MT translation proposal from the post-editing effort point of view. When a decision on the best overall software combination was made, this MT software was re-tested against all domains. Translators were asked to assign a quality score to each specific domain/sub-domain and suitability of domain documents for MT (Figure 2-4).

Sub-domain	MT proposal perceived quality
Informed consent form	Good
Hospital agreement	Good
Legal	Variable (acceptable)
Amendments	Not applicable
General texts, Institutions	Variable (acceptable)
Medical literature	Variable (insufficient)
Medicine	Acceptable
Other	Variable (acceptable)
Protocol	Good
Protocol + Informed consent form	Good
Pharmacy	Acceptable
Patient leaflet + Labelling	Acceptable
Technical	Good

Figure 2-4: MT quality per domain

Document statistics: based on experiments carried out internally, it was established that MT quality might be affected by the length, complexity, and quality of source segments. A research on finished projects found that 73% of company projects had less than 6,000 words (around 24 pages), 90% of the projects had less than 20,000 words (around 80 pages) and average sentence length was below 22 words.

Translation memory quality and size: an in depth review of TMs was carried out to establish general quality, reliability and size of segments, as well as overall TM size. The information was very useful to initiate actions on TMs given their importance for the corpus based APE approach being developed. For instance, many sentences were split to keep their length bellow certain size, some were deleted from the TM due to low quality, age or incorrect placement, domain and sub-domain were reviewed, etc.

In addition to what has already been mentioned, changes to the current CAT workflow were identified and implemented. Similarly, given the growing relevance expected for post-editing MT and previous experiences on the subject, the need for proper post-editing training, clear and concise post-editing guidelines and a fair post-editing MT rate was evident.

Migrating to MT+APE

Between 2007 and 2008, a number of procedures were tested to automate the workflow, reduce human errors and try to improve the quality of MT proposals. It consisted of a document pre-processing step, mainly implemented as Visual Basic macros. These macros were given to editors and project managers, not the translators. The macros included routines for automatically solving common problems, such as file format conversion, source text error correction (typos, incorrectly split sentences or words, etc.), placing headers and footers as running text, deactivate track changes, extracting images and tables to separate documents, converting tables to running text, fixing problems related to incorrect carriage returns, blank spaces, sub/superscripts, parentheses, bulleted lists, etc. In addition, regular expression macros were programmed to improve the quality of MT proposals (solving some basic issues) before it reached the translators. Later, all these macros served as the basis for a pre-processing stage in the MTAPE platform.

In 2008, a pilot project was designed to introduce SMT and APE; initial tests were conducted using the RBMT in place and a Moses system to handle the SMT and APE process. The SMT system was trained using the TMs available and selected source sentences were translated. Sentences were also translated by the RBMT system and then passed to the SMT for automatic post-editing (APE). APE results were compared to RBMT-only translations, SMT translations, and a reference human translation for the same segment. Translators were asked to check quality and expected post-editing effort, and a ranking was established. The APE system was found to provide better domain and client adaptability, and consequently increase the overall quality and allow lower post-editing effort than RBMT and SMT proposals. However, the test conclusions did not clearly show that post-editing effort was significantly lower.

At that time, the notion that a hybrid MT system (RBMT+STM) could potentially outperform a pure SMT or RBMT system in post-editing effort gained momentum (Isabelle et al., 2007). In the first months of 2009, a hybrid sequential platform (RBMT>SMT) was conceived and set up along with the ITI/PRLHT groups at the Universidad Politécnica de Valencia (Lagarda et al. 2009). The main goals pursued were to increase MT usage, reduce post-editing effort and cost, while at least maintaining prior quality levels. Although the company had been using MT for more than a decade, only a small proportion of projects were covered by MT. The main reasons were low quality (mainly due to low client terminology and domain adaptability), complex integration procedure and high post-editing effort.

A web interface was developed to allow easy management of MTAPE systems by non-technical users. The system included an automatic TM management and quality maintenance module, an automatic process to use TMs to generate corresponding application-specific training data (corpora) at different merge levels (domain, sub-domain, client, etc.), an automatic step to create application-specific MTAPE systems from each corpus, a coding method for TMs, corpora and MTAPE systems, a RMBT system, a SMT system (based on TMs). Later on, new modules added an automatic tunable method to pre-process source documents, including regular expression search and replace and file format conversion and a post-processing module for file/format conversion tasks. At this point, the company did not have enough resources to seriously fine-tune the SMT engine or test many different RBMT+SMT combinations to find the best option available.

A development-only environment was created. Translation quality of MT was tested using different language model levels: client level/sub-domain level/domain level. At client level, the SMT engine was trained using exclusively a translation memory whose segments belong to an individual domain (technical, scientific, etc.) of a single client of the company. At domain and sub-domain levels, the SMT engine was trained using all combined TMs from all clients for a specific domain or sub-domain (medicine, automotive, etc.). Sub-domain level is very similar to domain level, but more specific. The minimum TM usable quality size for training a model was established at 30,000 segments (after a human QA test on the different models), although models were trained using every single TM in order to have them available for experiments. Not surprisingly, it was detected that the domain-level model (several million segments) in general yielded best results. However, for some specific source documents, better results were achieved using a client or sub-domain level language model. Again, not enough resources were available for an in depth test.

External and internal development teams tested the application. Initial deployment and translation tests were done internally, by in-house translators and reviewers. Tight collaboration between the research centre (ITI – Universidad Politécnica de Valencia) and the company was critical for the success of the operation. A new workflow was designed in order to accommodate MTAPE. This is shown in Figure 2-5. Notice that all translation tasks make use of CAT tools, including MT.

Translators were allowed to reject the post-editing task altogether, if the quality of MT proposals was deemed too low for post-editing purposes. Because this approach let the translator decide whether or not to post-edit, it had a very positive impact on many aspects (final quality, attitude towards PEMT, delivery time, etc.). However, things did not always work as expected, and some translators still complained about low MT quality after finishing their assignments. This sometimes occurred

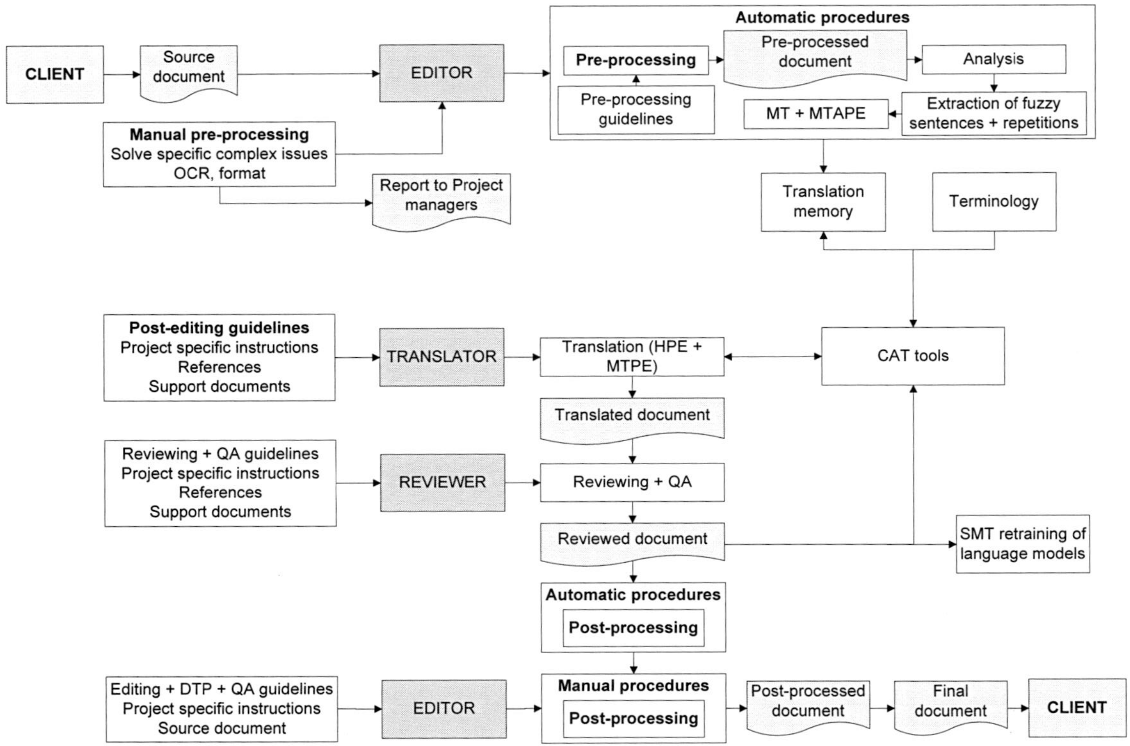

Figure 2-5: CAT+MTAPE workflow

because of the application setup, sometimes as result of the lack of proper instructions, and sometimes due to the translator's own idiosyncrasies.

The Search for Performance Indicators

Words per hour/day performance is probably the most widely used productivity indicator within the professional translation industry. It accounts for the number of source words (generally) translated over the selected period of time. Most translators know this performance indicator and may provide their productivity figure to the LSP. The LSP may use it as a way to estimate time to delivery of projects, decide which translators may be more suitable for a specific project, and split a task among many translators if needed. One of the problems faced when introducing MT was that measuring its benefits on productivity on a representative number of translators over long periods of time was very difficult to achieve. Almost all professional translators employed by the company were freelancers (97%), mostly working remotely from home (88%). The company had no control over their working environment (software, computer, monitor size, etc.). It was not possible to install specific tracking software on their computers. Although online CAT tools are becoming popular which may allow for easier productivity rate and post-editing effort tracking, most professional translators work on a locally installed CAT tool that does not offer such functionalities. The only information available was their feedback. As valuable as it is, it did not really provide valid productivity rates or post-editing effort figures. Internal translator productivity, on the other hand, was easily measured as there was complete control over their working environment and number of hours employed. However, they were few in number and they were not always available or involved in MT-related projects.

Because of these issues, additional key performance indicators (KPI) were needed to measure the benefits of PEMT, which could shed some light on productivity increase and post-editing effort. The approach was not perfect, but it gave us some clues and helped with aspects of strategy and corporate social responsibility, among other things.

Many KPIs were analysed and tested, but finally the following were effectively used in order to indirectly estimate the benefits of introducing MT. It should be noted that quality is measured on a constant basis as part of the workflow and auditing process of the company (ISO:9001, ISO:27001, UNE:15038); nevertheless, one specific quality KPI was also designed to analyse this aspect.

Average lead time of projects (days/year): *lead time* is the number of days required to complete a project, from the initial quote to the final delivery to the client. Figure 2-6 shows the yearly average lead time of all projects over recent years. Although MT is not the only factor affecting lead time (others being: workflow improvements, project length, etc.), a steady decrease can be observed over time. The lowest values correspond to periods with the highest rates of MT and workflow optimisation. Project length was constant over the ten years period measured, except for the low values observed in 2009. This was due to a very high number of short projects (one to three days) from a single client.

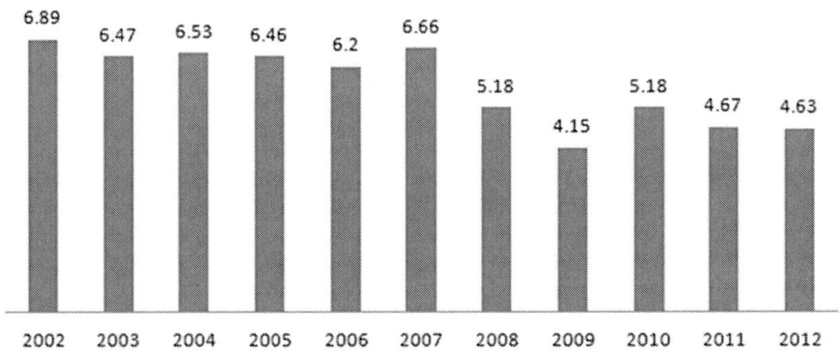

Figure 2-6: Average lead time of projects

Productivity versus lead time of projects: Figure 2-7 compares the lead time of all projects/MT projects against productivity (words delivered per project and day). Most projects in the period 2010–2012 were short and simple (only one delivery date). Curiously, while lead time globally decreased over the given time period, it seemed to converge for MTAPE and non-MT projects; at the same time, productivity globally increased. It is reasonable to think that this was due to a number of additional factors: better TM management (automatic and manual processing), better MT model re-training, increasing experience of translators with the platform, better post-editing guidelines, better filtering of candidate documents for MTAPE, better document pre-processing, and translator's training.

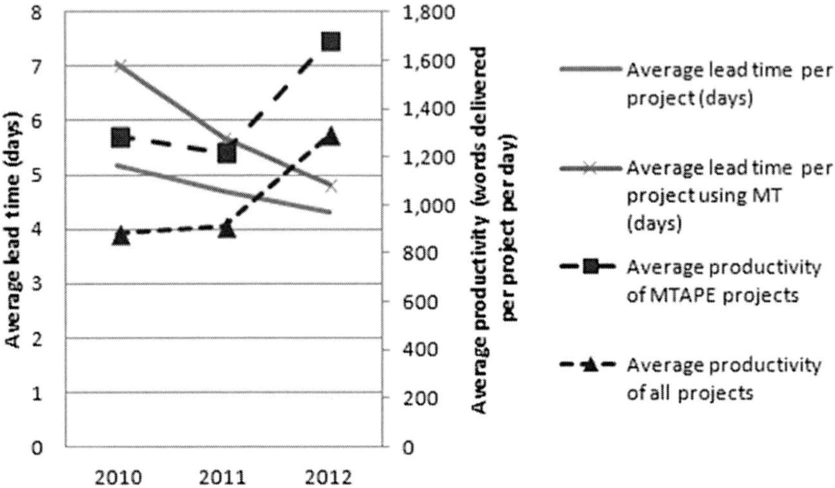

Figure 2-7: Average lead time of projects and productivity

Lead time versus MT productivity gain: while the average lead time decreased between 2010 and 2012, overall changes due to MT integration also benefited non-MT projects. As a result, the difference in productivity between projects with and without MT decreased over time. An increase of 86.90% was detected in average productivity (number of words delivered per day and project) of MTAPE projects compared to non-MT projects. Pre-processing methods and translation memory improvements had a very positive effect on both types of projects (Figure 2-8).

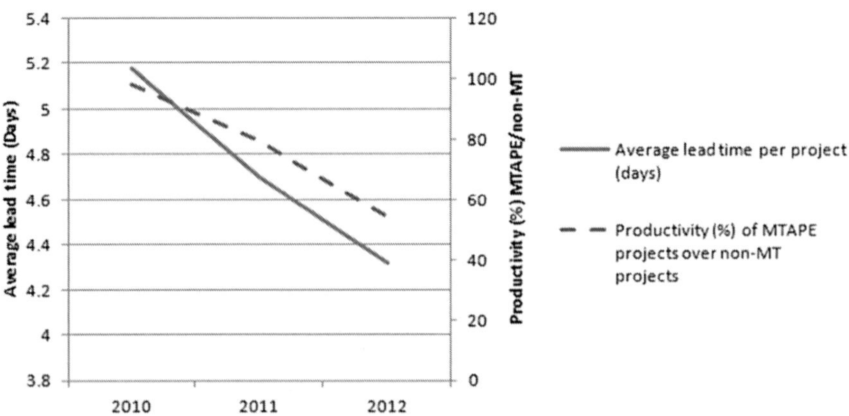

Figure 2-8: Average lead time vs. MT Productivity Gain

Word achievement rate: the difference between the number of source words provided to translators and the number of source words received from clients, divided by the number of source words received from clients, expressed as percentage, gives an idea on the benefits of the system at the TM level (sentence matching). Changes in workflow, better processing of TMs and better pre-processing of documents were in part due to the introduction of MT in the company. The implementation of manual and automatic TM processing stages to detect and correct errors in 2008, and a semi-automatic document pre-processing step had a very positive impact on training MT models for APE and CAT tool fuzzy matching. As a result, the number of CAT tool matches increased. Fewer segments were given to translators because more segments were recognised as perfect matches by the CAT tool. Figure 2-9 shows a significant increase of this KPI for all project types (with and without MT) in the period 2008–2012, when changes due to MTAPE were taking place.

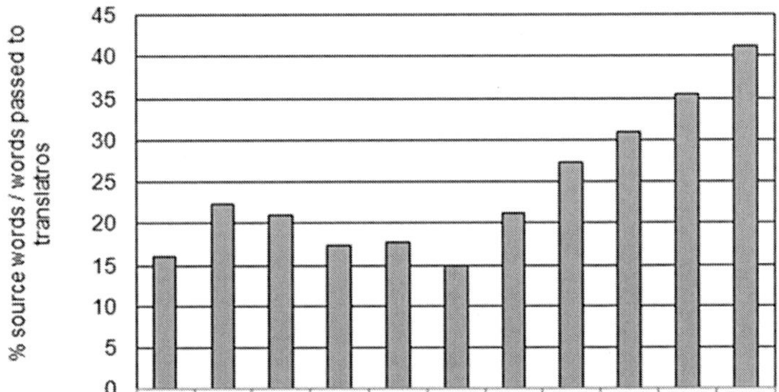

	2002	2003	2004	2005	2006	2007	2008	2009	2010	2011	2012
WORD ACHIEVEMENT RATE / ANUAL (%)	15.97	22.28	21.09	17.37	17.83	14.85	21.26	27.36	30.96	35.51	41.19

Figure 2-9: Annual word achievement rate

Looking at monthly word achievement rates for the year 2011 (Figure 2-10), it can be observed that achievement rates for MT projects are systematically 10% higher than for non-MT projects. In addition, both workflows benefit from the changes implemented and continue to improve over time.

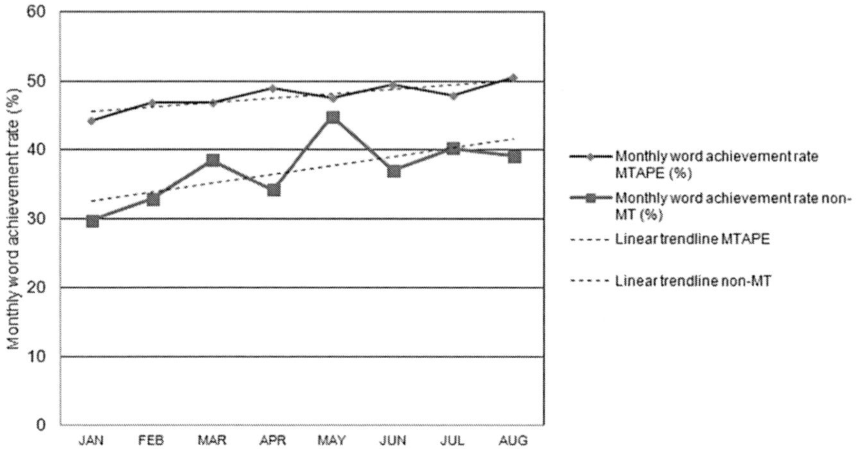

Figure 2-10: Monthly word achievement rates in 2011

One of the remaining questions was how quality had been affected by using MT in the translation workflow. Although most translations would go through a reviewing stage, quality was not directly registered. A manual annotation was ruled out given the effort and resources needed.

Quality of service versus Lead time: it was observed that the number of projects delivered on time and without non-conformities due to quality issues (ISO:9001 compliance) had been kept constant in the period 2010–2012. A 99.5% quality of service was achieved in the period 2010–2012 (Figure 2-11). The number of projects delivered per year on that period was over 4,000. There was practically no variation in the number of non-conformities. Non-conformity is registered when a client notice correlates with one or more issues in a project. It may also be registered as a result of internal procedures. It is important to mention that in a series of limited tests consisting of manual reviewing of final documents, an increase in absolute quality over time was observed. However, the level of quality was so high that it was difficult to establish significant differences between final translated documents produced with and without MT.

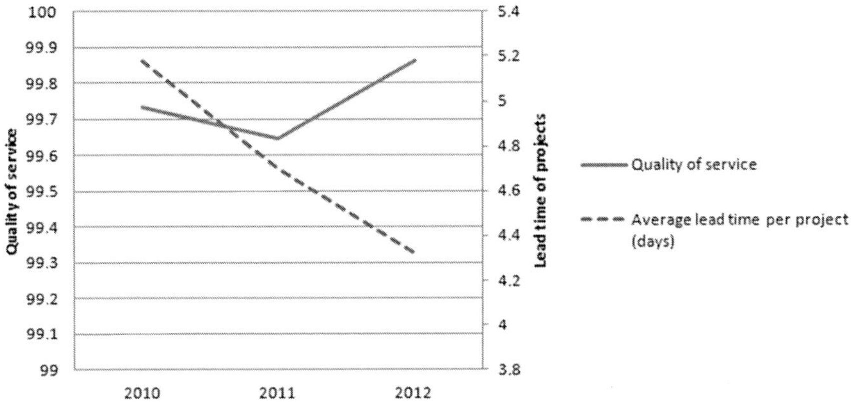

Figure 2-11: Quality of service (%) versus Lead-time

Conclusions

Change management and decision making is generally easier in a small business compared to a large company. In a small company, it is more feasible to try out new technologies and workflows. That is probably one of the reasons why this story was possible.

After integrating MTAPE and PEMT in the workflow, more projects were processed and more words per time unit were translated. Lead time was reduced significantly and quality was at least been maintained (and most likely improved) in the process. Changes in the workflow benefited MTAPE and non-MT projects. After more than a decade trying different strategies and technology combinations, a 35.5% PEMT coverage was reached (we recall that not all projects are good candidates for MT).

A number of other lessons were learned and they played a significant role in the process of integrating MT in the workflow. They are worth mentioning here even if for some of them no details are provided in this chapter due to space constraints. Figure 2-12 shows these key elements schematically.

Among the most crucial lessons, we emphasize the role of the translator/post-editor. They are the key piece of the change towards MT integration and interaction (Casacuberta et al. 2009). Another crucial point is the ability to measure how the company benefits from MT, including its workflow, employees, clients, external translators and partners, among others. The whole scenario should also improve over time.

Finally, tight collaboration between the research community and the professional translation community, between the translators and the company, and reachable goals that take into account the target audience, are essential to obtain sustainable results. However, this chapter tells a story that broadly is an example of the opposite: researchers, LSPs and translators are still separate communities for the most part. Each of them sees the technology from a different angle, although they share common goals and groups of interest. In days when translation may start to be seen as a right and a utility (Choudhury et al. 2013), if we are to research, develop, provide and integrate helpful tools that are easily adopted and rapidly embraced, links and cooperation among LSPs, translators and the research community are a must.

Figure 2-12: Some key elements of MT integration

Bibliography

Casacuberta, Francisco, Jorge Civera, Elsa Cubel, Antonio L. Lagarda, Guy Lapalme, Elliott Macklovitch, and Enrique Vidal. 2009. "*Human Interaction for High-Quality Machine Translation*". Commun. ACM 52(10):135–138.

Choudhury, Rahzeb, and Brian McConnell. 2013. Translation Technology Landscape Report. TAUS. Accessed October 2013. https://www.taus.net/reports/taus-translation-technology-landscape-report.

DePalma, Donald A. 2011. "*Trends in Machine Translation: Automated Translation Technology Finds a Seat at the Corporate Table*". Accessed October 2013. http://www.commonsenseadvisory.com/AbstractView.aspx?ArticleID=2154.

Hutchins, John. 2010. "Machine Translation: A Concise History". *Journal of Translation Studies* 13(1-2):29–70. *Special issue: The teaching of computer-aided translation*, ed. Chan Sin Wai.

Isabelle, Pierre, C. Goutte, and M. Simard. 2007. "Domain adaptation of mt systems through automatic post-editing". *Proceedings of MT Summit XI*. 255–261. Copenhagen, Denmark.

Koehn, Philipp. 2012. "*Computer Aided Translation*". Lecture, http://research.microsoft.com/apps/video/default.aspx?id=175933

Koehn, Philipp, and Jean Senellart. 2010. "Convergence of translation memory and statistical machine translation". *Proceedings of the Second Joint EM+CNGL Workshop*. 21–31. Denver, CO.

Koehn, Philipp, Hieu Hoang, Alexandra Birch , Chris Callison-Burch, Richard Zens, Rwth Aachen, Alexandra Constantin, Marcello Federico, Nicola Bertoldi, Chris Dyer, Brooke Cowan, Wade Shen, Christine Moran, and Ondřej Bojar. 2007. "Moses: Open source toolkit for statistical machine translation". *Proceedings of the 45th Annual Meeting of the ACL on Interactive Poster and Demonstration Sessions*. 177–180, Prague, Czech Republic.

Lagarda, Antonio, Vicente Alabau, Francisco Casacuberta, Roberto Silva, and Enrique Díaz-de-Liaño. 2009. "Statistical Post-Editing of a Rule-Based Machine Translation System." *HLT-NAACL (Short Papers)*. 217-220.

Maklovitch, Elliott. 2004. "The Contribution of End-Users to the TransType2 Project". *Proceedings of AMTA-2004*, Washington DC, September 2004

Wolf, Petra, and Ulrike Bernardi. 2013. "Hybrid Domain Adaptation for a Rule Based MT System". *Machine Translation Summit XIV*, Nice, France, 2–6 September 2013.

Notes

[1] I am really grateful for the help provided by the referees and the editors. Their comments and input highlighted many important points and guided me in lifting the overall quality of the chapter.
[2] Work carried out as research and innovation at two Language Service Providers in Spain. The author is currently working as a freelance consultant.
[3] http://blog.memsource.com/machine-translation-survey/.
[4] "QUality AssuRance Techniques for Enhancing multi-lingual Translation".
[5] An innovative interactive predictive translation system.
[6] "Statistical Multilingual Analysis for Retrieval and Translation".
[7] A translation workbench featuring Interactive translation prediction, Interactive editing and Adaptive translation models.
[8] MLIS 3005 Quartet (Quality assurance techniques for multi-lingual translation).

CHAPTER THREE

THE ROLE OF PROFESSIONAL EXPERIENCE IN POST-EDITING FROM A QUALITY AND PRODUCTIVITY PERSPECTIVE

ANA GUERBEROF ARENAS

Abstract

This study presents results on the impact of professional experience on the task of post-editing. The results are part of a larger research project where 24 translators and three reviewers were tested to obtain productivity, words per minute, and quality data, errors in final target texts, in the post-editing of machine translation (MT) and Fuzzy match segments (in the 85 to 94 range). The findings suggest that the incidence of experience on the processing speed is not significantly different since translators with more experience performed similarly to other very novice translators. Notwithstanding, when we looked at the final quality, translators with more experience made significantly fewer mistakes than those with less experience. However, if we observed the number of errors on the segments where translators used a MT proposal, the difference between experienced and novice translators was not significant, suggesting that the MT output had a levelling effect as far as errors was concerned.

Introduction

In this chapter, we present results on the impact of professional experience on the task of post-editing. These results are part of a larger research project where 24 translators were tested to obtain productivity, words per minute, and quality data, errors in final target texts, in the post-editing of machine translation (MT) and Fuzzy match segments (in the 85 to 94 range). We will discuss here the results on the participants' experience according to their responses in a post-assignment questionnaire and explain how they were grouped into different clusters in order to correlate firstly the experience with speed according to the words per minute in the different match categories: Fuzzy matches, MT matches (MT output) and No match and secondly, to correlate experience with the quality provided by measuring the errors marked by the three reviewers in each match category. Finally, conclusions will be drawn in relation to the experience and the resulting speed and number of errors.

Related work

There are several studies on the topic of post-editing in recent years exploring different aspects of this activity such as technical and cognitive effort: O'Brien (2006a, 2006b), Beinborn (2010) and Carl et al. (2011); productivity measurement and quality: Fiederer and O'Brien (2009), Flournoy and Duran (2009), García (2010, 2011), Plitt and Masselot (2010) and De Sutter and Depraetere (2012); post-editing effort and automatic metric scores: Offersgaard et al. (2008), Tatsumi (2010) and Koponen (2012), Tatsumi and Roturier (2010), O'Brien (2011), De Sutter (2012); confidence scores: Specia (2009a. 2009b, 2011) and He et al. (2010a, 2010b), to name just a few. However, there are fewer studies exploring experience in particular and its correlation with speed and numbers of errors. We would like to mention two studies in particular. De Almeida and O'Brien (2010) explore the possible correlation between post-editing performance and years of translation experience. This pilot experiment is carried out with a group of six professional translators (three French and three Spanish) in a live localisation project using Idiom Workbench as the translation tool and Language Weaver as the MT engine. Four translators had experience in post-editing while two others did not. To analyse this performance a LISA QA Model is used in combination with the GALE post-editing guidelines. The results show that the translators with the most experience are the fastest post-editors but they also make the higher number of preferential changes. Depraetere (2010) analyses text post-edited by ten translation trainees in order to establish post-editing guidelines for translators' post-editing training. The analysis shows that students follow the instructions given and they do not rephrase the text if the meaning is clear, the students "did not feel the urge to rewrite it" (ibid, 4), they are not, however, sufficiently critical of the content thus leaving errors that should be corrected according to the instructions. Depraetere points out that this indicates a "striking difference in the mindset between translation trainees and professionals" (ibid: 6). Despite the fact that this study is focused on students, we find that it might be applicable to junior translators who have been exposed to machine translation either during their training or from the beginning of their professional experience as opposed to more senior translators that might have experienced MT at a later stage in their professional life.

Finally, we would like to mention the pilot project that served as preparation for this larger research project (Guerberof 2008) with eight subjects. In this project, we found that translators' experience had an impact on the processing speed: translators with experience performed faster on average. When we looked at the number of years of experience in localisation, domain, tools and post-editing MT output, we observed an increasing curve up to the 5-10 year range and then a drop in the speed. The number of errors was higher in experienced translators by a very small margin, and there were more errors in MT segments. This pointed to the fact that experienced translators might grow accustomed to errors in MT output. On the other hand, translators with less experience had more errors in the segments they translated from scratch than in the MT segments, which seemed to indicate that MT had a levelling effect on their quality. We felt, however, that the sample of eight participants was a highly limiting factor. It was necessary to explore further the relationship between productivity, quality and experience with a greater number of participants.

Hypothesis

Localization has a strong technical component because of the nature of the content translated as well as the tools required to translate. On many occasions this experience is associated with speed, that is, the more experience in localisation, tools used and domain, the less time will be needed to complete a project. Therefore, our hypothesis proposes that the greater the experience of the translator, the greater the productivity in post-editing MT match and Fuzzy match segments. We also formulate a sub-hypothesis that claims that this technical experience will not have an impact on the quality (measured in number of errors) as was observed in the pilot project (Guerberof 2008).

Material and method

A trained Moses (Koehn et al. 2007) statistical-base engine was used to create the MT output. In order to train the engine, we used a translation memory (TM) and three glossaries. The TM used came from a supply chain management provider (IT domain) and it had 173,255 segments and approximately 1,970,800 words (English source). The resulting output obtained a BLEU score (Papineni et al. 2002) of 0.6 and a human evaluation score of 4.5 out of 5 points. The project involved the use of a web-based post-editing tool designed by CrossLang to post-edit and translate a text from English into Spanish. The file set used in the project was a new set of strings for the help system and user interface from the same customer and therefore different than the parallel data used to train the engine. It contained 2,124 words in 149 segments distributed as follows: No match, 749 words, MT match (the output), 757 words and Fuzzy match, 618 words from the 85 to 94 percent range. The 24 translators had the task to translate the No match and edit the MT and Fuzzy matches (they were not aware of the origin of each proposal). The final output was then evaluated by three professional reviewers, who registered the errors using the LISA QA model. The focus was on the number and classification on errors, and not on a Fail or Pass result for each individual translator.

Results

As part of the global project, we analysed the 24 translators' productivity and we observed no significant differences in speed or quality for processing either the MT segments or the TM segments. Moreover, there were wide ranges in the processing speed of MT outputs so we established the possibility that some of these MT segments might have been perfect matches that required no change while others required substantial work. When looking at the impact MT had on the final quality of the post-edited text, we concluded that in this experiment both the MT and TM proposals had a positive impact on the quality since the translators had significantly more errors in the No match category, translating on their own with an approved glossary, than in the MT and Fuzzy match categories. The qualitative analysis showed us that the high quality of the MT output was possibly one of the reasons for the translators showing fewer errors in the MT category than in the No match. It also showed that there were certain factors that might have influenced the translators' quality negatively: the fact that they could not go back to translated or post-edited segments, that they did not have a context for the segments, that the glossary was not integrated into the tool, that the source text contained ambiguous structures, and that the instructions might have been too vague for certain translators. These factors highlight several issues to consider when measuring quality, and when organising projects.

Finally, we analysed the data considering the translators' experience which is the focus of this chapter and we will be presenting these results in following sections.

Results on translators' experience

We are aware that the experience embraces several aspects of a translator's profile. For the purpose of this study, experience is defined as a combination of years of experience in localisation, subject matter, tools knowledge, post-editing, type of tasks performed, estimation of daily throughputs and average typing speed. The data were obtained from the questionnaire that was provided to the translators through SurveyMonkey upon completion of the assignment. The translators responded to the following questions:

- How long have you been working in the localisation industry?
- How long have you been using translation memory tools (such as SDL Trados, Star Transit, Déjà Vu)?
- How long have you been translating business intelligence software (such as SAP, Oracle, Microsoft)?
- How long have you been post-editing raw machine translated (MT) output?
- Please estimate the percentage, on average, that post-editing MT output represents in your work (considering the last three years)
- What tasks does your work involve? (You can choose more than one option).
- Please estimate your average daily throughput when you translate from scratch without any translation aid:
- What is your average typing speed? (Please, provide an estimate in words per minute).

We present a brief overview of their responses in order to understand better the experience of the participants before they are grouped into different clusters.

Answer Options	Response %
No experience.	0.0%
Less than 2 years.	0.0%
2 years or more, less than 4 years.	12.5%
4 years or more, less than 6 years.	12.5%
6 years or more, less than 8 years.	25.0%
8 years or more.	50.0%

Table 3-1: Experience in the localisation and TM tools

The responses indicate that they are professional translators with experience. All translators have more than two years' experience in the localisation industry and half of them have more than eight years.

Answer Options	Response %
Never.	8.3%
Less than 2 years.	8.3%
2 years or more, less than 4 years.	4.2%
4 years or more, less than 6 years.	29.2%
6 years or more, less than 8 years.	16.7%
8 years or more.	33.3%

Table 3-2: Experience in domain

The experience is more heterogeneous in this group in relation to the domain, business intelligence translation, but still only four translators have less than two years' experience or none.

Answer Options	Response %
Never.	25.0%
Less than 2 years.	29.2%
2 years or more, less than 4 years.	25.0%
4 years or more, less than 6 years.	8.3%
6 years or more, less than 8 years.	4.2%
8 years or more.	8.3%

Table 3-3: Experience in post-editing

The responses show that post-editing is a relatively new task for the translators in comparison with their experience in the other areas, 79.2 percent has no experience or less than four years' experience on the task.

Answer Options	Response %
0%	25.0%
1% to 25%	66.7%
26% to 49%	4.2%
50% to 74%	4.2%
75% to 90%	0.0%
91% to 100%	0.0%

Table 3-4: Estimated post-editing work in the last three years

We wanted to qualify the previous questions as some translators might have certain experience in post-editing but they might not perform it on a regular basis and we can see on Table 3-5, rows 1 and 2, that post-editing still does not represent a high percentage of work for them.

Tasks		No		Yes
Post-editing		37.50		62.50
Translating		4.17		95.83
Revising		12.50		87.50
Writing		83.33		16.67
Terminology work		62.50		37.50
Other		79.17		20.83

Table 3-5: Tasks performed

The 24 translators are more focused on translating and revising activities.

Answer Options	Response %
Less than 2000 words per day.	8.3%
Between 2100 and 3000 w/ per day.	70.8%
Between 3100 and 5000 w/ per day.	20.8%
More than 5100 words per day.	0.0%
I don't know	0.0%

Table 3-6: Estimated daily throughput

The majority selected the option between 2,100 and 3,000 words per day which is considered a standard metric in the industry and thus not surprising.

Answer Options	Response %
0-20 words per minute	8.3%
21-40 words per minute	16.7%
41-60 words per minute	41.7%
61-80 words per minute	20.8%
More than 81 words per minute	12.5%

Table 3-7: Estimated typing speed

All responses suggest that this is a group of 24 professional translators with different areas of expertise, and that there are three translators with considerable less experience than the remaining twenty-one. Most have experience using tools and some experience in post-editing MT output, although the task represents a low percentage of their work and has not been performed for a very long period of time. Finally, their working speed seems to be in accordance with the industry standard. Now, we should look into how these translators were grouped into clusters to test the hypothesis.

Grouping translators according to their experience

In order to distribute translators into different groups with similar experience, a multiple correspondences analysis was setup (Greenacre 2008). This enables us to represent all the data (responses from the questionnaire by all translators) as rows and columns in a table including active variables (the questions above) and showing illustrative variables (age and sex). These were then graphically represented as dots in a two dimensional map (biplot). Four groups (clusters) were found, with distinctive characteristics. To explain the complete statistical analysis is beyond the scope of this study, but we should mention that the factors are not pre-defined, as we plot the data to see how the different variables are related in order to understand this relation and hence define the clusters.

We obtained four clusters that are characterised as follows. Cluster 1 has experience in all the areas queried, but they have been doing these tasks for a shorter period of time than those in Cluster 2. The translators in this cluster have between six and eight years' experience in localisation and TM tools, between four and six years' experience in translating business intelligence and 50 percent of them have a speed ranging from 21 to 60 words per minute. Cluster 2 is the one with the most experience. The translators in this cluster have more than eight years' experience in the localisation industry, more than eight years' experience using TMs, more than eight years' experience in translating business intelligence and all translators in this cluster work in post-editing. Cluster 3 has experience in translation, but none or less experience in post-editing MT output. Finally, Cluster 4 is characterised by being young and having less professional experience. Both translators in this cluster have less than two years' experience translating business intelligence and they are less than 25 years old.

Experience vs. processing speed: Fuzzy match

The speed (words per minute) for the Fuzzy match segments processed by the translators is calculated taking the words per minute in Fuzzy match segments according to the translators' different clusters:

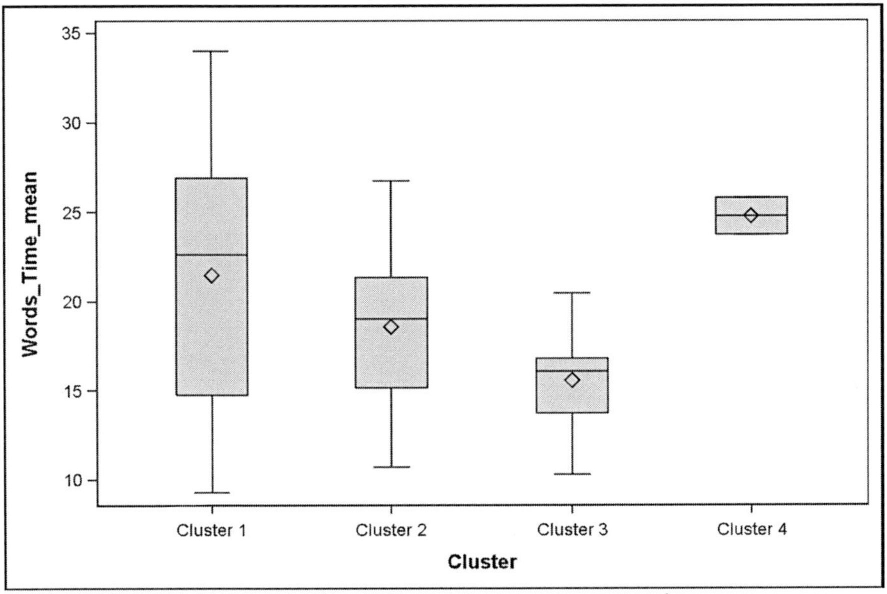

Figure 3-1: Processing speed in words per minute vs. Fuzzy match

Cluster 3, with no or little experience in post-editing, shows lower processing speed in Fuzzy match than the other clusters. Cluster 1, the second in overall experience, has a higher mean and median values than Clusters 2 and 3. Cluster 2, the most experienced, behaves similarly to Cluster 1 but slower than Cluster 4, which has a very homogeneous speed (only two translators) and the highest mean and median values. Let us look at the descriptive data in Table 3-8.

Cluster	Min	Median	Mean	Max	SD
1	9.29	22.65	21.49	34.03	8.41
2	10.73	19.05	18.59	26.74	4.95
3	10.33	16.07	15.58	20.48	3.37
4	23.75	24.76	24.76	25.78	1.43

Table 3-8: Processing speed vs. Fuzzy match

Cluster 1 has the second highest mean and median values with the highest deviation. Cluster 2 has slightly lower figures. Cluster 3 has the lowest values. Cluster 4 has the highest mean and median values and is the most homogenous group.

Therefore, if Fuzzy matches are examined in the clusters with more experience (1 and 2) the productivities are high. However, productivities are also high in Cluster 4, the one with the least experience. The interesting data point in this case is that Cluster 3, with no or little experience in post-editing, although with experience on the other areas, has a lower processing speed than the other three clusters. This might indicate that this particular cluster was slower when processing the data because their typing speed was slower (the two slowest typists are in this cluster) or because they invested more time in producing a better translation (we will see this in the following section when we look at the errors per cluster). But how did the clusters then behave with MT matches? Was this Cluster 3, with no experience in post-editing, also the slowest in this category?

Experience vs. processing speed: MT match

Figure 3-2 shows Cluster 4, with the least experience, seems to have taken full advantage of MT matches, with very high median and mean. Cluster 1 and Cluster 2, with the most experience, show similar values, although Cluster 1 seems to be slightly faster. There are translators in Clusters 1 and 2 that seem to have quite different speeds. Cluster 3, with no post-editing experience, has more homogenous values and again the lowest mean and median values. This might be understandable if they declare having no experience in post-editing MT.

Table 3-9 shows Cluster 4 as clearly having high processing speeds when dealing with MT matches. Cluster 3 has the lowest values if the mean and median values are considered, there is a maximum speed of 22.33 words per minute, the deviation here being lower than in Clusters 1 and 2. Clusters 1 and 2 have similar minim and maximum values, although Cluster 1 shows faster mean and median values.

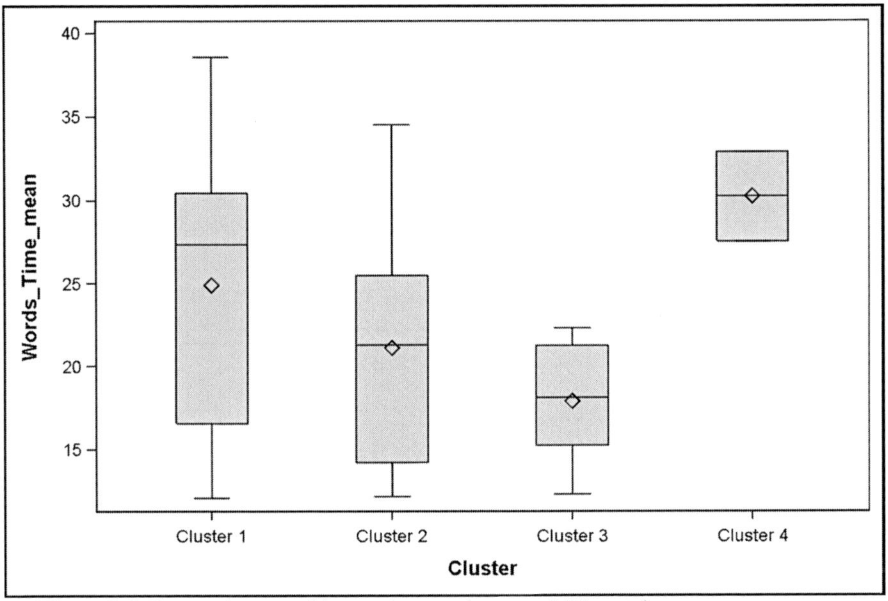

Figure 3-2: Processing speed in words per minute vs. MT match

Cluster	Min	Median	Mean	Max	SD
1	12.07	27.38	24.94	38.58	9.09
2	12.17	21.29	21.10	34.57	7.57
3	12.31	18.14	17.90	22.33	3.82
4	27.55	30.23	30.23	32.91	3.79

Table 3-9: Processing speed vs. MT match

If Cluster 4 shows the highest mean and median values, it seems to show quite the opposite of what we were trying to test. These translators are young and have very little experience but they seem to benefit considerably from MT. Nevertheless, we also see that specific experience could be a factor. Cluster 3, the slowest, had no or little post-editing experience. This seems to indicate that younger translators might find it easier to deal with MT post-editing because they might have had more contact with MT or TM outputs since they started working professionally (we saw, when defining the clusters, that these two translators had the same experience in localisation as in post-editing, which shows that they have almost a parallel experience in both areas, while more senior translators do not). At any rate, Clusters 1 and 2, with more experience, still have the highest values at 38.58 and 34.57 in words per minute respectively. Overall experience can have different influences. On the one hand, translators with more experience can perform well, and on the other, translators with less experience can also make good use of MT segments (possibly if exposed to or trained in machine translation post-editing).

It will be interesting to see how these four clusters perform when translating on their own, to find out if the different productivities were also related to their own (intrinsic) speed in No match words.

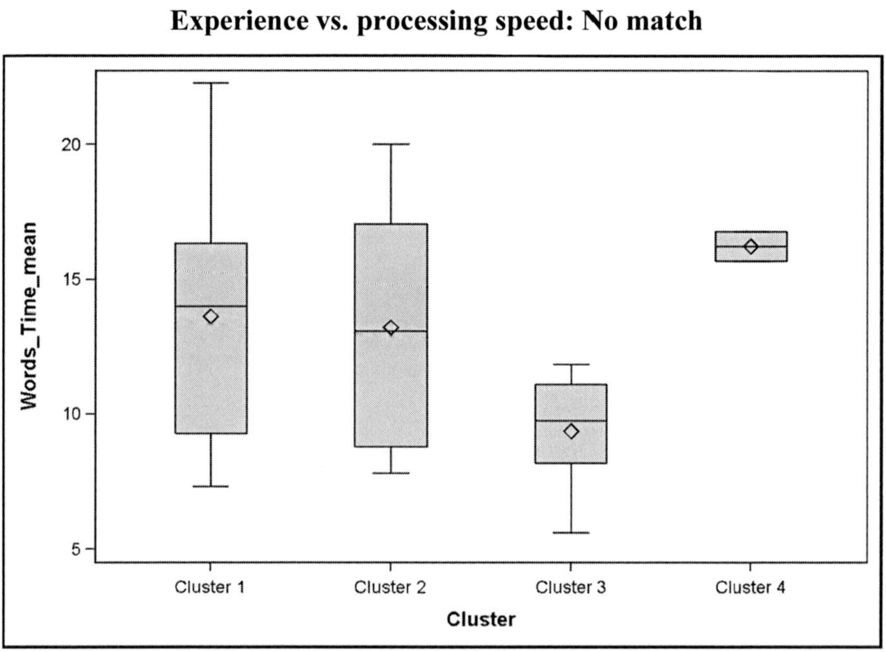

Figure 3-3: Processing speed in words per minute vs. No match

Cluster 4 has the highest mean and median values for the No match category. These two translators seem to work at a reasonable speed also when working without a translation aid. Cluster 1 is the second fastest in mean and median values and also seems to have the maximum value in words per minute. Cluster 2 has similar values with a wider range in the quartiles than Cluster 1. Cluster 3 is the group with the lowest mean and median values, and also includes the translator with the lowest value in all the clusters. Table 3-10 shows the descriptive data.

Cluster	Min	Median	Mean	Max	SD
1	7.32	14.00	13.61	22.29	5.00
2	7.80	13.08	13.20	20.00	4.70
3	5.60	9.75	9.37	11.85	2.24
4	15.69	16.24	16.24	16.78	0.77

Table 3-10: Processing speed vs. No match

Cluster 4 has the highest processing speeds if we look at the median and mean values, and also less deviation (only two translators). However, Cluster 1 has the maximum value followed by Cluster 2. The translators in Cluster 3 present lower values overall but less deviation that shows more homogeneity in the translators' speeds.

It seems understandable that Cluster 3 also had low processing speeds when working with MT and Fuzzy matches, since their baseline (No match translation) is within a low speed range. It is, therefore, not clear if their low productivity in the three match categories (Fuzzy, MT and No match) was due to their speed as translators, to lack of experience in post-editing MT output (the lack of familiarity with these types of errors might decrease their speed) or simply because they had spent more time in correcting errors. It is also interesting to note that all the translators that declare having an average typing speed of 0-20 words per minute are in this cluster.

By looking at the descriptive data it is difficult to know if experience made a statistically significant difference in processing speed. A linear regression model with repeated measures was applied to the data, taking logarithm of *Words per minute* as the response variable, and *Match category* and *Cluster* as explanatory variables. There are statistically significant differences ($F=169.91$ and $p<0.0001$) between the three translation categories: Fuzzy match, MT match and No match. This is exactly what we saw when we analysed productivity. However, there are no statistically significant differences between Clusters, and in the interaction between Clusters and Match category. From this model, mean value estimations were calculated taking the variable logarithm of *Words per minute according to the Match and Cluster*. We present the estimated mean value with their corresponding confidence intervals of 95 percent. The estimations are expressed in words per minute for a better understanding.

Cluster	Mean	Lower	Upper
1	18.09	14.27	22.91
2	16.46	12.99	20.86
3	13.46	10.24	17.89
4	22.95	14.30	36.84

Table 3-11: Estimated mean in words per minute per Cluster

Although the estimated mean for Cluster 4 is the highest, followed by Clusters 1, 2 and Cluster 3, there are no statistically significant differences between the four clusters. The gap between Cluster 3 and Cluster 4 is approximately nine words. The lower and upper intervals overlap with each other, showing that the translators in each cluster presented a variety of speeds not necessarily related to experience. This is contrary to the findings from De Almeida and O'Brien (2010) and our pilot project (Guerberof 2008) where faster translators were also the ones with more experience. However, the number of participants was smaller, and this made it difficult to see the effect experience had on speed. Table 3-12 shows the estimated mean again, but now showing the Match category and the Productivity gain with respect to No match.

Match	Cluster	Estimated mean	L	U
Fuzzy	1	19.85	15.56	25.32
Fuzzy	2	17.98	14.09	22.93
Fuzzy	3	15.26	11.52	20.21
Fuzzy	4	24.74	15.21	40.26
MT	1	23.31	18.28	29.74
MT	2	19.94	15.63	25.44
MT	3	17.54	13.24	23.24
MT	4	30.11	18.51	49.00
No match	1	12.79	10.02	16.31
No match	2	12.45	9.76	15.88
No match	3	9.11	6.88	12.07
No match	4	16.23	9.97	26.40

Table 3-12: Estimated mean according to Match and Cluster

Speed is always lower for Cluster 3, higher for Cluster 4, and similar for Clusters 1 and 2 in the three match categories. No match is significantly different for all clusters, while Fuzzy match and MT match show similar values, except with Cluster 4, where the MT match is slightly higher. To double-test the validity of the findings, non-parametric comparisons were set-up (Kruskal-Wallis analysis of variance) and we found no statistically significant differences between the Clusters according to the Match category if speed was considered.

Consequently, the first part of our hypothesis that says that the greater the experience of the translator, the greater the productivity in post-editing MT match and Fuzzy match segments is not supported in our experiment. Although Clusters 1 and 2, with more experience, show high values, Cluster 4, with less experience, also shows the highest mean and median results. Cluster 3, on the other hand, with no post-editing experience, shows lower speed values, but this was also the case in the No match category. Hence the reason could lie more in their own average typing speed or general processing speed than in the fact that they have no experience in post-editing MT matches.

In the same way that productivity needs to be linked to quality, experience needs to be related to productivity and to quality. Would Cluster 4 present more errors than Cluster 3, for example?

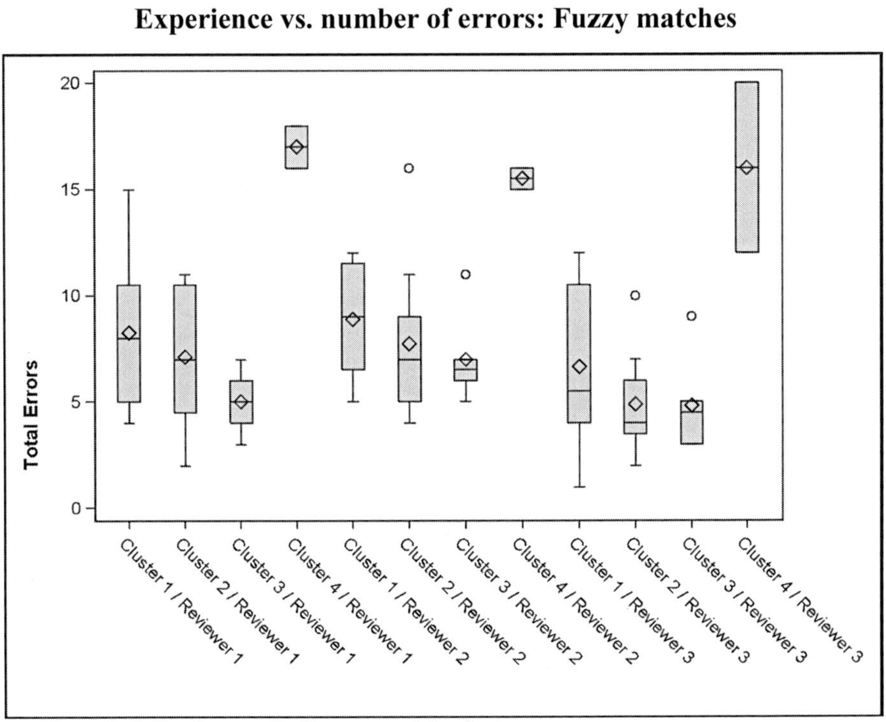

Figure 3-5: Total errors for Fuzzy match in clusters

Interestingly, Cluster 4 has the highest number of errors according to all three reviewers, indicating that this Cluster was the fastest if the mean value is considered, but it was not as rigorous or thorough when editing the Fuzzy match category. On the other hand, Cluster 3 has the lowest number of errors, indicating that this Cluster was the slowest but also thorough when processing the Fuzzy match segments. The differences between Clusters 1 and 2 are not pronounced.

Cluster + Rev		N	Mean	Median	SD	Min	Max
1	Rev 1	8	8.25	8.00	3.77	4	15
	Rev 2	8	8.88	9.00	2.90	5	12
	Rev 3	8	6.63	5.50	3.96	1	12
2	Rev 1	8	7.13	7.00	3.48	2	11
	Rev 2	8	7.75	7.00	3.99	4	16
	Rev 3	8	4.88	4.00	2.53	2	10
3	Rev 1	6	5.00	5.00	1.41	3	7
	Rev 2	6	7.00	6.50	2.10	5	11
	Rev 3	6	4.83	4.50	2.23	3	9
4	Rev 1	2	17.00	17.00	1.41	16	18
	Rev 2	2	15.50	15.50	0.71	15	16
	Rev 3	2	16.00	16.00	5.66	12	20

Table 3-13: Total errors for Fuzzy match in clusters

Cluster 4 has the highest mean values for all three reviewers, the highest median values, and the highest minimum and maximum values. The only similar maximum value is in Cluster 2. Cluster 3 has the lowest mean and median values from the three reviewers. However, the minimum and maximum values are very similar in these three clusters (1, 2 and 3), indicating that some translators had low or high values irrespective of the cluster they were in. When the type of errors is consulted, Cluster 4 made more mistakes in Terminology. This clearly indicates that translators in Cluster 4 gained speed because they tended not to check the glossary. They accepted the terminology as it was presented to them in the Fuzzy matches. We observe that Cluster 3 was slowest because they might have devoted more time to check the terminology against the glossary provided.

For Fuzzy matches, the results are rather clear. Cluster 4, with less experience and higher speed, left or made more errors in the segments according to the three reviewers. Cluster 3 made slightly less, although results for Clusters 1, 2 and 3 are quite similar. These results are interesting since they seem to signal a lack of attention to certain important aspects of the translation process in the more novice translators.

We suspect that this would be the case for the whole assignment, but let us have a look at the results for the MT matches in Figure 3-6.

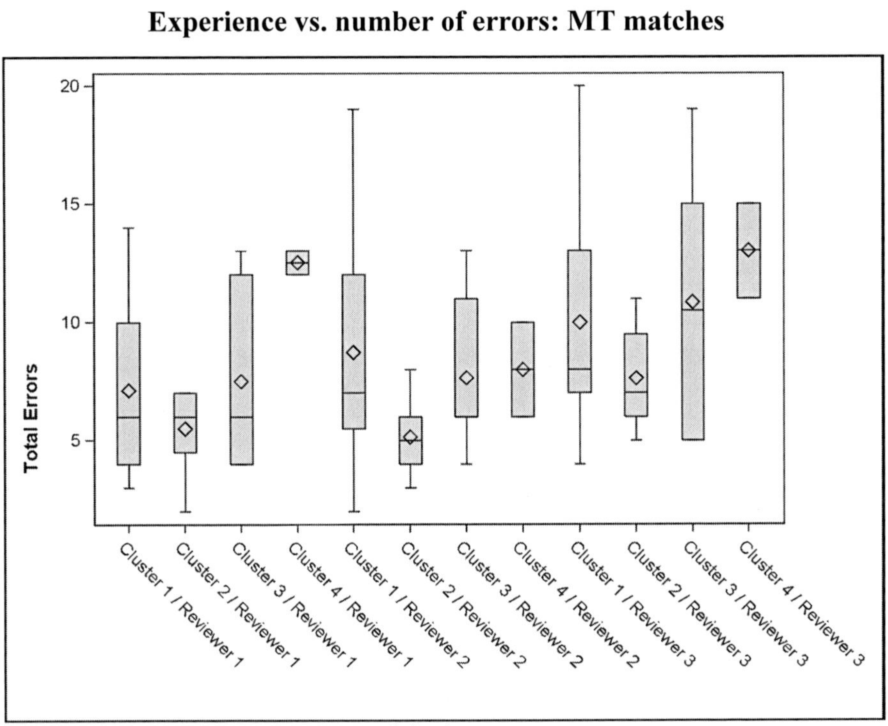

Figure 3-6: Total errors for MT match in clusters

These results are particularly interesting. In this case, the differences between the clusters are not as pronounced as with the Fuzzy matches. We think this is possible because some of the MT matches were perfect matches, with no changes required, and although translators can still introduce mistakes, it would be logical that if the translators in Cluster 4 had problems in terminology (failing to check the glossary consistently, and a certain lack of understanding of instructions), the perfect matches could help them lower the number of errors. Table 3-14 shows the descriptive data for MT match.

Cluster 2 has the lowest mean values and Cluster 4 the highest if we consider all three reviewers. However, not all the values are as different as what we saw in the Fuzzy match category. Cluster 4 has the highest minimum values, but the maximum values are to be found in Cluster 1. If we look at the type of errors each Cluster made the results are different from those found in Fuzzy matches. There are Terminology errors but here the majority of errors are on Language overall, according to all three reviewers. The reviewers seem to be of the opinion that not enough changes were made in the segments for them to be linguistically acceptable. Still the least experienced translators did not check the glossary with MT matches because they have almost an equal number of Terminology errors. Cluster 2, the most experienced, performed better with MT matches with fewer errors and fewer Language errors than the other clusters. Hence, this might indicate that experience is a factor when dealing with MT matches in terms of quality, but also that the differences in errors between the clusters were not as pronounced as in Fuzzy matches. Cluster 4 performed faster with MT matches and the number of errors was lower than with Fuzzy matches, and this might indicate that with translators who have less experience, high quality output MT might be a better option than translation memories below the 94 percent threshold.

Cluster + Rev		N	Mean	Median	SD	Min	Max
1	Rev 1	8	7.13	6.00	4.19	3	14
	Rev 2	8	8.75	7.00	5.60	2	19
	Rev 3	8	10.00	8.00	5.21	4	20
2	Rev 1	8	5.50	6.00	1.77	2	7
	Rev 2	8	5.13	5.00	1.64	3	8
	Rev 3	8	7.63	7.00	2.13	5	11
3	Rev 1	6	7.50	6.00	4.04	4	13
	Rev 2	6	7.67	6.00	3.50	4	13
	Rev 3	6	10.83	10.50	5.60	5	19
4	Rev 1	2	12.50	12.50	0.71	12	13
	Rev 2	2	8.00	8.00	2.83	6	10
	Rev 3	2	13.00	13.00	2.83	11	15

Table 3-14: Total errors for MT match in clusters

If translators behave differently with Fuzzy than with MT matches, how did they do without any translation proposal? Figure 3-7 shows the results for the No match category.

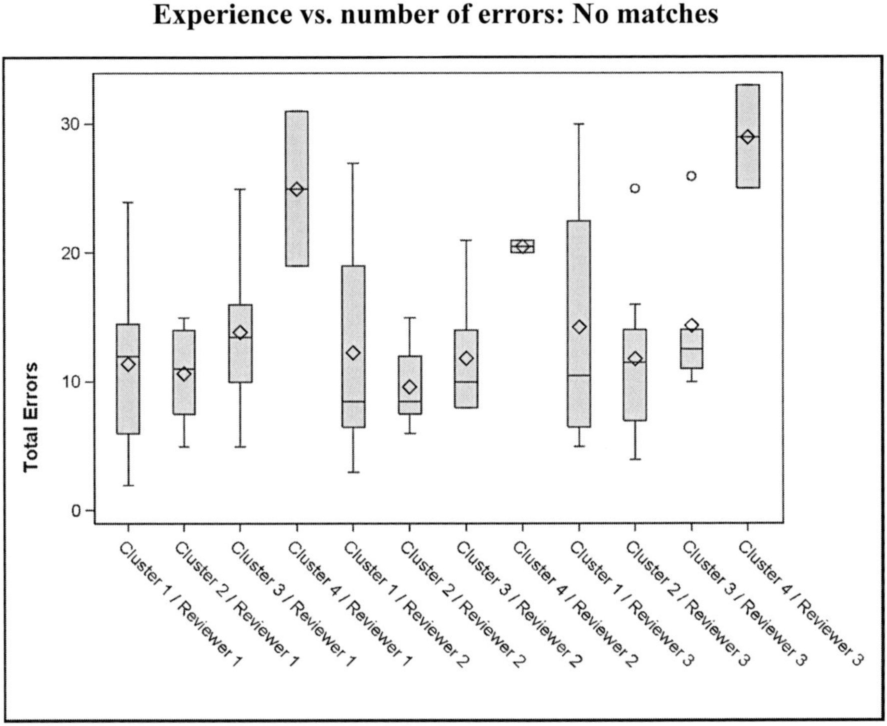

Figure 3-7: Total errors for No match in clusters

The results here are more similar to the Fuzzy match than to the MT match results. Cluster 4 clearly has the highest number of errors, and the other three clusters are very close in results. Once again, Cluster 2 seems to have the most homogenous data, thus indicating that this cluster did not have translators with extreme values as in Clusters 1 and 3. Table 3-15 shows the descriptive values for the No match category.

Cluster 4 clearly has the highest mean and median values according to all reviewers. They also have a very high minimum value. Cluster 3 has higher aggregated values, but all three clusters have similar median and mean values, showing that many translators have similar numbers of errors. If we look at the type of errors each Cluster made, the results are slightly different from those found for Fuzzy and MT matches. The majority of errors are in Language, followed by Terminology and Style. The reviewers seem to be of the opinion that the segments were not linguistically acceptable, as with MT matches. However, when we look at Cluster 4, the majority of errors are in Terminology. Once again, the glossary and the instructions were not followed correctly. The number of errors in Clusters 1, 2 and 3 are similar. This seems to point to the fact that translators with experience work better with the instructions given and are more thorough. This was also true for Fuzzy matches and to a lesser extent for MT matches.

Cluster + Rev		N	Mean	Median	SD	Min	Max
1	Rev 1	8	11.38	12.00	6.86	2	24
	Rev 2	8	12.25	8.50	8.38	3	27
	Rev 3	8	14.25	10.50	9.68	5	30
2	Rev 1	8	10.63	11.00	3.93	5	15
	Rev 2	8	9.63	8.50	3.11	6	15
	Rev 3	8	11.75	11.50	6.56	4	25
3	Rev 1	6	13.83	13.50	6.68	5	25
	Rev 2	6	11.83	10.00	5.04	8	21
	Rev 3	6	14.33	12.50	5.89	10	26
4	Rev 1	2	25.00	25.00	8.49	19	31
	Rev 2	2	20.50	20.50	0.71	20	21
	Rev 3	2	29.00	29.00	5.66	25	33

Table 3-15: Total errors for No match in clusters

Are these differences significant? We saw differences in speed but these were not statistically significant between the Clusters, so what will be the case for the number of errors? A Poisson regression model is applied with repeated measures taking the variable *Total errors* as the response variable and the offset as text length. Statistically significant differences are observed for the variable *Total errors* between the different Match categories: Fuzzy, MT and No match ($F=53.50$ and $p<0.0001$), as well as for the different clusters ($F=7.61$ and $p<0.0001$). Finally, statistically significant differences are observed in the interaction between Match categories and Clusters ($F=3.37$ and $p=0.0039$).

From this model, estimations of the mean values are obtained for the variable (total errors /text length) according to Match category with the corresponding interval levels of 95 percent. We present the results of these estimations but expressed in number of errors per segment length for better understanding. We consider the length of the original text (Fuzzy match, 618 words, MT match, 757 words and No match 749 words).

When we observe the interaction between Clusters and Match categories in Table 3-16, the results are interesting once again. Cluster 4 shows statistically significant differences in the Fuzzy match and No match categories. But in the MT match category, although the number of errors is higher, the confidence intervals overlap (row 8), showing that this difference is not statistically significant in this particular match category. So MT, in this instance, acted as a "leveller" in terms of errors for Cluster 4. The results are in line with the findings from De Almeida and O'Brien (2010) where more experienced translators were more accurate and also with Guerberof (2008) where MT had a levelling effect with novice translators.

Match	Cluster	Mean	SD	L	U
Fuzzy	1	7.41	0.74	6.08	9.03
Fuzzy	2	6.41	0.67	5.21	7.89
Fuzzy	3	5.42	0.69	4.21	6.96
Fuzzy	4	16.04	2.72	11.47	22.44
MT	1	8.07	0.79	6.65	9.79
MT	2	5.93	0.64	4.79	7.33
MT	3	8.37	0.94	6.70	10.45
MT	4	11.08	2.02	7.72	15.90
New	1	11.81	1.06	9.89	14.10
New	2	10.39	0.96	8.65	12.48
New	3	12.87	1.31	10.52	15.75
New	4	24.65	3.91	18.01	33.73

Table 3-16: Estimated mean of errors per match and cluster

The second part of our hypothesis claims that experience will not have an impact on the quality (measured in number of errors). Now, after going through the results, we find that this hypothesis is not supported by our data. In fact, the results show the opposite, that experience does play a part in the number of errors found. It is true that for Clusters 1, 2 and 3 there are no statistically significant differences, but there are for Cluster 4 that represented the novice group. The translators made more mistakes, mainly because they did not follow instructions and hence avoided the glossary, resulting in a higher speed but poorer quality. Interestingly, the number of errors was not as high in MT match segments, and this could be because some segments in MT required little change or because the terminology was already consistent with the glossary. Cluster 2, the most experienced, has fewer errors although these were not significantly lower. Cluster 3, with no experience in post-editing, performed worse in this category, showing again that training and experience in this task might help not only with respect to speed but also in quality.

Conclusions on the translators' experience

All the translators are professional translators who have varying experience in localisation and using tools and some experience in post-editing MT output, although the task represents a low percentage of their work and has not been performed for a very long period of time. Their working speed seems to be in accordance with industry standards and is quite homogeneous. A multivariate analysis was setup to distribute the translators into four different clusters to test our hypothesis. The results indicate that the incidence of experience on the processing speed is not significantly different. Translators with more years of experience performed similarly to other very novice translators. Translators with less or no experience in post-editing were the slowest cluster but again the differences were not significant. This seems to be different from our previous findings (Guerberof 2008) and from the findings by De Almeida and O'Brien (2010), although more in line with the findings in Tatsumi (2010). However, the numbers of participants in those studies are lower, to the extent that one post-editor has a great impact in the whole group, whereas in this project there were 24 translators. Further research is needed to draw definitive conclusions.

Our findings on errors are in line with those in De Almeida and O'Brien (2010). Translators with more experience made fewer mistakes than those with less experience. As Offersgaard et al. (2008) suggests a "good post-editor is an experienced proof-reader" (ibid: 156). The number of errors was significantly different between Cluster 4 (the novice group) and the other clusters with regards to Fuzzy and No match. The difference was higher but not significant for MT match. Also the type of errors made by the novice translators were mostly Terminology errors, as opposed to Language or Style as in the other clusters, indicating that these translators with less experience were less thorough with terminology and with instructions than were the more experienced ones. But this is not to say that they did not have more errors in the other categories as well. The MT output, however, seems to have had a levelling effect as far as errors is concerned. This might lead us to suggest that using high-quality MT output as opposed to Fuzzy matches below the 95 percent threshold might be advisable for translators with less experience, as there are more probabilities of having perfect matches in the proposed texts and hence of making fewer mistakes. Are novice translators more tolerant to errors in quality than senior translators? Our reviewers were senior translators and they might have a different idea of quality than the novice translators. Is the current review method adequate to establish a quality suitable for the market? Lagoudaki (2008) and Flournoy and Duran (2009) also suggest that inexperienced translators seem to be more tolerant of MT errors and structures than experienced ones. Similarly, Depraetere (2010) pointed out that translation trainees are more tolerant of MT errors. It might be that "new" generations of translators might have a different outlook on translation quality to that of senior translators. Finally, it was also observed that the cluster with the least or no experience in post-editing performs better with Fuzzy matches in terms of errors than with MT matches, and this seems to indicate that experience and training on post-editing might have a pay-off in terms of quality, although this might not be the only factor.

Bibliography

Beinborn, L. 2010. "*Post-Editing of Statistical Machine Translation: A Crosslinguistic Analysis of the Temporal, Technical and Cognitive Effort.*" Master of Science Thesis, Saarland University.

Carl, M., B. Dragsted, J. Elming, D. Hardt, and A.L. Jakobsen. 2011. "The Process of Post-Editing: A Pilot Study." *Proceedings of the 8th International NLPSC Workshop*. Frederiksberg, Copenhagen, August 20–21. Accessed June 2013. http://www.mt-archive.info/NLPCS-2011-Carl-1.pdf.

De Almeida, G., and S. O'Brien. 2010. "Analysing Post-Editing Performance: Correlations with Years of Translation Experience." *Proceedings of the 14th Annual Conference of the EAMT*. St. Raphael, May 27-28. Accessed June 2013. http://www.mt-archive.info/EAMT-2010-Almeida.pdf.

De Sutter, N. 2012. "MT Evaluation Based on Post-Editing: A Proposal." In *Perspectives on Translation Quality*, edited by Ilse Depraetere, 125–143. Berlin: Mouton de Gruyter.

De Sutter, N., and I. Depraetere 2012. "Post-Edited Translation Quality, Edit Distance and Fluency Scores: Report on a Case Study." *Proceedings of Journée d'études Traduction et qualité Méthodologies en matière d'assurance qualité*. Universtité Lille 3. Sciences humaines et sociales, Lille, February 3. Accessed June 2013. http://stl.recherche.univ-lille3.fr/colloques/20112012/DeSutter&Depraetere_2012_02_03.pdf.

Depraetere, I. 2010. "What Counts as Useful Advice in a University Post-editing Training Context? Report on a case study." *Proceedings of the 14th Annual EAMT Conference*. St. Raphael, May 27-28. Accessed June 2013. http://www.mt-archive.info/EAMT-2010-Depraetere-2.pdf.

Flournoy, R., and C. Duran 2009. "Machine Translation and Document Localization at Adobe: From Pilot to Production." *Proceedings of the MT Summit XII*. Ottawa, August 26–30. Accessed June 2013. http://www.mt-archive.info/MTS-2009-Flournoy.pdf.

García, I. 2010. "Is Machine Translation Ready Yet?" *Target* 22(1):7–21. Amsterdam and Philadelphia: John Benjamins.

García, I. 2011. "Translating by Post-editing: Is it the Way Forward?" *Machine Translation* 25(3):217–237. Netherlands: Springer

Greenacre, M. 2008. *La práctica del análisis de correspondencias*. (Spanish Translation of *Correspondence Analysis in Practice*, Second Edition). Madrid: Manuales Fundación BBVA.

Guerberof, A. 2008. "*Productivity and Quality in Machine Translation and Translation Memory outputs*." Masters Dissertation, Universistat Rovira i Virgili. http://bit.ly/1a83G9p.

He, Y., Y. Ma, J. Roturier, A. Way, and J. van Genabith. 2010a. "Bridging SMT and TM with Translation Recommendation." *Proceedings of the 48th Annual Meeting of ACL*. Uppsala, July 10–16. Accessed June 2013. http://www.mt-archive.info/ACL-2010-He.pdf.

He, Y., Y. Ma, J. Roturier, A. Way, and J. van Genabith. 2010b. "Improving the Post-editing Experience using Translation Recommendation: A User Study." *Proceedings of the 9th Annual AMTA Conference*. Denver, October 31–November 4. Accessed June 2012. http://doras.dcu.ie/15803/.

Koehn, P., H. Hoang, A. Birch, C. Callison-Burch, M. Federico, N. Bertoldi, B. Cowan, W. Shen, C. Moran, R. Zens, C. Dyer, O. Bojar, A. Constantin, and E. Herbst. 2007. "Moses: Open Source Toolkit for Statistical Machine Translation." *Proceedings of the Demo and Poster Sessions of the 45th Annual Meeting of the Association for Computational Linguistics (ACL '07)*. 177–180. Prague, Czech Republic.

Lagoudaki, E. 2008. "The value of Machine Translation for the Professional Translator." *Proceedings of the 8th AMTA Conference*. Hawaii: 262–269. Accessed June 2013. http://www.amtaweb.org/papers/3.04_Lagoudaki.pdf.

Koponen, M. 2012. "Comparing Human Perceptions of Post-editing Effort with Post-editing Operations." *Proceedings of the 7th Workshop on Statistical Machine Translation*. Association for Computational Linguistics, Montreal, June 7–8. Accessed June 2013. http://www.aclweb.org/anthology-new/W/W12/W12-3123.pdf.

O'Brien, S. 2006a. "Methodologies for Measuring Correlations between Post-editing Effort and Machine Translatability." *Machine Translation:* 37–58. Netherlands: Springer.

—. 2006b. "Eye-tracking and Translation Memory Matches." *Perspectives: Studies in Translatology*. 14(3):185-205

—. 2011. "Towards Predicting Post-Editing Productivity." *Machine Translation* 25(3):197–215. Netherlands: Springer.

—. 2012. "Towards a Dynamic Quality Evaluation Model for Translation." *Journal of Specialised Translation* 17. Accessed June 2013. http://www.jostrans.org/issue17/art_obrien.pdf.

Offersgaard, L., C. Povlsen, L. Almsten, and B. Maegaard. 2008. "Domain Specific MT Use." *Proceedings of the 12th EAMT Conference*. Hamburg, September 22–23. Accessed June 2013 http://www.mt-archive.info/EAMT-2008-Offersgaard.pdf.

Papineni, K., S. Roukos, T. Ward, and W.J. Zhu. 2002. "BLEU: A Method for Automatic Evaluation of Machine Translation." *Proceedings of the 40th Annual Meeting of the Association for Computational Linguistics* (ACL), Philadelphia, July 7–12. Accessed June 2013. http://acl.ldc.upenn.edu/P/P02/P02-1040.pdf.

Plitt, M., and F. Masselot. 2010. "A Productivity Test of Statistical Machine Translation Post-editing in a Typical Localisation Context." *The Prague Bulletin of Mathematical Linguistics*. Prague: 7–16. Accessed June 2013. http://ufal.mff.cuni.cz/pbml/93/art-plitt-masselot.pdf.

Snover, M., B. Dorr, R. Schwartz, L. Micciulla, and J. Makhoul. 2006. "A Study of Translation Edit Rate with Targeted Human Annotation." *Proceedings of the 7th Annual AMTA Conference*, Cambridge, August 8–12. Accessed June 2013. http://mt-archive.info/AMTA-2006-Snover.pdf.

Specia, L. 2011. "Exploiting Objective Annotations for Measuring Translation Post-editing Effort." *Proceedings of the 15th Annual EAMT Conference*. Leuven, May 30–31. Accessed June 2013. http://www.mt-archive.info/EAMT-2011-Specia.pdf.

Specia, L., N. Cancedda, M. Dymetman, M. Turchi, and N. Cristianini. 2009a. "Estimating the Sentence-Level Quality of Machine Translation Systems." *Proceedings of the 13th Annual Conference of the EAMT*, Barcelona. May 14–15. Accessed June 2013. http://clg.wlv.ac.uk/papers/Specia_EAMT2009.pdf.

Specia, L., C. Saunders, M. Turchi, Z. Wang, and J. Shawe-Taylor. 2009b. "Improving the Confidence of Machine Translation Quality Estimates." *Proceedings of the MT Summit XII*. Ottawa, August 26–30. Accessed June 2013. http://eprints.pascal-network.org/archive/00005490/01/MTS-2009-Specia.pdf.

Tatsumi, M. 2010. "*Post-Editing Machine Translated Text in A Commercial Setting: Observation and Statistical Analysis*." PhD Thesis, Dublin City University. http://doras.dcu.ie/16062/.

Tatsumi, M., and J. Roturier. 2010. "Source Text Characteristics and Technical and Temporal Post-editing Effort: What is their Relationship?" *Proceedings of the 2nd Joint EM+/CNGL Workshop "Bringing MT to the User: Research on Integrating MT in the Translation Industry"*. Denver, November 4. Accessed June 2013. http://www.mt-archive.info/JEC-2010-Tatsumi.pdf.

Turian, J., L. Shen, and I.D. Melamed. 2003. "Evaluation of Machine Translation and Its Evaluation." *Proceedings of the MT Summit IX*. New Orleans, September 23–27. Accessed June 2012. http://nlp.cs.nyu.edu/pubs/papers/turian-summit03eval.

PART II:

MICRO-LEVEL TRANSLATION PROCESSES

CHAPTER FOUR

POST-EDITED QUALITY, POST-EDITING BEHAVIOUR AND HUMAN EVALUATION: A CASE STUDY[1]

ILSE DEPRAETERE, NATHALIE DE SUTTER AND ARDA TEZCAN

Abstract

In this chapter, we address the correlation between post-editing similarity and the human evaluation of machine translation. We were interested to find out whether a high similarity score corresponded to a high quality score and vice versa in the sample that we compiled for the purposes of the case study. A group of translation trainees post-edited a sample and a number of these informants also rated the MT output for quality on a five-point scale. We calculated Pearson's correlation coefficient as well as the relative standard deviation per informant for each activity with a view to determining which of the two evaluation methods appeared to be the more reliable measurement given the project settings. Our sample also enabled us to test whether MT enhances the productivity of translation trainees, and whether the quality of post-edited sentences is different from the quality of sentences translated 'from scratch'.

Aims and general background

Different methodologies have been put forward to assess the quality of machine translation (MT) output, ranging from the human evaluation of attributes such as intelligibility and accuracy to the automated calculation of output quality (cf. e.g. White 2003 for an overview of different types of MT evaluation and evaluation methodology). The text similarity between the MT output and post-edited MT output has also been used as a measure to gauge MT quality, one of the general ideas being that the more similar the MT output is to the post-edited translation, the better the quality of the output. In this chapter, we will zoom in on post-editing similarity and human quality evaluation. We will report on a case study that addresses two questions:

- Is post-edited (PE) quality different from the quality resulting from human translation without the aid of any translation technology?
- Does the effort involved in post-editing a machine-translated segment correlate with the score resulting from human quality assessment? Put differently, if an informant gives a high quality score to an MT segment, does this assessment translate into minimal edit effort (in which case the similarity between the MT output and the post-edited segment is high) and vice versa: if an evaluator judges the MT output to be of low quality, is this assessment reflected in a more considerable edit effort (in which case there are many edits resulting in a low similarity between the MT output and the post-edited output?) What does the correlation reveal about the reliability of the two methodologies to measure the quality of the MT output?

We will first describe the project settings and we will then address the different research questions and formulate the conclusions to be drawn from the current project.

Project settings: Evaluation set, informants, evaluation tasks

The source text for this project was taken from a bilingual corpus of English-French texts that is available online at http://cabal.rezo.net/. It was compiled at the University of Poitiers for purposes of research in contrastive linguistics and it consists of 200 articles, mainly from *Le Monde Diplomatique*, supplemented with articles from *National Geographic*, *Time magazine*, *Courrier international* and a few chapters from novels by Jules Vernes, corresponding to a total of about 400,000 words. As we did not aim to evaluate the quality of the MT engine used but were rather interested in the correlation between post-editing similarity and human quality judgments on the one hand and the quality of post-edited translation on the other, our selection of a sample from the corpus was random in the sense that we did not have a specific domain or specific textual features in mind. We wanted to make sure that the sample was not too technical so that the informants' general background knowledge would be sufficient to understand the text and to produce a quality translation without having to invest too much time in researching the terminology. We used a rule-based system (Systran 7) to produce the output; twenty terms were added to the dictionary. We selected an excerpt from an article, 'The Unbeatable Body' from *National Geographic* that reports on the ways in which athletes work towards enhancing their performance. The sample consisted of 3,045 English source words, corresponding to 181 segments. The French translation available online (*Le corps : repousser toujours plus loin ses limites*) was used as a reference translation.

The informants who participated in the project were translation trainees from the University of Lille 3, who were registered in the second year of a Master's course in computer-aided translation and project management. They had all followed a course on MT in which the history of MT, the evaluation of MT, types of MT, controlled languages and post-editing were covered. The course also involved the presentation of some MT use cases. The following topics were discussed during the session on post-editing:

- Definition of post-editing
- Different types of post-editing (rapid, minimal, full (Allen 2003))
- A critical discussion of the notion of 'necessary/unnecessary changes' on the basis of Guzmàn (2007) and some further examples

Two of the fifteen students who participated were non-native speakers of French. All participants carried out a productivity evaluation task; six of them also evaluated the MT output (human quality assessment task). As will be described below, an experienced professional translator who also teaches translation courses at Master's level evaluated the translations produced (during the productivity evaluation) by the six informants who did the quality assessment.

The informants worked in a web-based environment developed by CrossLang which presents the source text segment by segment.

A productivity evaluation task requires the informant to translate the source segment if the target box is empty and to post-edit it if the target box contains a pre-translation generated by the MT engine (cf. Figure 4-1). The tool measures the time spent translating or post-editing each segment. This set-up makes it possible to calculate the average throughput (in words per hour) for both activities (translation from scratch and post-editing).

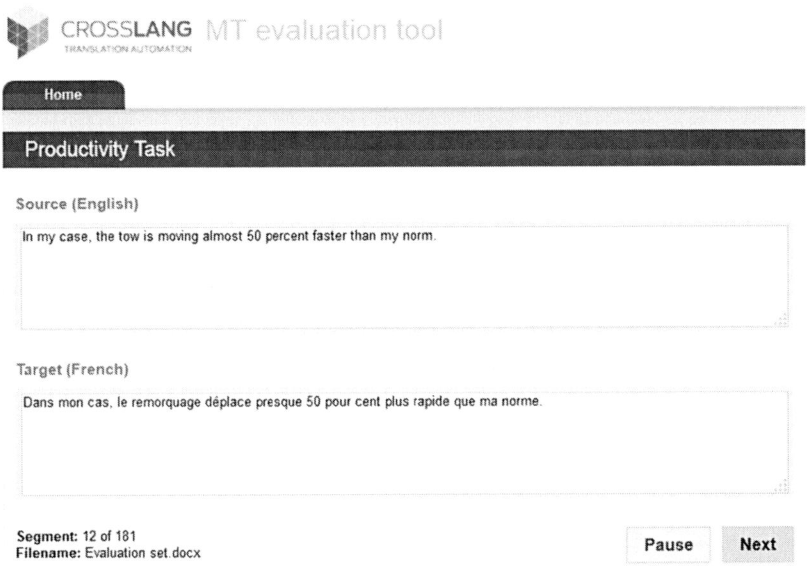

Figure 4-1: CrossLang web-based evaluation platform – productivity task

For this project, half of the segments were pre-translated with MT; for half of them there was no input from MT and the informants had to translate directly from the source text ('translation from scratch'). The instructions were to produce a high-quality translation. In other words, 'full post-editing' (Allen 2003) was required. No mistakes could be left uncorrected; the quality had to equal that of a 'manual' translation without input from MT. In the context of the experiment reported, pre-translated target segments and empty target segments alternated: for one subgroup of informants, the even segments were MT-translated and had to be post-edited; the uneven segments presented a source segment which the informants had to translate from scratch. For the second subgroup of informants, the uneven segments were pre-translated and the even segments had to be translated from scratch. We designed the experiment in this way to make sure that we had several post-edited versions of the target text at our disposal and several versions of the text that had been translated without input from MT.

It was technically not possible for the informants to go back to previous segments for revision. Once the segment had been saved by clicking on 'next (segment)', it could not be opened again. It was possible though to interrupt the post-editing activity in order to take a break by

clicking on 'pause'. The participants' productivity was calculated as follows: the system measures the time spent by each informant on the individual segments. The total time spent on each subset, that is, the post-edited subset and the 'translation-from-scratch' subset, was divided by the total number of words in the subset. The average time spent per word which results from this calculation was then extrapolated to the average number of words processed per hour within the corresponding subset.
The next step in the experiment involved a quality evaluation: six of the informants who participated in the first exercise also evaluated the quality of the MT output in a similar web-based environment. In this case, the informant was each time presented with a source segment and the corresponding MT output and (s)he had to assign a score (out of 5) corresponding to the quality observed (cf. Figure 4-2).

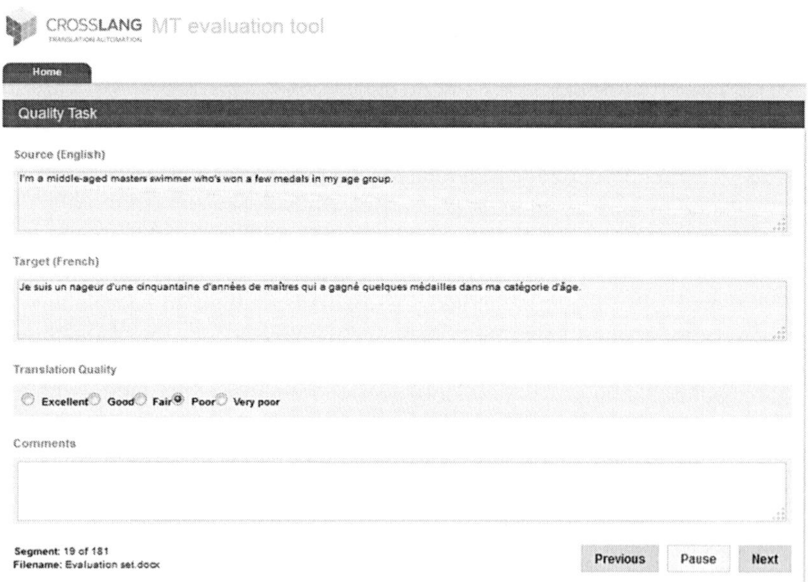

Figure 4-2: CrossLang web-based evaluation platform – quality task

Finally, the translations produced in the productivity task by the same set of six informants were evaluated in the same interface by a professional translator who also teaches translation courses at Master's level. More details will be provided about the rating scale below.

Productivity evaluation

It has been established in several (business and academic) case studies that the use of MT enhances translators' productivity (cf. e.g. Offersgaard et al. 2008, de Almeida and O'Brien 2010, Plitt and Masselot 2010, Plitt 2012, Guerberof 2012). However, in the experiment described in Carl et al. (2011), the use of MT did not result in a significant productivity increase. The authors believe that this may have been partly due to the low number of participants in the tasks; they also point out that while the translators were experienced, none of the post-editors had experience with the use of CAT tools or post-editing. Likewise in García's (2010) study, the use of MT pre-translations did not produce a statistically significant productivity increase; here the informants were 'educated bilinguals with an interest in translation, but not professional translators' (2010, 10). The most important difference in terms of project settings relates to the profile of the project participants: with the exception of García (2010), they were professional translators in previous studies whereas in our experiment, they were novice translators in the final stages of their training. The domains, the language pairs involved and the size of the corpus are further parameters which differ across the case studies. We first wanted to find out to what extent our results are in line with observations about productivity enhancement in previous research, further steps in our project being the comparison of the quality of both types of output (post-edited translation vs. translation from scratch) and the calculation of the correlation between human quality judgements and similarity scores.

Productivity increase?

In the project at hand, we compared the productivity when post-editing MT output with the productivity when translating from scratch. We were interested in finding out if MT makes novice translators more productive. Figures 4-3 and 4-4 provide details for each of the informants. On the basis of the methodology explained earlier, the average words per hour translated from scratch/post-edited by each informant was calculated:

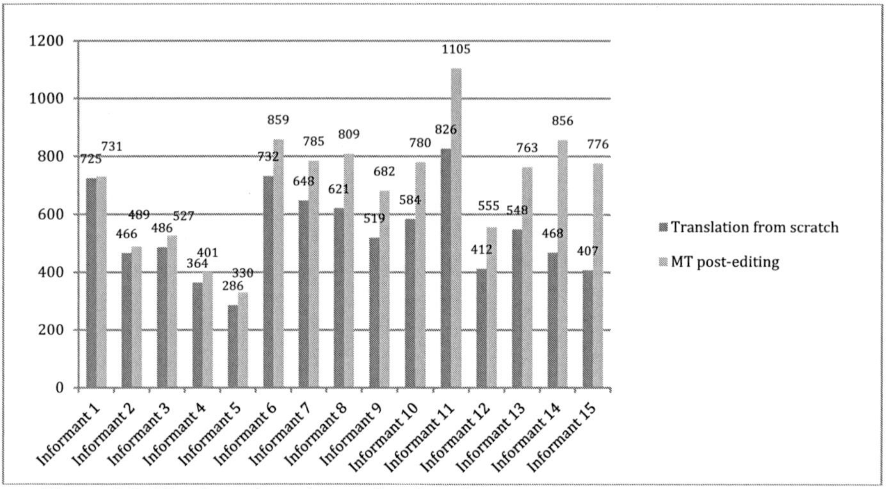

Figure 4-3: Number of words translated per hour

Figure 4-4 gives an overview of the productivity increase in percentages. No matter how fast or slow thc informants work, in all cases, there is an increase of productivity during post-editing, ranging between 1% and 91%:

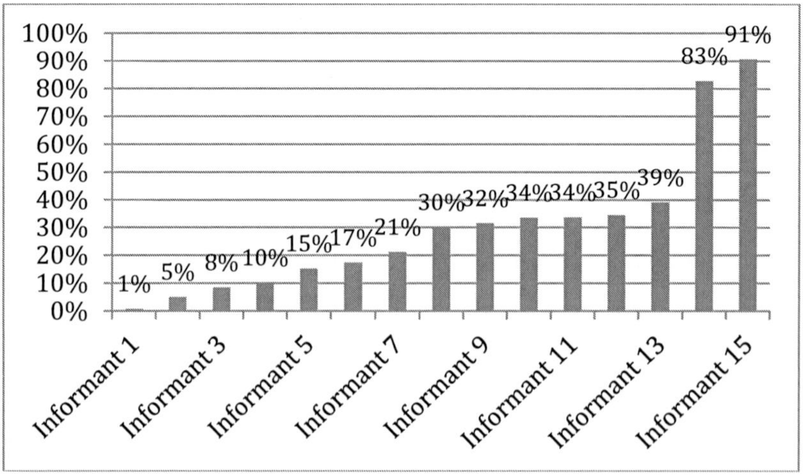

Figure 4-4: Productivity increase in percentages

Informant 14 and informant 15 are non-native speakers of French; the productivity enhancement of 83% and 91% shows that they benefit most from MT. This observation suggests that given this experimental set-up, MT is particularly beneficial to people whose proficiency in the target language is not optimal. In order not to bias the results, we excluded these two informants when calculating the average productivity enhancement for all informants. Figure 4-5 shows the average throughput per hour with and without the aid of MT (on the basis of the results from the 13 native speakers who participated):

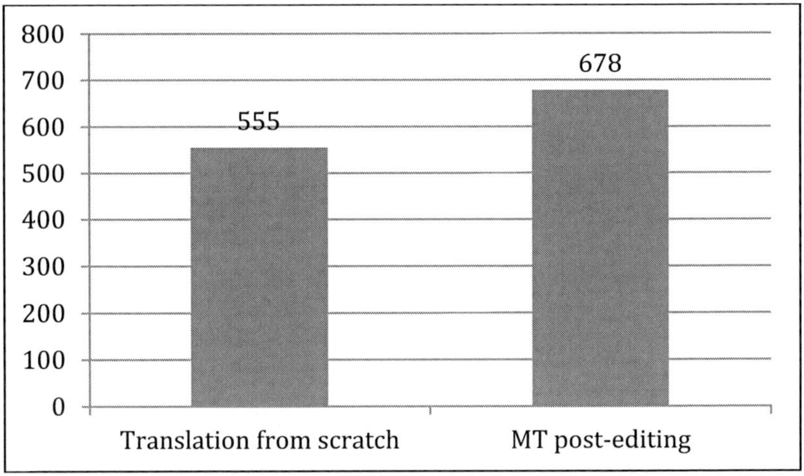

Figure 4-5: Average throughput in words per hour

The average productivity increase is 22%.[2,3] In comparison with the studies cited earlier, the average throughput increase in our experiment is lower. The throughputs for previous studies are summarised here for comparison purposes:

- Offersgaard et al. 2008: 67%
- de Almeida and O'Brien 2010: 170%
- Plitt and Masselot 2010: 72%
- Guerberof 2012: 37%

A variety of factors may explain the differences observed, the profile of the informants (experienced translators in the cases cited vs. novice translators in this project) no doubt being among the most important ones. It also needs to be added that in the case of de Almeida and O'Brien

(2010), the figures result from the extrapolation of post-editing time per word, on the basis of a corpus of 150 words, to number of post-edited words for an 8-hour working day. As the authors point out themselves (cf. also O'Brien 2011), this extrapolation presupposes that it is possible to sustain a very high post-editing productivity over a full working day; actual values are likely to be lower though due to the need for post-editors to take breaks from what can be a complex cognitive task. Also, the calculation of average throughput does not bring out the potential differences between language pairs, MT engines or domains. For instance, Plitt (2012) mentions a productivity increase of 131% for French compared to 42% for Chinese.

Quality of post-edited translation

While the results of the experiment as such confirm that MT has a positive impact on average throughput, we were particularly interested in determining whether the productivity increase that goes hand in hand with the use of MT did not result in a decrease in translation quality. If it did, then it would be clear that the potential of MT is limited.

Various techniques were used in previous studies to detect potential quality differences between post-edited output and 'human translation'. Fiederer and O'Brien (2009) asked 11 raters to assess the output in terms of accuracy, clarity and style on a 4-point scale. The assessment revealed no significant differences between the two types of translations in terms of clarity; the post-edited output did significantly better in terms of accuracy, but the 'human translations' scored significantly higher than the post-edited translations in terms of style. In Plitt and Masselot (2010), the majority of the final translations (including both 'post-editing jobs' and 'translation jobs') were evaluated by the Autodesk linguistic quality assurance team and all the jobs were rated as average or good, which means that they would have been published as is. Overall the proportion of sentences in which errors were flagged was higher for the translation jobs than for the post-editing jobs. In Daems et al. (2013), both the post-edited translations and human translations of a sample of journalistic texts (four texts ranging between 260 to 288 words) post-edited or translated by translation trainees[4] were annotated for 'adequacy' and 'accuracy', each parameter being associated with a specific set of translation error types. Their conclusion is that even though the type of error seems text-dependent, overall (for three of the four texts), the quality of the post-edited text was judged to be higher than that of the human translation. In a similar way, Guerberof observes that '[t]ranslators made more errors when translating without a proposal and made a very similar number of errors when editing text from MT or TM [Translation Memory] segments from the 85–94% range' (2009, 165). In Carl et al. (2011), seven evaluators ranked four candidate translations (two 'manual' translations and two post-edited translations). While the post-edited segments were ranked better than the 'manual' segments, the difference was not significant. In García (2010), the output was evaluated by two markers who gave a score out of 50 on the basis of guidelines of the Australian National Accreditation Authority for Translators and Interpreters (NAATI); the 'from MT' mode was favoured in 59% of cases, the overall mark being 33.8/50 for translation 'from ST' and 36.4 for translation 'from MT'.

We used two different methods to shed light on the question of the quality of post-edited translations. First, we selected six informants and asked a professional translator who also teaches translation courses at Master's level to evaluate the translations.[5] As explained earlier, the evaluation was done in the same environment as the productivity evaluation, the difference being that the translator was each time presented with a target segment that had either been translated from scratch or post-edited by the informant; the evaluator did not know which part of the text was post-edited MT output. The professional translator/assessor evaluated the six translations, and for each of them a score ranging from 1 to 5 was given to a total of 181 segments. We explained that 1/5 corresponded to a very poor translation, 5/5 meant the translation was excellent, 3/5 being a score reflecting average quality, 2/5 being worse than average but not very poor and 4/5 corresponding to better than average but not excellent quality. We chose this professional translator as an evaluator because of her wide experience, not only as a translator (14 years) but also as a translation course instructor (7 years) at Master's level.

The subgroup of informants was determined as follows: we made sure that the translations (a) represented the range of possible productivity increases (relatively low, relatively high) and that they (b) represented the range of translation rates (slow, average, fast):

Informant	Translation throughput	Post-editing throughput	Productivity increase	Profile
Informant 2	466	489	5%	Average speed – low increase
Informant 4	364	401	10%	Average speed – low increase
Informant 5	286	330	15%	Low speed – average increase
Informant 7	412	555	21%	Average speed – average increase
Informant 9	519	682	32%	Average speed - high increase
Informant 11	826	1105	34%	High speed – high increase

Table 4-1: Informant profiles based on average throughput and productivity increase

On the basis of the scores given by the translator/course instructor, we calculated an average score per informant for the post-edited text and the 'translation from scratch' part of the sample. The results are represented in Figure 4-6:

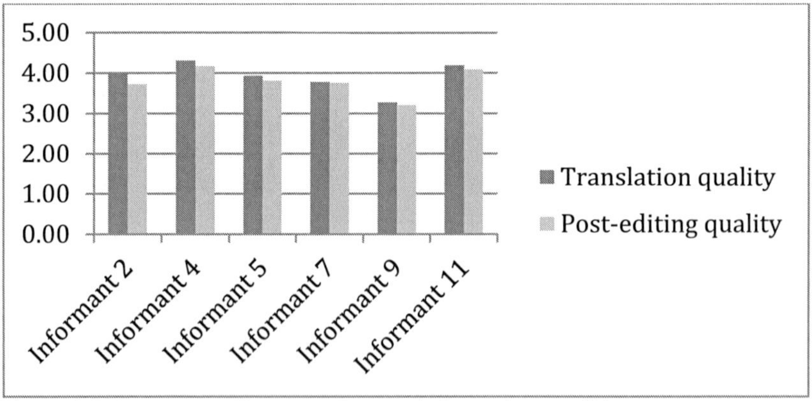

Figure 4-6: Average quality scores for translation and post-editing

The differences visualised in Figure 4-6 are based on the scores in the Table 4-2:

Informant	Translation quality (average)	Post-edited quality (average)	Difference (percentage on a score of 5)
Informant 2	3.98	3.73	-5%
Informant 4	4.31	4.17	-2.8%
Informant 5	3.93	3.81	-2.4%
Informant 7	3.78	3.76	-0.4%
Informant 9	3.27	3.21	-1.2%
Informant 11	4.19	4.09	-2%
Overall average	3.91	3.79	-2.4%

Table 4-2: Quality assessment of translations by a translator/translation course instructor

In all six cases, the quality of the translation from scratch is rated higher than that of the post-edited segments. The differences show a maximal decrease of 5% for informant 2 and an average decrease of 2.4%. In order to detect and measure, in a different way, potential quality differences between the 'translation from scratch' segments and the post-edited segments, we also compared the final translation produced by the informants with the human reference translation available online, the assumption being that the latter is of good quality, and that therefore, a distinct difference in similarity may be indicative of a quality difference. Based on the similarity scores for each individual segment in the two categories (translation from scratch and post-editing), we calculated the average similarity with the reference translation for the part that was translated from scratch as well as for the part that was generated by post-editing the MT output. We used the similar text algorithm that calculates the similarity between two strings based on character matches as described in Oliver (1993). The higher the percentage, the more similar the segments; 100% similarity means that the two segments are identical.

On average, similarity is roughly 60% with the reference translation. As is clear from Figure 4-7, the translation from scratch and the post-edited measures do not differ substantially: the difference in similarity with the reference translation between the translation from scratch and the post-edited translation is indeed minimal, that is, between 0% and 4%. In one out of six cases, the score is the same. In two (informants 7 and 11) out of the five remaining cases, the post-edited version is just slightly more similar to the reference translation than the translated version.

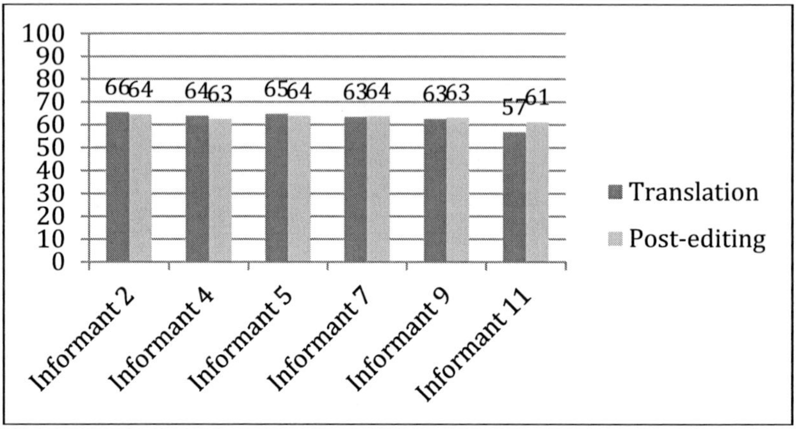

Figure 4-7: Similarity between translated/post-edited versions and reference translation

Even though we did not do the quality comparison 'translation from scratch vs. post-edited translation' for the whole set of informants, on the basis of the sample examined, we can conclude that the difference in quality level between the post-edited version and the human translation is minimal. In other words, it seems that the MT post-editing does not jeopardize the final translation quality in this project, a conclusion which is in line with the general tendency observed in previous work.

Correlation between post-editing effort and human MT quality evaluation

The project data also enabled us to analyse some aspects of post-editing behaviour.[6] We were particularly interested in finding out whether the similarity between the MT output and the post-edited version of the MT output correlated with human evaluation scores: as a subset of six informants both post-edited the sample and evaluated the MT output, it was possible to compare the results of both evaluation types.

Human evaluation of MT quality

The six informants whose translations were evaluated by a translator were also asked to rate the quality of the MT output segment by segment by assigning scores ranging from 1 (very poor) to 5 (excellent). The informants had some useful experience of translation quality evaluation: they had received input about the quality of the translations they produced during their training, they had followed a course on revision and a session on the evaluation of MT, during which several *n*-point scales for the evaluation of MT, such as the 5-point scale used in the DARPA evaluations (cf. e.g. White 2003), and those in Caroll (1966) and Nagao et al. (1985) had been presented. Even though the informants were told to trust their translation intuition when assigning scores, the following, more explanatory rating scale was also put at their disposal in case they wanted some guidance in terms of the scoring system to be applied. This scale is inspired by the 5-point scale used in the DARPA evaluations and various descriptions of quality levels used in the industry.

Values	Description
Excellent (5)	Read the MT output first. Then read the source text (ST). **All** meaning expressed in source fragment appears in the translation fragment. Your **understanding is not improved** by reading the ST because the MT output is satisfactory and would not need to be modified (**grammatically correct/proper terminology is used**/maybe not stylistically perfect but fulfills the main objective, i.e. transferring accurately all information).
Good (4)	Read the MT output first. Then read the source text. **Most** meaning expressed in source fragment appears in the translation fragment. Your **understanding is not improved** by reading the ST even though the MT output contains **minor grammatical mistakes** (word order/punctuation errors/word formation/morphology). You would **not need to refer to the ST** to correct these mistakes.
Fair (3)	Read the MT output first. Then read the source text. **Much** meaning expressed in source fragment appears in the translation fragment. However, your **understanding is improved** by reading the ST allowing you to correct **minor grammatical mistakes** in the MT output (word order/punctuation errors/word formation/morphology). You would **need to refer to the ST** to correct these mistakes.
Poor (2)	Read the MT output first. Then read the source text. **Little** meaning expressed in source fragment appears in the translation fragment. Your **understanding is improved considerably** by reading the ST, due to **significant errors** in the MT output (textual and syntactical coherence/textual pragmatics/word formation/morphology). You would have to **re-read the ST a few times to correct** these errors in the MT output.
Very poor (1)	Read the MT output first. Then read the source text. **None** of the meaning expressed in source fragment appears in the translation fragment. Your **understanding only derives from reading the ST**, as you could not understand the MT output. It contained serious errors in any of the categories listed above, including wrong POS. You could only produce a translation by dismissing most of the MT output and/or re-translating from scratch.

Figure 4-8: Description of the rating scale for the evaluation of MT output

The hypothesis for this part of the experiment is as follows: if an informant judges the quality to be perfect (5/5), there should be no need to post-edit. In a similar way, if the quality is bad (1/5), the similarity between the MT output and the post-edited version should be rather low. Potential correlations like these were not discussed with the informants. As the quality evaluation task took place two months after the productivity task, it can be assumed that their evaluation behaviour was not consciously monitored by their post-editing behaviour. In other words, the informants were not aware that we were testing the potential correlation (or not) between human evaluation and post-editing effort.

Figure 4-9 gives an overview of the average quality of the MT output as assessed by the informants.

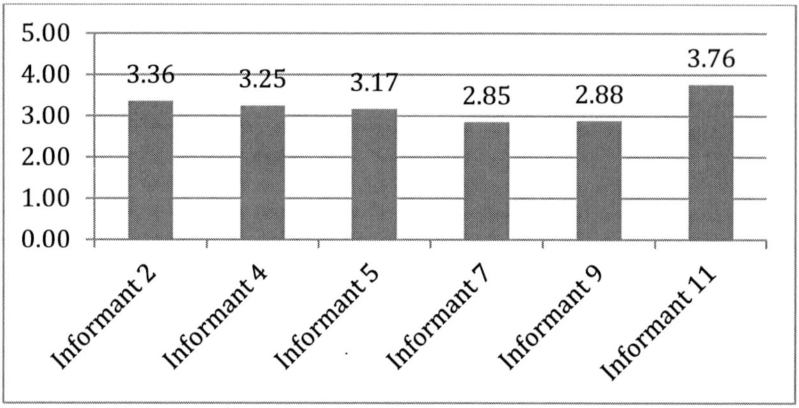

Figure 4-9: Human quality assessment of MT output

The average similarity score between the MT output and the post-edited output for each of the informants was as follows:

	Average similarity score
Informant 2	81.89
Informant 4	77.11
Informant 5	76.09
Informant 7	81.08
Informant 9	81.19
Informant 11	76.63

Table 4-3: Average similarity score per informant

Scoring behaviour of informants

First, we checked the overall scoring behaviour of the informants. Table 4-4 gives an overview of the number of segments, also in percentages, that were given a score of 1, 2, 3, 4 and 5 respectively by each of the informants:

	1		2		3		4		5	
Informant 5	13	7%	39	22%	63	35%	36	20%	30	17%
Informant 7	21	12%	55	30%	53	29%	34	19%	18	10%
Informant 2	11	6%	24	13%	69	38%	43	24%	34	19%
Informant 9	33	18%	42	23%	45	25%	35	19%	26	14%
Informant 11	3	2%	20	11%	49	27%	56	31%	53	29%
Informant 4	6	3%	33	18%	68	38%	57	31%	17	9%
Overall average		10%		24%		38%		29%		20%

Table 4-4: Human evaluation results by six informants

The overall picture that emerges is that informants 7 and 9 are most critical about the quality of the MT output (cf. the relatively high number of segments that get a score of 1/5); however, this does not mean that they are critical of MT quality in general: the number of segments they give a rating of 5 is not the lowest compared to the other informants. Informant 11 rates almost 30% of the segments as 'excellent'; this is a far higher number compared to the other informants. Informant 4 appears to be a very cautious and careful assessor, both in terms of giving a very bad and a very good score. On average, half of the segments get a score of 4 or 5. The data seem to confirm that quality evaluation is subjective (cf. e.g. Secară 2005, Fiederer and O'Brien 2009) and that it is necessary to work with multiple informants.

Bearing in mind these evaluation profiles, we looked in more detail at the post-editing effort for the segments that at least one of the informants graded as 1 or as 5. Post-editing effort is a textual similarity measure between the MT output and the post-edited version of the MT output. A score of 100% means that the informant did not make any corrections. The lower the score, the more corrections are needed and as such we can assume that the MT output generated by the engine was not very good.[7] Note that each informant post-edited half of the segments and translated half of the segments from scratch. In other words, it is only for half of the segments per subset that we can calculate the similarity of MT output and post-edited output. Informants 2, 5, 7 were assigned subset A (even segments post-edited, uneven segments translated from scratch); informants 4, 9 and 11 were assigned subset B (uneven segments post-edited, even segments translated from scratch). In the sections below, we focus on the informants' assessment of excellent and bad quality. We comment on the human evaluation scores and post-editing effort. For each of the bands (band 1 and band 5), we compared post-editing behaviour across informants. We also assessed the trustworthiness of post-editing similarity as compared to human quality evaluation on the basis of the calculation of the correlation between the two scores and the standard deviation for each method of evaluation.

High quality score and post-editing behaviour

As shown in Table 4-5, 34 segments out of a total of 181 were given a score of 5 by at least one of the informants. In 14 cases, they unanimously agree on a score of 5/5; in 10 cases, only two informants gave a score of 5/5; in the remaining 10 cases, only 1 informant graded the output as excellent. Given that informant 11, who has the highest number of good quality segments, and informant 9, who has the highest number of low quality segments evaluated the same data set, there is more diversity in the scores in subset B than among those in subset A. All in all, and taking into account the evaluation profiles, the informants' views on excellent quality are rather in agreement, with two exceptions: in two cases, informant 9 gives a score of 1 (seg. 168) and a score of 2 (seg. 94) to segments that informant 11 graded both as 5 and informant 4 as 4 and 3 respectively. Given that the similarity score of informant 9 is higher than that of the other two informants, we feel that informant 9 may have temporarily got the grading system confused, taking 1 as the top score rather than the lowest score.

For 23 out of the 34 top rated segments, the similarity score is similar. The segments with a difference in similarity score of more than 10% between one informant vs. the two others are in bold.

What is most striking though is that a score of 5 does not mean that no changes are made to the segments. They may be minimal, but as is clear from Table 4-5, 21 out of 34 segments (that were given a score of 5 by at least one informant) have been post-edited by all three informants. Among the 14 segments that were given a score of 5 by the three informants, there are only 2 segments which have not been post-edited by any of the informants; 3 of them have not been post-edited by two informants, and 8 segments have not been post-edited by one of them.

The edit rates in bold in Table 4-5 show that it is especially informant 5 in the first group and informant 4 in the second group whose post-editing behaviour is different from the other informants in the group. In order to get a better insight into the post-editing behaviour in the 11 cases in which there is a difference of at least 10% in similarity score between one informant vs. the two others, we have listed the source segment, the MT output and the three post-edited versions in Appendix 1.

	Informant 5		Informant 7		Informant 2	
Seg. number	Similarity score	Quality score	Similarity score	Quality score	Similarity score	Quality score
13	100	5	98.97	5	98.97	5
35	91.01	5	93.85	5	93.26	5
37	89.04	5	85.61	3	97.22	3
41	**74.53**	5	93.51	3	93.51	5
43	88.14	5	98.28	4	94.92	5
45	97.63	5	94.6	4	90.61	5
49	100	5	94.04	3	100	5
59	100	5	100	5	100	5
65	90.83	5	100	5	92.59	5
85	**49.32**	5	100	5	100	5
113	**66.23**	5	82.28	4	100	5
143	**79.68**	5	100	5	100	5
177	73.63	5	80.42	4	**94.44**	5
	Informant 9		Informant 11		Informant 4	
14	97.14	5	97.14	5	97.14	5
22	100	5	100	5	100	5
26	92.75	5	100	5	84.93	5
34	74.14	3	88.27	5	82.84	4
40	84.08	3	71.72	5	**51.35**	4
46	92.13	5	93.92	5	91.12	5
76	100	5	88.61	5	**65.12**	4
86	100	5	**86.9**	5	98.53	5
92	**96.93**	3	85.12	5	86.75	4
94	88.29	**2**	78.4	5	88.29	3
98	85.89	3	81.99	5	**66.67**	4
108	98.85	5	100	5	94.19	5
122	91.43	5	88.26	5	96.48	4
128	96.88	5	98.02	5	86.86	4
146	82.76	5	71.64	5	**50.85**	5
150	88.89	3	83.13	5	78.55	4
160	75.93	3	74.61	5	75.85	3
168	93.33	**1**	89.64	5	84.97	4
170	89.28	3	80.56	5	80.47	5
172	87.39	3	86.44	5	82.25	3
178	94.38	5	100	5	94.38	5

Table 4-5: Comparison of quality scores and similarity scores of good quality segments

While a detailed analysis of post-editing strategies is beyond the scope of this article (cf. e.g. De Almeida and O'Brien 2010), the following observations may shed some light on the differences in post-editing distance observed in these segments. Informant 4 and informant 5 worked at a low to average speed and the increase in productivity was low to average (10% and 15% respectively). The finding that emerges here is that informant 4 is finding it hard to settle on a translation; she seems as cautious when translating from scratch/post-editing as when assigning evaluation scores; even for the segments that this informant rates as 5, she fine-tunes the output. As is clear from Table 4-2, the post-edited output of informant 4 receives the highest overall quality score from the professional translator-assessor. So one could argue that in this case, the extensive editing has a beneficial effect on the quality of the output. In the case of informant 5 though, this effect is not as obvious; with an average score of 3.81 for the post-edited output, she is seeded 3rd out of 6 in terms of overall quality achieved.

Low quality score and post-editing behaviour

A total of 33 segments were given a score of 1/5. What is striking on the low quality end of the data set is that the scores vary more across evaluators: it is only in one out of 33 cases that the three informants agree that the quality equals 1/5; in six out of 33 cases two informants gave a score of 1. As pointed out above, the rather opposite evaluation profiles of informant 11 and informant 9 may partly explain the divergences as well as the fact that there are proportionally more 'bad' segments in data set B (20) than in data set A (13).

Low human scores do not necessarily mean that the MT output is useless, even though, of course, a higher number of edit operations is required. As was already pointed out, informant 9 has a proportionally high number of segments with a low evaluation score. The scores she assigned may well be too low taking into account the number of edits made, which is overall very similar to the number of edits made by the other informants.

In Table 4-6, the segments in bold are those for which there is a difference of more than 10% in similarity score between one informant vs. the two others:

	Informant 5		Informant 7		Informant 2	
Seg. number	Similarity score	Quality score	Similarity score	Quality score	Similarity score	Quality score
7	85.11	2	75.71	1	75.71	3
25	76.33	3	66.67	1	76.33	1
57	56.93	2	56	1	52.71	2
75	76.47	3	66.67	1	64.54	1
77	61.83	2	71.32	2	63.49	1
79	69.21	1	77.59	2	72.26	2
93	68.15	2	76.75	1	68.4	2
111	**30.77**	3	76.92	1	72.53	2
115	65	1	75.21	2	74.78	1
117	63.93	1	61.9	1	63.87	1
121	59.39	1	57.39	1	56.88	2
133	69.69	2	69.96	2	60.26	1
153	63.83	3	72.25	1	65.89	2
	Informant 9		Informant 11		Informant 4	
2	80.6	3	**69.23**	1	80.6	3
24	68.46	1	66.83	2	70.34	2
28	71.93	1	73.35	3	69.89	2
30	56.16	1	**45.07**	2	72.05	1
38	54.22	2	52.29	2	47.44	1
56	52.47	1	55.15	3	46.31	2
58	90.48	1	**69.9**	3	88.1	2
68	66.15	1	61.92	2	**47.64**	1
74	79.27	1	72.02	3	73.2	3
78	81.79	1	78	4	78.26	3
82	70.45	1	58.17	2	67.6	2
84	81.61	1	76.92	3	79.3	4
88	61.7	1	**37.38**	2	62.56	2
102	63.22	1	53.33	3	72.15	2
116	90.36	1	89.15	3	81.63	2
142	81.42	1	80.85	3	**47.65**	3
152	86.29	1	81.48	4	75.62	3
168	93.33	1	89.64	5	84.97	4
176	80.18	1	**43.37**	3	67.82	4
180	67.35	1	**41.45**	3	67.11	2

Table 4-6: Comparison of quality scores and similarity scores of poor quality segments

The relatively divergent quality scores of the segments on the poor quality side are not observed at the level of post-editing: the differences of the similarity score between MT output and post-edited MT output here are less obvious. The number of segments where the difference between MT output and post-edited MT output is more than 10% (9) (between one informant and the two others) is about the same as the number of segments (11) with a similarly divergent score in Table 4-5. These examples have been listed in Appendix 2. The finding that emerges here is that it is informant 11, the fastest post-editor/translator with a very high productivity increase who has edited the segments most thoroughly.

Correlation similarity scores and quality scores

As a final step in the experiment, we tried to assess the relative reliability of the two methods of MT evaluation (human evaluation vs. similarity between MT output and post-edited MT output).

The corpus compiled enabled us to measure the level of correlation between the similarity scores and the quality scores per informant. We used Pearson's Correlation Coefficient to measure the correlation. As half of the segments were translated from scratch and half were post-edited, the calculations are based on the comparison of the similarity scores and quality scores for 90 segments. In other words, what we want to measure here is if the human evaluation scores given to the MT output for each segment and the post-editing effort for the same segment is in line for each informant. A high correlation coefficient indicates that a high score is strongly related with low post-editing effort (in other words high similarity between the MT output and the post-edited MT output) and a low correlation coefficient indicates that there is small or negligible relationship between high evaluation scores and post-editing effort. The results, which are summarized in Table 4-7, show that the two values have low to moderate correlation depending on the informant.

	Correlation coefficient
Informant 5	0.29
Informant 7	0.61
Informant 2	0.63
Informant 9	0.40
Informant 11	0.57
Informant 4	0.44

Table 4-7: Correlation between similarity score and human quality scores

We also calculated the relative standard deviation for the similarity scores and quality scores per informant. As can be observed from Table 4-8, the post-editing behaviour of the informants seems to point to less fluctuation than human evaluation behaviour: the relative standard deviation in similarity scores is around half of the deviation in human quality scores.

	Deviation PE score	Deviation quality score
Informant 5	17%	35%
Informant 7	13%	38%
Informant 2	14%	24%
Informant 9	14%	44%
Informant 11	18%	26%
Informant 4	15%	29%

Table 4-8: Deviation PE score and deviation quality score

The overall conclusion that can be drawn from these data is that post-editing behaviour fluctuates less than human evaluation behaviour; cf. Table 4-7 (Pearson's correlation coefficient) and Table 4-8 (Deviation post-editing score and deviation evaluation score). Unless there is extensive training and instruction about quality levels, the subjectivity inherent in any evaluation is likely to remain a challenge in the context of human evaluation. Given the observation that post-editing behaviour is more consistent across informants and the low to moderate correlation between post-editing behaviour and human evaluation scores, it seems that post-editing similarity is a more reliable measurement than human evaluation for gaining further insight into MT quality levels when the MT output is used in the context of full post editing.

Conclusion

In this paper, we have reported on a case study that involved the post-editing of an MT-translated text sample by translation trainees. The experiment has revealed the following findings:

- The productivity increased on average by 21.5% (post-edited translation vs. translation from scratch). It may be concluded that MT enhances the translator's productivity, even if they are in the initial stages of their careers.
- For a sample of six informants, the post-edited output and the translation from scratch were assessed by a professional

translator/course instructor and the differences in quality turned out to be minimal. The calculation of the similarity between the post-edited output and the translation from scratch on the one hand, and a reference translation on the other, did not reveal major differences. This seems to justify the conclusion that, in the context of this project, the use of MT does not impact in a negative way on the quality of the final translation.

- For a sample of six informants, the post-editing effort (based on the similarity score between MT output and post-edited output) of the segments was compared to human evaluation scores of MT quality and it appears that the former is more stable across informants than the latter. This leads to the tentative conclusion that post-editing effort (measured as similarity with a reference translation) can be considered a more objective measure than a 5-point human evaluation scale measuring the quality of an MT engine.

Bibliography

Allen, Jeff. 2003. "Post-editing." *Computers and Translation. A Translator's Guide*, edited by Harold Somers, 297–317. Amsterdam/Philadelphia: John Benjamins Publishing Company.

Carl, Michael, Barbara Dragsted, Jakob Elming, Daniel Hardt, and Arnt Lykke Jakobsen. 2011. "The Process of Post-editing: a Pilot Study." *Proceedings of the 8th International NLPSC Workshop. Special Theme: Human-Machine Interaction in Translation,* edited by Bernadette Sharp, Michael Zock, Michael Carl and Arnt Lykke Jakobsen, 131–142. Copenhagen Studies in Language 41. Frederiksberg: Samfundslitteratur.

Carroll, John B. 1966. "An Experiment in Evaluation the Quality of Translations." *Language and Machines: Computers in Translation and Linguistics. A Report by the Automatic Language Processing Advisory Committee*, edited by John R. Pierce and John B. Carroll et al., 67–75. Washington DC: National Academy of Sciences. National Research Council.

Daems, Joke, Lieve Macken and Sonia Vandepitte. 2013. "Quality as the Sum of its Parts: a Two-Step Approach for the Identification of Translation Problems and Translation Quality Assessment for HT and MT+PE." *Proceedings of MT Summit XIV Workshop on Post-editing Technology and Practice (WPTP-2)*, edited by Sharon O'Brien, Michel Simard and Lucia Specia, 63–71. Allschwil: The European Association for Machine Translation.

De Almeida, Gisela and Sharon O'Brien. 2010. "Analysing Post-Editing Performance: Correlations with Years of Translation Experience." *Proceedings of the 14th Annual Conference of the EAMT*, edited by François Yvon and Viggo Hansen. St. Raphael.

Fiederer, Rebecca and Sharon O'Brien. 2009. "Quality and Machine Translation: A Realistic Objective?" *The Journal of Specialised Translation* 11: 52–74.

García, Ignacio. 2010. "Is Machine Translation Ready yet?" *Target* 22(1):7–21.

Guerberof, Ana. 2012. *Productivity and Quality in the Post-Editing of Outputs from Translation Memories and Machine Translation*. PhD Thesis, Universitat Rovira I Virgili.

Guzmàn, Rafael. 2007. "Manual MT Post-Editing: "If it's not Broken, don't Fix it!"" *Translation Journal*, Volume 11.4, October, 2007. Accessed 22 October 2013. http://translationjournal.net/journal/42mt.htm

Nagao, Makoto, Jun-ichi Tsujii and Jun-ichi Nakamura. 1985. "The Japanese Government Project for MT." *Computational Linguistics* 11:91–109.

O'Brien, Sharon. 2011. "Towards Predicting Post-editing Quality." *Machine Translation* 25(3):197–215.

Offersgaard, Lene, Claus Povlsen, Lisbeth Almsten and Bente Maegaard. 2008. "Domain Specific MT Use." *Proceedings of 12th EAMT Conference*, edited by John Hutchins and Walther v. Hahn. 150–159. Hamburg.

Oliver, Ian. 1993. *Programming Classics: Implementing the World's Best Algorithms*. New Jersey: Prentice Hall PTR.

Plitt, Mirko. 2012. "*Observations on MT Quality: Results from Post-editing and Raw MT Usability Tests at Autodesk.*" 3e Journée d'études 'Traduction et Qualité', University of Lille 3, 3 February 2012. Accessed 22 October 2013. http://stl.recherche.univ-lille3.fr/colloques/20112012/Mirko_Plitt_Lille_2012_02_03.pdf

Plitt, Mirko and François Masselot. 2010. "A Productivity Test of Statistical Machine Translation Post-Editing in a Typical Localisation Context." *The Prague Bulletin of Mathematical Linguistics* 93:7–16.

Secară, Alina 2005. "Translation Evaluation – a State of the Art Survey." In *eCoLoRe-Mellange Workshop Proceedings*. Accessed 10 October 2013. http://ecolore.leeds.ac.uk/

White, John S. 2003. "How to Evaluate Machine Translation." In *Computers and Translation. A Translator's Guide*, edited by Harold Somers. 211–244. Amsterdam: John Benjamins Publishing Company.

Appendix 1. High quality segments with a similarity difference of at least 10% between one informant vs. the two others

(1) ST (seg. 41): This will be repeated after each set to measure my lactate level.
MT: Ceci sera répété après chaque ensemble pour mesurer mon niveau de lactate.
informant 5: Cette opération aura lieu après chaque étape pour mesurer mon niveau de lactate. (**74.53**%)[8]
informant 7: Ceci sera répété après chaque série pour mesurer mon niveau de lactate. (93.51%)
informant 2: Ceci sera répété après chaque série pour mesurer mon niveau de lactate. (93.51%)

(2) ST (seg. 85): It's only 60 percent strength.
MT: C'est seulement 60 pour cent de force.
informant 5: Il ne représente que 60% de force. (**49.32**%)
informant 7: C'est seulement 60 pour cent de force. (100%)
informant 2: C'est seulement 60 pour cent de force. (100%)

(3) ST (seg. 113): She'd probably just compliment me on the beautiful splash.'
MT: Elle me complimenterait probablement juste sur la belle éclaboussure. »
informant 5: Elle m'aurait certainement juste complimenté sur la belle éclaboussure. » (**66.23**%)
informant 7: Elle se contenterait probablement de me complimenter sur la belle éclaboussure. » (82.28%)
informant 2: Elle me complimenterait probablement juste sur la belle éclaboussure. » (100%)

(4) ST (seg. 143): Less than three seconds later, like an arrow, each diver pierces the surface with barely a splash.
MT: Moins de trois secondes plus tard, comme une flèche, chaque plongeur perce la surface avec à peine une éclaboussure.
informant 5: Moins de trois secondes plus tard, chaque plongeur, tel une flèche, transperce la surface de l'eau avec à peine une éclaboussure. (**79.68**%)
informant 7: Moins de trois secondes plus tard, comme une flèche, chaque plongeur perce la surface avec à peine une éclaboussure. (100%)

informant 2: Moins de trois secondes plus tard, comme une flèche, chaque plongeur perce la surface avec à peine une éclaboussure. (100%)

(5) ST (seg. 177): 'It's difficult to stay at this level'; she admits, 'but I have a strong mind.
MT: « Il est difficile de rester à ce niveau, » elle admet, « mais j'ai un esprit fort.
informant 5: « C'est difficile de maintenir ce niveau, » admet-elle, « mais je suis forte d'esprit. (73.63%)
informant 7: « Il est difficile de se maintenir à ce niveau, » admet-elle, « mais j'ai un mental d'acier. (80.42%)
informant 2: « Il est difficile de rester à ce niveau, » admet-elle, « mais j'ai un esprit fort. (**94.44**%)

(6) ST (seg. 40): Next, the technician pricks my earlobe for a drop of blood.
MT output: Après, le technicien pique mon lobe de l'oreille pour une goutte de sang.
informant 9: Après, le technicien pique mon lobe de l'oreille pour recueillir une goutte de sang. (84.08%)
informant 11: Le technicien pique ensuite mon lobe pour prélever une goutte de sang. (71.72%)
informant 4: Le technicien prélève ensuite une goutte de sang sur mon lobe d'oreille. (**51.35**%)

(7) ST (seg. 76): Also, I don't finish my strokes.
MT output: En outre, je ne finis pas mes courses.
informant 9: En outre, je ne finis pas mes courses. (100%)
informant 11: En outre, je ne finis pas mes mouvements. (88.61%)
informant 4: De plus, je ne finis pas mes mouvements de bras. (**65.12**%)

(8) ST (seg. 86): The strongest guy in the world can't do what we do.
MT: Le type le plus fort au monde ne peut pas faire ce que nous faisons.
informant 9: Le type le plus fort au monde ne peut pas faire ce que nous faisons. (100%)
informant 11: Le type le plus fort du monde n'est pas capable de faire ce que nous faisons. (**86.9**%)
informant 4: Le type le plus fort du monde ne peut pas faire ce que nous faisons. (98.53%)

(9) ST (seg. 92): I see Wilhite at work at the American Open Championships - a qualifying event for the Olympics - in Tacoma, Washington.
MT output: Je vois Wilhite au travail aux championnats ouverts américains - un événement de qualification pour les Jeux Olympiques - à Tacoma, Washington.
informant 9: Je vois Wilhite au travail aux championnats libres américains - un événement de qualification pour les Jeux Olympiques - à Tacoma, Washington. (**96.93**%)
informant 11: Je vois Wilhite à l'œuvre au Championnat Américain Open (un événement de qualification pour les Jeux Olympiques) à Tacoma, Washington. (85.12%)
informant 4: Je vois Wilhite au travail au championnat Open américain - une épreuve de qualification pour les Jeux Olympiques - à Tacoma, dans l'état de Washington. (86.75%)

(10) ST (seg. 98): 'Wilhite will lift ten million pounds in 80,000 reps between now and 2004.'
MT output: « Wilhite soulèvera dix millions de livres dans 80.000 reps d'ici 2004. »
informant 9: « Wilhite soulèvera dix millions de livres au bout de 80.000 répétitions d'ici 2004. » (85.89%)
informant 11: « Wilhite soulèvera 10 millions de livres, soit 80 000 répétitions, d'ici à 2004. (81.99%)
informant 4: « D'ici 2004, Wilhite soulèvera cinq millions de kilos en 80 000 mouvements. » (**66.67**%)

(11) ST (seg. 146): It's hard to learn.
MT output: Il est difficile d'apprendre.
informant 9: C'est difficile à apprendre. (82.76%)
informant 11: C'est un sport difficile à apprendre. (71.64%)
informant 4: L'apprentissage est difficile. (**50.85**%)

Appendix 2. Low quality segments with a similarity difference of at least 10% between one informant vs. the two others

(12) ST (seg. 111): What worked for me was humor.
MT output: Ce que travaillé pour moi était l'humeur.
informant 5: C'est l'humour qui a fait ma force. **(30.77%)**
informant 7: Ce qui fonctionnait pour moi, c'était l'humeur. (76.92%)
informant 2: Ce qui a fonctionné pour moi c'était l'humour. (72.53%)

(13) ST (seg. 2): "Can I break a record?"
MT: « Peux je casse un record? »
informant 9: « Puis-je battre un record ? » (80.6%)
informant 11: « Suis-je capable de battre un record ? » (**69.23**%)
informant 4: « Puis-je battre un record ? » (80.6%)

(14) ST (seg. 30): Whether fast-twitchers or slow, however, elite athletes take human performance to a notch we lesser mortals can only imagine.
MT: Si rapide-twitchers ou ralentissez, cependant, les athlètes d'élite nous portent à activité humaine à une entaille que peu de mortels peuvent seulement imaginer.
informant 9: Qu'il s'agisse de fibres à fibrillation rapide ou lente, les athlètes d'élite amène la performance humaine à un niveau dont nous autres pauvres mortels, pouvons seulement rêver. (56.16%)
informant 11: Toutefois, qu'ils possèdent des fibres à contraction lente ou rapide, les athlètes d'élites parviennent à un niveau de performance dont nous, simples mortels, pouvons seulement rêver. (**45.07%**)
informant 4: Qu'il s'agisse de fibres à contraction rapide ou lente, cependant, les athlètes d'élite mènent la performance humaine à un niveau que peu de mortels peuvent seulement imaginer. (72.05%)

(15) ST (seg. 58): The water feels as thick as mud.
MT: L'eau se sent aussi épaisse que la boue.
informant 9: L'eau me semble aussi épaisse que la boue. (90.48%)
informant 11: J'ai l'impression que l'eau est aussi épaisse que de la boue. (**69.9%**)
informant 4: L'eau semble aussi épaisse que de la boue. (88.1%)

(16) ST (seg. 68): ‘It's like getting goose bumps with acid in every one, along with deep burning in the lungs and the sensation of dragging lead weights behind you instead of logs.’
MT output: « Elle est comme faire avancer la chair de poule avec de l'acide dans chacun, le burning profond dans les poumons et la sensation des poids de déplacement d'avance derrière vous au lieu des rondins. »
informant 9: « C'est comme avoir la chair de poule à l'acide, associé à une brûlure profonde dans les poumons et la sensation de traîner du plomb derrière soi plutôt que du bois. » (66.15%)
informant 11: « C'est comme si tu avais la chair de poule et que chaque pore contenait de l'acide. Il y a également une sensation de brûlure profonde dans les poumons et l'impression de traîner derrière soi des morceaux de plomb au lieu de rondins. » (61.92%)
informant 4: « C'est comme si j'avais une chair de poule acide sur tout le corps, comme si mes poumons brûlaient en profondeur et comme si je tirais de lourdes charges de plomb à la place de mes jambes. » **(47.64%)**

(17) ST (seg. 88): We can all spring up and slam-dunk a basketball from a dead standstill under the hoop.’
MT output: Nous pouvons tout prendre naissance et smasher un basket-ball d'un arrêt mort sous le cercle. »
informant 9: Nous pouvons tous, à l'arrêt, pousser et smasher une balle de basket dans le panier. » (61.7%)
informant 11: Au basket, tout le monde est capable de sauter et de réaliser un dunk à partir d'un point mort sous le cerceau. » **(37.38%)**
informant 4: « Nous sommes tous capables de nous soulever et de smasher un ballon de basket à partir d'un point d'arrêt sous le panier. » (62.56%)

(18) ST (seg. 142): Then comes a slow, graceful lifting of the arms, a leap skyward, and a twisting, somersaulting dance with gravity.
MT output: Vient ensuite une lente et gracieuse levée de bras, un saut vers le ciel et une torsion, comme une danse acrobatique avec la gravité.
informant 9: Viens alors un lever lent et gracieux des bras, un saut vers le ciel, et une culbute vrillée chorégraphiée avec la gravité. (81.42%)

informant 11: Vient alors un levage lent et gracieux des bras, un saut vers le ciel. Effectuant des rotations et des sauts périlleux, le plongeur danse avec la gravité. (80.85%)
informant 4: D'un mouvement gracieux, elles lèvent alors lentement les bras, bondissent vers le ciel, jouent avec la gravité d'une vrille et d'un saut périlleux. **(47.65%)**

(19) ST (seg. 176): Today Loroupe, petite at four feet eleven and 86 pounds, runs 120 miles a week.
MT output: Aujourd'hui Loroupe, petit à quatre pieds onze et 86 livres, court 120 milles par semaine.
informant 9: Aujourd'hui Loroupe, petite avec ses quatre pieds onze (1, 25 mètres) et 86 livres (39 kg), court 120 milles (193 km) par semaine. (80.18%)
informant 11: Menue (150 cm pour 39 kgs), Loroupe parcourt désormais 193 km par semaine. **(43.37%)**
informant 4: Aujourd'hui Loroupe, petit gabarit de 40 kgs pour 1 m 50, court 200 km par semaine. (67.82%)

(20) ST (seg. 180): She promised that if he sent her and her brother to boarding school, she would stop, but coaches there insisted otherwise.
MT output: Elle a promis que s'il envoyait son et son frère à l'internat, elle s'arrêterait, mais donnerait des leçons particulières là insisté autrement.
informant 9: Elle a promis que s'il l'envoyait elle et son frère à l'internat, elle s'arrêterait, mais qu'autrement les entraîneurs d'ici insistaient. (67.35%)
informant 11: Elle a promis qu'elle arrêterait si son père acceptait de l'envoyer, ainsi que son frère, en internat, mais les entraîneurs en ont décidé autrement. **(41.45%)**
informant 4: Elle a promis que s'il l'envoyait à l'internat avec son frère, elle s'arrêterait, mais les entraîneurs là-bas avaient insisté pour qu'elle continue. (67.11%)

Notes

[1] We are grateful to the anonymous referees and to the editors for their very useful input on the manuscript of this chapter.

[2] There is a productivity increase of 29% if the non-native speakers are included.

[3] A control test was carried out with a second group of informants with a similar background. Twelve students participated in the second experiment. For reasons that had to with the availability of the students, a smaller portion of the original source text was used (2,023 words, 125 segments). As is clear from the table below, the productivity increase was similar:

Informant group	1	2
Number of informants	13	12
Size source text sample	3,045	2,023
Number of segments	181	125
Post-editing throughput in words per hour	678	792
Translation from scratch throughput in words per hour	555	654
Productivity increase	22%	21%

Table 4-9. Comparison results informant group 1 and informant group 2.

[4] The output was produced by 16 Master's students of translation taking a general translation course; they did not have any experience with post-editing and they did not receive specific training. While the authors report a faster throughput in the case of post-editing (2013, 68), no detailed figures are provided.

[5] While we are aware that it would have been beneficial to the experiment to work with a pool of evaluators, due to funding limitations we could not have the output assessed by more than one evaluator.

[6] Even though all informants worked on the same pre-translations, we noticed that some informants made a lot of edits and others did not. Differences in the number of edits are considered to be pointing to differences in post-editing behaviour.

[7] As pointed out before post-editing effort is based on the Similar_Text algorithm that calculates the similarity between two strings as described in Oliver (1993).

[8] A high similarity score means that there are relatively few differences between the MT output and the post-edited text whereas a low similarity score indicates that the difference is considerable. A score of 100% means that the two texts are the same.

CHAPTER FIVE

THE HANDLING OF TRANSLATION METADATA IN TRANSLATION TOOLS

CARLOS S. C. TEIXEIRA

Abstract

In this chapter, we map out how five translation tools present translation metadata. Although the spectrum of possible metadata elements runs to hundreds, the five tools combined display only around 15 such elements. We raise the question of whether this set of metadata elements and the way they are presented constitute the best combination in terms of translator productivity and translating effort. We take Pym's minimalist approach to translation competence and extrapolate it as a model for the translation process, indicating how translation tools can contribute to the generation-selection steps of this process.

Introduction

Current translation workflows increasingly involve the need to take into account translation suggestions coming not only from translation memories (TMs) and terminology databases but also from machine translation (MT) engines. In this relatively new scenario, the border between TM-assisted translation and MT post-editing is becoming blurred, as statistical MT engines are fed with large bilingual corpora and with the results of translation projects. For the same reason, it becomes increasingly relevant to know where translation suggestions come from and to have some indication of the quality or confidence associated with the suggestions. The presence or absence of metadata on a given translation suggestion is believed to have an impact on performance, but the exact mechanisms of such an impact are still to be determined.

In a recent issue of *The Tool Box Newsletter* (Zetzsche 2013), a memoQ advertisement reproduces an (implicitly complimentary) testimonial by a customer stating that "[…] it seems like a video game with so many options and levels to discover!" It is actually not uncommon to find similar statements in industry magazines about the usefulness of metadata: "The translator is helped by metadata in that he or she sees what to translate and what not, sees the suggested translations provided by TM or MT and so on" (Anastasiou 2010, 51). The question is whether an interface that looks like a video game can actually make your work more productive. Is it not the case that too much information can be distracting? How can we find a balance? Is it better to define the metadata items that are more likely to increase translator productivity, and display only those? Or is it better to display the highest possible number of metadata items, which each translator will be able to filter (and this ability may even increase with tool familiarity)? Alternatively, is it better to display virtually no metadata, so as to have translators focus on the target text? We could perhaps change our productivity paradigm and consider that fun (like video games) can actually be part of the equation, where some productivity would happily be lost for the sake of task satisfaction (or even job satisfaction). The goal of this chapter is to discuss some concepts and ideas that could help to find answers to those questions.

Translation metadata

Metadata can be generally defined as "data about data" (Anastasiou & Vázquez 2010, 257) and can come in many forms depending on the application. Translation metadata, as we use the term in this study, is the information that appears on the interface of a translation tool to inform the user about several aspects of a translation task, in addition to the source text. By translation tool here we mean what has elsewhere been called CAT (Computer-Aided Translation) tool or Translation Environment Tool (TEnT)[1], i.e. an integrated, computer-based environment for translating electronic files. Figure 5-1 displays a typical interface of such a tool.

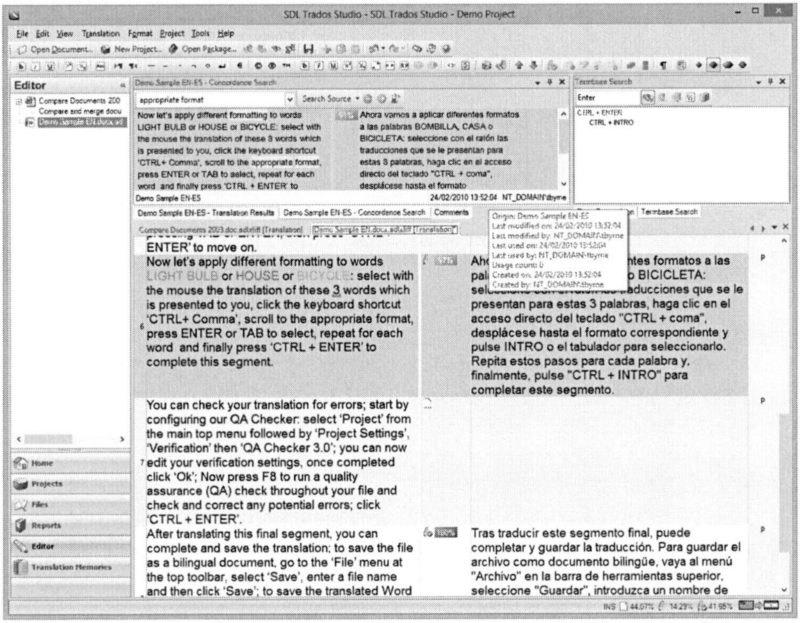

Figure 5-1: The SDL Trados Studio editing environment showing several elements of translation metadata.

As can be seen in Figure 5-1, translation metadata can include:[2]

- The language pairs involved in the file(s) being translated, usually indicated by country flags or language abbreviations.
- Translation progress statistics, such as the percentage of translated, reviewed or remaining segments.
- The state of segments, including:
    - "translation status" (translated, not translated, automatically propagated, reviewed, pending, approved, etc.);
    - original provenance (whether the translation was typed from scratch or was post-edited from an MT feed or from a TM match (exact, fuzzy match, etc.)).
- Terminology suggestions from term bases (glossaries): Typically, text portions identified by the tool as terms are highlighted in the source text, with the corresponding translations and additional information displayed in a separate pane.
- Variables and entities: Similarly to the above, tags, numbers, times, units, etc. are identified and highlighted.

- Type of textual element being translated: These include headings, regular paragraphs, list items, footnotes, table cells, etc. They can typically be indicated through text formatting within the segment, with a letter or code next to the segment, through a preview pane, or a combination of those elements.
- Segment number, line number (in the file), number of characters or words in the source/target segment.
- Typing aids in the form of automatic text (generated either from a predefined list or from glossary or TM matches), which also display as on-screen information.
- Automatic indicators for spelling mistakes or other potential editing mistakes (such as tag and number misplacements).
- Indications of whether a segment is the result of two or more segments being manually joined or if two or more segments were originally a single segment that was manually split.
- Information about translation suggestions, including their origin or provenance (whether a suggestion comes from a translation memory —and which—or a machine translation engine—and which), and in the case of translation memories: project-specific, historical (author, date of creation, date of modification, etc.) and linguistic information (fuzzy match levels, differences between source texts, etc.).

This last type of metadata—information about translation suggestions —is the focus of this chapter, as we aim to discuss to what extent the wealth of information available on screen might help or hinder the translator's work.

Metadata in translation tools

In this section, we map which metadata elements related to the translation suggestions are present in typical translation tools and expose how those elements are displayed. To this end, we have analysed five translation tools: four of them can be said to be mainstream—SDL Trados Studio, memoQ, Wordfast Pro and Déjà Vu, while one has more restricted use—IBM TranslationManager (formerly known as TM/2). The reasons for nonetheless choosing IBM TranslationManager are: (1) it was one of the first translation tools to be created in the early 1990s and its graphical user interface has remained virtually unchanged since its first Windows version in the late 1990s; (2) despite its dated interface it is still used for all IBM localisation projects, involving hundreds of translators around the world; (3) we have some empirical data from a recent translation process experiment using the tool. The reasons for choosing the four other tools are their widespread adoption and the availability of trial versions with full functionality for testing the features we needed.

We could certainly have covered additional tools, including open-source tools such as OmegaT, Virtaal and OpenTM2, but we believe the discussions are of a general nature and can be extended to any other tool working under the same principles. Our main focus is not on specific tools or on the current state of the translation tool market, but on the usability principles that govern the development and use of translation tools in general, as far as metadata is concerned.

In what follows, the results of our study will be divided into two broad categories: provenance metadata and translation memory metadata. The second category is then sub-divided into project-specific, historical and linguistic metadata.

Provenance metadata

Table 5-1 presents the first metadata elements we were able to identify in the tools, which we are grouping under the general name of *provenance metadata*. These elements include:

- Type of origin: an indication of whether a translation suggestion comes from a translation memory, a machine translation engine or is the result of fragment assembly (TM sub-segmental matches combined using MT algorithms).
- TM name, for translation memory matches.
- TM location, for translation memory matches.
- MT engine name, for machine translation feeds.

In the case of tools that offer assembled suggestions—Déjà Vu and memoQ, we have inferred from the documentation and from usage that the origin indicated on screen is the translation memory from which the longest sub-segmental match is retrieved. This is why we are presenting no separate column for this element, as this metadata goes together with "TM name".

In Table 5-1, the number "1" in a cell indicates that a particular tool displays the corresponding metadata element. A dash ("-") indicates that the tool does not display that element (feature not available).

Tool name	Type of origin	TM name	TM location	MT engine name
SDL Trados Studio	1*	1	1	1
memoQ	1†	1	-	1
Wordfast Pro	1*	1	-	1
Déjà Vu X2	1‡	1	1	1
IBM TM	1*	1	-	-

Notes:
* colour codes + letters
† colour codes + symbols
‡ colour codes

Table 5-1: Provenance metadata displayed in five TM tools

Type of origin: All five tools have a way of indicating whether a translation suggestion comes from a translation memory or from a machine translation engine. All of them use colour codes to indicate this, while Trados, Wordfast and IBM TM also use letters—"AT" (meaning 'Automatic Translation'), in the case of Trados; "MT" in the case of Wordfast; and "m" in the case of IBM TM)—and memoQ uses symbols.

Name of translation memory or machine translation engine: When a translation suggestion comes from a translation memory, all tools display the name of the TM for the selected suggestion. When it comes to translation suggestions coming from an MT engine, Trados, memoQ, Wordfast and Déjà Vu display the name of the originating engine. IBM TM is the exception here, because of the way it integrates machine translation.

Trados, memoQ, Wordfast and Déjà Vu are able to connect to on-line MT services such as Google Translate, Microsoft Translator (Bing), WorldLingo, SDL ATS, SDL BeGlobal, iTranslate4.eu, LetsMT, Systran and PROMT. This allows translators to obtain translation suggestions from those engines in real time, e.g. while translating a specific segment. IBM TM does not offer this option. In order to integrate MT into the translation workflow, the user (usually a project manager or "file handler") has to send the relevant segments for pre-translation to a machine translation engine or service and then use the resulting translated segments as a regular translation memory in the folder (a translation project, in IBM's jargon). Translation suggestions from segments pre-translated through this process will always contain an "m" flag to indicate they are not regular TM matches.

Translation memory location/type: All five tools under study offer the possibility for more than one translator to use the same translation memory simultaneously. This is typically done by sharing a translation memory on a local network or by making a translation memory available on a remote server. Of the five tools, Trados and Déjà Vu indicate whether the TM from which the translation suggestions were obtained are exclusive/local or shared/remote. In memoQ, Wordfast and IBM TM, this information must be inferred from the name of the translation memory.

Translation memory metadata

When a translation suggestion comes from machine translation, no further metadata is displayed other than the engine name. Therefore, the remaining metadata elements displayed by all five tools concern translation memory matches. These elements can be roughly subdivided into three categories, which we are tentatively naming "project-specific", "historical" and "linguistic" metadata.

Project-specific metadata comprise information such as file name, project name, client name and subject domain of the text from which a translation suggestion was produced. Historical metadata concern the time and date when a translation segment was created, changed or used; the name of the person who created, modified or used it; and the number of times that segment was used. Linguistic metadata indicate the similarities between the text in the source segment being translated and the text in the source segment(s) of the translation memory(ies) from which translation suggestions were produced. Tables 5-2, 5-3 and 5-4 offer an overview of how translation memory metadata are displayed across the five tools.

Tool name	File	Project	Client	Subject
SDL Trados Studio	-	-	-	-
memoQ	3	1	1	3
Wordfast Pro	-	-	-	-
Déjà Vu X2	1	1	1	1
IBM TM	2	-	-	-

Legend:
1: item visible at first sight by default
2: item visible at first sight after configuration change
3: item visible after user action
-: item not available

Table 5-2: Project-specific translation metadata displayed in five TM tools

Project-specific translation metadata

Reference source file: A possible project-specific metadata element is the name of the file that was being translated when a bilingual segment was created (first stored) in the translation memory or last changed/used. Déjà Vu shows this information at first sight by default, IBM TM if the corresponding option is selected in the configurations, and memoQ only in the Concordance window.

Project and client: Other metadata elements in the same category are the names of the project and the client associated with the TM segment. memoQ and Déjà Vu show this information by default, while the three other tools do not offer this feature.

Subject: The last project-specific element found in the tools was the name of the subject (i.e. topic, domain) related to a particular project. Déjà Vu shows this metadata by default, while memoQ shows it in the Concordance window only. The other tools cannot display metadata about the subject of a TM segment.

Tool name	Time			Author			Usage count
	Last change	Last usage	Creation	Last change	Last usage	Creation	
Trados	1	3	3	1	3	3	3
memoQ	1	-	-	1	-	-	-
Wordfast	1	-	-	3	-	-	-
Déjà Vu	1	-	-	1	-	-	-
IBM TM	-	1	-	-	-	-	-

Legend:
1: item visible at first sight by default
3: item visible after user action (hover text or mouse click)

Table 5-3: Historical translation metadata displayed in five TM tools

Historical translation metadata

Translation memory segment time: Three possible types of metadata related to the time of a translation memory segment were found in the different systems: creation date and time, last modification date and time, and last usage date and time. Trados, memoQ, Wordfast and Déjà Vu display the *last modification* date and time. IBM TM displays the *last usage* date (but not the time), and this is actually the only time-related metadata displayed by that tool. This implies that the tool developers take an approach that treats the acceptance of a TM match (even without changing it) as equivalent to the change of an existing TM match. Trados can also display information about the last usage (date and time), but this is in the form of hover text (the user has to move the mouse to a specific position and wait until the additional metadata are displayed in a floating text box). None of the tools displays the *creation* date and time of a TM segment at first sight. Trados can display this metadata as hover text.

Translation memory segment author: As is the case with date and time, the author of a translation memory segment can be displayed, indicating who created, modified or used a TM segment. Trados is the only tool that displays the *creation* author of a TM segment, and only as hover text. The author of the *last modification* is displayed at first sight by Trados, memoQ and Déjà Vu, and as hover text by Wordfast. The author who last used a TM segment can only be identified in Trados, which displays this metadata as hover text. IBM TM displays no information at all about the author of a TM segment.

Usage count: Trados is the only tool, of the five under study, that is able to indicate the number of times a TM segment has been used. This refers to activity occurring since the translation memory was created. Usage count is displayed as hover text.

Tool name	Type of match					Source text	Text diffs‡
	Exact match	Fuzzy match (%)	Context match	Repeat match	Assembled match		
Trados	1	1	1	1	-†	1	1
memoQ	1	1	-*	-*	1	1	1
Wordfast	1	1	-*	-*	-†	1	~
Déjà Vu	1	1	1	1	1	1	1
IBM TM	1	1	-*	-*	-†	1	1

Notes:
* Displays as a regular Exact match
† Feature not available
‡ Text differences between current source segment and TM source segment
Legend:
1: item visible at first sight by default
~: item inconsistently indicated
-: item not available

Table 5-4: Linguistic translation metadata displayed in five TM tools

Linguistic translation metadata

Type of match: All five tools under investigation display metadata indicating whether a translation suggestion is an exact match or a fuzzy match. For fuzzy matches, they all display the degree of fuzziness as a percentage.

Each tool can display additional metadata depending on the tool's algorithms for retrieving matches from the memory. For example, Déjà Vu and Trados are able to check whether the previous and/or following segment in the translation memory is the same as the previous and/or following segment in the text being translated; an "exact match" that meets these conditions is deemed to have a higher degree of confidence than a non-contextual (actually, non-co-textual) exact match. The tools indicate this kind of suggestion—named "guaranteed match" and "context match", respectively—with a specific flag. Déjà Vu and memoQ are also able to assemble segment matches by locating sub-segmental matches and assembling those using MT algorithms built into the tools. The suggestions that are generated through this process are indicated with a specific flag.

Textual differences: When a suggested translation is a fuzzy match, all the tools indicate the textual differences between the current source segment and the source segment found in the translation memory. This is typically indicated as revision marks (e.g. struck-through text for deletions, underlined text for insertions, etc.), similar to the Track Changes feature in Microsoft Word. Wordfast highlights changes in yellow, but it is not always clear what text portions have been deleted or inserted.

Empirical research on the use of metadata

Based on what was presented in the previous section, it is worth noting that the only metadata elements that are displayed by all tools are the following:

- source text;
- provenance of translation suggestion (MT or TM);
- TM name;
- TM match type (exact, fuzzy, etc.);
- textual differences between current source segment and TM source segment (with different levels of detail).

This leads us to assume that most tool manufacturers—either knowingly or unknowingly—have concluded at some point that this is the most relevant set of metadata to be displayed. However, empirical research on the actual usefulness of translation metadata is still very scarce.

Morado Vázquez (2012) compares the behaviour of translators working in three different scenarios: (A) without any translation memories; (B) with a translation memory but without metadata; and (C) with a translation memory and basic metadata elements, mostly project-specific. She uses screen recording and keystroke logging for measuring translation speed and the LISA QA model for assessing translation quality. Her process data indicate that in terms of both speed and quality there is no significant difference between scenarios B and C. In scenario A translators were slower and produced translations of lower quality than in B and C. When it comes to self-reporting data from questionnaires, however, most participants indicate that they prefer to have access to the metadata and even believe they can translate faster and better when proper metadata is available (contradicting the actual performance data).

Using similar data collection methods, we have reported (see Teixeira 2011) on a pilot experiment that compares translator performance between two environments: one that presents a selected set of metadata elements (the five points listed above) and another environment with no metadata. Our results indicate that there is a difference in speed and typing activity depending on the types of translation suggestions and on the presence or absence of metadata. However, results varied between the only two participants of the experiment, indicating that there might be no single answer as to whether or how particular metadata elements affect the translation process. This seems to depend on the task being performed ("pure" MT post-editing, "pure" TM translation, combined TM/MT translation, revision, etc.), on the translator's personal editing style and technology awareness, on the type of matches that are more frequent in a project (e.g. ratio of exact matches and high-percentage fuzzy matches over MT feeds and low-percentage fuzzy matches) and so on.

Other research studies not dealing directly with translation metadata can also shed some light on the topic. O'Brien (2006) compares the performance of translators exposed to translation suggestions coming from TM vs. MT when translation metadata is available. One of her findings is that "cognitive load [and processing speed] for machine translation matches is close to fuzzy matches of between 80–90% value" (op. cit., 185). For fuzzy matches above 90%, including exact matches, TM processing is faster and requires a lighter cognitive load than MT processing, whereas the opposite happens for fuzzy matches below 80%.

When looking at speed and quality in an environment without translation metadata, Guerberof (2009) finds "that translators have higher productivity and quality when using machine translated output than when processing fuzzy matches [at any percentage level] from translation memories" (op. cit., 11). In the case of speed, her findings thus contradict those obtained by O'Brien (2006), although the studies are not directly comparable, as they used different texts, language pairs, MT engines and participants.

What seems to be a common finding in most translation process studies is a great intersubject variation. This can be noticed in the statistical dispersion of the data presented as well as in several comments: "Individual differences in the translation and post-editing process were observed for almost all process characteristics examined" (Krings 2001, 549); "productivity seems to be subject dependant" (Guerberof 2009, 19).

Discussion

In his minimalist approach, Pym (2003, 489) models (human) translation competence as follows:

- The ability to generate a series of more than one viable target text (TT_1, TT_2 … TT_n) for a pertinent source text (ST);
- The ability to select only one viable TT from this series, quickly and with justified confidence.

If we include translation technology in this model, we can argue that the suggestions obtained from translation memories and machine translation help translators in the first sub-process (generation of viable target text options). The information about the suggestions (which we have been calling translation metadata) might help in the second sub-process, i.e. the selection of the best suggestion.

So what are the factors that play a role in the decision-making process of selecting a translation suggestion? Research is still incipient in trying to understand which pieces of metadata are taken into account (or even simply looked at) when translators are at work. Trying to be deductive, one could suggest that in order to increase productivity (i.e. reduce the time it takes to make a decision for each segment) and reduce effort, translators develop strategies that somehow rank the information that is worthwhile acting upon. And the key strategy here could be to identify the trustworthiness of information, as trust can be seen as a mechanism that helps to reduce complexity and effort (see Pym 2012, 147, citing Luhman).

The order of presentation of matches is definitely an important decision factor, and this order is automatically calculated by the tool based on predefined criteria (order of priority of translation memories, date of segment in the translation memory, etc.). A second important factor is the linguistic information about the suggestions, i.e. the textual differences between the source text in the segment being translated and the matching source text in the translation memory. A third factor taken into account in the selection sub-process of translation is the project-specific and historical metadata about the translation suggestions, i.e. for which domain or project or customer they were created, when they were created or modified or used, and who created or modified or used them. Karamanis et al. (2011) corroborate the usefulness of this type of translation memory metadata in collaborative scenarios.

An excess of metadata, however, is likely to have a negative effect on productivity, and this is why in practice the tools present much less metadata than they are able to. For example, the XLIFF[3] localisation standard "includes 37 elements, 80 attributes and 269 pre-defined values. That makes a total of 386 items […]" (Morado Vázquez 2012, 32). When combined, the XLIFF standard (for bilingual files), the TMX[4] standard (for translation memories) and the newer ITS[5] standard (for multilingual Web content) encompass hundreds of possible elements and attributes, either fixed or customisable. However, as we have seen, only a reduced subset of all those possible elements are actually used in the various tools and displayed to translators.

Today, each particular tool attracts its customers based on a number of factors, such as reputation, visual appeal of the graphical user interface, file formats supported and, certainly, its price tag. Although none of the tools shows all possible metadata items or hides them all, we have seen that they offer little variation in the basic set of metadata they display and in the way this metadata is displayed. In a hypothetical scenario, a translation tool could allow for enhanced customisation or personalisation. That is, the tool could allow translators to choose what best fits their particular translating style among an expanded set of metadata elements and screen configuration options or it could even automatically adapt to each translator's usage pattern.

As O'Brien (2012) points out, it would also be interesting to have cognitive ergonomics play a more prominent role in the development of translation tools. This calls for more translation oriented research on human-computer interaction in general, and translator-computer interaction in particular, to help understand how metadata affect cognitive processes during translation. After all, is it equally effective to visualise a match type through colour codes, letters, or both?

Finally, translation tools could benefit from advances in the field of MT quality estimation (Specia 2011), by including metadata related to MT suggestions. If, for example, an MT suggestion contained information on its "degree of confidence" or highlighted areas of uncertainty in the text, this could help translators make decisions when choosing between different suggestions and could help them adapt their editing strategies when post-editing the suggested translation.

Conclusion

In today's competitive world of commercial translation, productivity is a key factor for staying in business, be it for translation buyers, translation companies, individual translators or translation tool manufacturers. In this chapter we have focused on a particular aspect of computer-aided translation tools that, based on grounded suspicion and preliminary empirical evidence, is believed to have an impact on translator productivity—translation metadata.

Pym's minimalist model of translation competence describes the translation process as consisting of two cognitive sub-processes: one that generates translation options and another that chooses the most suitable of those options. We have argued that when translation tools are included in the translation process, they contribute to both sub-processes: by producing and displaying several suggestions, and by providing information (metadata) about the suggestions that help translators make choices among the many options.

That said, several questions emerge on how (many) translation suggestions should be generated and how the corresponding metadata should be presented, if the goal is to get the most productivity from the tools, preferably with reduced effort.

Current translation tools are able to generate relevant suggestions from many different sources: from multiple translation memories, including public TM repositories; from multiple glossaries, including public term banks; from multiple machine translation engines, either generic, domain-specific or custom-built; and the tools can even assemble translation suggestions based on a combination of those different sources. The question on the generation side is which and how many of those suggestions to present. While the highest possible number could be an answer in restricted cases, too many options would definitely be a time drain in hectic localisation projects.

The second question concerns the translation metadata to present, and trying to shed some light on this issue has been the focus of this chapter. We have analysed five translation tools—which we believe are representative of the whole spectrum of existing tools—and observed that: (1) they display different amounts of translation metadata, although there is a core of items (mainly of linguistic nature) that are common to all of them; (2) they present those items in different ways, i.e. in different parts of the screen, in different shapes and sizes, etc.; (3) most of the metadata presented is related to translation memory matches, and virtually no information is displayed for machine translation suggestions (except for the name of the engine that generated them). Although we have limited the scope of this chapter to drawing attention to the potential usefulness of translation metadata, we hope to be able to also contribute some empirical evidence in the near future, as the result of our on-going research.

As for the third aspect mentioned above, namely the absence of metadata for MT suggestions, we propose that the current research on MT quality estimation is bound to contribute some practical implementations, possibly by including quality estimation scores and highlighting areas of uncertainty in the suggested translation.

As far as the product interfaces of translation tools are concerned, we believe that personalisation/customisation should play a key role, so that a single tool can adapt or be adapted to different work styles. Finally, we hope that research on human-computer interaction will help to design translation software with more visually ergonomic, thus more productive, user interfaces.

Acknowledgments

This chapter was written with the support of a Marie Curie research grant from *TIME—Translation Research Training: An integrated and intersectoral model for Europe*, a research consortium sponsored by the European Commission under its Seventh Framework Programme (FP7).[6] I would like to thank Anthony Pym, David Orrego Carmona, Alberto Fuertes Puerta, Sharon O'Brien and two anonymous reviewers for their suggestions on previous versions of the manuscript.

Bibliography

Anastasiou, Dimitra. 2010. "Open and Flexible Localization Metadata." *MultiLingual* June 2010:50–52.

Anastasiou, Dimitra, and Lucía Morado Vázquez. 2010. "Localisation Standards and Metadata." In *Communications in Computer and Information Science* 108. *Metadata and Semantic Research*, edited by Salvador Sánchez-Alonso and Ioannis N. Athanasiadis. 255–74. Berlin; Heidelberg: Springer.

Guerberof, Ana. 2009. "Productivity and Quality in the Post-Editing of Outputs from Translation Memories and Machine Translation." *Localisation Focus* 7(1):11–21.

Karamanis, Nikiforos, Saturnino Luz, and Gavin Doherty. 2011. "Translation Practice in the Workplace: Contextual Analysis and Implications for Machine Translation." *Machine Translation* 25(1): 35–52.

Krings, Hans. 2001. *Repairing Texts: Empirical Investigations of Machine Translation Post-Editing Processes*. Edited by G. S. Koby. Ohio: Kent State University Press.

Morado Vázquez, Lucía. 2012. "An Empirical Study on the Influence of Translation Suggestions' Provenance Metadata." PhD diss., University of Limerick.

O'Brien, Sharon. 2006. "Eye-Tracking and Translation Memory Matches." *Perspectives: Studies in Translatology* 14(3):185–205.

—. 2012. "Translation as Human-Computer Interaction." *Translation Spaces* 1:101–122.

Pym, Anthony. 2003. "Redefining Translation Competence in an Electronic Age. In Defence of a Minimalist Approach." *Meta* XLVIII (4):481–497.

—. 2012. *On Translator Ethics: Principles for Mediation Between Cultures*. Amsterdam/Philadelphia: John Benjamins.

Specia, Lucia. 2011. "Exploiting Objective Annotations for Measuring Translation Post-Editing Effort." In *Proceedings of the 15th Conference of the European Association for Machine Translation*, edited by Mikel L. Forcada, Heidi Depraetere, and Vincent Vandeghinste. 73–80. Accessed October 28, 2013. http://clg.wlv.ac.uk/papers/EAMT-2011-Specia.pdf

Teixeira, Carlos S. C. 2011. "Knowledge of Provenance and its Effects on Translation Performance in an Integrated TM/MT Environment." In *Proceedings of the 8th International NLPCS Workshop – Special theme: Human-Machine Interaction in Translation. Copenhagen Studies in Language* 41, edited by Bernadette Sharp, Michael Zock, Michael Carl, and Arnt Lykke Jakobsen, 107–118. Copenhagen: Samfundslitteratur. Accessed October 28, 2013. http://www.mt-archive.info/NLPCS-2011-Teixeira.pdf

Zetzsche, Jost. 2013. "The Tool Box Newsletter – A Computer Newsletter for Translation Professionals." Issue 13–1–218. Accessed February 24, 2013. http://www.internationalwriters.com/toolkit/current.html

Notes

[1] This second term was coined by Jost Zetzsche: http://www.translatorstraining.com/mat/cat/cat_preview.htm

[2] We are referring here solely to the translation editing environment, where documents are actually translated, as translation tools usually have separate sub-environments for managing projects, for dealing with files within the projects, for configuring terminology databases, etc. and those sub-environments present their own sets of metadata.

[3] http://www.oasis-open.org/committees/tc_home.php?wg_abbrev=xliff#overview

[4] http://www.gala-global.org/oscarStandards/tmx/

[5] http://www.w3.org/TR/its20

[6] http://eu-researchprojects.eu/time

CHAPTER SIX

ANALYSIS OF POST-EDITING DATA: A PRODUCTIVITY FIELD TEST USING AN INSTRUMENTED CAT TOOL

JOHN MORAN, DAVID LEWIS AND CHRISTIAN SAAM

Abstract

A lack of strong correlation between post-editing effort as measured by string distance measures like Levenshtein and post-editing time combined with the difficulties of obtaining reliable time sheets from busy translators who do not have the time to record when they are actually translating and when they are working on related tasks has made it difficult to gather reliable data to measure the impact of machine translation on translator speed. Unfortunately current commercial CAT tools do not record time data in a manner that facilitates further in-depth analysis to measure productivity gains from machine translation. In this chapter we will present the iOmegaT Translator Productivity Testbench. The central component of the testbench is an adapted CAT tool that can be used to record translator activity data for further analysis. The system is compatible with Trados, a commonly used CAT tool as well as a number of other enterprise Translation Management System formats. It is available at no cost to researchers who wish to gather translation process field data from working translators. We will discuss previous work on MT productivity testing, detail our motivation for developing the testbench and discuss results from one of a number of productivity tests we have carried out using the software. The most important of these is accounting for translator self-review and the risk that failing to do so may overstate the utility of MT by some margin.

Introduction

Post-editing of Machine translation (PEMT) has been shown to increase translation speed relative to human translation (HT) (Plitt and Masselot, 2010, Federico et al., 2012, Guerberof, 2009). In general, it is possible to measure this speed difference by simply recording the average number of words post-edited by a translator in a given day and comparing it with a record of the average number of words translated per day without machine translation (MT). However, this practice of self-reporting on time worked and word count assumes that tasks that do not contribute to a daily word count like terminology research, answering e-mail etc. take the same amount of time each day, or that busy translators will accurately record time spent actually translating. As data gathered using this kind of self-reporting cannot be easily verified a number of researchers have adopted an approach where time data is gathered at the segment level (Plitt and Masselot, 2010, Federico et al., 2012, Guerberof, 2009).

In this chapter we will outline a number of approaches taken by previous researchers to carry out such MT productivity tests based on segment level time data. We will then present the *iOmegaT Translation Productivity Testbench*. This is a system based on an existing popular open-source Computer Aided Translation (CAT) tool called OmegaT. It records various events along with timestamps for those events as a translator works within a version of OmegaT, which is used by many translators around the world. By adapting an existing open-source CAT tool we did not have to develop a CAT tool from scratch. SDL Trados is the CAT tool normally used by the translators who carried out the productivity test to translate similar material.

With some additions we found that OmegaT proved to be sufficiently similar to Trados to be used as a temporary replacement CAT tool for the purposes of productivity testing. This made it possible for us to gather large quantities of field data from professional translators working directly or indirectly for Welocalize - a large translation company and CNGL (Centre for Next Generation Localisation) industrial partner. Welocalize are a translation supplier for Autodesk, a large software publisher who have been using machine translation to lower translation costs for a number of years, and whose content was translated in this field test.

In the results section we will discuss data we have gathered thus far using the iOmegaT Testbench and we will compare our approach and results to a similar study reported by Autodesk (Plitt and Masselot, 2010).

Motivation

Zhechev (2012) and Tatsumi (2009) have shown that a number of edit distance measures calculated on machine translation (MT) output before and after post-editing correlate moderately with time spent. Tatsumi found that the GTM (General Text Matcher) distance measure correlated best with PE time where Pearson's r=.56. Zhechev found that GTM correlated with PE time with a value of Spearman's ρ=.57. Though Tatsumi did not examine Levenshtein-based string similarity measures similar to those found in CAT tools, Zhechev found that a hybrid character based and word based fuzzy score correlated slightly better with a value of r=.609.

This lack of a strong correlation between edit distance and PE time could lead to a misleading impression with regard to the impact of MT on translator productivity where only edit distance and not time is recorded. Plitt and Masselot (2010) highlighted this risk in their description of one of the largest post-editing productivity tests carried out to date. Their study found that the post-editor who changed the most segments was also the fastest in terms of PE throughput. Though not reported in the paper, this was also the translator with the best quality assessment (QA) score.

This was mirrored in data gathered using self-reporting in commercial post-editing projects at Welocalize, where different string similarity measures were found to correlate very loosely with self-reported post-editing time. It was unclear if the lack of clear correlation was a result of inaccuracies in self-reporting of working times or a lack of strong correlation between string distance measures and PE time.

Unfortunately, PE time data is difficult to gather using current commercial CAT (Computer Aided Translation) tools. In describing their motivation for the PET post-editing and machine translation evaluation Aziz et al. (2012) report that segment level time data is difficult to record from translators working in the field using commercial CAT tools and list a number of well-known commercial CAT tools they tested that lack the ability to record segment level time data.

While most CAT tools record timestamps when segments are added to a translation memory (TM) and this can be read from a TMX (Translation Memory Exchange format) export of the project TM, this timestamp is overwritten if a TM match is added with the result that 100% and repetition segments will only record the last time value. Also, there is no timestamp recorded in TMX when a segment is opened. It is only recorded when the segment is added to the TM.

Thus, while HT and MT segment types could be categorized in advance and matched against a TMX file later using source segment text to estimate PEMT versus HT time values for translations carried out in Trados, in the longer term we believe that instrumentation of an open-source CAT tool is a better approach. It is more accurate and we can gain more insights into how a segment was translated within the CAT tool than we could by analysing TMX export timestamps.

Finally, using an open-source application instead of a proprietary CAT tool allowed us to add or remove functionality within the CAT tool. A more in-depth discussion of the motivation behind the testbench is presented in Moran and Lewis (2010).

Previous Work

In recent years a number of studies have been carried out in which translator speed was measured during PEMT. Guerberof (2009) used a web-based editor developed and hosted by a language technology consultancy called CrossLang[1] to gather HT, PEMT and fuzzy-match segments in the 80% to 90% range without informing the translator of the segment type (MT or fuzzy-match). Plitt and Masselot (2010) took a similar approach using an in-house web-based editing environment they developed to test MT productivity. They only measured time for HT and MT segments and not translation memory (TM) matches. The target segment field was empty for HT segments so translators were implicitly aware of the segment type. Neither of these translation environments provide the features that translators have come to expect in CAT tools, e.g. concordancing, terminology matching. Hence, productivity tests that use this approach can incur a high financial cost as translated segments are not round-tripped back into the translation workflow. At least in the Autodesk study, translations were discarded after the productivity test as, irrespective of MT, the method used to gather them had a negative impact on translation quality. This cost has the effect of reducing the quantity of data that can be gathered.

Two researchers carried out time studies of sentence level time data using monitoring technology external to the CAT tool. Tatsumi (2009) uses a specially developed third-party macro to capture key-logging data that is then parsed to capture segment transition times in Trados. O'Brien (2011) uses an eye-tracker with a proprietary Computer Aided Translation (CAT) tool to report on PE time. Both of these approaches require manual analysis to report on segment level time data so it is time consuming to analyse a large quantity of segments.

The approach most similar to our own is that taken by Federico et al. (2012) who describe how they used a Trados plugin connected to a server that provides MT and TM matches to measure segment time. Unfortunately, this software is not available for commercial or academic use as it uses timestamps recorded on an internal company server. In addition the system uses timestamps recorded on a server that is not running on the translator's PC so request-response delays between the Trados client and the TM/MT server must influence time measurements to a small but nevertheless unpredictable extent. They only measure single session edits whereas iOmegaT can sum editing time across any number of visits to a segment to record self-review time.

In contrast to these CAT tool based approaches, a number of applications that can measure sentence or segment level time data are available at no cost to researchers. Translog[2] is an example of such a system. It is often used in tandem with eye-tracking software to gather digital translation process data, as, for example, in Doherty et al. (2010). This approach is normally used on shorter texts of around 300 words in a controlled testing environment (Carl, 2012). PET (Aziz et al. 2012) is an offline open-source editor that measures sentence time data and also provides a configurable means for translators to annotate or label sentences from different MT systems. TransCenter (Denkowski and Lavie 2012) is an open-source web-based translation editor that measures sentence post-editing time as well as the number of keystrokes used in a segment and other annotation data. Unfortunately, none of these freely available systems provides translation aids commonly found in CAT tools. For this reason they are not suitable for gathering activity data related to MT on a large scale from translators working in the field as the aids to translation found in CAT tools, terminology matching, concordancing, fuzzy matching etc. do not just aid words per hour productivity but terminological consistency also.

The iOmegaT Translation Productivity Testbench

The iOmegaT Translation Productivity Testbench is a system we have developed to record fine-grained activity data from professional translators working in the field.

It comprises:

1) The iOmegaT CAT tool

This is an adapted version of the free open-source OmegaT CAT tool that has been developed over the past decade. A number of translators and programmers support the application mainly on a volunteer basis. It is an active project with new features added regularly. Per year download numbers for the application have been steadily growing over the past years suggesting increasing popularity. It also has a growing user support mailing list with approximately 1,400 subscribers. Though it is unclear how many of the translators who download the tool use it as their only CAT tool, we are aware of a number of translators and translation agencies who use it as their only CAT tool. These factors combined suggested that the application was sufficiently reliable and featured for use in field tests.

We have added a logging function to record various events within the CAT tool along with millisecond level timestamp information for these events. We refer to this logging as *instrumentation* because it serves a different function to normal software application logs. In general these events are logged in a manner that facilitates segment-level replay using a replayer component that is currently at an early prototype stage. This component is available for free including source code to academic researchers.

2) The iOmegaT Analytics Component

This component imports, interprets and reports on this instrumentation data. This component is not freely available but we can provide access to results from it in an SQL database at no cost to academic researchers. It is currently the focus of a commercialisation feasibility study in Trinity College Dublin and has been licensed to large buyers of machine translation services who use the system to establish word-based prices for post-editing services.

3) The iOmegaT Middleware Component

This component is used to reformat files for translation from external sources into OmegaT and back again. This component is also available at no cost to academic researchers for field tests, for example where iOmegaT is used instead of Trados as a CAT tool.

Method

In this section we will outline how we carried out the Autodesk productivity test and describe how iOmegaT gathers translator activity data. The productivity test reported here differs from a regular commercial translation project in a number of respects:

1) Per language, two translators translated the same source text. We were not privy to translator identity and anonymous IDs were used. Translation was carried out from English into 11 languages so 22 translators took part in the productivity test. Except for Japanese all translators translated the same source text.
2) In most cases translators were using a CAT tool that was new to them. To ease disorientation, all translators were given a small sample translation task to complete the day before the productivity test to give them time to familiarise themselves with the new CAT tool.
3) The time period for the test we are reporting on here was two working days including normal breaks et cetera. Translators were not expected to translate all segments in the project.

The texts were typical help files found in Computer Aided Design software. Unlike similar systems for large-scale analysis of segment level time data, iOmegaT records but does not control the sequence in which translators work in segments. In the results section we will show that this approach still generates data that can be used for the purposes of MT productivity testing.

By default iOmegaT opens project files in the numerical order that corresponds to the natural order of the files for translation but a translator can override this. When a translator enters a segment for the first time (i.e. it has not been added to the writeable translation memory stored in project_save.tmx) the translator is shown either an empty segment (HT) without a segment status message, or a pre-filled segment with one of the status messages listed in Table 6-1.

Offline MT inserted in target
Fuzzy match inserted in target
100% match inserted in target – WARNING PLACEHOLDER MISMATCH
100% match inserted in target

Table 6-1: iOmegaT status bar messages

In iOmegaT, if a translator returns to a segment that was added to the writeable translation memory (TM) the status "Already translated" is shown. HT segments are segments that do not appear in the read-only MT file or any TM.

As the translators in the Autodesk study normally use Trados for their work we compared OmegaT to Trados in order to ensure that translators were presented with similar information in both CAT tools. We also carried out speed tests using screen recordings that we replayed later in slow motion. We found that TM matching speeds and terminology database matching speeds were slightly faster for OmegaT than for Trados. For the examples we tested, concordance speed was significantly faster in OmegaT. In light of the functional comparison, we made a number of changes to OmegaT, e.g. we added an offline MT feature based on a read-only TMX file stored locally and the status messages shown in Table 6-1.

Below is a summary of the features, changes and training assets that were added to OmegaT:

- We added XML instrumentation to capture time and other data from the CAT tool (e.g. terminology matches, keystroke data).
- We removed non-essential menu items and the user manual to reduce disorientation in iOmegaT, an unfamiliar CAT tool.
- We recorded training videos for translators. In total these were less than ten minutes viewing time.
- We added an auto-download function triggered by the File | Open dialog in the main OmegaT menu.
- We adapted an existing Java webstart[3] version of OmegaT so that the iOmegaT CAT tool could be started from a web page rather than using a traditional application installer.
- We added a feature that shows translators the status of each segment, e.g. fuzzy match or MT (see Table 6-1).
- We changed the order in which files were opened from alphabetical to numerical.
- We provided an information sheet for translators taking part in the Autodesk study according to Trinity College Dublin ethical approval guidelines.
- We developed a separate parser and analyser that parses the XML output by iOmegaT and imports segment session data into a database for further analysis and visualisation.

In order to evaluate the translators' perception of the usability of the CAT tool we asked them to fill out a non-mandatory questionnaire with a set of standard questions (Brooke 1996) after the productivity test had been completed. Ten translators chose to fill it out. The answers were on a scale of 1 to 5, where 1 was "Strongly disagree" and 5 was "Strongly agree".

Question	Average
I found OmegaT unnecessarily complex	1.6
I think that I would like to use OmegaT frequently	3
I thought OmegaT was easy to use	4
I found the various functions in OmegaT were well integrated	3.4
I thought there was too much inconsistency in OmegaT	2.4
I think that I would need the support of a technical person to be able to use OmegaT in my own work	1.8
I would imagine that most people would learn to use OmegaT very quickly	4.2
I found OmegaT very cumbersome to use	1.8
I needed to learn a lot of things before I could get going with OmegaT	1.7

Table 6-2: Responses to iOmegaT questionnaire

iOmegaT segment session data

An example of the kind of data we gathered is shown in Figure 6-1 for the post-edit shown in Table 6-3 for German. The text is typical of the kind of technical, software help text translated and post-edited during the productivity test.

Source	*In this section the options are described that can be used with the <x0/>cmdjob <x1/>command.*
Before	*In diesem Abschnitt werden die Optionen beschrieben, können Sie mit dem Befehl <x0/>cmdjob <x1/>verwendet.*
After	*In diesem Abschnitt werden die Optionen beschrieben, die Sie mit dem Befehl <x0/>cmdjob <x1/>verwenden können.*

Table 6-3: Sample segment before and after post-editing.

```
<SegmentSession sourceIndex="14">
<SourceText>This section describes the options you can use with the <x0/>cmdjob
<x1/>command.</SourceText>
<PreeditText>null</PreeditText>
<Events>
<LogEvent Action="segmentOpen" Time="1363874598949"/>
<LogEvent Action="insertCharUp" Utf8Value="110" CharacterTyped="n" Cursor="-
83" Time="1363874598953"/>
<LogEvent Action="mtMatchPlacement" In diesem Abschnitt werden die Optionen
beschrieben, können Sie mit dem Befehl <x0/>cmdjob <x1/>verwendet.="In diesem
Abschnitt werden die Optionen beschrieben, können Sie mit dem Befehl
<x0/>cmdjob <x1/>verwendet." MTsystem="123456789" Time="1363874599029"/>.
<LogEvent Action="segmentClose" Time="1363874641632"/>
</Events>
<PostEditTarget>In diesem Abschnitt werden die Optionen beschrieben, die Sie mit
dem Befehl <x0/>cmdjob <x1/>verwenden können.</PostEditTarget>
<Comment postEditTime="42"/>
```


Figure 6-1: Some XML data from the first editing session of the source segment with a segmentIndex value of 14


```
<SegmentSession sourceIndex="14">
<SourceText>This section describes the options you can use with the <x0/>cmdjob
<x1/>command.</SourceText>
<PreeditText>In diesem Abschnitt werden die Optionen beschrieben, die Sie mit
dem Befehl <x0/>cmdjob <x1/>verwenden können.</PreeditText>
<Events>
<LogEvent Action="segmentOpen" Time="1363874646601"/>
<LogEvent Action="alreadyTranslated" TargetMatch="In diesem Abschnitt werden
die Optionen beschrieben, die Sie mit dem Befehl <x0/>cmdjob <x1/>verwenden
können." Time="1363874646605"/>
<LogEvent Action="segmentClose" Time="1363874659343"/>
</Events>
<PostEditTarget>In diesem Abschnitt werden die Optionen beschrieben, die Sie mit
dem Befehl <x0/>cmdjob <x1/>verwenden können.</PostEditTarget>
<Comment postEditTime="12"/>
</SegmentSession>
```


Figure 6-2: Some XML data from the second editing session of the source segment with a segmentIndex value of 14

Figures 6-1 and 6-2 show some of the XML data that is gathered for a segment in which MT is post-edited and then worked on a second time. The Time attribute value is the number of milliseconds since January 1st 1970. The postEditTime attribute in the Comment element was included to improve readability of the XML output in its raw form. The analytics component does not process them. In this case the post-edit required 42 seconds for the first edit and 12 seconds on the second visit. An early version of iOmegaT maintained back-compatibility with Translog so that keystrokes gathered in iOmegaT could be replayed in that application but we have since developed our own user activity data replay component as a prototype. Although there are overlaps in terms of some aspects of the data format this back-compatibility has since not been maintained.

A key feature of iOmegaT is the ability to take into account translator self-review. We will discuss the importance of this in the Results section below. Figure 6-2 shows an example of this kind of self-review. The translator returned to the segment with a segmentIndex value of "14" after approximately five seconds but did not type any text.[4] The segmentIndex value is unique for each source file in the OmegaT project that was sent to the translator so we can record multiple editing sessions by appending new segment session edit data to the XML file that is unique to the source file and keeping note of the segmentIndex value. We call this the segment visit count. In this example the visit count is 2. This means a manual search for the text "segmentIndex="14" would show that string appears twice in the instrumentation file.

With regard to data quantity, although compressed textual data contains a minimum amount of redundant data, we chose to use longer descriptive attributes and element names despite the fact that this uses more disk space. This makes the XML data easier to read for humans. For example, 25,300 segment editing sessions from approximately 44 days of productivity test data gathered from 22 translators in 11 languages for the Autodesk productivity test required approximately 1.5 GB of disk space prior to compression, but only 190 MB when compressed. As productivity data is a new type of data that is related to earnings we felt it was preferable to have a format that can be read and interpreted by translators so that they are better equipped to decide if this is data they are comfortable sharing, despite the fact that this design decision results in greater use of disk space and bandwidth to transfer the data.

Results

In this section we will show some visualisations of the data gathered using the approach of not locking segments, where translators were free to move around at will from segment to segment and file to file in the translation project.

Figure 6-3 shows general progression patterns for segments with typing activity. Though translators were located in different time zones and began the tests at different times, here all times have been normalised to start at the same point in time. Vertical lines indicate that a translator jumped from one segment to another that was not near it. Horizontal lines indicate a period of inactivity. We can see how most activity is grouped into two working days starting on the morning of June 19th 2012 and starting again on the morning of June 20th with the expected periods of inactivity between working days. We hope this visualisation will be useful in that it should correlate with patterns a translator expects to see in their own activity data. Longer term we hope it may help them plan for breaks in their work.

Progression speed can be seen more clearly in Figure 6-4 where temporal information is normalised to unit time which we call editing steps. The horizontal axis therefore only represents indexical progression in terms of editing steps from one segment to the next. Linear progression at an even speed would result in a slope equal to a diagonal from the bottom left corner to the top right corner through a field in the grid. Steeper slopes mean segments were omitted in forward jumps, shallower slopes mean backtracking by backward jumps. Spikes represent jumps to and from segments that are at a distance from the original segment. As expected, we see that translators progress reasonably linearly through segments during typing phases. All segment types are conflated in this figure. We present it here as a prototype visualisation. It is a step towards determining sections of text that slow down or speed up translator progress for PEMT or HT. We hope to be able to use variations on this visualisation alongside text categorization techniques to spot patterns where MT is hindering rather than helping translators in terms of translation speed in production translation projects where iOmegaT is used.

Figure 6-5 shows the production speed as a function of source text segment length. The fitted curves suggest that the optimum sentence length for both translation and post-editing is between 20 and 30 words in the English source language. This is similar to the value of 22 found by Plitt and Masselot (2010).[5] This similarity is unsurprising as both file content and translator profiles are similar and the same MT implementation was used to produce the MT proposals.

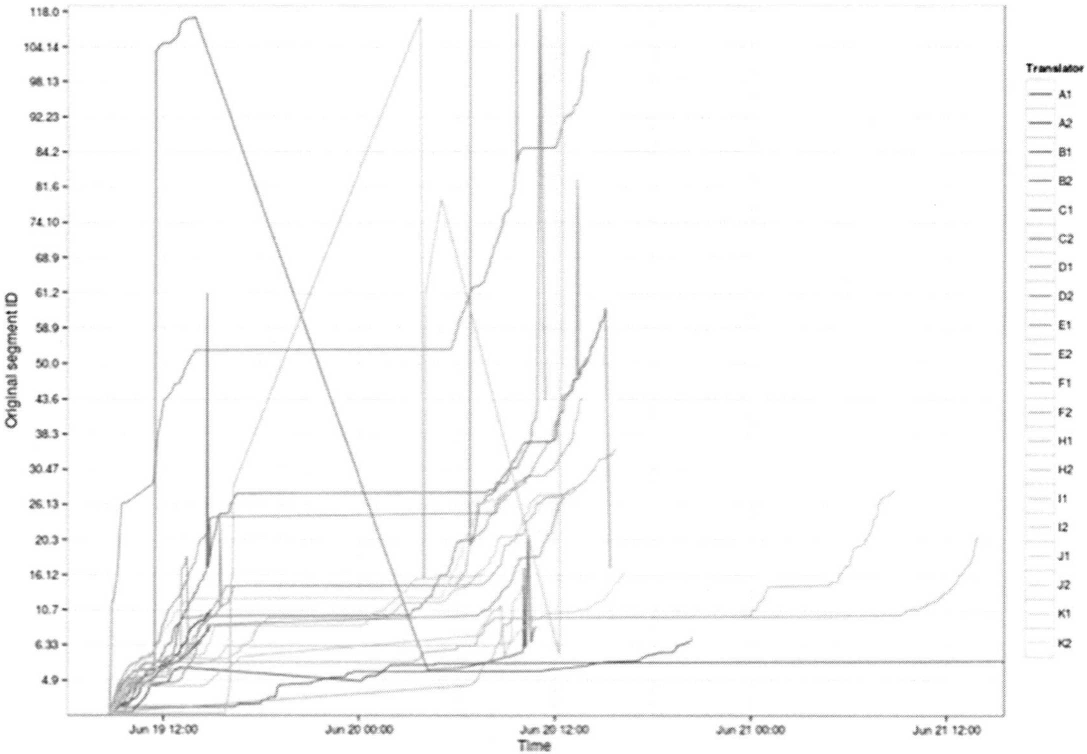

Figure 6-3: Time of day progression pattern for segments with typing activity

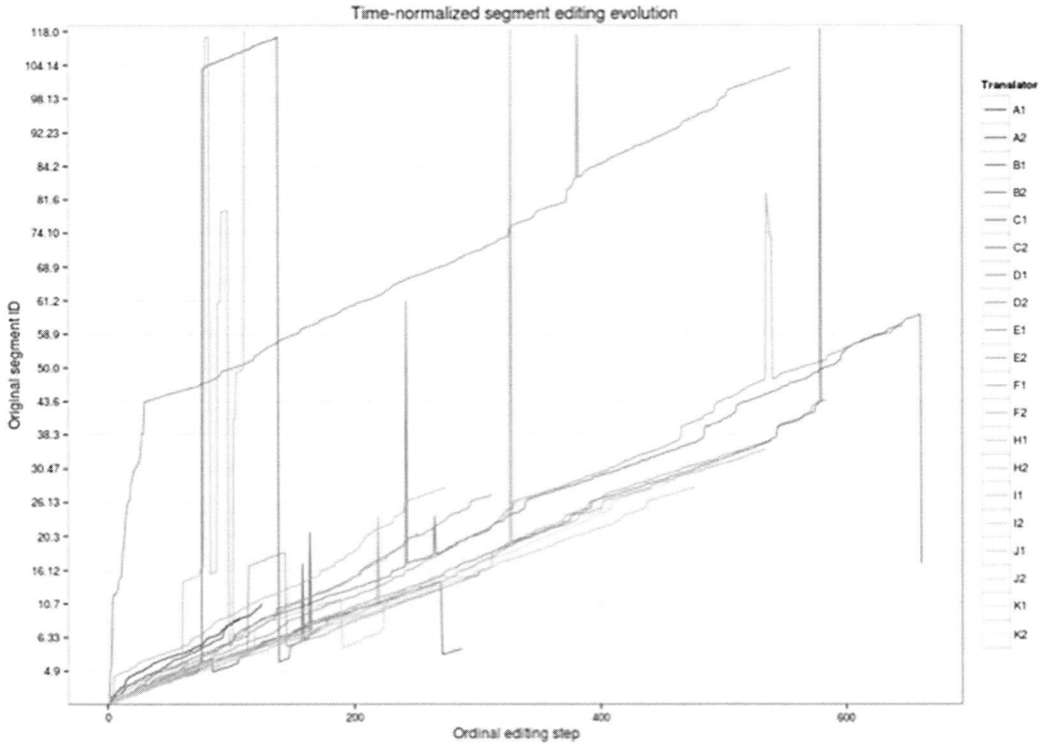

Figure 6-4: Time normalised progression pattern for segments with typing activity

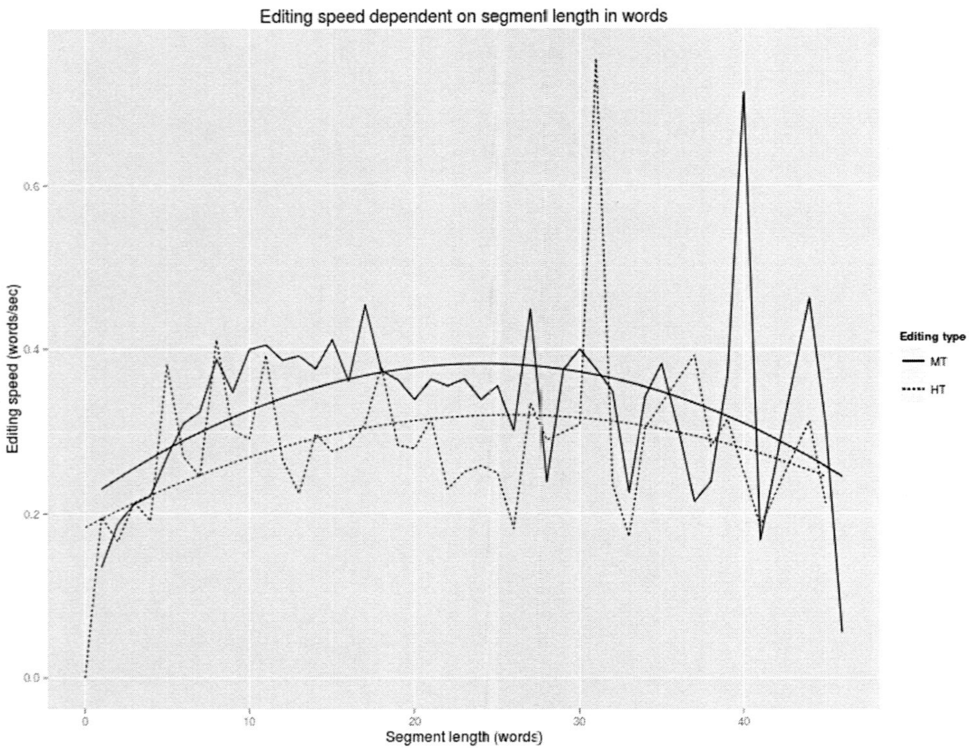

Figure 6-5: Production speed relative to segment length in words

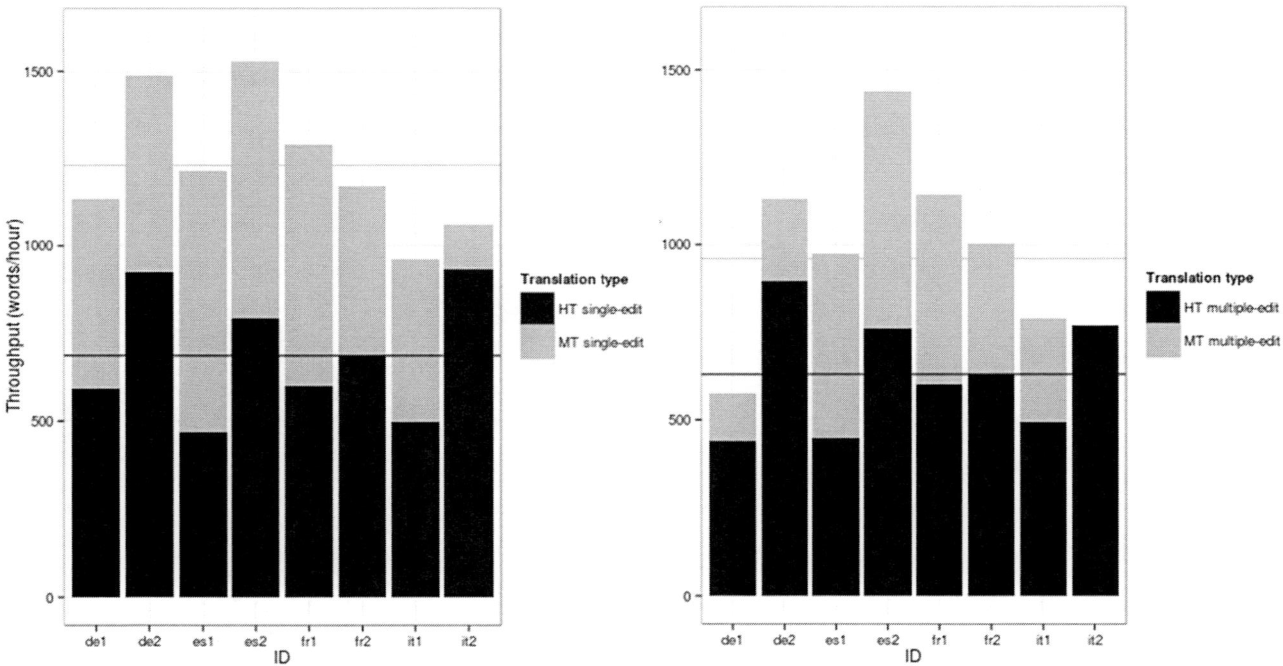

Figure 6-6: HT versus MT single-edit (left) and multiple-edit (right) throughput

In Figure 6-6, each vertical bar refers to an individual translator, e.g. de1 translated and post-edited from English into German.

We have limited the language pairs in this figure to English to French, Italian, German and Spanish as these were the language pairs presented by Plitt and Masselot (2010). On average in total across all these languages for the two day productivity test each translator translated 1,003 words in 'HT' mode plus 5,418 words post-editing using MT. We do not count words that were fuzzy matches, 100% matches or repetitions (which were auto-propagated).

As can be seen in the figure on the left hand side of Figure 6-7, when only single-session edits are compared between studies, our single-session MT throughput was 1,231 words per hour (WPH) while Plitt and Masselot's was approximately 1,100 WPH. In our study a single session is defined as a session in which typing occurred when the segment was opened for the first time. Where a segment was opened but no typing occurred we ignore the data. Where a segment was reopened, whether typing occurred or not we ignore the data. This self-review activity is accounted for in the multiple session analysis.

Our single session HT throughput was 687 WPH while theirs was around 600 WPH. It is not surprising that these numbers are similar as translator profile, source text and the MT system used are similar or indeed identical. However, our system also records subsequent segment sessions. Obviously, times summed over a number of segment sessions must exceed times for just the first session. Thus, relative to single session time we would expect to see a dampening effect on HT and MT throughput values.

When total time is summed for multiple sessions, which includes self-review time where some typing or no typing occurred, the MT throughput in our study is 271 WPH lower than single-session MT. Indeed, it reverses the picture for translator it2, who seems to be faster post-editing when only the first editing session is accounted for, specifically 931 WPH HT versus 1,059 WPH MT. When self-review is accounted for using multi-session time data, MT impeded it2 relative to HT by 152 WPH.

Only accounting for single-session data we see an 80% increase for MT versus HT. However, when multiple sessions are accounted for this average throughput increase for MT for the four language pairs shown is reduced to 54%. Thus, if we only measure single session edit times in projects where MT aids throughput but increases self-review time, we run the risk of overstating the utility of MT as a means of increasing throughput by some margin. This has obvious implications when discussing per-word pricing for PEMT with suppliers and customers.

A note on translation quality

Translation speed data is only relevant to productivity after quality has been assessed. The analysis provided here is two dimensional in that word count and time were analysed. However, a translation productivity must account for quality to have a full three dimensional model.

Spot-checks were carried out after the productivity test and in most cases the QA (Quality Analysis) result was a fail for the project as a whole. No distinction was made between HT and PEMT during this check. However, most errors were attributable to lack of adherence to terminology that was not provided in the termbase. Some translators reported spending less time on manual terminology lookup as they were aware that the translations would be discarded after the test and the QA results would not be entered in any Welocalize databases. MT has been used in Autodesk translations for a number of years and QA procedures to evaluate quality for PEMT relative to HT are mature and the translators' ability to supply high quality translation when post-editing the MT system used to provide proposals has already been proven. The gap in knowledge that we seek to address with our software is translation speed under different conditions so this was the focus of our discussion.

Future work

There are a number of areas that require further investigation. For future productivity tests we hope to be able to measure productivity in real rather than simulated translation projects using an iOmegaT workflow that supports round-tripping of file formats both into and out of iOmegaT. This means we will be able to gather speed data for longer periods of time. In this scenario the cost of carrying out the tests will be much reduced as the translations would be sold to the client and not discarded, as was the case here. Alongside more stringent QA we plan to look at patterns across several productivity tests to look for correlations between high MT utility and other factors.

With regard to the data already gathered, we also hope to be able to carry out blind testing to see if linguists can guess which segments were post-edited and which were manually translated. We also plan to examine the large difference in self-review time for MTPE versus HT in more detail. It is a surprising result as once a segment has been translated or in the case of MT post-edited or accepted without editing for the first time by a translator it is marked as "Already translated". When a translator returns to the segment, it is not possible for that person to tell from information in the CAT tool if it was originally post-edited MT or HT.

Regarding the analytics component, we plan to look at patterns across several productivity tests to look for correlations between high MT utility and other factors. We also plan to extend the Analytics Component to look for actionable patterns like changes in tag placement, underuse of do-not-translate lists and changes to glossary entry proposals.

In terms of software development we intend to publish the source code for iOmegaT along with a formal description of the format used to record translator activity data within this tool. We plan to further develop our prototype replay component. We also plan to make a version of the analytics component available as a web-application at no cost to academic researchers in the field of translation process research and provide them with structured translation process data in SQL format for further analysis. The iOmegaT Testbench is currently available for commercial use at a cost. It is available as an offline standalone application for commercial enterprises who wish to carry out MT productivity tests without sharing sensitive data with any third party. In the future we plan to make it available for companies that can share data with a third-party as a less expensive web application.

Summary

In this chapter we presented the motivation for iOmegaT, an instrumented offline CAT tool that can be used to evaluate the utility of MT for translators working in the field. We compared some data gathered using this software to a previously described productivity test carried out on similar MT output using a locked segment approach. We provided comparative data with a previous productivity test to support the argument that locking segments is not required to gather MT productivity data and showed that in our data a locked segment approach to productivity testing risks overstating MT utility relative to HT because translator self-review activity across multiple segment editing sessions is not taken into account and a naïve single session analysis would have overstated our MT utility score by 26%.

Acknowledgements

This research is supported by the Science Foundation of Ireland (SFI) (grant 07/CE/I1142) as part of the Centre for Next Generation Localisation (www.cngl.ie) at Trinity College, Dublin and some development has been funded by a Technology Innovation Feasability Study grant also from SFI.

The work presented here results from an ongoing collaboration between CNGL and David Clarke, Laura Casanellas Luri and Olga Beregovaya, employees of Welocalize, a CNGL industrial partner. We would also like to express a debt of gratitude to the OmegaT development and support community and to Autodesk for allowing us access to their data.

Bibliography

Aziz, Wilker, Castilho, Shelia. and, Specia, Lucia, 2012. "PET: a Tool for Post-editing and Assessing Machine Translation." In *Proceedings of the Eight International Conference on Language Resources and Evaluation (LREC'12)*. Istanbul, Turkey: European Language Resources Association (ELRA).

Brooke, John., 1996. "SUS-A quick and dirty usability scale." *Usability evaluation in industry*, 189, p.194.

Carl, Michael., 2012. "The CRITT TPR-DB 1.0: A Database for Empirical Human Translation Process Research." In *AMTA 2012 Workshop on Post-Editing Technology and Practice*. San Diego. Available at: http://amta2012.amtaweb.org/AMTA2012Files/html/11/11_paper.pdf [Accessed March 24, 2013].

Denkowski, Michael. & Lavie, Alon, 2012. "TransCenter: Web-Based Translation Research Suite.". In *AMTA 2012 Workshop on Post-Editing Technology and Practice Demo Session*. p. 2012. Available at: http://www.cs.cmu.edu/afs/cs/Web/People/mdenkows/pdf/transcenter-amta2012.pdf [Accessed March 24, 2013].

Doherty, Stephen., O'Brien, Sharon, & Carl, Michael., 2010. "Eye tracking as an MT Evaluation Technique." *Machine Translation*, 24(1), pp.1–13. Available at: http://www.springerlink.com/index/10.1007/s10590-010-9070-9 [Accessed February 4, 2011].

Federico, Marcello, Cattelan, Alessandro, Trombetti, Marco, 2012. Measuring "User Productivity in Machine Translation Enhanced Computer Assisted Translation." In *Tenth Biennial Conference of the Association for Machine Translation in the Americas*. Available at: http://amta2012.amtaweb.org/AMTA2012Files/papers/123.pdf [Accessed March 25, 2013].

Guerberof, Ana, 2009. "Productivity and Quality in MT Post-editing." In *Proceedings of MT Summit XII*. Ontario, Canada.

Moran, John & Lewis, David., 2010. "Unobtrusive Methods For Low-cost Manual Evaluation of Machine Translation." In *Tralogy*. Paris. Available at: http://lodel.irevues.inist.fr/tralogy/index.php?id=141.

O'Brien, Sharon, 2011. "Towards Predicting Post-editing Productivity." *Machine Translation*, 25(3), pp.197–215. Available at: http://www.springerlink.com/index/10.1007/s10590-011-9096-7.

Plitt, Mirko. & Masselot, Francois., 2010. "A Productivity Test of Statistical Machine Translation Post-Editing in a Typical Localisation Context." *The Prague Bulletin of Mathematical Linguistics*, (93), pp.7–16.

Tatsumi, Midori, 2009. "Correlation Between Automatic Evaluation Metric Scores, Post-editing speed, and Some other Factors." *Proceedings of MT Summit XII*, (2001), pp.332–339. Available at: http://www.mt-archive.info/MTS-2009-Tatsumi.pdf [Accessed February 4, 2011].

Zhechev, Ventsislav, 2012. "Machine Translation Infrastructure and Post-editing Performance at Autodesk." In *AMTA 2012 Workshop on Post-Editing Technology and Practice (WPTP 2012)*. San Diego, USA, pp. 87–96. Available at: http://amta2012.amtawcb.org/AMTA2012Files/html/5/5_paper.pdf.

Notes

[1] www.crosslang.com

[2] http://www.translog.dk

[3] http://www.oracle.com/technetwork/java/javase/tech/index-jsp-136112.html

[4] The insertChar events where "n" and "p" were typed are command-and-control keyboard sequences in OmegaT where "n" is typed along with an operating system specific meta-key to move to the next segment. Any non-alphanumeric key is represented by "*".

[5] Like Plitt and Masselot, in our analysis we excluded segments with a session time exceeding five minutes for the single session analysis and seven minutes in the multiple session analysis. We also found that these cut-off points excluded most outliers where translators may have taken a break from work. We also make the assumption that these cut offs will apply as often to MT segments as HT segments.

CHAPTER SEVEN

INVESTIGATING USER BEHAVIOUR IN POST-EDITING AND TRANSLATION USING THE CASMACAT WORKBENCH

JAKOB ELMING, LAURA WINTHER BALLING AND MICHAEL CARL

Abstract

This article presents the CASMACAT workbench and findings from the first post-editing and translation experiments conducted with it. The CASMACAT workbench is a web-based computer-aided translation (CAT) tool with extensive logging of user behaviour including eye tracking. Analyses are based on more than 90 hours of English to Spanish post-editing and translation performed by professional translators. Findings support an average time saving of 25% from post-editing machine translation over translation from scratch. This is especially interesting in light of the fact that the processed texts stem from the less restricted domain of newspaper articles. Not surprisingly, we also find that the time saving to a large degree depends on how many keystrokes the post-editor performs. Interestingly, this is a much better predictor than edit distance between the machine translation output and the final translation product, which is often used in the literature. Also, the post-editor has to produce a relatively high number of keystrokes before post-editing no longer pays off compared to translation from scratch.

Introduction

Machine translation (MT) has received much attention over the last decades, especially due to the statistical approaches that have made the technology available to a wider audience, most notably through the translation services provided free of charge by companies such as Google, Microsoft and Yahoo.Research within MT has to a large degree been evaluated by different automatic and manual text-based quality evaluation metrics such as BLEU (Papineni et al., 2002) and translation ranking (Callison-Burch et al., 2007). These metrics provide a measure of quality either by comparing MT to human-produced reference translations or by having a human directly provide a grade.

Recently, the practical use of MT has begun to receive more attention. The focus here is no longer on how good fully automatically produced translations are, instead interest is directed towards how the MT output can be used, and what value it provides in a human translation or post-editing situation. The focus is thus directed towards questions such as: What is the required level of quality if MT is to be useful for post-editors? How should MT output be presented and used to increase productivity for translators? How can MT systems best help the translator? How does the process of post-editing MT differ from the process of translation?

To provide a solid basis for answering such questions, the EU 7th framework project CASMACAT aims at designing, implementing and evaluating an advanced MT post-editing workbench together with exhaustive logging facilities. Advanced MT post-editing includes visualisation of translation confidence, interactive predictive MT (Alabau et al., 2012), adaptive and incremental learning (Martínez-Gómez et al. 2012) and other facilities which will be included in successive versions of the workbench. As numerous novel functions and configuration possibilities are added to the workbench, the conglomeration of processes involved in translation becomes increasingly complex, while the actual task of translation hopefully becomes easier. The investigation procedure can no more rely on introspection and user questionnaires. Instead, in order to facilitate the investigation of how advanced translation assistance tools are used, the CASMACAT workbench provides a complete key-logging and eye-tracking protocol. This allows the analysis of user behaviour on a fine-grained level as well as research into cognitive aspects of translation processes. In a later section, the CASMACAT project is described in greater detail.

In this chapter, we start by giving some more background on the nature and goal of these studies, and then introduce the first version of the CASMACAT workbench which was used to collect the data that are analysed in this chapter. The presented version of the CASMACAT workbench was developed to conduct a first field trial in a translation agency which allowed us to collect 90 hours of translation and post-editing data. We present three different analyses to evaluate the field trial data, comparing translation and post-editing time as well as gaze behaviour and to determine factors that predict post-editing time.

Background

Even though post-editing as a field has been revitalised only in the past few years, the first post-editing experiments were already conducted in the 1980s. According to Guerberof Arenas (2012), post-editing processes and post-editing profiles were described in the early 80s based on MT implementations in big organisations such as the EU and the Pan American Health Organization. Today, most MT systems offer a post-editing interface (e.g. ProMT, Systran), and translation memories include possibilities to use MT proposals for segments where there are no or only low fuzzy matches (e.g. SDL Trados, Transit, Across, OmegaT etc. (see Moran et al, this volume).

While early investigations found no increase in productivity for post-editing (e.g. Krings, 2001), more recent studies have shown a benefit in the form of time savings for post-editing compared to translating from scratch. Although Groves and Schmidtke (2009) note the MT "quality itself is only one of several important factors influencing productivity" they observe that, as Microsoft's machine translation improves, the "productivity gains increase from 5-10%, to 10-20%, for selected languages." Plitt and Masselot (2010) describe a 17-57% time saving on a software localisation project. Impressive time savings between 50% and 68% are reported by Roukos (2012) for English-Spanish translation of IBM content in a Translation Services Center.

In a recent interview, Fred Hollowood, research director of Symantec Corporation, states that "[i]n our product documentation we are experiencing throughput improvements in the region of 50% to 100% in various languages. That is to say that a translator is able to post-edit in excess of 5,000 to 6,000 words a day in some languages on a well-formed source."[1]

Several other studies confirm these findings (Flournoy and Duran, 2009; Tatsumi 2010). While in a previous study (Carl et al 2011) we could not support these findings, in our current study we see an average time saving from using post-editing of 24.6%[2] across comparable segments. However, our study is different from previous ones, as in those cases MT is reported to give time savings in restricted, technical domains, while in our study, translation is performed in the very general domain of newspaper articles. This is not only interesting from a research point-of-view. In commercial companies doing media intelligence, newspaper articles or summaries of these are often translated for multilingual companies. Our finding also confirms Koehn's (2012) suggestion that MT output has reached a level of quality for many languages and texts which makes it suitable for post-editing.

However, metrics that assess whether MT quality is sufficient to make it suitable for post-editing are hard to come by. In an attempt to find a metric for MT quality that is meaningful for translators and post-editors, O'Brien (2011) suggests a correlation between processing speed and cognitive measures of effort using eye tracking. While the "average fixation time and count are found to correlate well with the scores for groups of segments" there are likely more factors that play a role, including visualization of machine generated translation knowledge, as mentioned above.

In order to investigate several aspects that may have an impact on the post-editing process, the CASMACAT workbench builds on experience from the Translog tool (Jakobsen 1999). Translog is a logging tool for studying reading and writing processes especially in translation. The CASMACAT workbench complements the key-logging and eye-tracking abilities of Translog with a browser-based front-end and an MT server in thc backcnd. Thc main advanccs of thc tool arc that:

1. it uses web-based technology which allows for easy portability across different machine platforms and versions,
2. it gives a realistic translation session by both visually and functionally resembling commercial translation tools,
3. it allows for direct integration of translation technologies such as interactive or regular machine translation, supplemented with confidence estimation.

Characteristics 1) and 3) are properties the CASMACAT workbench shares with, e.g., the Caitra tool (Koehn 2009), but Caitra does not allow for the same detailed analysis of the user behaviour, since user action logging is minimal.

Similar tools to study translation behaviour in depth have been developed in different contexts. The iOmegaT tool implements Translog-style user behaviour logging (but with no eye tracking) in the open-source CAT tool OmegaT[3] (Moran 2012, Moran et al., this volume). A great advantage of this tool is that it is integrated in a proven CAT tool environment, but the tool is not web-based, it does not facilitate more advanced MT features, and so far no session replay function is available.

The PET tool (Aziz et al., 2012) also logs Translog-style user behaviour information without eye tracking. The tool facilitates direct user feedback for each translated segment. It differs from the CASMACAT workbench in that it is not web-based, does not facilitate session replay, and has no online MT connection, and does not allow for advanced MT features, like interactive MT.

Browser-based web applications, as in CASMACAT, do not require special installations on the client side. While the software runs on a remote server, users only need to open a web page in their browsers and can start working immediately. On the one hand, this allows for greater user mobility as translators can work from any computer and any location that provides a connection to the internet. On the other hand, a centralised administration means a reduction in administration and configuration costs for organisations, and eliminates the differences in configuration for each user, while a central help-desk may be established to answer user requests.

However, web-based applications also have a cost on the engineering side, not only with respect to security issues, but with respect to the complexity of the software, as multiple programming languages and techniques have to be integrated and advanced keyboard logging and eye tracking (as in CASMACAT) are not fully supported by the current browser technologies.

The CASMACAT workbench

The CASMACAT workbench is the core product of the EU 7th framework project CASMACAT[4] (*Cognitive Analysis and Statistical Methods for Advanced Computer Aided Translation*) running from November 2011 to November 2014. The main goal of the project is to build the next generation translator's workbench to improve productivity, quality, and work practices in the translation industry. The tool is especially useful for examining the effects of integrating MT technology in the translation process, in particular how it affects the behaviour of the human translator. The extensive logging allows the development of the workbench to be shaped by how users actually work with the tool. During the lifetime of the project, three versions of the workbench will be released. The version described in this chapter is the first prototype, which includes only the most basic translation and post-editing features. Key features of the tool are: **open-source web-based technology**, extensive **logging of user behaviour** including eye tracking, and **exact replay** of the translation session.

The CASMACAT workbench provides basic CAT tool functionality and basic MT integration. It produces a full log of user activity data (UAD) and has a function to replay a translation session. Future versions will contain more advanced MT utilisation such as interactive MT and confidence scores for the MT-produced translations.[5]

The main functionality of the CASMACAT workbench is a web-based CAT tool. The entry point is a web page that the users log into using a personal user name and password. This allows for easy control over users, their profiles, the translation tasks they are assigned, and records of their translation sessions.

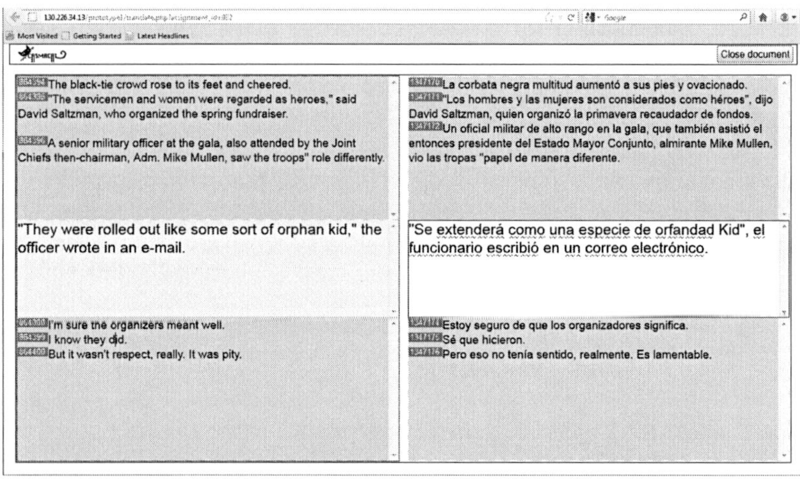

Figure 7-1: Screenshot of the first prototype CASMACAT workbench

Once the user has logged on and selected an assignment, the text opens up in the actual CAT tool. Figure 7-1 shows the first prototype of the CASMACAT workbench. The source text appears in segments on the left and the target text on the right. The white box in the middle of the screen contains the segment that is currently being edited by the translator. Shortcut keys are used for functions such as navigating between segments. The translation field can be pre-filled by machine translation through a server connection or left empty for translation from scratch.

An essential part of the CASMACAT workbench is its exhaustive logging functionality. This opens up new possibilities of analysing the translator's behaviour both in a qualitative and quantitative manner. The extensive log file contains entries of the translator's activity in the form of all the events that have occurred in the session (keystrokes, mouse activity, cursor navigation, as well as gaze behaviour if an eye tracker is connected). This logging data can be used to analyse and model the translation process at a higher level. Aziz et al. (this volume) use CASMACAT logging data to assess difficulties in post-editing "based not only on the type of edit (deletion, insertion, substitution), but also on the words being edited".

The extensive logging information allows for a translation session to be replayed on the screen. This important feature lets the researcher visually gain insight into the choices made by the translator during the translation and post-editing session. This is an insight that may not only be used to characterise how the translator works, but also locate where improvements to the workbench might be helpful to the translator.

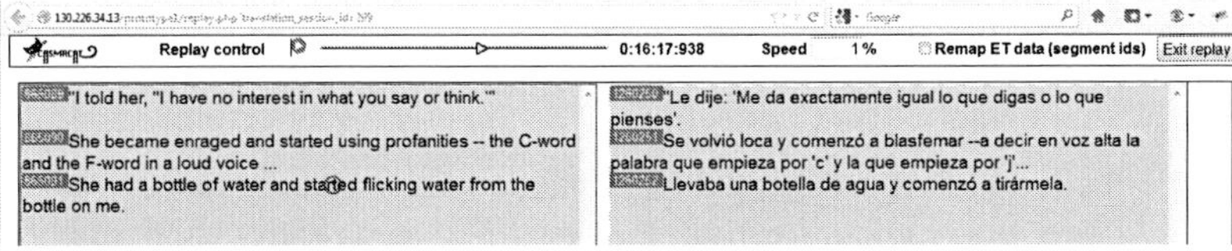

Figure 7-2: Screenshot of the replay functionality in the first prototype CASMACAT workbench

Figure 7-2 shows the menu bar of the replay session. Post-editing sessions can be positioned at certain points; they can be replayed at different speeds to investigate particular translation patterns. The red circle indicates where the user is currently looking; in this case on the source word "started".

The CASMACAT workbench logging data is exported to its own internal XML format and a Translog-II compatible format (Carl and Jakobsen 2009), which allows it to be analysed and visualised with the toolkit that is distributed with a Translation Process Research Database (TPR-DB). At the time of writing, the TPR-DB contains more than 900 translation, post-editing and other text production sessions which amounts to more than 200 hours of UAD. The TPR-DB is publicly available and can be obtained from the TPR-DB webpage[6].

An analysis of the first CASMACAT field trial

In this section we describe and analyse the post-editing and translation UAD that were collected with the CASMACAT workbench in the first field trial during June and July 2012. 25 news texts from the 2012 WMT workshop[7] were translated from English into Spanish by five professional translators, where each translator translated or post-edited between 17 and

19 documents (but never saw each document more than once). The texts contained between 371 and 1716 words with an average of 728 words. This resulted in more than 90 hours of post-editing and translation data.

For post-editing, the texts were automatically pre-translated with the University of Edinburgh's MT system that was used in the experiments for the 2012 WMT workshop. An Eyelink 1000 was used to collect 20 hours of gaze data for one of the five translators.
Post-editors were instructed how to post-edit the pre-translated segments:

- Use as much of the raw MT output as possible
- Aim for a grammatically, syntactically and semantically correct translation.
- Don't worry if style is repetitive.
- Ensure that key terminology is correctly translated
- Ensure that no information has been accidentally added or omitted.
- Basic rules regarding spelling, punctuation and hyphenation apply.
- Don't worry about formatting (rules for bold or italics should not be applied).
- Make changes only where absolutely necessary, i.e. correct words or phrases which are nonsensical, wrong or ambiguous.

These guidelines should NOT be applied if:

- Raw MT does not make any sense and it would take longer to post-edit than to translate from scratch.
- There are multiple errors that require re-arranging most of the text.

In such cases post-editors should proceed to translate from scratch.

A detailed discussion of the post-editing guidelines and an evaluation of the retrospective interviews is found in Mesa-Lao (2012). The five participants in the evaluation of the first CASMACAT prototype were professional translators with more than three years of experience working for different language service providers (LSPs). The Vendor Management team at CELER Soluciones SL[8] selected these five post-editors based on having English to Spanish as their main language pair and having proven experience with this particular company in post-editing projects over the previous 15 months. No previous domain knowledge on the topics treated in the news items being post-edited was required. Their age or gender was not considered relevant to the task. On the background of their professional experience, the produced translations can be expected to conform to the post-editing brief, so that we did not consider necessary to conduct a final quality control of the post-edited texts.

In this section we give three main perspectives on the data: first we investigate different parameters that predict differences in translation and post-editing speed. This analysis uses texts that were translated and post-edited by different translators. It shows that a normalised post-editing keystroke ratio predicts the production time ratio.

The second perspective discusses properties of the gaze data that were collected from one translator. They suggest that less effort is spent on reading and understanding the source text while post-editing compared to translation.

The third analysis looks in more detail at the variables that influence the post-editing process, including those variables that were only relevant for post-editing.

Production speed in translation and post-editing

A first comparison of translation and post-editing data was carried out based on 30 segments that were post-edited by all five participants and 115 segments that were translated by all five participants. Figure 7-3 is based on this aggregation, where we use only segments that had been encountered by all five participants doing the same task (either translation or post-editing) in order to allow comparison between participants and tasks, without introducing variations in segments. The more detailed analyses are based on larger numbers of segments, as described below. The study was not designed with this explicit comparison in mind and we therefore get unequal numbers; however, 30 segments is still a reasonable high number, compared for instance to the number of participants in this and other translation experiments.

Figure 7-3 shows translation and post-editing speeds for the five translators. The figure indicates that i) faster translators are also faster post-editors, and ii) that all participants experienced an average increase in productivity when post-editing machine translation compared to translating from scratch. The average time saving across participants is 25%.

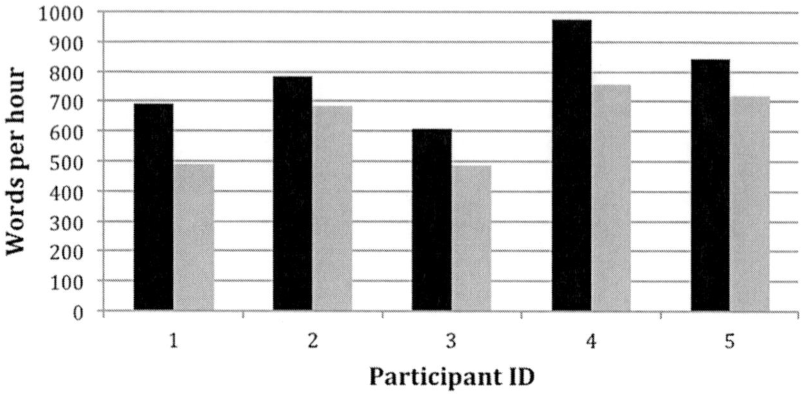

Figure 7-3: Productivity for each participant when translating (grey) and post-editing (black) measured in average words per hour.

To understand this result in more detail, we investigate under which conditions post-editing is faster than translation. Our dependent variable in this analysis is the ***production time ratio***: the mean post-editing time per sentence divided by the mean translation time per sentence, across different translators for the same source sentences. This ratio is 1 when mean translation time and mean post-editing time are equal, below 1 when post-editing is faster and above 1 when post-editing is slower. We had 590 different sentences which had been both translated and post-edited by different translators. This number was reduced to 586 segments after removing four data points that were clear outliers either in terms of the dependent variable production time ratio or the explanatory variables described below.

The *production time ratio* between translation and post-editing may be influenced by a whole range of variables – characteristics of the participants, the texts, the system and the process – some of which we have at our disposal for the analysis. Most of the variables we investigated have a positive skew: for each variable, most of the observations are clustered at the lower end of the scale with observations at the higher end of the scale being few and far between. This type of distribution is frequently found for lexical statistical and psychometric variables, but may distort the analysis. The standard remedy is to perform transformations of the variables in order to avoid the harmful effects of potential outliers. In this analysis and the analysis of the post-editing data, we mostly used the square root transformation, but in the case of the dependent variables, which were both time measurements that are typically quite strongly skewed, a logarithmic transformation was necessary. Which transformations were used is indicated in the relevant tables and figures.

We constructed the regression model in a stepwise fashion, including one variable at a time and discarding it if non-significant. We started with the least important variables and ended with the ones that are most central to the present investigation.

We investigated the following explanatory variables in a linear regression model using the R Language and Environment for Statistical Computing (R Development Core Team, 2011):

- the number of characters in the source sentence
- the number of characters in the MT output
- the number of characters in the final translation
- the number of keystrokes performed in post-editing
- the number of keystrokes performed in translation
- the edit distance between the MT output and the final version of the post-edited translation (Levenshtein distance).

Some of these variables are very highly correlated, for instance the numbers of characters in source sentence, MT output and final translation, and for that reason could not reasonably be included in the model at the same time. However, as it turned out, none of these variables were significant, making the multi-correlation problem irrelevant.

In fact, most of the explanatory variables turned out to be non-significant. In some cases we looked at ratios instead of raw measures. In analogy with our dependent variable *production time ratio*, we considered the ratio of keystrokes in post-editing to the number of characters in the MT output, the ratio of keystrokes in translation to the number of characters in the final translation, and the ratio of keystrokes in post-editing to keystrokes in translation.

The only explanatory variable that turned out significant in our analysis was the ***post-editing keystroke ratio***, the ratio of keystrokes in post-editing to number of characters in the MT output. In other words, the *post-editing keystroke ratio* is a variable indicating the number of keystrokes that were used to produce the final translation, normalised for the length of the given sentence in the MT output.

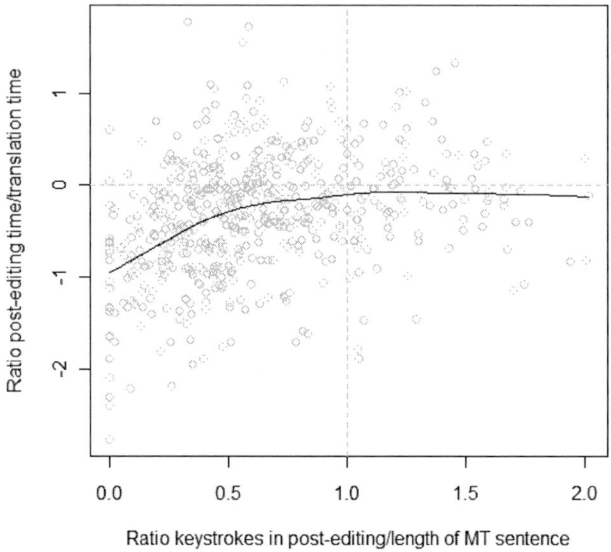

Figure 7-4: Correlation between time *production time ratio* (vertical) and the *post-editing keystroke ratio* (horizontal)

This variable had a significant non-linear effect, accounting for just under 16% of the variance in the time ratio ($R^2 = 0.1589$). The effect is illustrated in Figure 7-4 which shows each observation as a grey circle. The black line is a non-parametric (lowess) smoother indicating the relation between number of keystrokes divided by length of MT output on the horizontal axis and the production time ratio on the vertical axis. The dependent variable time ratio on the vertical axis is on a log scale, which means that 0 indicates a ratio of 1 (translation and post-editing requiring the same amount of time), with values below 0 indicating that post-editing is faster and values above 0 that translation is faster. The plot shows that for the majority of sentences, post-editing is faster, but the reverse also holds in some cases. The lowess smoother indicates that the post-editing advantage decreases as more keystrokes per MT character are produced. This effect flattens out around 0.5, i.e. when the post-editorproduces about half as many keystrokes as the number of characters in the relevant MT output, and asymptotes completely around 1, when the post-editing translator produces as many keystrokes as there are characters in the MT output.

The keystroke measure only takes into account text modifying keyboard activities (deletions and insertions) and ignores text navigation.

In contrast to other similar measures (e.g. Balling and Carl, 2013) this metric uses the real number of keystrokes produced: if an entire word or phrase is marked and deleted by a single keystroke, this will count only as one event. The measure leaves thus unspecified how much of the text was actually modified (deleted).

One interesting aspect of Figure 7-3 is that all the way up to post-editing keystroke ratio 1, there is a clear overweight of points indicating that post-editing is faster than translation, i.e. data points below 0 on the vertical time ratio axis. This is interesting because a keystroke ratio of 1 means that the post-editor has typed exactly as many keystrokes as there were characters in the raw MT output. That is, the translators are likely to have replaced most of the MT suggestion, but still they are saving time. This may be due to a priming effect, where the words suggested by MT activate relevant translation candidates and thereby reduce the time needed to locate these.

The regression model analysing the ratio of post-editing time to translation time is summarised in Table 7-1. It shows the intercept, the estimated intercept, and its spread in the first line; this corresponds roughly to the place where the lowess smoother in Figure 7-4 crosses the vertical axis, i.e. the time ratio value when the explanatory variable relative keystrokes is 0. The next two lines together describe the slope of the relation between the dependent variable time ratio and the explanatory variable relative key strokes, corresponding (again, roughly) to the shape of the lowess smoother in Figure 7-4. The linear and quadratic terms are both necessary in order to describe a non-linear (parabola-shaped) effect.

	Estimate	Std. Error	t-value	p-value
Intercept	-0.94512	0.06533	-14.467	<0.0001
RelativeKeyStrokesPE (linear)	1.62715	0.18484	8.803	<0.0001
RelativeKeyStrokesPE (quadratic)	-0.71061	0.10991	-6.466	<0.0001

Table 7-1: The linear regression model analysing production time ratio as a function of relative keystrokes in post-editing, i.e. the number of keystrokes produced in post-editing divided by the number of characters in the MT output. The adjusted R2 of the model is 0.1589.

Interestingly, the model making use of the *post-editing keystroke ratio*, i.e. the regression model summarised in Table 7-1, was substantially better than a model using the more traditional edit distance measure: the model reported in Table 7-1 had an adjusted R^2 of 0.1589, while a parallel model replacing relative post-editing keystroke ratio with relative edit distance (the edit distance between MT output and the final version divided by the number of characters in the final version) had an adjusted R^2 of 0.122. Neither number is particularly impressive, probably because there are a number of variables that we cannot take into account and - as in most behavioural experiments - a lot of noise. Nonetheless, the difference between the two analyses is substantial.

We see the post-editing keystroke ratio as a more interesting and relevant measure than edit distance because it indicates the effort actually expended by the translator, rather than the absolute distance between the MT output and the final text. This interpretation is confirmed by the difference in goodness of fit of the models.

Gaze data in translation and post-editing

As mentioned above, we also have gaze data but only for one of the translators in the CASMACAT field trial corpus. This unfortunate fact is the result of flaws in the experimental design as well as data that had to be discarded and participants that did not show up. It is problematic because it means that we cannot generalise beyond this one participant; we nonetheless discuss the data briefly here as we think the patterns seen are potentially interesting.

As shown in Figure 7-1, the CASMACAT workbench places the source text on the left and the target text on the right so that the translated segments of both texts are horizontally aligned. Both texts are plotted from top to bottom. Only one segment, the so-called current segment, can be edited; this appears in the centre of the screen. The past, already translated text is above the current source segment, while the future text to be translated (or post-edited) appears below the current target segment.

There are thus six different regions on the CASMACAT workbench in which the gaze can be detected. The logging data indicate for each gaze sample on which of these six segments it was located, together with the closest character to the fixation. Figure 7-5 illustrates where the participant spent gaze time during translation (grey) and post-editing (black). Besides the six windows of the workbench, there is a final category ("other") which most often will mean that the participant is looking off screen, e.g., at the keyboard. The figure is based on more than 20 hours of data collection from the participant who had eye movements recorded.

Since these data represent translation behaviour of a single participant, it is impossible to draw general conclusions, but the pattern is suggestive of a difference between the two tasks. The participant spends more time looking at the current translation being revised during post-editing, while looking more at the current source and off screen during translation.

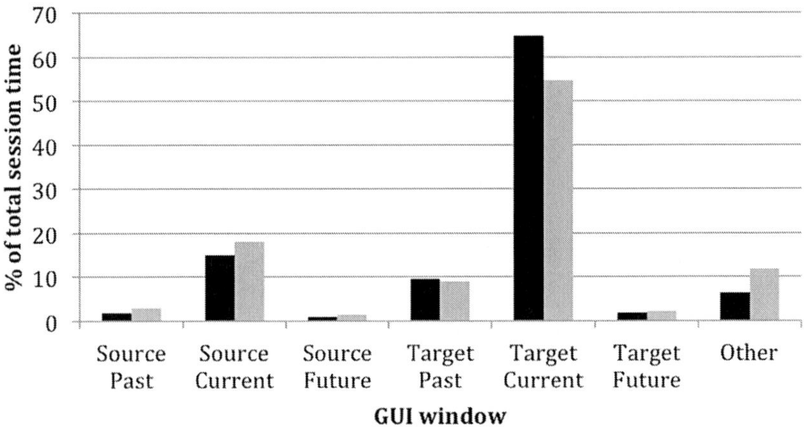

Figure 7-5: Gaze point distribution across GUI windows for translation (grey) and post-editing (black) measured in the percentage of total session time spend on each window.

The observation that the translator had more gaze activity on the current source segment when translating than when post-editing may be explained by the fact that a translation suggestion is already presented for post-editing, so less inspiration from looking at the source is needed. Similar findings are also confirmed by a previous study (Carl et al. 2011, 140) who speculate that "Manual translation seems to imply a deeper understanding of the ST, requiring more effort and thus longer fixations" on the source segment.

The reason that the translator looks more off-screen when translating than when post-editing is likely to be the higher keyboard activity during translation, requiring the participant to look more at the keyboard (the average keystroke count for a segment is 87 for post-editing and 212 for translation).

Besides modelling the tasks of translation and post-editing, eye-movement differences like these may be instrumental for future design of the workbench layout. It may, for instance, suit post-editing activities better to give more visual prominence to the current target segment.

Post-editing analysis

In addition to comparing gaze and production time in post-editing and translation, we analyse factors which have an impact on post-editing time, using some of those variables that are only relevant for post-editing. Instead of operating with the ratio between mean translation time and mean post-editing time, we look at the time that each participant needed to post-edit each of the sentences he/she worked with. This configuration allows us to avoid working with averages, which are not unproblematic, but requires that we deal with the dependence between the observations – the fact that we have several versions of some of the sentences and many sentences from each translator – in a different way. We do that by including crossed random effects for participants and sentences in our analysis, a linear mixed-effects regression model (Bates, Maechler and Bolker, 2011), which models the dependencies between participants and sentences by allowing the intercept to vary for each participant and each sentence. Apart from the random intercepts, we built the model in the same stepwise fashion as the standard linear model used for the task comparison above.

The potential explanatory variables fall into two groups. Firstly, the length in characters of the texts:

- the number of characters in the source sentence
- the number of characters in the MT output
- the number of characters in the final translation

These variables were extremely highly correlated (all r's > 0.97). Such high correlations make it unfeasible to include more than one of the three variables, and we chose the number of characters in the source sentence as the most fundamental of the three.

The second cluster of variables has to do with the changes made to the MT output:

- standard edit distance between MT output and final translation
- the number of keystrokes typed
- the number of words that were revised (words changed, deleted or added).

These variables are also highly correlated with r-values around 0.9, but nonetheless related to somewhat different aspects of the process. We start with the number of keystrokes (preferred over edit distance for the reasons mentioned in the previous section) and then investigate whether the number of words explain any additional variance. Though high pairwise correlations between variables may be problematic, including that between the number of keystrokes typed and the number of words revised, a more important measure is the overall collinearity in the model, which in this case was acceptable with a condition number (see Baayen, 2008: 181ff) of approximately 15. All three explanatory variables were square root transformed in order to avoid harmful effects of potential outliers, while the dependent variable post-editing time was more strongly skewed and therefore logarithmically transformed. In Figure 7-6, the dependent variable is backtransformed from the log scale for ease of interpretation.

	Estimate	MCMC mean	HPH95 lower	HPD95 upper	p
Intercept	8.9315	8.9475	8.6501	9.2346	0.0001
Number of source characters (sqrt)	0.0743	0.0705	0.0599	0.0813	0.0001
Number of keystrokes (sqrt, linear)	0.1665	0.1761	0.1508	0.2004	0.0001
Number of keystrokes (sqrt, quadratic)	-0.0037	-0.0040	- 0.0049	-0.0031	0.0001
Number of words revised (sqrt)	0.1091	0.1011	0.0576	0.1461	0.0001

Table 7-2: Summary of fixed effects in the mixed-effects analysis of post-editing time. The model also included random intercepts for participant (standard deviation estimated at 0.2262) and sentence (standard deviation estimated at 0.2145). The residual standard deviation was estimated at 0.3361.

The regression model analysing post-editing time as a function of the different explanatory variables is summarised in Table 7-2. The table shows the effects of source sentence length in characters, keystrokes typed, and the number of words revised. The table shows the effect of each of the variables when the other variables are taken into account;

correspondingly, the illustrations of effects in Figure 7-6 are partial effects plot, showing the effect of each variable when the other variables in the model are held constant. The linear and quadratic effects of number of keystrokes together describe the shape of the relation between post-editing time and number of keystrokes; they should therefore be interpreted together and are plotted together in Figure 7-6.

Table 7-2 shows the names of the variables in the first column and the estimated effect size in the second column. The subsequent columns are the output of a 10,000 Markov chain Monte Carlo (MCMC) simulations based on the data and the model; the p-values and credible intervals produced in this way are argued to be more appropriately conservative than p-values and confidence intervals based on the t-distribution (Baayen, Davidson and Bates, 2008). The third column is the mean estimate of the effect size across the MCMC samples, the next two columns show the higher posterior density intervals, which are credible intervals which correspond to standard 95% confidence intervals. The final column shows the p-value associated with each explanatory variable.

One requirement of regression models such as the one used here is that the residuals of the model (the difference between each actual observation and the model's prediction for that point) should be (approximately) normally distributed. The residuals of the model initially fitted showed a strong departure from normality, and we therefore trimmed the model to exclude large standardised residuals (outside the interval -2.5 to 2.5). This procedure removed 26 data points, corresponding to 2.4%, and resulted in an improved distribution of residuals and a better fitting model.

The top left panel of Figure 7-6 shows the effect of the number of characters in the source sentence; quite as we would expect, post-editing time is higher for longer source sentences, partly because longer sentences tend to take longer time, but it may also be a result of longer source sentences leading to low MT quality.

The next panel of Figure 7-6 shows the effect of the number of keystrokes. Here, we see a flattening out of the effect that is not dissimilar to what we observed in the task comparison reported in the previous section. Apparently, the time cost of additional editing becomes quite low, once you reach a certain (very high) threshold of around 400 keystrokes (corresponding to the squareroot transformed value 20). This variable is not normalised against any of the length measures, instead we include the length of the source segment in the analysis.

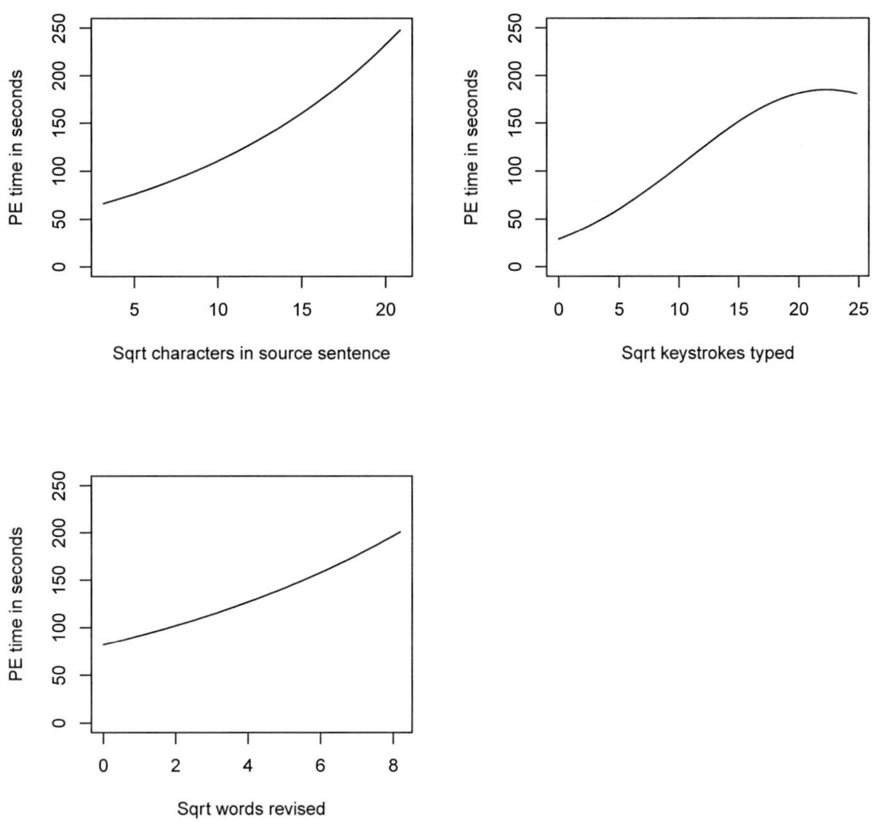

Figure 7-6: Partial effects plots of the number of source sentence characters, the number of keystrokes typed and the number of word revised.

Finally, the bottom left panel shows that the number of words revised interestingly has an effect over and above the effect of the number of keystrokes typed, in spite of the relatively high correlation between the two. This means that for two settings where the post-editor has typed the same number of keystrokes, the one where editing has been restricted to fewer words, will be faster. The effect may be caused by a lower mental cost from having to evoke fewer concepts when dealing with fewer words. Again, we leave out standard edit distance for two reasons: firstly, because the number of keystrokes typed is a better predictor than edit distance, and secondly, because the number of words revised had an effect over and above that of number of keystrokes typed, while edit distance did not.

Conclusion

We have presented the CASMACAT workbench; a web-based CAT tool with extensive logging of user behaviour including both keylogging and eye tracking. In addition to quantitative analysis, the tool opens up the possibilities of very detailed qualitative analysis through the accurate replay of translation sessions.

Findings from the first field trial using the CASMACAT workbench were also presented. The analysis builds on more than 90 hours of English to Spanish post-editing and translation performed by professional translators.

The experiments show an average time saving of 25% from post-editing machine translation over translation from scratch. This is especially promising in light of the fact that the processed texts stem from the relatively unrestricted domain of newspaper articles.

The analysis shows that the time saving to a large degree depends on how many keystrokes the post-editor performs. This finding does not surprise, but it is interesting that the number of keystrokes is a much better predictor than edit distance, which is typically used in the literature. In addition the post-editor has to produce a lot more keystrokes in post-editing than could have been expected before it no longer pays off to post-edit rather than translate from scratch.

As mentioned above, the current study analyses data that were collected with the first prototype of the CASMACAT workbench. The main focus for this prototype has been on developing the logging and replay functionality into a basic post-editing user interface. The project runs for another two years where the workbench will evolve with more advanced post-editing functions. For the next release of the CASMACAT workbench much work will be put into adding machine translation-based support for the translator and improving the user interface.

For the further development of the workbench, the CASMACAT project will be teaming up with another EU 7th Framework project, MATECAT.[9] The core product of the MATECAT project is an open-source web-based CAT tool. CASMACAT will integrate its logging and replay functionality in addition to advanced machine translation-based support into the MATECAT CAT tool. This synergy will lead to an ecologically much more realistic translation scenario than what is provided by the current basic user interface. This development thus opens up the possibility of a range of naturalistic investigations of translation and post-editing, with the potential to give us a deeper understanding of both processes.

Acknowledgments

This work was supported by the CASMACAT project funded by the European Commission (7th Framework Programme).

Bibliography

Alabau, Vicent, Luis A. Leiva, Daniel Ortiz-Martìnez, and Francisco Casacuberta. 2012. "User Evaluation of Interactive Machine Translation Systems." *Paper presented at the* 16th EAMT Conference, Trento, Italy, May 28-30.

Aziz, Wilker, Sheila Castilho, and Lucia Specia. 2012. "PET: a Tool for Post-editing and Assessing Machine Translation". *Proceedings of the Eight International Conference on Language Resources and Evaluation (LREC'12).* http://www.lrec-conf.org/proceedings/lrec2012/pdf/985_Paper.pdf

Baayen, R.Harald. 2008. *Analyzing Linguistic Data. A Practical Introduction to Statistics using R.* Cambridge: Cambridge University Press.

Baayen, R. Harald, Doug Davidson, and Douglas H. Bates. 2008. "Mixed-effects modeling with crossed random effects for subjects and items." *Journal of Memory and Language* 59: 390-412.

Balling, Laura Winther, and Michael Carl. 2014. "Production Time Across Languages and Tasks: A Large-scale Analysis using the CRITT Translation Process Database". In *The development of translation competence: Theories and methodologies from psycholinguistics and cognitive science*, edited by Aline Ferreira and John Schwieter, Cambridge Scholars Publishing, forthcoming.

Bates, Douglas H., Martin Maechler, and Ben Bolker. 2011. *lme4: Linear mixed-effects models using S4 classes.* R package version 0.999375-42. Downloaded 6 September 2011 from <http://CRAN.R-project.org/package=lme4>.

Callison-Burch, Chris, Cameron Fordyce, Philipp Koehn, Christof Monz, and Josh Schroeder. 2007. "(Meta-) Evaluation of Machine Translation". *Proceedings of the Second Workshop on Statistical Machine Translation* 2007: 136-158.

Carl, Michael, Barbara Dragsted, Jakob Elming, Daniel Hardt, and Arnt Lykke Jakobsen. 2011. "The Process of Post-Editing: A Pilot Study." *Copenhagen Studies in Language* 41: 131-142.

Carl, Michael, and Arnt Lykke Jakobsen. 2009. "Towards statistical modelling of translators' activity data " *International Journal of Speech Technology* 12(4): 125-138.
Flournoy, Raymond, and Christine Duran. 2009. "Machine translation and document localization at adobe: From pilot to production." *MT Summit XII: proceedings of the twelfth Machine Translation Summit.* http://www.mt-archive.info/MTS-2009-Flournoy.pdf
Groves, Declan, and Dag Schmidtke. 2009. "Identification and analysis of post-editing patterns for MT." *MT Summit XII: Proceedings of the Twelfth Machine Translation Summit.* http://www.mt-archive.info/MTS-2009-Groves.pdf
Guerberof Arenas, Ana. 2012. "Productivity and quality in the post-editing of outputs from translation memories and machine translation." PhD dissertation, Universat Rovira i Virgili, Tarragona.
Koehn, Philipp. 2012. "Computer Aided Translation." Guest lecture at Microsoft, http://research.microsoft.com/apps/video/default.aspx?id=175933
—. 2009. "A web-based interactive computer aided translation tool." *Proceedings of the ACL-IJCNLP 2009 Software Demonstrations:* 17-20.
Krings, Hans. 2001. *Repairing Texts: Empirical Investigations of Machine Translation Post-Editing Processes.* (edited by Geoffrey S. Koby). Kent, Ohio: The Kent State University Press.
Jakobsen, Arnt Lykke. 1999. "Translog documentation." *Copenhagen Studies in Language* 24: 149-184.
Martínez-Gómez, Pascual, Germán Sanchis-Trilles, and Francisco Casacuberta. 2012. "Online adaptation strategies for statistical machine translation in post-editing scenarios." *Pattern Recognition* 45(9): 3193-3203.
Mesa-Lao, Bartolomé. 2012. "The next generation translator's workbench: post-editing in CASMACAT v.1.0." Paper presented at the 34th Translating and the Computer Conference, ASLIB, 29-30 November.
Moran, John, 2012. "Experiences instrumenting an open-source CAT tool to record translator interactions." Paper presented at the *International Workshop on Expertise in Translation and Post-editing: Research and Applications*, Copenhagen, Denmark, August 17-18.
Moran, John, David Lewis, and Christian Saam. This volume. "Analysis of post-editing data: A productivity field test using an instrumented CAT tool."
O'Brien, Sharon. 2011. "Towards predicting post-editing productivity." *Machine Translation* 25(3): 197-215.

Papineni, Kishore, Salim Roukous, Todd Ward, and Wei-Jing Zhu. 2002. "BLEU: a method for automatic evaluation of machine translation". *Proceedings of the 40th Annual Meeting on Association for Computational Linguistics* 2002: 311-318.

Plitt, Mirko, and François Masselot. 2010. "A Productivity Test of Statistical Machine Translation Post-Editing in a Typical Localisation Context." *The Prague Bulletin of Mathematical Linguistics* 93: 7-16.

R development core team. 2011. *R: A Language and Environment for Statistical Computing*. Version 2.13.1. Downloaded September 6, 2011, http://www.r-project.org.

Roukos, Salim. 2012. "Document-Specific Statistical Machine Translation for Improving Human Translation Productivity." Invited Talk given at Cicling, 13th International Conference on Intelligent Text Processing and Computational Linguistics, Delhi, India, March 11-17.

Tatsumi, Midori. 2010. "Post-editing machine translated text in a commercial setting: Observation and statistical analysis." PhD dissertation, Dublin City University. http://doras.dcu.ie/16062/

Notes

[1] http://www.upf.edu/materials/bib/docs/iula/multilingual/multilingual201101-dl.pdf

[2] Time saved percentage = 100 – avr-PE-time/avr-T-time*100

[3] www.omegat.org

[4] www.casmacat.eu

[5] See the CASMACAT web page http://www.casmacat.eu/

[6] http://bridge.cbs.dk/platform/?q=CRITT_TPR-db

[7] www.statmt.org/wmt12

[8] Celer Solutiones (http://www.celersol.com/) is a Madrid-based translation company and partner of the Casmacat project.

[9] www.matecat.com

CHAPTER EIGHT

SUB-SENTENCE LEVEL ANALYSIS OF MACHINE TRANSLATION POST-EDITING EFFORT

WILKER AZIZ, MAARIT KOPONEN AND LUCIA SPECIA

Abstract

Machine translation (MT) post-editing is becoming a common practice in the translation industry as a faster and cheaper way of producing high quality translations. Compensation models based on the percentage of edits necessary to fix the raw MT are becoming popular. MT post-editing has also been used as a way of assessing MT quality through productivity tests measuring post-editing time or edit distance between the raw MT and its post-edited version. In all these scenarios, post-editing time and edit distance metrics have been used as a proxy to post-editing effort: the higher the average word post-editing time and/or percentage edits, the higher the effort needed to edit the raw MT. However, average time or edit distance can be affected by a number of elements that make it difficult to reliably quantify and understand post-editing effort. For example, pauses in editing have an effect on time, while edit distance cannot capture cognitive effort or the fact that some edits are more difficult than others. In addition, these measures are oblivious to the fact that post-editing effort may depend on the complexity of the source text, as opposed to the MT quality only. In this chapter, we examine data post-edited by a number of translators using time measurements at the sub-sentence level to localise complex edits. Our analysis searches for patterns of edits with certain linguistic constructions on the source language that lead to cases of high post-editing effort.

Introduction

As Machine Translation (MT) becomes widely available for a large number of language pairs and the demand for faster and cheaper translations increases, its adoption is becoming more popular in the translation industry. However, it is well known that except in very narrow domains with dedicated MT systems, automatic translations are far from perfect. A common practice is thus to have human translators performing post-editing of such translations. Following the tradition of compensation models based on fuzzy match level scores in translation memory systems, metrics of edit distance between the raw machine translation and its post-edited version have started to be adopted as pricing models for MT post-editing by a number of companies, e.g. MemSource.

Post-editing has also been attracting increasing attention from researchers and users of MT as a way of evaluating the quality of automatic translations or comparing machine and human translation through productivity tests. Metrics include post-editing time (Plitt and Masselot, 2010, Sousa et al., 2011), edit distance metrics like TER (Snover et al., 2010), as well as standard MT evaluation metrics based on string-matching between the MT output and its post-edited version. String-matching metrics like BLEU (Papineni et al., 2002) have proved to correlate significantly better with human assessments of quality when computed having a post-edited version of the automatic translation as reference. The letter "H" is commonly used to denote these "human" targeted variants of the metrics, e.g. HTER (Snover et al., 2006).

In the above mentioned scenarios, edit distance and time measurements are used as proxies for post-editing effort. However, post-editing effort is a complex concept which consists of different but highly interconnected aspects: temporal, technical and cognitive (Krings, 2001). Edit distance metrics such as HTER compute the minimum number of edits between the system output and its post-edited version. It cannot fully capture the effort resulting from post-editing. Certain operations can be more difficult than others, based not only on the type of edit (deletion, insertion, substitution), but also on the words being edited. The metrics do not generally differentiate the reasons for edits, so that edits due to incorrect morphological variants or function words are treated the same way as more complex edits such as fixing an untranslated content word. Recently, Koponen (2012) conducted an error analysis on post-edited translations with HTER and 1-5 scores assigned by humans for post-editing effort. A number of cases were found where post-edited translations with low HTER (few edits) were assigned low scores (indicating high post-editing effort), and vice-versa. This seems to indicate that certain edits require more cognitive effort than others, which is not captured by HTER. While variants of such metrics assigning weights for specific edits or classes of words can be implemented (Snover et al., 2010; Blain et al., 2011), a careful and systematic linguistic analysis is necessary to identify classes of words/segments that are complex to post-edit.

Post-editing time can reflect not only the technical effort needed to perform the editing, but also the temporal and cognitive effort required to detect errors and plan the necessary corrections. We have recently conducted a study focusing on measuring post-editing time as a way of quantifying the cognitive effort involved in post-editing (Koponen et al., 2012). The study involved English-to-Spanish translations from several different MT systems on a news corpus, and focused on discrepancies between post-editing time and HTER: sentences with long editing time but relatively few edit operations (low HTER) and not excessively high number of words. We identified different groups of errors in the automatic translations and correlated them to error typologies believed to represent different levels of cognitive difficulty involved in fixing them. Our findings suggest that shorter editing times seem to be associated with errors ranked cognitively easiest, which include word form errors, synonym substitutions, and simple incorrect word substitutions with correct part-of-speech. On the other hand, substitutions involving an incorrect part-of-speech or an untranslated word, errors related to idiomatic expressions and word order, especially when reordering crosses phrase boundaries, seem to be connected with longer edit times. However, because time and edit measurements were only available at the sentence level, the analysis to localise errors had to be performed manually. As a consequence, this was a very small scale study and its findings become difficult to generalise. In addition, it focused on errors in the translation, disregarding aspects of the source text that may have had an impact on post-editing effort.

In this chapter, we focus on the analysis of segments that have been post-edited within a sentence: a *production unit* (PU) (see the section "The CASMACAT Workbench"). We use the field trial data collected with the CASMACAT workbench as dataset (Elming et al., 2013), which provides data segmented utilising such production units. Instead of pre-selecting potentially interesting PUs based on time and HTER discrepancies, we consider all PUs and search for patterns of linguistic constructions in the source segments that best explain the variance in post-editing time of their corresponding target segments. This analysis is done using Principal

Component Analysis (Jolliffe, 2002), which allows much larger volumes of data to be examined automatically.

The remainder of this chapter is organised as follows. Section "Related work" presents previous attempts to measure post-editing effort. Section "Sub-sentence level analysis" describes the dataset, the motivation for sub-sentence analysis based on source segments, the variables considered and method used in our analysis. Section "Results" shows the results of this analysis.

Related work

A common approach to quantifying post-editing effort is the use of semi-automatic MT evaluation metrics such as HTER that measure the similarity or distance between the MT system output and its human post-edited version at the level of sentences. In an attempt to quantify different levels of editing effort, Blain et al. (2011) introduce the Post-Editing Action (PEA), a new unit of PE effort which is a more linguistically-founded way of measuring a traditional edit distance. In their approach, rather than treating each edited word as a separate action, PEAs incorporate several interrelated edit operations. For example, changing a noun propagates changes to its attributes (number, gender) which are then treated as one action. This approach has the disadvantages that it is hardly generalisable across languages, and it requires an annotated corpus to train a model to classify PEAs for new texts.

A recent strand of work has been using post-editing *time*, particularly for comparing MT to human translation (Plitt and Masselot, 2010), but also for comparing different types of tools to supprt human translation (Sousa et al., 2011), or different types of texts translated by an MT system, e.g. translations produced from controlled language texts versus naturally occurring texts (Temnikova and Orasan, 2009; Temnikova, 2010).

Tatsumi (2009) examines the correlation between post-editing time and certain automatic MT evaluation metrics. She finds that the relationship between these two types of metrics is not always linear, and offers some variables such as source sentence length and structure as well as specific types of dependency errors as possible explanations.

Focusing on target segments, Doherty and O'Brien (2009) use an eye-tracker to log the fixation and gaze counts and time of translators while reading the output of an MT system. Overall translation quality was quantified on the basis of the number and the duration of fixations. Results show that fixation counts correlate well with human judgments of quality. Doherty, O'Brien and Carl (2010) further investigate the use of various eye tracking measures as an MT evaluation method. Gaze time and fixation count on a sentence-level show medium strength correlation with human evaluation, whereas fixation duration shows weaker correlation and no significant connections are found for pupil dilation data. O'Brien (2011) measures correlations between MT automatic metrics and post-editing productivity, where productivity is measured using an eye tracker. Processing speed, average fixation time and count are found to correlate well with automatic scores for groups of sentences.

With respect to translatability features, Bernth and McCord (2000) present certain features of source sentence analysis to be used for calculating a "translation confidence index", or a measure of confidence for the quality of a given MT system's translation. It is argued that source analysis plays the most important role in the translation process and therefore source text features are central for the confidence index. The suggested features include segment length, combinations of certain potentially ambiguous parts-of-speech, non-finite verbs, combinations of certain phrase categories, and sentences where obligatory arguments are missing in the parse tree. The translation confidence index based on penalties given to the selected features is tested by setting a threshold for usable translations and comparing the set of sentences selected by the index to those selected by a human translator. The results show agreement in 66.7% of the cases.

Bernth and Gdaniec (2002) describe characteristics that decrease translatability of texts by MT systems and suggest ways of writing for MT that improves translatability. The suggestions are based on practices of interactive MT and controlled languages, and involve 26 rules related to grammar, ambiguity, spelling, style and file characteristics such as markup.

Underwood and Jongejan (2001) describe a tool for assessing machine translatability and source text features based on specific parts-of-speech and part-of-speech patterns as well as lexical ambiguity. Features used for calculating the translatability index involve segment length – both very long (> 25 words) and very short (< 3 words) segments are identified as problematic – and the presence or absence of specified POS tags, such as absence of finite verb in the segment, or presence of nominal compounds or prepositional phrases.

It should be noted that this prior work on translatability features has been carried out focusing on rule-based machine translation (RBMT). SMT systems and RBMT systems are known to produce somewhat different types of errors. On the other hand, from the perspective of post-editing and using units larger than individual words, the patterns may not be as different. For example, the PEA patterns found by Blain et al. (2011) for SMT and RBMT are overall very similar. Specifically, for both systems, the majority of post-editing actions relates to noun phrases rather than verb phrases, with noun meaning being the most common type of change.

O'Brien (2005) discusses the suitability of different approaches to studying post-editing effort and translatability features. The approaches considered include Think-Aloud Protocols, keyboard logging and Choice Network Analysis (CNA). In CNA, the translations produced by multiple translators are compared and source text items with multiple different translations are assumed to indicate cognitive difficulty. An analysis of sample data using keyboard logging shows that a connection can be found between some potentially difficult source text features identified using CNA and the pauses recorded by keyboard logging, suggesting increased cognitive effort.

Our first experiment for investigating potentially difficult cases (Koponen et al., 2012) utilised English-to-Spanish machine translated sentences post-edited by eight post-editors. We focused on finding sentences that required a long time to edit and could therefore be expected to contain errors that are particularly difficult for the editor to correct. Potentially interesting examples of post-edited translations were selected for long duration (seconds-per-word) and low HTER for each post-editor separately, providing 32 sample sentences. A comparison set of 32 sentences with similar sentence length and similar HTER but short-to-average seconds-per-word editing time was also selected. The sample sentences were then manually analysed against an error classification (Temnikova, 2010) for MT by ranking the error categories according to how cognitively costly they are assumed to be. This experiment suggested that certain types of errors assumed to be cognitively more difficult occurred more often in the sentences with long editing times. Such errors include errors related to idioms and word order. In addition, we hypothesised that specific part-of-speech errors may be linked to longer edit times, and some differences were observed with regard to content words (verbs, nouns, adjectives) versus function words (articles, prepositions).

To the best of our knowledge, no previous work focuses on using post-editing time at the sub-sentence level to analyse different types of post-editing effort based on the source segments.

Sub-sentence level analysis

The CASMACAT workbench

Our previous experiment (Koponen at al., 2012) suggested some features that might be useful in assessing post-editing effort. However, as sentences often contain many different types of errors and edits, it is difficult to be certain about which edits, specifically, are causing most effort for the editor. For this reason, we moved to examining segments within sentences.

For this purpose, we utilised the data collected during the first field test trial of the CASMACAT workbench (Elming et al., 2013). This field trial dataset consists of 25 English newspaper documents from the WMT12 workshop data, translated or post-edited into Spanish by five translators. The MT system used was a statistical MT system by University of Edinburgh (see Elming et al. 2013 for a detailed description of the dataset). For our experiment, only the post-editing data was used, resulting in 5-9 documents per editor. One document had been post-edited by all five editors, seven by two editors, and nine by a single editor. Three files (identifiers P01_P04, P01_23, and P04_P11) were excluded from the analysis because their markup was compromised by errors. Altogether, we analysed 622 sentences with 2297 production units (see description below).

The CASMACAT data logs include the source text, MT output and post-edited version(s), tokenisation and source-target alignment information, as well as the types of edits performed: insertions, deletions, edit durations and pauses. Coherent sequences of typing (insertions and deletions) logged by the workbench have been put together by a few heuristics into *production units* (PU). A production unit is defined by Carl and Kay (2011) as a sequence of successive (insertion and deletion) keystrokes that produce a coherent passage of text. The boundary between two PUs is indicated by either a delay of a given length (1000 milliseconds in the CASMACAT data) or a movement to a new location in the text. These PUs have further been mapped onto the aligned source and target tokens involved. More specifically, the log files provide the following information for each PU:

- **DURATION**: the total duration in seconds;
- **PAUSE**: the pause before starting the next PU;
- **I**: the total number of inserted characters;
- **D**: the total number of deleted characters;

- **EDITS**: the total number of insertions + deletions (char-based).

The PU is similar to the *production segment* defined by Alves et al. (2010, 125) as passages of target text produced between pauses. The production segments can then be mapped back to the source segments to which they relate. While these segments are not identical to *translation units*, defined as source text segments that are identified by pause intervals and that reflect the translator's focus at a given time, Alves et al. (2010, 124-125) argue that they momentarily capture and correlate with translation units.

Motivation

Example 1, taken from the CASMACAT field trial data, illustrates the type of information we can learn by examining units at the sub-sentence level. The example first shows the sentence identifier, source sentence (ST), its automatic translation (MT), post-edited version (PE), total duration of editing without pauses (and with pauses), total number of edits (character based), and the HTER score between the MT and its post-edited version. The words changed between the MT and the PE versions are bold-faced.

	Segment: P03_P24_s908089
ST	The deal was disclosed in a joint statement issued after Secretary of State Hillary Rodham Clinton met with Belarusan Foreign Minister Sergei Martynov on the sidelines of a security summit here.
MT	El acuerdo fue **consignado** en una declaración conjunta emitida después de que la **secretaria** de Estado Hillary Rodham Clinton se **reunió** con el **ministro** de Relaciones Exteriores Sergei Martynov **Belarusan al margen** de una cumbre sobre seguridad aquí.
PE	El acuerdo fue **anunciado** en una declaración conjunta emitida después de que la **Secretaria** de Estado Hillary Rodham Clinton se **reuniese** con el **Ministro** de Relaciones Exteriores **bielorruso** Sergei Martynov **en las actividades subsidiarias** de una cumbre sobre seguridad **celebrada** aquí
Total duration: 22.64 s (without pauses)/347.664 s (with pauses) Total edits (char): 112, HTER score: 0.19	

Example 1: Source text, machine translation, its post-edited version and log from the CASCAMAT field trial data

Overall, the quality of the machine translated sentence is relatively good: more than 80% of it has been used as such, as reflected by the low HTER score. Moving from this general information to the PUs logged by the CASMACAT workbench allows a much more informative perspective on the edits performed. The changes of *consignado* ('assigned') to *anunciado* ('announced, disclosed'), *secretaria* to *Secretaria* ('Secretary'), *reunió* ('met' – past tense) to *reuniese* ('met' – imperfect tense), *ministro* to *Ministro* ('Minister') and the addition of *celebrada* ('held') each form their own PUs with relatively short editing durations. The other three PUs are more interesting, as they take up most of the editing time:

1. insertion: *bielorruso* + deletion: *Belarusan al margen*
   – DURATION 7.649 s, PAUSE 87.207 s
2. insertion: *en*
   – DURATION: 0.487 s, PAUSE: 162.297 s
3. insertion: *las actividades subsidiarias*
   – DURATION: 7.101 s, PAUSE: 3.199 s

It appears that this part of the sentence with three consecutive PUs caused most problems for the editor. Tracking the sequence of events we can see that after correcting the untranslated and misplaced *Belarusan* by inserting the word *bielorruso* ('Belarusan'), the editor then deletes *al margen* ('on the margins of') in one consecutive unit together with *Belarusan*. Next, the editor pauses for 87 seconds before starting a correction by typing *en*, then pauses again for 162 seconds before inserting *las actividades subsidirias* ('subsidiary activities') as a translation for the English *on the sidelines*.

Observing what these words relate to on the source text, we see that they are the translation of an idiomatic expression ('on the sidelines'), which had been translated literally. In addition, these units occur in the middle of a long sequence of noun phrases, prepositional phrases, and finally one lone adverbial phrase, the combination of which might be somewhat difficult to understandin the source text. The complexity is increased by the elision of a verb between *summit* and *here* (meaning *summit which was held here*), which the editor explicitates in the post-edited version.

Based on the fact that not all edits within a sentence are necessarily equal in terms of effort, the purpose of the experiments in this chapter is to examine how time varies in post-editing units within sentences in order to identify particularly time-consuming post-editing situations. Further, by analysing source text features of the PUs with long edit durations, we aim to uncover the types of source text features that lead to difficult to time-consuming edits.

Source text and post-editing effort features

To cover the potential complexity which arises from the source text, we examine a variety of source text features. Certain source text features have generally been suggested as being problematic in prior research in machine translatability (see "Related work"). These features may be to some extent language- and system-specific (generally English as a source language), although Bernth and Gdaniec (2002) argue that the overall principles of their rules would be applicable across languages. Commonly cited source text features affecting machine translatability include:

- Sentence length, with both very long and very short sentences suggested as problematic;
- Specific part-of-speech (POS) combinations, such as noun+noun, noun+adjective;
- Specific phrase types, such as prepositional phrases and sentence-initial adverbial phrases;
- Specific phrase combinations, such as multiple consecutive noun phrases or prepositional phrases;
- The absence of predicate verbs or obligatory arguments of the predicate;
- The presence of non-finite verbs – particularly gerunds and when they occur as arguments of another verb.

As noted in the section "Related work", earlier work has mainly addressed automatic translations produced following the rule-based MT paradigm. Although the statistical MT approach used in our study is generally known to produce somewhat different types of errors than rule-based MT, the example of Blain et al. (2011) suggests that for sequences longer than individual words, the overall patterns may not differ as much. Therefore, we were interested in seeing whether these same features can be found in time-consuming PUs relating to SMT.

We are firstly interested in seeing whether the time spent on editing an individual PU is connected to features of the sentence it appears in, such as the number of tokens in the sentence, the number of different phrases or the number of predicates and their arguments, which could indicate that the overall sentence is complex. Following from our motivation for investigating sub-sentence units, we are interested in examining features of the individual PUs. One hypothesis was that more effort would be involved in PUs that relate to more central elements of the sentence (verbs, verb phrases and predicates, or nouns, noun phrases and core arguments of predicates), or their combinations. On the other hand, some other elements such as prepositional phrases were suggested as problematic in the translatability literature. To investigate these issues, we extracted various features related to the number of arguments, chunks (phrases) and various POS patterns at the sentence- and PU-level. More detailed information was also obtained for verbs to examine if patterns related to verb type (finite vs types of non-finite verbs). Since the occurrence of a verb as an argument of another verb could signal overall complexity, this was also selected as a feature. Named entities, for example names of people or organisations, were also used as a feature.

For generating the source text features of the PUs, the source texts were automatically tagged with SENNA (Collobert et al., 2011) to obtain POS tags, named entities (NE), chunks (phrases), and semantic role labels (SRL). The features were then extracted based on regular expressions.

The other group of variables needed for the analysis refers to the effort indicators, here provided based on logs from edits made to the MT output. We are mostly interested in logs of the duration of the edit, but we also take into account the number of characters edited. In addition to the absolute numbers of seconds or characters involved in editing, another way to examine features of a PU is to analyse how these numbers relate to the average numbers of seconds or characters in editing. For this purpose, we calculated the average of DURATION and EDITS for all the PUs in a given document. The PUs in each document were then labelled in terms of how many standard deviations above or below the document average they represented for each variable. The PUs were classified in standard deviation ranges from -3 to 3 by 0.5 intervals. For sentence-level analysis, we used TERp (Snover et al., 2010) to calculate the sentence-level HTER score. Altogether, the set of features used in the analysis contains both sentence- and PU-level features as follows.

Sentence-level features:

- **SNT_ORI_PUS**: total number of PUs in the CASMACAT log;
- **SNT_DURATION/SNT_DUR**: total editing duration without pauses (accumulated over all PUs in the sentence);
- **SNT_TDURATION**: total editing duration including pauses (accumulated over all PUs in the sentence);
- **SNT_EDITS**: total number of edits (character based);
- **SNT_I**: total number of insertions (character based);

- **SNT_D**: total number of deletions (character based);
- **SNT_STOKENS**: number of source tokens;
- **SNT_PHRASES**: number of source phrases;
- **SNT_PREDICATES/SNT_PRED**: number of source verbs in the SENNA parse;
- **SNT_ARGS**: number of arguments in the SENNA parse;
- **SNT_COREARGS**: number of core arguments in the SENNA parse;
- **SNT_MODARGS**: number of modifying arguments in the SENNA parse;
- **SNT_RELARGS**: number of relative arguments in the SENNA parse;
- **SNT_HTER**: the sentence HTER score (MT against PE).

PU-level features:

- **DURATION/DUR**: editing duration of the PU not including pauses;
- **DCLASS**: PU duration classification according to deviation from the document average (-3 to 3 standard deviations);
- **PREPAUSE**: the duration of the pause that precedes the editing of a PU;
- **TDURATION/TDUR**: total editing duration value including PREPAUSE;
- **EDITS**: total number of edits;
- **I**: number of insertions in characters;
- **D**: number of deletions in characters;
- **REVISIONS**: the number of original PUs merged into a PU;
- **STOKENS**: number of tokens in the PU;
- **POSTYPES**: number of unique POS categories in the PU;
- **VB, NN, JJ, RB, MD, TO, DT, PR, IN, CC, W**: number of specific POS categories in the PU for verbs, nouns, adjectives, particles, modal verbs, infinitival *to*, determiners, pronouns, prepositions, coordinating conjunctions and relative pronouns;
- **VBNI**: number of verb participles VBN or past tense VBD in the PU and binary feature **bVBNI** (0 = zero occurrences; 1 = 1+ occurrences);
- **ING**: number of gerunds and binary feature **bING**;
- **TO_VB**: number of TO+VB sequences and binary feature **bTO_VB**;

- **MD_VB**: number of MD+VB sequences and binary feature **bMD_VB**;
- **W_MD_VB**: number of W*+VB* sequences, possibly with MD in between them and binary feature **bW_MD_VB**;
- **NN_NN**: number of NN+NN sequences and binary feature **bNN_NN;**
- **NN_JJ**: number of NN+JJ sequences and binary feature **bNN_JJ**;
- **VBNI_NN**: number of sequences VBG/VBD/VBN+NN and binary feature **bVBNI_NN**;
- **NE**: number of named entities and binary feature **bNE**;
- **CHUNKS**: number of phrases;
- **VP, NP, PP, ADJP, ADVP, PRT, SBAR**: number of occurrences of each phrase category in the PU;
- **VP_PP**: number of sequences of this type of POS and binary feature **bVP_PP**;
- **VP_ADJP**: number of sequences of this type and binary feature **bVP_ADJP**;
- **NP_ADJP**: number of sequences of this type and **bNP_ADJP**;
- **NP_NP**: number of sequences of this type and binary feature **bNP_NP**;
- **NP_PP**: number of sequences of this type and binary feature **bNP_PP**;
- **PP_PP**: number of sequences of this type and binary feature **bPP_PP**;
- **PREDICATES**: number of predicates in the PU;
- **ARGS**: total number of arguments (for all possible predicates) that overlap with that PU;
- **COREARGS, MODARGS, RELARGS**: numbers of each type of arguments that overlap with the PU;
- **bVinARG**: binary feature for verb within another verb's argument;
- **VXCARG**: for cases where the PU contains a verb that is also part of another verb's core argument, the number of overlapping core arguments and binary feature **bVinCARG**;
- **VXMARG**: same as VXCARG but for modifying arguments and binary feature **bVinMARG**;
- **VXRARG**: same as VXCARG but for relative arguments and binary feature **bVinRARG**.

Principal Component Analysis

To analyse the relationships among the variables described in the previous section, and particularly the relationship between the source-text features and measurements of time and edits, we use Principal Component Analysis (PCA) (Jolliffe, 2002), a very popular technique to visualise high dimensional feature spaces such as the one we have in this chapter, with nearly 100 features.

Each point in our high dimensional space is described in terms of the many features we consider. Visualising these data points and reasoning about how they distribute and relate across the feature space becomes an issue as we are limited to simultaneously understand 2-3 dimensions. PCA provides a convenient compact representation (which we can limit to 2-3 dimensions) with a minimum loss of expressiveness compared to the original feature space. PCA has been extensively used in the literature of text, speech and image processing to visualise data, as well as to provide more aggressive and lossy compression for dimensionality reduction.

In a nutshell, PCA rotates the coordinates of the original feature space until it finds a configuration in which most of the variance of the data can be explained with as few as possible dimensions called "principal components" (PCs). Formally, it finds the space of projections that maximises the variance of the projected data points (or minimises the projection errors). This results in PCA being so popular for dimensionality reduction (and therefore visualisation); it finds a lower dimensional representation that still accommodates all data points with minimum loss.

If two features are independently very important to explain the variance of the data points, they will have very distinguishable values projected onto the first PCs. On the other hand, if they are highly correlated, possibly redundant, or are less important in explaining the data's variance, they will be highly confusable with respect to the first two PCs and PCs other than the first two will discriminate them.

We use PCA to inspect what source language patterns (our source features) correlate well with post-editing effort. Since we do not have gold standard labels for cognitively demanding PUs, we study the different patterns' correlation to post-editing features such as duration and character-level number of edits.

Results

We concatenated the CASMACAT data from all five editors involved in the CASMACAT field trial and used R's *prcomp* function[1] to obtain the principal components and features' projections. We proceeded by identifying features that correlate the most with notions of post-editing effort such as post-editing time and edits. We used R's *biplot* function to visualise the projected data points onto the two first PCs: PC1 and PC2. The choice of two PCs here is motivated by the fact that we can easily visualise and interpret PC1 vs PC2 in a 2D space.

Figure 8-1 shows the projections of **sentence level features** onto the first two PCs explaining 72.92% of the data's variance. A data point in the Figure represents a post-edited sentence. The vectors are the projections onto PC1 and PC2 of sentence level HTER, total number of edits (insertions and deletions), the total duration (including pauses), the total number of interventions (i.e. number of PUs) and the number of tokens, phrases and predicates in the sentence. The origin of the projected feature vectors is the mean of the features those vectors represent. Orthogonal vectors are poorly correlated, while parallel vectors are strongly correlated. As we do not have gold standard labels, we are looking for features that can be used to explain phenomena such as high HTER, high duration and other indicators of post-editing effort. Moreover we are interested in inspecting PUs with interesting values for those features.

Interesting observations can be made about Figure 8-1. Note that indicators of post-editing effort (SNT_HTER, SNT_EDITS, SNT_ORI_PUS and SNT_DURATION) project positively onto PC2, especially SNT_HTER projects almost exclusively onto PC2. On the other hand, indicators of sentence length (SNT_STOKENS, SNT_PHRASES and SNT_PRED) project negatively onto PC2. This means that PC2 discriminates between sentences which require many individual fixes (SNT_ORI_PUS), which are time-consuming (SNT_DURATION), which require significant typing (SNT_EDITS), and which require many edit operations (SNT_HTER) from those which are simply long. Note also the vectors SNT_TDURATION (total duration) and SNT_STOKENS (total length): they are positively correlated with respect to PC1 (their projections onto PC1 point in the same direction), and they present a negative correlation with respect to PC2 (their projections onto PC2 have opposite directions). Therefore only for very small absolute values of PC2, that is, when correlation is governed by PC1, we will observe that lengthier sentences imply more post-editing time. This suggests that we typically observe a positive correlation between duration and length for cases with low post-editing effort: in these cases the correlation between length and duration could be reflecting the relation between length and reading time. For example, the dashed circle (top-left corner) in Figure 8-1 highlights many of the cases of high HTER and low post-editing time in short sentences and the dotted circle (bottom-right corner) highlights lengthy time-consuming sentences with low HTER.

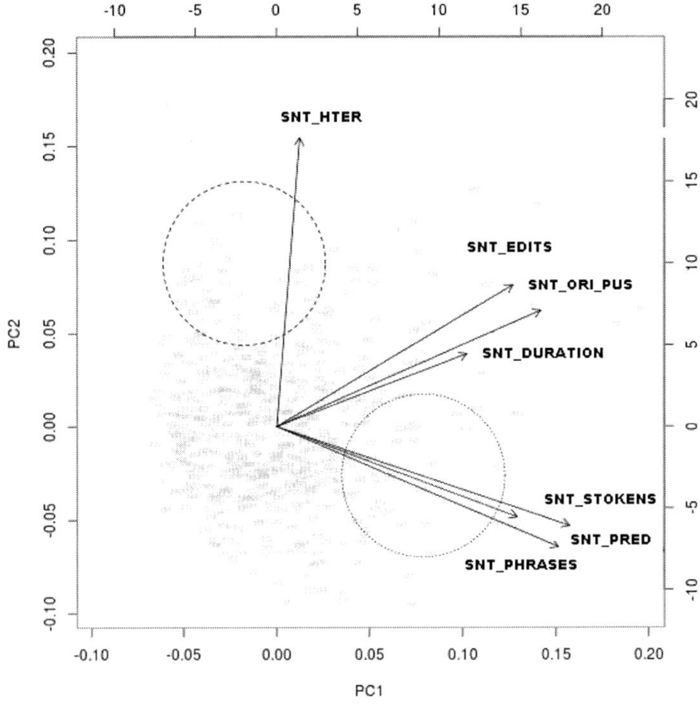

Figure 8-1: Sentence-level features

Following from our motivation for **sub-sentence analysis**, hereafter we only present plots where a data point is a PU. As we previously mentioned, our PUs are different from CASMACAT's original PUs: we have merged multiple CASMACAT PUs overlapping in terms of source or final tokens. Therefore, a PU is the set of CASMACAT PUs which represents all the interventions in a region of the text. In this sense, our PUs are similar to macro translation units defined by Alves et al. (2010), where a micro unit corresponds to a single sequence of edits and a macro unit contains all the micro units related to the same region of text but occurring at different times during the editing process.

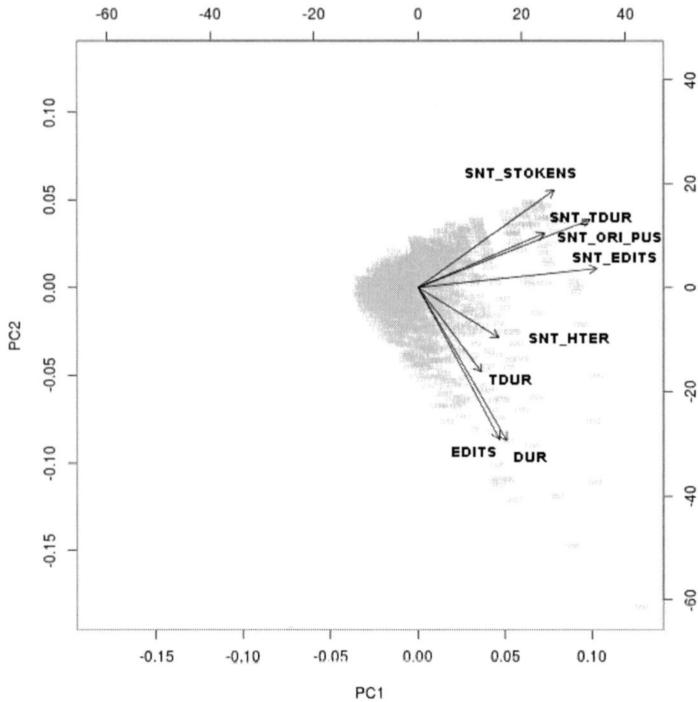

Figure 8-2: Sentence and sub-sentence level features

Figure 8-2 shows projections onto PC1 and PC2 of sentence level features (HTER, amount of typing, total duration including pauses, length and amount of interventions) and features of the PUs (duration with and without pauses and amount of typing) explaining 61.61% of the data's variance. The total amount of typing SNT_EDITS projects almost exclusively on PC1, that is, PC1 tells us about the amount of typing that post-editing a sentence requires. PC2 discriminates the amount of typing as a function of at least two other aspects: i) one related to total length, total duration and number of interventions in the sentence as a whole (top half), and ii) another that relates to the total HTER and the duration and amount of typing of individual PUs (bottom half). PC2 seems to decouple localised effort from accumulated effort, that is, PUs that are individually time-consuming from those happening in longer sentences which sum up to high post-editing times. Long sentences might take longer due to a high number of less time-consuming PUs found altogether. Again, HTER correlates better with time and typing related to individual PUs than to cumulative sentence level indicators.

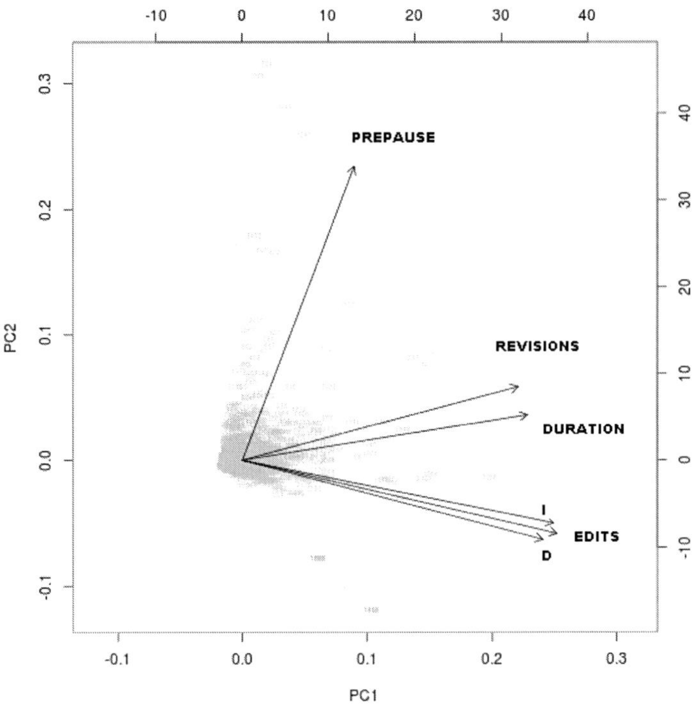

Figure 8-3: Post-editing effort features

Figure 8-3 shows the projections of the post-editing features (that is, number of revisions, duration without pause, pause prior to each revision, number of edits, insertions and deletions) onto the first two PCs explaining 85.92% of the data's variance. The first interesting observation is that the pause prior to editing correlates very poorly to the character-level edits performed. In general, interpreting pauses is difficult. As noted, for example, by Alves et al. (2010), based on the pause and editing information alone, we cannot tell whether the pause is related to the segment edited after the pause – reading new text, planning, consulting external resources for translation alternatives – or to assessing the text already produced. This poor correlation, however, does reiterate the fact that the amount of editing following the pause does not explain it alone. We see that with respect to PC1, duration and edits are well correlated, which is due to the way PUs are defined in CASMACAT: a PU boundary is defined as a delay of 1000ms or more without keyboard activity. On the other hand, PC2 separates PUs that require more revisions and are more time-consuming from those requiring some amount of typing which is not necessarily slow to perform. Moreover, there is a stronger correlation between insertions and duration than between deletions and duration.

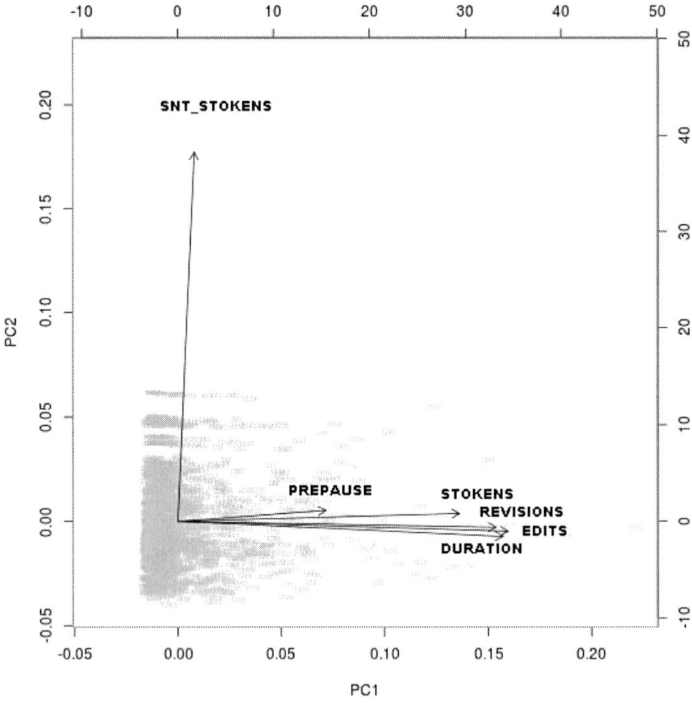

Figure 8-4: Post-editing effort features and source length

Figure 8-4 shows the projections onto PC1 and PC2 of the post-editing features, the length of the PU and the length of the sentence where the PU occurs. PC1 and PC2 explain 68.17% of the data's variance. Features of the PU correlate strongly with PC1, including the length of the PU (source tokens), while the length of the sentence projects almost exclusively onto PC2. Basically PC1 tells us how time-consuming and lengthy a PU is, while PC2 discriminates PUs happening in long sentences from those happening in short sentences. In other words, there is very little correlation between the length of a sentence and how time-consuming individual PUs are, as we have mentioned before. This shows us that post-editors in the CASMACAT field trial worked on localised edits, that is, edits whose duration does not necessarily depend on the whole sentence. This seems to suggest that it is possible to decouple sentence length from the difficulty of each PU in terms of how time-consuming and how many edits (character level insertions and deletions) it requires. This corresponds to similar observations that when translating, translators do not process the translation as whole sentences but rather in smaller units (see Alves et al. 2010).

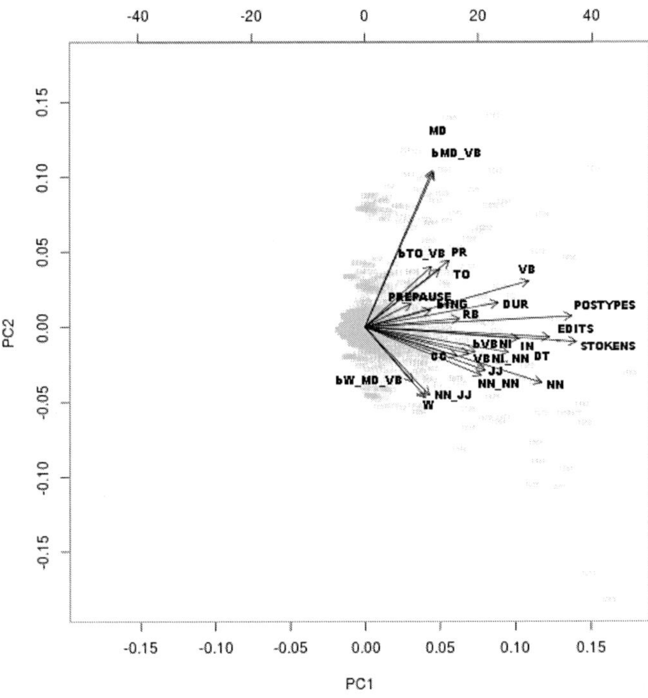

Figure 8-5: Post-editing effort and POS features

Figure 8-5 shows the projections onto PC1 and PC2 of the post-editing features and the POS features of the PUs (24 features in total). PC1 and PC2 can explain 38.74% of the data's variance. In order to maximise the data variance that the two first components can explain, PCA does not discriminate well among some feature groups (other principal components discriminate features that look redundant in the plot, for instance the first nine PCs explain 75.46% of the variance). Some features in Figure 8-8-5 are indeed interdependent by definition (e.g MD and bMD_VB, TO and bTO_VB, bVBNI and VBNI_NN, W and bW_MD_VB).

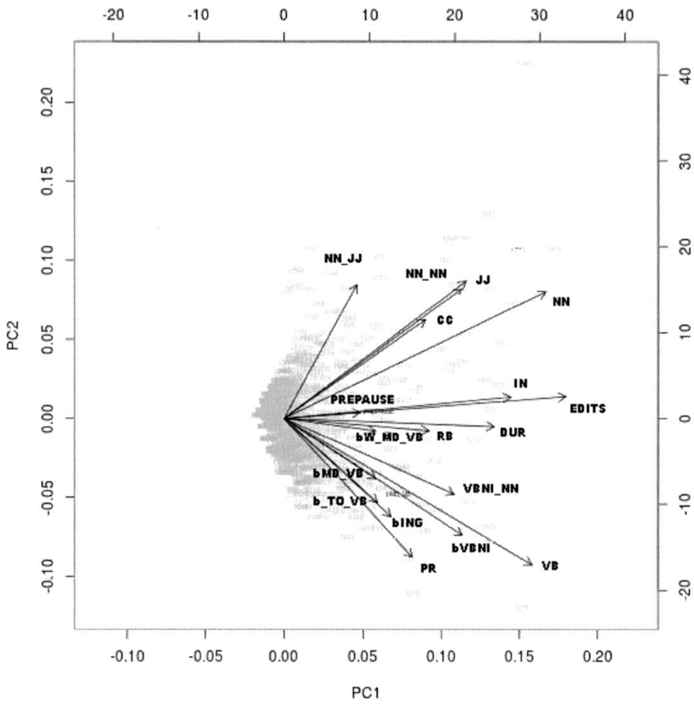

Figure 8-6: A closer look at POS features

Figure 8-6 shows a more fine-grained analysis of POS features. It shows that duration and edits project the most onto PC1, i.e., PC1 generally reflects effort in terms of time and edits. PC2 discriminates between PUs related to verbs (bottom half) and PUs related to nouns (top half). It also seems to indicate that PUs involving verbs are slightly more time-consuming, given how PUs in the verb group (data points in the bottom-right corner) project more on duration than PUs in the noun group, while PUs related to nouns require slightly more typing.

Editing an individual verb alone is not necessarily time-consuming. For instance, in Example 1 given in the section ”Motivation”, we saw two PUs involving only the source verbs *disclosed* and *met*, both of which had short editing times. Instead, these may be cases where the PU consists of multiple words, one of them being a verb. In some cases, the presence of a verb in the PU might indicate problematic cases. One example could be an idiom, as in the PU *though it falls short of being* (segment P03_P17_s907722, edit duration 8.512 s, preceding pause 32.346 s).

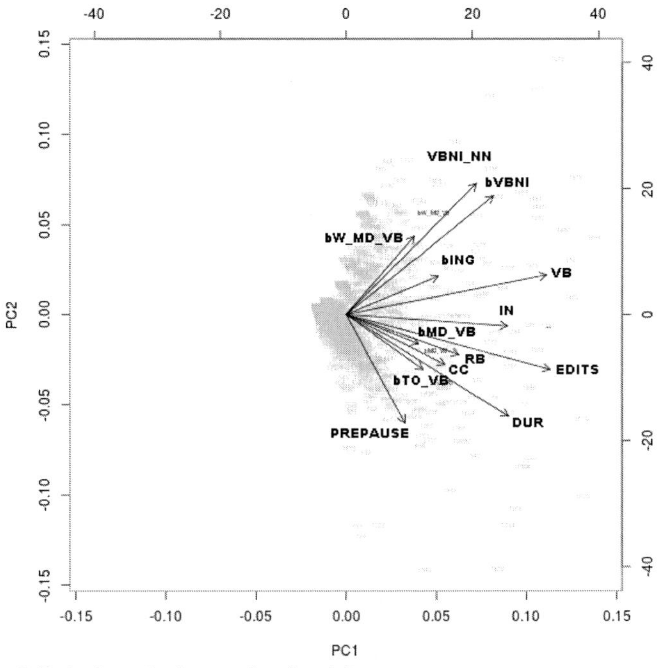

Figure 8-7: A closer look at verb-related features

Figure 8-7 provides a closer look at the features in the verb group. PC1 tells us about the presence of verbs (VB projects mostly onto PC1). PC2 separates PUs depending on the type of verbs they contain. It seems that the presence of modal verbs, adverbs and coordinating conjunctions leads to time-consuming PUs more often than gerunds and other non-finite verbs. This finding is slightly surprising, in that non-finite verbs are often among features suggested as problematic for MT. A more detailed analysis of the MT and PE would be necessary to identify the actual changes made, but perhaps the presence of adverbs or coordinating conjunctions as part of the PU may indicate wider-reaching edits requiring reordering, for example.

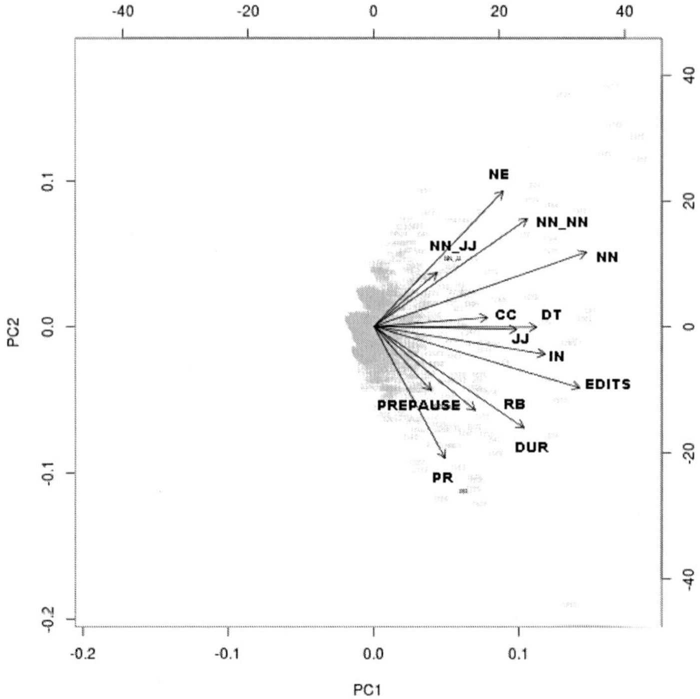

Figure 8-8: A closer look at noun-related features

Figure 8-8 details the features in the noun group plus the named-entity feature. PC2 discriminates PUs with pronouns and prepositions from those basically composed of nouns (including named-entities) and adjectives. The presence of pronouns in the PU projects more on to duration than sequences of nouns and named-entities. Pronouns are by nature more ambiguous, so perhaps some of the duration can be explained by the greater need to analyse the context when editing a unit containing a pronoun.

It is important to highlight that many of these features (both related to verbs and nouns) present a somewhat strong correlation with duration. This provides a good indication that methods to classify PUs in terms of their duration should consider these features. Moreover they present a positive correlation, which corroborates previous work based on linguistic analysis.

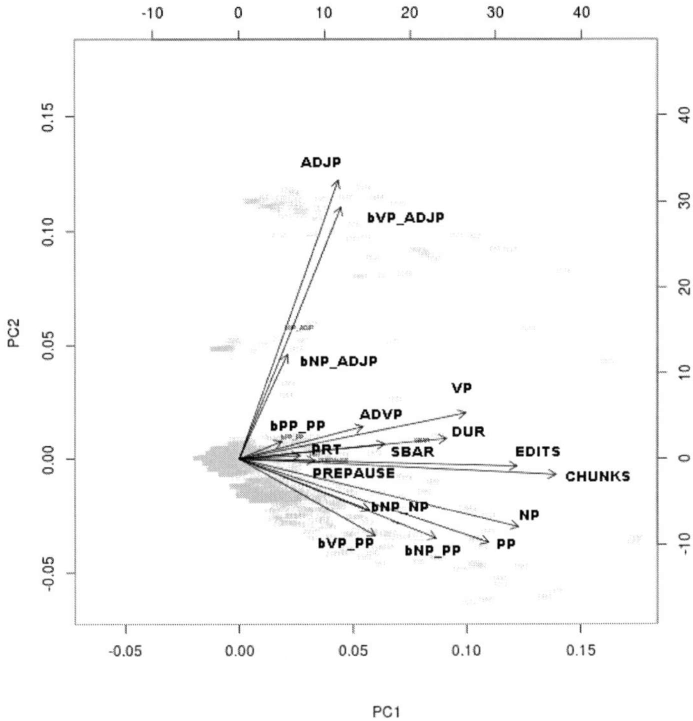

Figure 8-9: Post-editing effort and phrase category features

Figure 8-9 shows the projection onto the first two PCs of the post-editing features and features extracted from a shallow parser with respect to the PUs. PC1 and PC2 explain 40.34% of the data's variance. PC1 reflects mostly the duration, amount of typing and the number chunks of the PUs. Observe that most syntactic features show some degree of positive correlation with duration. PC2 separates PUs according to their syntactic content essentially into two groups: one with PUs containing adjuncts and another with PUs containing more core categories.

In the first group it is interesting to see how VB+ADJP projects much more onto duration than NP+ADJP and there are quite a few data points corroborating that. This is connected to the observation from Figure 8-8-6 that the presence of verbs is more correlated with duration than the presence of nouns. The second group seems more populated and the features there correlate well with duration, such as the presence of a VP and sequences of NPs. This reflects the fact that NPs and VPs are more often obligatory arguments in a sentence than other types of phrases.

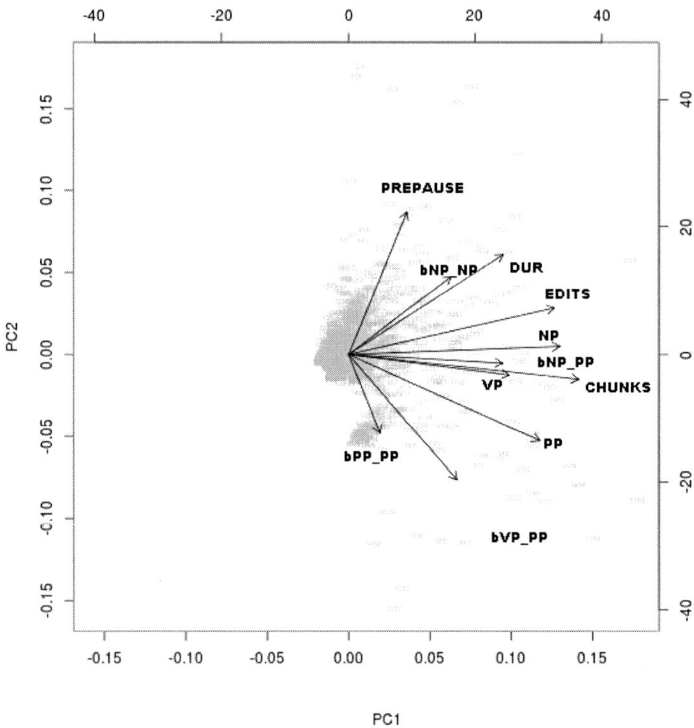

Figure 8-10: A closer look at main phrase categories

In Figure 8-10 PC2 discriminates between PUs that contain NPs (top half) and those that contain PPs and VPs (bottom half). Duration and edits are explained by a compromise between PC1 and PC2: the top-right corner contains PUs that are time consuming and require many edits. Typically consecutive NPs make a sentence more difficult to parse and they do show strong correlation to duration and pause prior to editing. One example of this can be seen in the passage *(competing) against the Billy Childs Ensemble's rich chamber-jazz* (P04_P10_s908627, DURATION: 12.314 s, PREPAUSE: 87.148 s). Such combinations of NPs (and in this case, also PP) can be problematic for the MT system and lead to errors previously identified as difficult, for example, word reordering crossing the phrase boundaries.

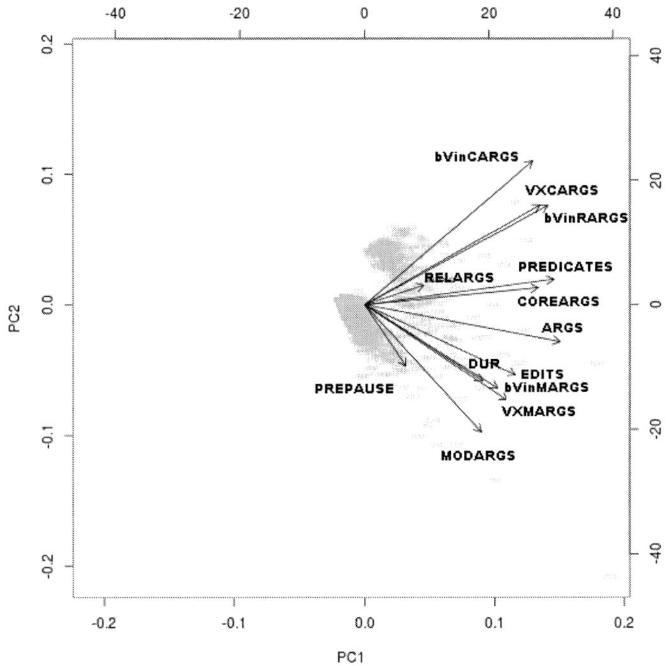

Figure 8-11: Post-editing effort and semantic roles features

Figure 8-11 shows the projection onto PC1 and PC2 of the post-editing features and the SRL features explaining 51.61% of the data's variance. The number of predicates and arguments project the most on PC1, while PC2 covers the type of arguments that the PU (fully or partially) contains. There is a positive correlation between the number of arguments (ARGS) and duration. Modifying arguments in general and the presence of a verb within a modifying argument of another verb also appear to correlate with duration and edits.

Many of the PUs involve several words and may contain combinations of the features identified as difficult. For example, the passage *uses an iTunes-like system to deliver games* (segment P03_P26_s907891), where the PU consists of the words *like system to deliver* (DURATION: 6.535 s, PREPAUSE: 99.265 s) combines some of the features discussed above: a compound noun (NN+JJ+NN) followed by an infinitival construction (TO+VB) as an argument of the predicate *uses*. The PU also involves two different arguments of the predicate, and as noted, the number of arguments inside a PU is also correlated with duration.

Conclusions

The goal of this study was to examine edits with certain linguistic constructions on the source language at the sub-sentence level that lead to cases of high post-editing effort.

The experiments led to a number of interesting findings. Sub-sentence features provide more informative cues about actual editing effort, helping locate edits that are more costly within sentences. They seem promising for error classification, and potentially also for error prediction. In terms of specific features, POS (see Figures 8-5 and 8-6) and phrase categories (see Figures 8-9 and 8-10) seem the most informative features, particularly when compared to semantic role labels. This can be due to the relatively better performance of tools for POS tagging and phrase chunking in comparison to tools for semantic parsers.

Our experiments evidenced a gap between HTER and post-editing time (see Figure 8-2). This corroborates our previous work (Koponen et al., 2012) showing that HTER does not fully capture post-editing effort by giving equal importance to all edits. On the other hand, we observed a modest correlation between sentence length and post-editing time overall, which again should be expected to an extent (in that longer sentences at least take more time to read). Nevertheless we showed that such correlation is not strong, and is mostly observed in cases of low post-editing effort (see Figure 8-1). Therefore, we must not take it as a rule or make it a general assumption.

With respect to specific linguistic constructions, our findings suggest some connection between PUs containing verbs and difficulty in post-editing (see Figure 8-6). While PUs consisting only of a single verb are not necessarily time-consuming, the presence of a verb inside the PU may indicate difficulty with a central part of the sentence, for example in the case of idiomatic expressions, or overall sentence complexity as with verbs as arguments of another verb. However, specific verb types such as gerunds and other non-finite verbs, which have been suggested as problematic for MT systems, appeared less strongly connected to PU duration than modal verbs, for example (Figure 8-7). On the other hand, other patterns such as sequences of consecutive noun phrases may require effort to correctly parse the head-modifier relations. The effort related to specific linguistic patterns may be partly due to the fact that they are problematic for the MT system, as suggested in earlier work on machine translatability, and partly due to the fact that they also require more effort from humans to arrive at the correct interpretation.

Future work includes: (a) further sub-sentence level analysis using target language features based on both the original MT and its post-edited version, which will require some form of alignment between source and the MT and/or its post-edited version; (b) attempting to predict post-editing effort at the PU level using the linguistic patterns defined here, a finer-grained version of current work on quality estimation based on source features only (Specia et al., 2010; Sánchez-Martínez, 2011), or on source and target features (Specia et al., 2009); (c) making better use of the pause information, particularly in terms of connecting pauses to cognitive effort (possibly with the help of eye-tracking data); (d) analysing *fixation units*, rather than *production units*, as produced by eye-tracking logs, once they are made available by CASMACAT, since these will be more decoupled from chararacter-based edits.

For readers interested in further analysing our processed version of the CASMACAT dataset, it is available for download from http://pers-www.wlv.ac.uk/~in1676/resources/casmacat.tar.gz. The tar contains the pre-processed and parsed data (using SENNA), the extracted feature sets, HTML files that allow for manual inspection of individual data points, and the plots shown in this chapter in higher resolution.

Bibliography

Alves, Fabio, Adriana Pagano, Stella Neumann, Erich Steiner, and Silvia Hansen-Schirra. 2010. "Translation units and grammatical shifts. Towards an integration of product-and process-based translation research." In *Translation and Cognition*, edited by Gregory M. Shreve and Erik Angelone, 109-142. Amsterdam/Philadelphia: John Benjamins Publishing Company.

Aziz, Wilker, Sheila C. M. Sousa, and Lucia Specia. 2012. "PET: A Tool for Post-editing and Assessing Machine Translation." *Proceedings of the 8th International Conference on Language Resources and Evaluation.* 3982-3987.

Bernth, Arendse, and Claudia Gdaniec. 2002. "MTranslatability." *Machine Translation* 16: 175-218.

Bernth, Arendse, and Michael C. McCord. 2000. "The Effect of Source Analysis on Translation Confidence." *Proceedings of the 4th Conference of the Association for Machine Translation in the Americas.* 89-99.

Blain, Frédéric, Jean Senellart, Holger Schwenk, Mirko Plitt, and Johann Roturier. 2011. "Qualitative Analysis of Post-Editing for High Quality Machine Translation." *Proceedings of the MT Summit XIII.* 164-171.

Carl, Michael, and Martin Kay. 2011. "Gazing and Typing Activities during Translation: A Comparative Study of Translation Units of Professional and Student Translators." *Meta* 56(4): 952-975.

Collobert, Ronan, Jason Weston, Leon Bottou, Michael Karlen, Koray Kavukcuoglu, and Pavel Kuksa. 2011. "Natural Language Processing (almost) from Scratch." *Journal of Machine Learning Research* 12: 2493-2537.

Doherty, Stephen, and Sharon O'Brien. 2009. "Can MT Output be Evaluated through Eye Tracking?." *MT Summit XII*. 214-221.

Doherty Stephen, Sharon O'Brien, and Michael Carl. 2010. "Eye Tracking as an Automatic MT Evaluation Technique." *Machine Translation* 24(1):1-13.

Elming, Jakob, Laura Winther Balling, and Michael Carl. 2013. "Investigating User Behaviour in Post-Editing and Translation using the CASMACAT Workbench." *This volume*.

Jolliffe, I. T. 2002. *Principal Component Analysis* (2nd Ed.). New York: Springer.

Koponen, Maarit. 2012. "Comparing Human Perceptions of Post-Editing Effort with Post-Editing Operations." *Proceedings of the Seventh Workshop on Statistical Machine Translation.* 181-190.

Koponen, Maarit, Wilker Aziz, Luciana Ramos, and Lucia Specia. 2012. "Post-Editing Time as a Measure of Cognitive Effort." *Proceedings of the AMTA 2012 Workshop on Post-editing Technology and Practice.* 11-20.

Krings, Hans P. 2001. *Repairing Texts: Empirical Investigations of Machine Translation Post-Editing Processes*, edited by Geoffrey S. Koby. Kent, Ohio: Kent State University Press.

O'Brien, Sharon. 2005. "Methodologies for Measuring the Correlations between Post-Editing Effort and Machine Translatability." *Machine Translation* 19(1): 37-58.

—. 2011. "Towards Predicting Post-Editing Productivity." *Machine Translation* 25(3): 197-215.

Papineni, Kishore, Salim Roukos, Todd Ward, and Wei-jing Zhu. 2002. "BLEU: a Method for Automatic Evaluation of Machine Translation." *Proceedings of the 40th Annual meeting of the Association for Computational Linguistics*. 311-318.

Plitt, Mirko, and François Masselot. 2010. "A Productivity Test of Statistical Machine Translation Post-Editing in a Typical Localisation Context." *The Prague Bulletin of Mathematical Linguistics* 93: 7-16.

Sánchez-Martínez, Felipe. 2011. "Choosing the Best Machine Translation System to Translate a Sentence by Using only Source-Language

Information." *Proceedings of the 15th Annual Conference of the European Association for Machine Translation*. 97-104.
Snover, Matthew, Nitin Madnani, Bonnie Dorr, and Richard Schwartz. 2010. "TER-Plus: Paraphrase, Semantic, and Alignment Enhancements to Translation Edit Rate." *Machine Translation* 22(2-3): 117-127.
Snover, Matthew, Bonnie Dorr, Richard Schwartz, Linnea Micciulla, and John Makhoul. 2006. "A Study of Translation Edit Rate with Targeted Human Annotation." *Proceedings of the 7th Conference of the Association for Machine Translation in the Americas*. 223-231.
Sousa, Sheila C. M., Wilker Aziz, and Lucia Specia. 2011. "Assessing the Post-Editing Effort for Automatic and Semi-Automatic Translations of DVD subtitles." *Proceedings of the Recent Advances in Natural Language Processing Conference*. 97-103.
Specia, Lucia, Dhwaj Raj, and Marco Turchi. 2010. "Machine Translation Evaluation Versus Quality Estimation." *Machine Translation* 24(1): 39-50.
Specia, Lucia, Marco Turchi, Nicola Cancedda, Marco Dymetman, and Nello Cristianini. 2009. "Estimating the Sentence-Level Quality of Machine Translation Systems." *Proceedings of the 13th Annual Meeting of the European Association for Machine Translation*. 28-35.
Tatsumi, Midori. 2009. "Correlation Between Automatic Evaluation Metric Scores, Post-Editing Speed, and Some Other Factors." *Proceedings of the MT Summit XII*. 332-339.
Temnikova, Irina. 2010. "A Cognitive Evaluation Approach for a Controlled Language Post-Editing Experiment." *Proceedings of the 7th International Conference on Language Resources and Evaluation*. 3485-3490.
Temnikova, Irina, and Constantin Orasan. 2009. "Post-Editing Experiments with MT for a Controlled Language." *International Symposium on Data and Sense Mining, Machine Translation and Controlled Languages*. 249-255.
Underwood, Nancy L., and Bart Jongejan. 2001. "Translatability Checker: A Tool to Help Decide Whether to Use MT." *Proceedings of MT Summit VIII*. 363-368.

Notes

[1] We use feature scaling (*scale.=TRUE* in R).

CHAPTER NINE

THE INFLUENCE OF POST-EDITING ON TRANSLATION STRATEGIES

OLIVER ČULO, SILKE GUTERMUTH, SILVIA HANSEN-SCHIRRA AND JEAN NITZKE

Abstract

Though not always warmly welcomed, post-editing has recently emerged as a major trend in translation. The very nature of post-editing, namely revising machine translation output, poses specific problems to translators and one could expect this new kind of process to interfere with the strategies translators usually apply. The pilot study presented here investigates whether this is the case. It involved 12 professional translators and 12 translation students all working from English (L2) into German (L1), translating or post-editing a number of texts according to a permutation scheme. Post-edited and human-translated texts were compared and analysed for possible interferences occurring due to the post-editing task. Some individual cases are presented in this chapter and indications for future research given.

Introduction

The term *translation strategy* refers to procedures or methods applied by translators, including those used to circumvent typical problems or avoid common errors in translation. Picking the right strategy at the right time is one of the many challenges in translation, and one would hope that when liberated from the most basic translation task, i.e. without the need to start a translation from scratch but only revising an existing translation, translators could invest more in assuring that the right strategies were followed.

A special type of translation revision is the case of post-editing machine translation output. Machine translation (MT) output is still quite error-prone, and poses very specific problems, as it sometimes may "hit the nail on the head", but in other cases may completely fail the translation of a simple word.

The pilot study presented here investigates how the challenge of revising MT output interferes with translation strategies.

In the following, we will give a brief overview of MT and what kind of challenges it is still facing. Then, we will introduce the topic of post-editing and explain the setting in which the pilot study was conducted as well as the study setup. The next section presents some of the findings in relation to selected strategies and problems. We go on with discussing the findings, and finally conclude the chapter by suggesting lines of further research.

Machine Translation

With the advent of online machine translation tools like Babelfish and Google Translate, machine-translated texts have become an information source for the general public. Another factor for the recent success of MT systems both in research and everyday life is the fact that statistical machine translation (SMT) systems can be created easily and quickly for new language pairs given a minimum amount of parallel data. For European languages, for instance, there is a vast collection of data in the OPUS corpus (Tiedemann 2012), stemming from transcribed speeches of the European Parliament or other sources like translated newspaper texts.

One of the major problems of SMT systems is their quality with regard to grammatical correctness. Hybrid MT approaches are trying to tackle this and other problems mainly from two angles:

- SMT systems which incorporate linguistic information of various kinds and to various degrees (e.g. in dependency treelet translation, Ding and Palmer 2005; Quirk et al. 2005)
- Rule-based MT systems which add statistical components especially with regard to lexical choice (e.g. Žabokrtský et al. 2008; Haugereid and Bond 2012)

Including MT in the translation pipeline has become popular amongst companies for various reasons. This solution is cost-efficient in two ways: As mentioned, setting up an SMT has become very easy (cf. e.g. MOSES toolkit, Koehn et al. 2007), and an SMT system can process a vast amount of data. On the technical side, (S)MT systems are more flexible than translation memories (TM), as they translate on the sub-sentential level, i.e. they can create partial or even full translations for sentences they have never seen, something a TM is not capable of.

Despite these efforts, certain translation problems are still hard to tackle for SMT. For instance, certain typological contrasts are hard to translate even for students of earlier semesters. Let us take a look at the following sentence pair, adapted from the CroCo corpus (Hansen-Schirra et al. 2012):

(1) ST: *Tray 1 holds up to 125 sheets.*
TT: *In Fach 1 können bis zu 125 Blatt eingelegt werden.*
(`Into tray 1 can up to 125 sheets be inserted.`)

Here, we see a typical divergence between English and German: *Tray 1*, the non-agentive subject in English, cannot be translated into the subject in German, as German is very restrictive with regard to non-agentive subjects (cf. Hawkins 1986). Here, a typical strategy of translators is to realise *Tray 1* as a prepositional object in German (lit. *In tray 1*), and to accommodate the main verb of the sentence accordingly (*can be inserted* instead of *holds*).

When we attempt a translation of the sentence above using Google Translate or the web-based demo version of SYSTRAN, we get the following results:

TT – Google Translate: *Fach 1 können bis zu 125 Blatt.*
(`Tray 1 can up to 125 sheets.`)
TT – SYSTRAN: *Behälter 1 halten zu 125 Blättern.*
(`Container 1 hold to 125 sheets.`)

Interestingly, Google produced the closest match. *Tray* is translated correctly as *Fach* and not as *Behälter* `container`, and the atypical plural of *Blatt* `sheet` (usually *Blätter*, but here the uncountable mass plural *Blatt*), which is common in technical contexts, is used. Also, though the sentence is ungrammatical because the main verb is missing, the auxiliary construction using *können* that we see in the corpus example is already half-produced. However, *Tray 1* is still translated as the subject *Fach 1*, and an accommodated verb like *inserted* (or anything similar) is completely missing.

It is in such cases that post-editing, i.e. correction of the MT output by a human translator, is necessary. The pilot study presented here does not discuss the efficiency and effort of post-editing, but looks into translation strategies (like the transfer into a prepositional object in example (1)) that are usually observed in human translation and how these are affected by the post-editing process. At the same time we briefly look into how observations and results from post-editing studies may be valuable feedback for the improvement of MT systems. We thus contribute to a field in which some pilot studies have been performed (Groves and Schmidtke 2009; Tatsumi 2009).

The Increasing Role of Post-editing

For a long time, post-editing was not considered part of the translation practice in translation science. It is even claimed that the rudimentary MT output in the early years helped to develop translation as a science because it proved that the transfer between two languages is much more complex than assumed (Prunč 2007: 31). However, PE has moved into focus as a more efficient and cost-effective method of translation, because of the growing demand for translational services due to globalization. Recent major improvements of the MT quality have also contributed to this focus shift towards the use of so-called post-editing machine translation (PEMT) in the translation industry. PEMT is on its way to become a generally accepted, separate part of the translational landscape.

PEMT can satisfy customer's needs with respect to time and quality by offering several levels of post-editing. The so-called *light* or *fast post-editing* delivers the main content in a comprehensible and accurate form with only essential corrections (O'Brien et al. 2009, O'Brien 2010a). By contrast, the result of *full* or *conventional post-editing* is indistinguishable from a translation from scratch by a human translator (Wagner 1985). PEMT can be particularly suited for closely related language pairs and text domains with a considerable amount of redundancy or controlled language (cf. Fiederer and O'Brien 2009, O'Brien 2010b) such as product manuals, technical documentation or specialized translation (e.g. Aymerich 2005, Kirchhoff et al. 2011).

PEMT is dependent on high quality MT output in order to increase productivity and efficiency (Specia 2011). From a practical point of view, this high quality MT needs to be incorporated into translational environments to facilitate translator workflow and minimize the post-editing effort. This PEMT workflow requires additional skills (O'Brien 2002:100, Wagner 1985:73,76) different to those a classical translator training generally provides, therefore it has to be acknowledged as a 'separate branch' in educational curricula.

So, PEMT is increasingly becoming subject not only to the translation industry, but also to scientific research in many fields. Nonetheless, many professional translators are sceptical towards PEMT and some image-boosting of the post-editing task may be necessary to achieve a wider acceptance among them.

New Translational Environments

As shown above, MT is gaining ground among globally acting companies and organizations, researchers and in day-to-day life. However, dependent on several factors such as text type or language pair, MT output can still be quite "unpredictable" (Cattelan 2013) despite constant efforts to improve its quality. Besides these quality issues, another reason for the weak acceptance of MT amongst professional translators we assume is the lack of proper tools incorporating the different translational tasks into a single collaborative, interactive human-machine workflow. Such a platform where MT and CAT tools work hand in hand with human translator activity would facilitate the translation process and hence increase translator efficiency and productivity.

Several web-based projects like CAITRA[1] (Koehn 2009), PET[2] (Aziz et al. 2012), CASMACAT[3] and MateCat[4], partly in joint efforts, are trying to fill this gap. Features like self-tuning, user-adaptive and informative MT are integrated in MateCat (Federico et al. 2012). CASMACAT focuses on visualization and enhanced user-friendly input methods and aims at "cognitive analysis that provides insight into the human translation process to guide our development of a new workbench for translators." (Ortiz-Martínez et al. 2012).

The CRITT TPR database

The project presented here is a contribution to the CRITT TPR database being developed at the CRITT/CBS[5] using translation process research methods such as keystroke logging, eyetracking and retrospective questionnaires to investigate and analyse cognitive aspects of translator behaviour and to provide the basis for the development of a new translation respectively post-editing environment.

The experimental design included six English general purpose source texts taken from British newspapers[6] and translated or post-edited into five different target languages: Chinese, Farsi, German, Hindi and Spanish using three different translation tasks. The texts were a) translated from scratch by a human translator (HT), b) machine-translated via Google Translate, then post-edited by a human translator with the source text available (PE) and c) machine-translated via Google Translate and edited by a human translator without access to the source text (ED).

All data presented in the study were obtained by using the data acquisition software Translog-II[7] (Jakobsen 1999, Carl 2012a) developed at the CRITT, a Tobii® eyetracker and questionnaires.

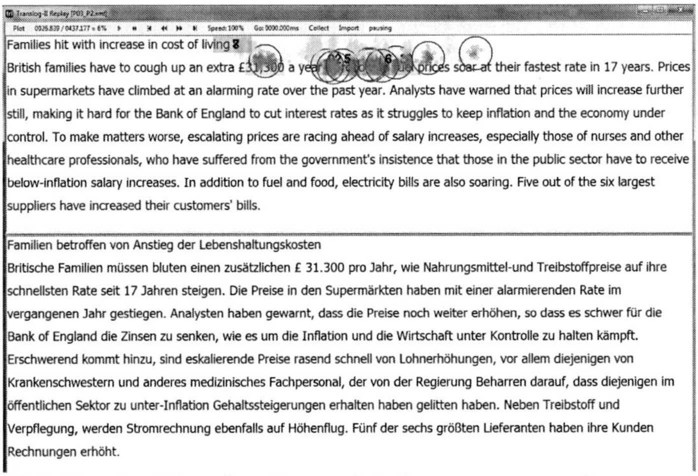

Figure 9-1: Translog-II interface. Dots and circles represent gaze data.

With its split-screen feature (see Figure 9-1) Translog-II provides a user-friendly interface for all three translational tasks, because source and target text can be presented simultaneously. The option to connect an eyetracker enables Translog-II to record gaze data in addition to keyboard and mouse activity. Saved into XML format and fed into a database, the data can be easily processed and analysed in various ways (Carl 2012a+b).

Each participant had to work with all six texts, finally producing two target texts per task i.e. two translations from scratch, two post-edited and two edited texts.

Source text length ranged between 110 and up to 161 words, so they would fit into the Translog split-screen without scrolling. Avoiding scrolling is necessary for precise eyetracking.

English-German study

The English-German contribution to the CRITT TPR database was collected in cooperation with the Faculty of Translation Studies, Linguistics and Cultural Studies of the Johannes Gutenberg-University of Mainz in Germersheim, Germany. It involved 12 professional translators and 12 translation students all working from English (L2) into German (L1) according to a pre-defined permutation scheme to ensure all six texts were processed equally often (see permutations in Table 9-1).

Trans-lator	Translating from scratch (HT)		Post-editing with source text (PE)		Editing without source text (ED)	
T1	HT1	HT2	PE3	PE4	ED5	ED6
T2	HT3	HT4	PE5	PE6	ED1	ED2
T3	HT5	HT6	PE1	PE2	ED3	ED4
T4	(…)					

Table 9-1: Distribution of texts per translator and translation task.

The participants were allowed to use the internet for task-related search and they were provided with a short definition of post-editing together with a set of 'general post-editing rules' pointing out that they were expected to make only essential corrections and to retain as much of the raw translation as possible, i.e. to perform *light post-editing* (O'Brien et al. 2009).

Additionally, two questionnaires were presented to gather information about the participants and their experience with MT and post-editing prior to the experiment. Right after the experiment, participants were asked to evaluate their performance on the tasks, including judgements of the MT output with respect to grammaticality, style, accuracy and overall assessment. There was no time limit given, the average time needed to fulfil the tasks was around 1.3 hours.

Qualitative evaluation of MT post-editing

The impact of post-editing on translation strategies

The term **local translation strategies** designates strategies that are used for single translation decisions, i.e. on clause, phrase or word level, on the level of rhetorical structure or of paragraph organisation. The term local translation strategy is opposed to **global translation strategies**, which refer to strategies for translation of texts as a whole (Bell 1998:188), e.g. referring to determination of the text type and the norms associated with it, but also to goals like terminological consistency.[8]

When comparing the results of human from-scratch translation, post-editing and editing, we found some striking differences in how constructions used in the English original text (ST) but not typical for German were translated into German. The cases reported in this section point in two different directions: First, they indicate that the phenomenon of interference from the source language is more prominent when not translating from scratch, and second, they indicate that translation teaching needs to focus more on (post-)editing strategies, something that e.g. O'Brien (2002) has already pointed out.

In the following, we will be looking at individual examples of the impact of post-editing on translation strategies to highlight our point. We do not distinguish between students and professionals, as errors and interferences appear in all translations regardless of the professional background of the participants. The problems listed here will be discussed in a broader translation theoretical context below.

Interference is one of many phenomena often observed in translations: The grammatical or lexical structures of the source language have an impact on the target language production. This may happen, for instance, if a proverb is translated literally, but the literal translation is not understood in the same way in the target language. In order to avoid interference, translators may choose to use a completely different wording in the translation.

In the following sentence pair, the English original starts with the PP *In a gesture* which, in this example, is completely changed. The literal translation *In einer Geste* is not idiomatic for German; some translators chose to use the idiomatic version *Mit einer Geste* `with a gesture`, others went for a totally different rendering of the initial phrase:

(2) *In a gesture sure to rattle the Chinese Government, Steven Spielberg pulled out of the Beijing Olympics to protest against China's backing for Sudan's policy in Darfur. (ST)*
Als Zeichen des Widerstands gegen die Chinesische Regierung... (HT)
'As sign of opposition against the Chinese government...'

The literal translation appears both in edited and in post-edited versions of the translation. At the same time, the idiomatic translation *Mit einer Geste* is produced by translators in all three tasks. In edited versions, some translations are completely changed (which is the case in half of the human translations). These results show how MT output might trigger interference effects in the (post-)edited texts.

	HT (8)	ED (8)	PE (7)
Unidiomatic translation *(In einer Geste)*	0	4	5
Idiomatic translation *(Mit einer Geste)*	4	2	2
Neither	4	2	0

Table 9-2: Figures for unidiomatic, idiomatic and re-worded translations of *In a gesture*.

Consistency in translation is ensured by various global strategies like determining a terminology to be used, backtracking during translation, or including a drafting phase in the translation workflow. As PE already constitutes the (first) drafting phase, one would hope that it would aid the goal of reaching consistency in a text.

Let us look at the following sentence pair which consists of an original English title of a newspaper article plus its first sentence and one post-edited translation and its gloss:

(3) *Killer nurse receives four life sentences. Hospital nurse C.N. was imprisoned for life today for the killing of four of his patients. (ST)*
Killer-Krankenschwester zu viermal lebenslanger Haft verurteilt. Der Krankenpfleger C.N. wurde heute auf Lebenszeit eingesperrt für die Tötung von vier seiner Patienten. (PE)
'Killer woman-nurse to four times life-long imprisonment sentenced. The man-nurse C.N. was today for lifetime imprisoned for the killing of four of-his patients.'

Besides issues of lexical choice there are some problems in the target text that are noteworthy. First, the post-editor fails to edit the first occurrence of *nurse* such that it reflects in German that this is a male nurse (*Krankenpfleger* rather than *Krankenschwester*). The second occurrence was edited accordingly, facilitated by the fact that the gender of the nurse is made explicit by the pronoun *his*. Second, we have another case of interference: The syntax in the German sentence reflects the English sentence as it leaves the *for*-PP at the end. This is ungrammatical in German, as the main verb *eingesperrt* should be in sentence-final position.

When looking at the distribution of these errors as shown in Table 9-3, the picture seems very clear: These two specific errors only occur in the post-editing task. Interestingly, the playback of the translation sessions in Translog-II reveals that in the HT-task four of the translators first translated *nurse* as *Krankenschwester* (female nurse) and revised it during the translation of the rest of the text. The remaining three translators read the whole text first or did searches on the topic in the internet, before they started translating. Therefore, they translated *nurse* correctly right at the beginning. We get very similar results for the editing-sessions: Four of the editors changed other words/phrases first, before they realised that *Krankenschwester* was not correct, while the other three editors started editing after they read the MT output and corrected *Krankenschwester* right away.

	HT (7)	ED (7)	PE (8)
Error 1*: Krankenschwester*	0	0	4
Error 2*: Main verb not final*	0	0	5

Table 9-3: Distribution of errors over HT, ED, and PE (number of total instances in brackets).

So far, it appears that participants produced better final texts in the editing tasks than in the post-editing task. The last example shows that this accounts only for certain cases. Not surprisingly, when the MT output contains translations that are wrong with respect to content, editors have problems recognizing those, whereas post-editors can easily correct those mistakes, because they can refer to the source text. Editing, in contrast to post-editing, could thus also be referred to as "blind editing".

Let us have a look at another sentence from the source text with its MT parallel:

> *(4) Increasing mobility and technological advances resulted in the increasing* exposure *of people to cultures and societies different from their own. (ST)*
> *Zunehmende Mobilität und der technologische Fortschritt führte zu der zunehmenden* Gefährdung *von Personen... (MT)*

`Increasing mobility and the technological progress resulted in the increasing endangerment of people... `

Here, the MT produced a content-related error on the word level, translating *exposure* with *Gefährdung* 'endangerment'. This error did not occur in HT, and also all seven post-editors recognized the error in the MT output and changed it into a correct translation. However, the editing group had difficulties recognizing the mistake: Four did not edit the word at all, two changed something, but the content was still wrong and two edited the phrase in a way that the content was correct afterwards. For the latter, the replays show that editing *Gefährdung* into a correct version took a lot of effort. The first participant marked *Gefährdung* and then needed over 40 seconds to decide on a solution. During this time, (s)he did not edit another part of the MT, but read the text before and after *Gefährdung* repeatedly. The second participant changed *Gefährdung* in the first revision phase – after long considerations – into the verbal construction *bedroht wurden* ('were threatened') and only in the second revision phase into *ausgesetzt waren* ('were exposed'), which is an acceptable translation of *exposure*. A deeper investigation of the replay revealed that both had used online dictionaries to first retrieve the back-translation of *Gefährdung* into *exposure*, in order to then weigh the options of the various potential, more fitting translations of *exposure*.

	HT (8)	**ED (8)**	**PE (7)**
Incorrect translation (*Gefährdung*)	0	4	0
Incorrect translation (other)	0	2	0
Correct Translation	8	2	7

Table 9-4: Figures for correct and incorrect translations of *exposure*.

Evaluating MT with post-editing process data: finite and non-finite clauses

The discussion in the previous section makes clear that the quality of the (post-)editing heavily depends on the quality of the MT output. As a consequence, the intensity of (post-)editing effort could be used as a measure of MT quality, as has been done before (cf. e.g. Doherty et al. 2010). We will attempt this in the following.

Since MT systems cannot compensate for typological contrasts between source and target languages with adaptation strategies, we assume that such contrastive differences trigger interference effects and errors in the MT output. The correlation of linguistic features of the source text with post-editing efforts and strategies has already been tested for other language pairs (e.g. Temnikova 2010). Text 3 of our experiment comprises a relatively high proportion of non-finite clauses (ten non-finite clauses and ten finite clauses), which cannot be translated literally into German since this grammatical feature is less productive in German than in English. This leads to two hypotheses: first, we assume that errors due to interference effects show up for non-finite clauses and secondly, these interference effects might cause longer processing times for the post-editing task, especially given that non-finite clauses are more ambiguous than finite clauses (not indicating tense, modality, etc.) making it necessary for the (post-)editor to make decisions on these aspects.

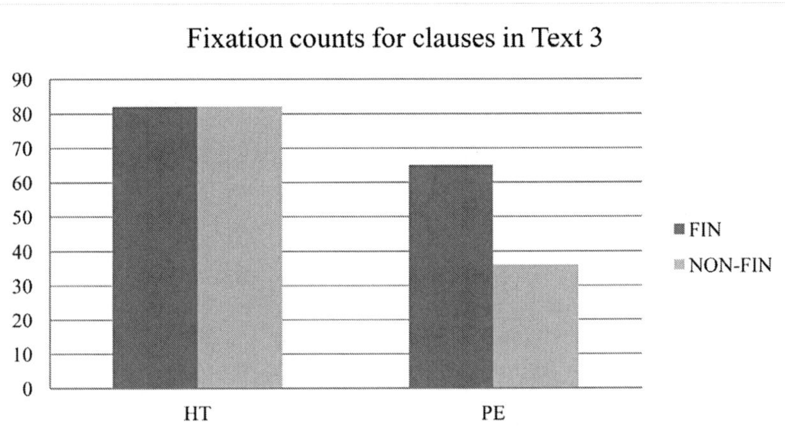

Figure 9-2: Fixation counts for finite and non-finite clauses.

Figure 9-2 shows the average total fixation count for finite (FIN) and non-finite (NON-FIN) clauses across all participants for text 3. The values for the translation task (HT) are nearly identical for the two clause types. By contrast, for the post-editing task (PE), the fixation count is higher for finite clauses compared to non-finite ones. This disconfirms our second hypothesis that non-finite clauses – constituting a contrastive gap – might cause longer processing times in PE. A closer look at the MT output shows that the first hypothesis is also rejected: non-finite clauses do not trigger interference effects or errors in the MT. In contrast, MT quality for non-finite clauses is so good (see examples below) that the MT output does not need any modifications, which is reflected in reduced source text reading, i.e. fewer fixations.

ST: *to end the suffering*	MT: *um das Leiden zu beenden*
ST: *Although emphasizing that*	MT: *Obwohl betont wird, dass*
ST: *to protest against*	MT: *um gegen ... zu protestieren*
ST: *in the wake of fighting flaring up again in Darfur*	MT: *im Zuge des Kampfes gegen ein erneutes Aufflammen in Darfur*

Similar observations are also reported by Aziz et. al (this volume) who find that some non-finite verbs are less time consuming to post-edit than other word forms, despite the fact that non-finite verbs have been suggested problematic for MT systems.

Discussion

Table 9-5 briefly summarises the observations made in our pilot study and adds some translation theoretical considerations. For instance, the translation of *nurse* in example (2) as *Krankenpfleger* is, in terms of translation universals, an **explicitation** (cf. e.g. Baker 1995). The word *nurse* is ambiguous with regard to gender, but the gender of the person has to be explicitated in the German translation; in this case, the use of the male form is correct. Explicitation can happen on various levels (grammar, semantics, etc.) and can be operationalized in diverse ways (cf. e.g. Steiner 2012), but clearly the post-editing task interferes with this operation. A future task will be to further investigate how this and other universals are influenced by the post-editing task.

As for the translation of *In a gesture* in example (3), the task description saying that only the most basic corrections should be made is assumed to be a major factor leading to the unidiomatic translation *In einer Geste*. In terms of global translation strategies, this could be characterised as **overt translation** (House 1997), where features of the original can be clearly identified in the translation, as opposed to cases of covert translation. In terms of text function, we could speak of a documentary translation (cf. e.g. Nord 2006) which aims to remain closer to the translation, as opposed to an instrumental translation which is more oriented towards the recipient and target culture. The question arises, as above with regard to universals, how the post-editing task, or rather the various types of post-editing, relate to translation theoretical concepts and how this could be used e.g. in translator training, also in the field of post-editing.

Ex.	Standard strategy	Error	Occurs in	Hypothesis
(2)	covert translation (cf. House 1997)	interference: *In a gesture* unidiomatically translated as *In einer Geste*	PE (5/7), ED (4/8)	task description: only make most basic corrections
(3)	ensuring lexical consistency; explicitation (cf. Baker 1995)	*nurse* is not consistently translated as *Krankenschwester* `female nurse`	PE (4 out of 8)	non-backtracking post-editing style (cf. Carl et al. 2011)
(3)	adaption to contrastive differences	main verb not moved to sentence final position	PE (5/8)	interference
(4)	preserve invariant semantic content	*exposure* wrongly translated as *Gefährdung* `endangerment`	ED (4/8)	missing source for proper disambiguation

Table 9-5: Summary of observations and potential causes for errors

At this point, we attempt some hypotheses with regard to why the numbers discussed above point in the directions we describe here. From the perspective of quality and correctness, the HT task produced good results in all tasks discussed here. The translators pretty much worked in their standard setting and could thus rely on all the strategies and methods they acquired – whether taught or self-taught – to tackle potential problems, among them matters of consistency (example 2, translation of *nurse*), idiomaticity (example 3) or grammatical contrast (example 2, placement of the main verb). Also, they did not have to deal with potentially erroneous material as in the ED and PE task (as in example 4, where the editors were at a clear disadvantage).

We could assume that PE should yield just as good results as HT, as the source text is available in both tasks. This was clearly not always the case. We would suggest two possible causes. First, the problem of cognitive load: in PE, the translators are required to analyse *two* texts at once, one of them – the MT output – partially of very bad quality. Nuances of collocational or grammatical structures may well slip through the filter (the filter here being the post-editors) in such a process. Second, the task setup: When asked to only make essential corrections, post-editors might decide that a formula like *In einer Geste* may be unidiomatic, but is "good enough" to be understood. We would need, though, to focus our study (e.g. the retrospective interviews) more specifically on such cases in order to understand the real causes.

The examples above lead to the assumption that errors and interference effects in the target texts might be triggered by the MT output. Thus, one of the conclusions to be drawn, as also suggested by O'Brien (2002), is that post-editing should be taught as an additional competence for translators in order to minimize interferences. In fact, translation revision (of human-made translations) usually is part of the curriculum, but post-editing MT output has its own challenges. We would suggest that in order to be able to successfully deal with MT output, it is at least helpful, if not vital, to have basic knowledge of the inner workings of an MT system and with that of its limitations and typical potential errors.

Conclusion and Outlook

Our pilot study reveals various points at which post-editing can interfere with strategies usually applied by human translators in from-scratch translations. We have linked the relevant phenomena to translation theoretical concepts, in order to facilitate further investigations and possible solutions, e.g. with regard to translator training. Future studies will explore further links and also investigate whether there are strategies typical for or even unique to the post-editing task.

In terms of MT assessment, our test shows that the processing effort during the source text reading task is rather low for high-quality MT since the post-editor does not have to check the meaning of the source text in order to understand the translation. As a consequence, low fixation durations can be an indicator of good MT quality. Future research will explore more deeply how eyetracking in connection with post-editing can be used systematically in order to assess MT quality.

Bibliography

Aymerich, Julia. 2005. "Using Machine Translation for Fast, Inexpensive, and Accurate Health Information Assimilation and Dissemination:

Experiences at the Pan American Health Organization." In *Proceedings of the 9th World Congress on Health Information and Libraries*. Salvador - Bahia, Brazil.

Aziz, Wilker, Sousa, Sheila C. M., and Specia, Lucia. 2012. "PET: a Tool for Post-editing and Assessing Machine Translation." In *Proceedings of the The Eighth International Conference on Language Resources and Evaluation*. Istanbul, Turkey.

Baker, Mona. 1995. "Corpora in Translation Studies: An Overview and Some Suggestions for Future Research." *Target* 7 (2): 223–243.

Bell, Roger I. 1998. "Psychological/cognitive Approaches." In *Routledge Encyclopedia of Translation Studies*, edited by Mona Baker. London & New York: Routledge.

Carl, Michael, Barbara Dragsted, Jakob Elming, Daniel Hardt, and Arnt Lykke Jakobsen. 2011. "The Process of Post-editing: a Pilot Study." In *Proceedings of the 8th International NLPSC Workshop. Special Theme: Human-machine Interaction in Translation*, edited by Bernadette Sharp, Michael Zock, Michael Carl, and Arnt Lykke Jakobsen, 131–142. Copenhagen Studies in Language 41. Frederiksberg: Samfundslitteratur.

Carl, Michael. 2012a. "Translog-II: A Program for Recording User Activity Data for Empirical Translation Process Research." In *Proceedings of The Eighth International Conference on Language Resources and Evaluation*. Istanbul, Turkey.

—. 2012b. "The CRITT TPR-DB 1.0: A Database for Empirical Human Translation Process Research." In *Proceedings of the AMTA Workshop on Post-editing Technology and Practice*, edited by Sharon O'Brien, Michel Simard, and Lucia Specia, 9–18. San Diego, USA.

Cattelan, Alessandro. 2013. "A Fair Rate for Postediting." Accessed September 27, 2013, http://thebigwave.it/words-on-the-fly/post-editing-rate/.

Ding, Yuan, and Martha Palmer. 2005. "Machine Translation Using Probabilistic Synchronous Dependency Insertion Grammars." In *Proceedings of the 43rd Annual Meeting of the ACL*, Ann Arbor, 541–8.

Doherty, Stephen, Sharon O'Brien, and Michael Carl. 2010. "Eye Tracking as an MT Evaluation Technique". In *Machine Translation* 24 (1): 1-13.

Federico, Marcello, Alessandro Cattelan, and Marco Trombetti. 2012. "Measuring User Productivity in Machine Translation Enhanced Computer Assisted Translation." In *Proceedings of AMTA 2012*.

Fiederer, Rebecca, and Sharon O'Brien. 2009. "Quality and Machine

Translation - A Realistic Objective?" In *Journal Of Specialised Translation* (11): 52-74.

Groves, Declan, and Dags Schmidtke. 2009. "Identification and Analysis of Post-editing Patterns for MT." In *MT Summit XII: Proceedings of the Twelfth Machine Translation Summit*, 429–436. Ottawa, Canada.

Hansen-Schirra, Silvia, Stella Neumann, and Erich Steiner. 2012. *Cross-linguistic Corpora for the Study of Translations. Insights from the Language Pair English-German*. Berlin: De Gruyter.

Haugereid, Petter, and Francis Bond. 2012. "Extracting Semantic Transfer Rules from Parallel Corpora with SMT Phrase Aligners." In *Proceedings of the Sixth Workshop on Syntax, Semantics and Structure in Statistical Translation*, 67–75. Jeju, Republic of Korea: Association for Computational Linguistics.

Hawkins, John A. 1986. *A Comparative Typology of English and German. Unifying the Contrasts*. London: Croom Helm.

House, Juliane. 1997. *Translation Quality Assessment. A Model Revisited.* Tübingen: Gunter Narr Verlag.

Hvelplund, K.T. 2011. *Allocation of Cognitive Resources in Translation: An Eye-Tracking and Key-Logging Study.* PhD diss., Copenhagen Business School. Frederiksberg: Samfundslitteratur.

Jakobsen, Arnt Lykke. 1999. "Translog Documentation." In *Copenhagen Studies in Language 24*, 149–184. Frederiksberg: Samfundslitteratur.

Kirchhoff, Katrin, Anne M Turner, Amittai Axelrod, and Francisco Saavedra. 2011. "Application of Statistical Machine Translation to Public Health Information: a Feasibility Study." *Journal of the American Medical Information Association* 18 (4): 473–478.

Koehn, Philipp. 2009. "A Web-Based Interactive Computer Aided Translation Tool." In *Proceedings of the ACL-IJCNLP 2009 Software Demonstrations*. Suntec, Singapore.

Koehn, Philipp, Hieu Hoang, Alexandra Birch, Chris Callison-Burch, Marcello Federico, Nicola Bertoldi, Brooke Cowan, et al. 2007. "Moses: Open Source Toolkit for Statistical Machine Translation." In *Proceedings of the Annual Meeting of the Association for Computational Linguistics (ACL)*. Prague, Czech Republic.

Koller, Werner. 2001. *Einführung in die Übersetzungswissenschaft*. Narr Studienbücher. Tübingen: Gunter Narr.

Nord, Christiane. 2006. "Translating for Communicative Purposes Across Culture Boundaries." In *Journal of Translation Studies* 9 (1): 43–60.

O'Brien, Sharon. 2002. "Teaching Post-editing: a Proposal for Course Content." In *Sixth EAMT Workshop*, 99–106. Manchester, U.K. http://www.mt-archive.info/EAMT-2002-OBrien.pdf.

—. 2010a. "Introduction to Post-Editing: Who, What, How and Where to Next?" In *Proceedings of AMTA 2010*. Denver, Colorado.

—. 2010b. "Controlled Language and Readability." In *Translation and Cognition*, ed. Shreve, Gregory and Angelone, Erik, 143–168. American Translators Association Scholarly Monograph Series XV.

O'Brien, Sharon, Johann Roturier, and Giselle de Almeida. 2009. "Post-Editing MT Output Views from the Researcher, Trainer, Publisher and Practitioner." In *MTS 2009, Machine Translation Summit XII*. Ottawa, Ontario, Canada.

Ortiz-Martínez, Daniel, Germán Sanchis-Trilles, Francisco Casacuberta Nolla, Vicent Alabau, Enrique Vidal, José-Miguel Benedí, Jesús González-Rubio, Alberto Sanchís, and Jorge González. 2012. "The CASMACAT Project: The Next Generation Translator's Workbench." Madrid, Spain. Accessed June 28, 2013. https://prhlt.iti.upv.es/aigaion2/attachments/iberspeech_casmacat.pdf-853f76aaa6b9abc89756cf22d3dbe858.pdf

Prunč, Erich. 2007. *Entwicklungslinien Der Translationswissenschaft: Von Den Asymmetrien Der Sprachen Zu Den Asymmetrien Der Macht*. Vol. 14. Frank & Timme GmbH.

Quirk, Christopher, Arul Menezes, and Colin Cherry. 2005. "Dependency Treelet Translation: Syntactically Informed Phrasal SMT." In *Proceedings of the 43rd Annual Meeting of the ACL*, edited Ann Arbor, 271–79.

Schreiber, Michael. 1993. *Übersetzung Und Bearbeitung : Zur Differenzierung Und Abgrenzung des Übersetzungsbegriffs*. Tübinger Beiträge Zur Linguistik ; 389. Tübingen: Narr.

Specia, Lucia. 2011. "Exploiting Objective Annotations for Measuring Translation Post-editing Effort." In *Proceedings of the 15th Conference of the European Association for Machine Translation*, ed. Mikel L. Forcada, Heidi Depraetere, and Vincent Vandeghinste, 73–80. Leuven, Belgium.

Steiner, Erich. 2012. "Methodological Cross-fertilization: Empirical Methodologies in (Computational) Linguistics and Translation Studies." In *Translation: Computation, Corpora, Cognition, 2(1)*.

Tatsumi, Midori. 2009. "Correlation Between Automatic Evaluation Metric Scores, Post-editing Speed, and Some Other Factors." In *The Twelfth Machine Translation Summit (MT-Summit XII)*, 332–339. Ontario, Ottawa, Canada.

Temnikova, Irina. 2010. "A Cognitive Evaluation Approach for a Controlled Language Post-Editing Experiment". In *7th International Conference on Language Resources and Evaluation*. Valletta, Malta.

Tiedemann, Jörg. 2012. "Parallel Data, Tools and Interfaces in OPUS." In *Proceedings of the Eight International Conference on Language Resources and Evaluation (LREC'12)*, ed. Nicoletta Calzolari (Conference Chair), Khalid Choukri, Thierry Declerck, Mehmet Uğur Doğan, Bente Maegaard, Joseph Mariani, Jan Odijk, and Stelios Piperidis. Istanbul, Turkey: European Language Resources Association (ELRA).

Wagner, Emma. 1985. "Post-editing Systran – A Challenge for Commission Translators." In *Terminologie Et Traduction,* (3).

Žabokrtský, Zdeněk, Jan Ptáček, and Petr Pajas. 2008. "TectoMT: Highly Modular MT System with Tectogrammatics Used as Transfer Layer." In *Proceedings of WMT 2008*.

Notes

[1] An experimental 'Web-Based Interactive Computer Aided Translation Tool' developed by the Machine Translation Group at the University of Edinburgh. URL: http://www.caitra.org/ (last accessed June 10th, 2013).

[2] PET: Post-editing Tool. URL: http://pers-www.wlv.ac.uk/~in1676/pet/index.html (last accessed June 10th, 2013).

[3] Cognitive Analysis and Statistical Methods for Advanced Computer Aided Translation. URL: http://www.casmacat.eu (last accessed June 10th, 2013).

[4] Machine Translation Enhanced Computer Assisted Translation. URL: http://www.matecat.com (last accessed June 10th, 2013).

[5] CRITT is the "Center for Research and Innovation in Translation and Translation Technology" at Copenhagen Business School, Denmark. URL: http://www.cbs.dk/en/CRITT (last accessed June 10th, 2013).

[6] Texts partly taken from: Hvelplund (2011).

[7] Translog II. URL: http://130.226.34.13/resources/translog-II.html (last accessed June 10th, 2013)

[8] Different terms are used for this differentiation, e.g. procedure vs. method (cf. Koller 2001, Schreiber 1993 for a discussion in greater detail).

CHAPTER TEN

GAZE BEHAVIOUR ON SOURCE TEXTS: AN EXPLORATORY STUDY COMPARING TRANSLATION AND POST-EDITING

BARTOLOMÉ MESA-LAO

Abstract

The main purpose of this research is to explore the differences between translation and post-editing of texts through the analysis of gaze activity. A group of six professional translators translated and post-edited four different texts from English into Spanish while their eye movements were being tracked. The aim when comparing these two different modalities was to study the effects on eye movement behaviour when reading the same text for two different purposes, i.e. translation vs. post-editing. The questions was whether translating results in different degrees of visual attention to the source text in comparison with the attention devoted to it by the translator while post-editing a machine-generated translation of the same text. Four different measures were registered during the process in order to make comparisons between reading during translation and reading during post-editing: (i) task time, (ii) number of fixations, (iii) total gaze time duration, and (iv) transitions between source and target areas on the monitor screen.

Introduction

Machine translation (MT) has achieved remarkable improvement in recent years due to advances in the field of Natural Language Processing. The availability of systems capable of producing fairly accurate translations has increased the popularity of MT, and many traditional Computer-Aided Translation (CAT) tools, based on translation memory technology, now include MT. This new MT feature in CAT tools enables their use as a post-editing workbench where the human translator is provided with a machine generated draft of the source text whenever nothing is retrieved from the translation memory. In this context, MT is thus not an end in itself, but a valuable asset to be further exploited by human translators to improve their productivity.

Now that post-editing MT increasingly plays a role in the translation industry, there are many questions to be addressed. Much progress has been made in almost thirty years since Vasconcellos and León (1985) first mentioned post-editing as it is known today. Nevertheless, there is still a great need for further research into the skills required for post-editing, the development of workbenches that can better serve MT post-editing, the generation of empirically based pricing models for this new service, and the design of quality standards.

In the light of the increasing use of MT in the translation industry, the main motivation of this study is to explore some of the differences between translation and post-editing by means of an experiment using eye-tracking. The main aim was to investigate visual attention, measured through eye-movements, on identical source texts while performing two different tasks: (i) translation from scratch and (ii) post-editing a machine-generated draft. Both tasks share the common goal of rendering meaning from one language to another but follow quite different processes.

Firstly, this exploratory study was conducted to start building the initial hypothesis that there are differences in how visual attention is distributed and managed when reading a source text in the above mentioned tasks. Secondly, we were also interested in discovering different reading patterns depending on the aim of the task in preparation of further studies using a larger sample.

This chapter is further motivated by the conviction that research on how translators behave when translating as opposed to post-editing can certainly inform the design of translation support tools based on gaze information. Information on how and when to display the source text on a translation/post-editing workbench can be grounded in empirical studies like this one. Similarly, the results of such a study can also have an impact on pedagogical principles for training future post-editors.

Background

The possibility of tracking translators' gaze patterns across source and target texts opens up an exciting research area that can certainly yield new insights in the field of translation studies. There is a long history of applying eye-tracking techniques in reading studies going back to the late

19th century. Since the mid-1970s such techniques have been used extensively in studying cognitive processes underlying reading behaviour (Jensen, 2008: 157).

Drawing on the seminal work of Just and Carpenter (1980), analyses based on the eye-mind hypothesis suggest that eye fixations can be used as a window into instances of effortful cognitive processing. Following this hypothesis, the assumption is that eye-movement recordings can provide a dynamic trace of where a person's attention is being directed, an assumption that is often today taken for granted by eye-movement researchers. Eye tracking, when used to study reading behaviour, has generally been applied to reading of individual words, phrases, or sentences (e.g. Rayner and Pollatsek 1989; Rayner 1998; Radach *et al.* 2004), but more recently also to longer texts (Hyönä *et al.* 2003, Radach *et al.* 2004, Jakobsen and Jensen, 2008). A number of papers have documented that variables such as word familiarity (Williams and Morris 2004), word predictability (Frisson *et al.* 1999), word length and complexity (Kliegl *et al.* 2004; Bertram and Hyönä 2003; Rayner and Duffy 1986), and lexical and syntactic ambiguity (Juhasz and Rayner 2003) all affect fixation duration.

More recently, eye-tracking has also been applied in experimental studies on translation. Pioneering research has been conducted by O'Brien (2006, 2008) in parallel with the EU-funded Eye-to-IT project[1] which aimed at exploring, describing and learning from translation processes using eye-tracking methods. The works of Dragsted and Hansen (2008), Jakobsen and Jensen (2008), Sharmin *et al.* (2008), Pavlović and Jensen (2009), Alves et al. (2009, 2011), Hvelplund (2011), Carl and Kay (2011), and Carl and Dragsted (2012), among others, have shown that tracking the eye movements of subjects when either reading a text prior to translation, or during translation itself, produces useful user activity data which can be further interpreted in combination with other types of experimental data (Alves et al. 2011: 175). In such studies, eye fixations are shown to occur in different areas of interest in the source and target texts depending on different variables (i.e. language directionality, reading purpose, cognitive activity involved, etc.). These studies provide new insights about reading and writing in translation.

Further research is still needed on how reading patterns differ according to reading purposes, or according to the way reading is sometimes combined concurrently with other language-related activities. As stated by Jakobsen and Jensen (2008), the main focus in reading research has been on lexical processing and on reading short strings of words, while less attention has been paid to eye movement behaviour during continuous reading and reading for different purposes. The connection between previous studies and the present findings will be outlined in the results and discussion sections below.

Method

Taking for granted the eye-mind hypothesis formulated by Just and Carpenter (1980), that gaze on a stimulus indicates attention to that stimulus, this study was devised in order to find out to what extent reading a source text while translating results in different degrees of visual attention, compared to the attention devoted to the source text by the translator while post-editing a machine-generated translation of the same text. Four different measures were registered during the translation/post-editing process in order to make comparisons between reading in/for translation and reading in/for post-editing: (i) task time, (ii) number of fixations[2], (iii) total gaze time duration[3], and (iv) transitions[4] between source and target areas on the monitor screen.

Apparatus

A Tobii T60 remote eye-tracker was used to register the eye movements. Texts were displayed in 17 point Tahoma font and double spacing on a 17" LCD screen at 1280 x 1024 pixels. The average viewing distance aimed at was 50-60 cm from the screen, but no head or chin rest was used.

The software used as a translation and post-editing environment was Translog-II (Carl 2012a). This software was originally developed for researching human translation processes by means of key-logging (Jakobsen 1999), but nowadays it also records gaze data as a result of the EU-funded Eye-to-IT project.

The MT engine used to produce raw MT output for the post-editing tasks was Google Translate.

Source texts

The six source texts used in this exploratory study belong to the CRITT TPR database[5], a publicly available database containing user activity data of translator behaviour (Carl 2012b). All of them were newspaper articles slightly modified for the purpose of this research (see Appendix A). Three of the texts in this study (Texts 1, 2 and 3) were selected and used by Hvelplund (2011) in his research on the allocation of cognitive resources in translation. The number of characters in the texts varied between 641 and 712; the number of words varied between 100 and 148, and the average word length varied between 4.55 and 5.6 characters. The average word count per sentence varied between 14.8 and 33. Differences in the number of sentences varied between 4 and 10.

As stated by Hvelplund (2011: 221), it is difficult to assess the level of difficulty of a source text for translation, since the level of difficulty it poses for translation can vary between individual translators. It depends very much on their routines, skills and specialisation (Jensen 2009: 62-63). This holds all the more when MT is involved because the outputs for post-editing can vary considerably in quality. Using the quality of the output given by the MT engine as a parameter to measure difficulty, two external evaluators with experience in the field of post-editing grouped Text 1 (T1) and Text 5 (T5) as the least complex/difficult, Text 2 (T2) and Text 6 (T6) as moderately complex/difficult, and Text 3 (T3) and Text 4 (T4) as the most complex/difficult to post-edit. This is used as the difficulty index in this study, and it is therefore important to remember that text difficulty is seen from a post-editing perspective. Although this classification can be problematic when applied to translation from scratch, it matches the classification made by Hvelplund (2011) for T1, T2 and T3 when it comes to text difficulty from the translation point of view.

Participants

A group of six professional translators aged between 21 and 55 volunteered to perform the two tasks under experimental conditions. All of them had a degree in translation studies and English (L2) to Spanish (L1) was their main language pair. The average translation experience for the six participants in the study was seven years (range 1–20). When asked about previous experience in post-editing, all of them stated that they had performed post-editing assignments as part of their work as professional translators.

Procedure and design

Each participant in the study translated and post-edited four different texts from English to Spanish while their eye movements were being tracked. First participants were informed about the test procedure and then the eye-tracker was calibrated for the participant's eyes. Each participant translated two texts from scratch and post-edited two further texts.

Task 1: Translation from scratch. This task was a traditional written translation assignment. The participants' written translation was produced in a split-screen window below the window in which the source text was displayed.

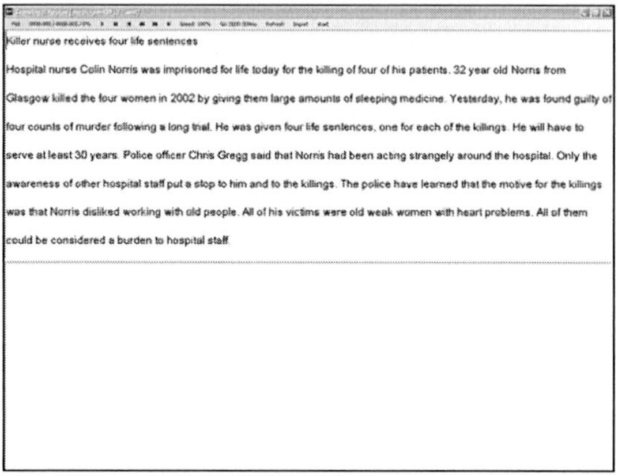

Figure 10-1: Translation editing environment in the study (Translog-II interface).

Task 2: Post-editing a machine generated translation. This task required participants to work on the raw output generated by the MT engine as a preliminary target text. It was a traditional post-editing assignment where translators were not forced to work on a sentence by sentence level.

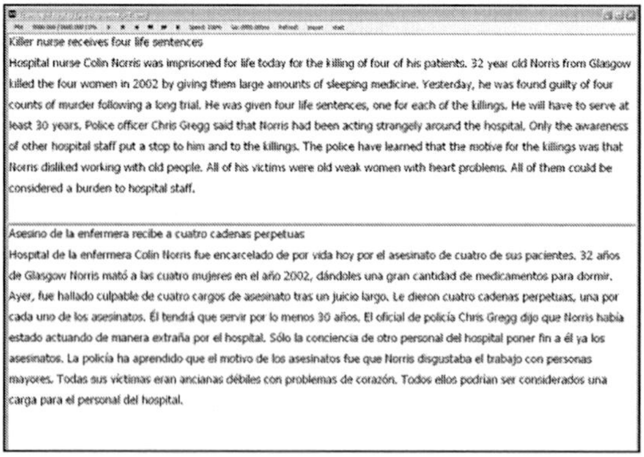

Figure 10-2: Post-editing environment in the study (Translog-II interface).

To facilitate eye-tracking measurements, texts were fully displayed to avoid any need for participants to scroll in either the source or at the target text window.

In an attempt to unify editing criteria among participants, all of them were instructed to follow these post-editing guidelines with specifications of the quality expected:

- Retain as much raw MT translation as possible.
- Do not introduce stylistic changes.
- Make corrections only where absolutely necessary, i.e. correct words/phrases that are clearly wrong, inadequate or ambiguous according to Spanish grammar.
- Make sure there are no mistranslations with regard to the English source text.
- Don't worry if the style is repetitive.
- Publishable quality is expected.

Since all the participants in this study were professional translators, the only guideline provided to the participants for the translation task was to produce an equivalent text of publishable quality.

As a means of neutralising any skewing effects caused by differences in the texts, the task-text combination was rotated systematically so that participants had to translate or post-edit four of the six texts involved in this exploratory study in different combinations.

The design of this exploratory study can be seen in Table 1[6].

Participant	**Task 1: Translation**		**Task 2:Post-editing**	
	First	Second	Third	Fourth
P01	T1	T2	T3	T4
P02	T5	T6	T1	T2
P03	T3	T4	T5	T6
P04	T2	T1	T4	T3
P05	T6	T5	T2	T1
P06	T4	T3	T6	T5

Table 10-1: Task and text distribution in the study.

Each text was translated and post-edited twice by different professional translators. In sum, the variables in the study were as follows:

- *Independent variables*: two different reading modalities (source text reading in translation and source text reading in post-editing). In addition to task, a secondary independent variable in this study is text difficulty based on the quality of the MT provided for post-editing.

- *Dependent variables*: (i) task time, (ii) number of fixations, (iii) total gaze time duration, and (iv) transitions between source and target areas on the monitor screen.

Participants were asked to carry out all tasks at the speed with which they would normally work in their everyday work as professional translators. No time constraint was imposed and no use of external resources (dictionaries, Internet, etc.) was allowed during the translation/post-editing process.

Findings and analysis

In this section, findings are presented separately for each of the two tasks regarding the four dependent variables in the study. In order to account for differences in text length, dependent measures involving time and fixation count were normalized for the number of words in the relevant source text. These values are shown in square brackets in the different tables. Given the small size of the sample of this exploratory study, no inferential statistics have been used and only descriptive statistics will be presented.

Task time

As can be seen from Table 10-2, translators were always faster in the post-editing task. The start of the task was calculated from the moment the participant opened the project and the task was considered as finished when the participant pressed the button ‘stop logging’ in the Translog-II.

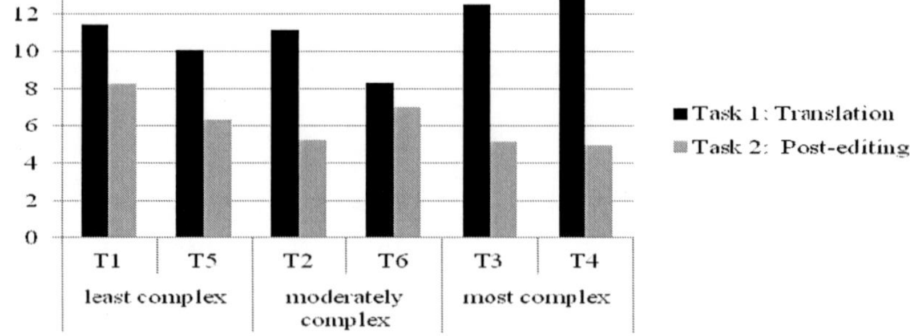

Figure 10-3. Average task times in minutes per text complexity [task time in seconds per word in brackets].

One of the most noticeable task time differences was that involving those texts considered the most complex/difficult to post-edit (T3 and T4). It seems reasonable to think that post-editing poor MT output takes longer. However, according to these preliminary results, post-editing the most difficult texts, here measured as the poorest MT output, does not necessarily lead to longer task time.

When looking at average task times across different participants, those who were slower when translating were not necessarily slower when post-editing (e.g. P04 and P06). There seems to be greater inter-subject variability regardless of the difficulty involved in post-editing (see Table i in Appendix B for precise times for participants, tasks and texts).

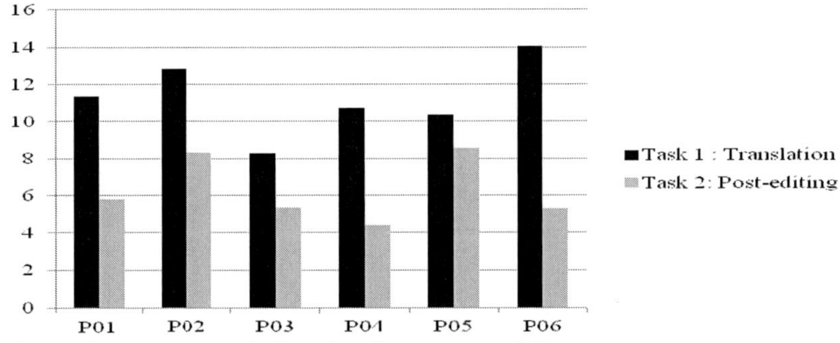

Figure 10-4. Average task times in minutes per participant.

Fixation count

Analysing the log files from Translog-II, it was possible to discriminate between fixations in the source and target text area and calculate the number of fixations in each area (see Table 10-2).

Overall, the post-editing task resulted in much fewer fixations on the source text than the translation task. In translation tasks, the average fixation count in the source text for all participants per text was 1464 (range 1016 - 2298). In the case of post-editing, fixation counts on the source text decrease considerably. The number of fixations in the source text decreases to an average of 667 (range 424 - 1182). Most of the translators (except for P01 and P04) had twice as many fixations on the target text than on the source text when post-editing (see Table ii in Appendix B for details on fixation counts for participants, tasks and texts).

	Task 1: Translation					Task 2: Post-editing				
	fixations on source	%	fixations on target	%	TOTAL	fixations on source	%	fixations on target	%	TOTAL
T1	1715 [11.59]	64.62	939	35.38	2654	690 [4.66]	24.19	2163	75.81	2853
T2	1527 [10.83]	60.05	1016	39.95	2543	477 [3.38]	26.81	1302	73.19	1779
T3	1804 [13.67]	54.01	1536	45.99	3340	652 [4.94]	54.29	549	45.71	1201
T4	1857 [18.57]	50.11	1849	49.89	3706	951 [9.51]	59.92	636	40.08	1587
T5	1085 [8.89]	37.48	1810	62.52	2895	733 [6.01]	35.43	1336	64.57	2069
T6	1046 [8.79]	38.77	1652	61.23	2698	535 [4.50]	28.62	1334	71.38	1869

Table 10-2. Average fixation count per text in source and target areas [fixations per word in the texts are in brackets].

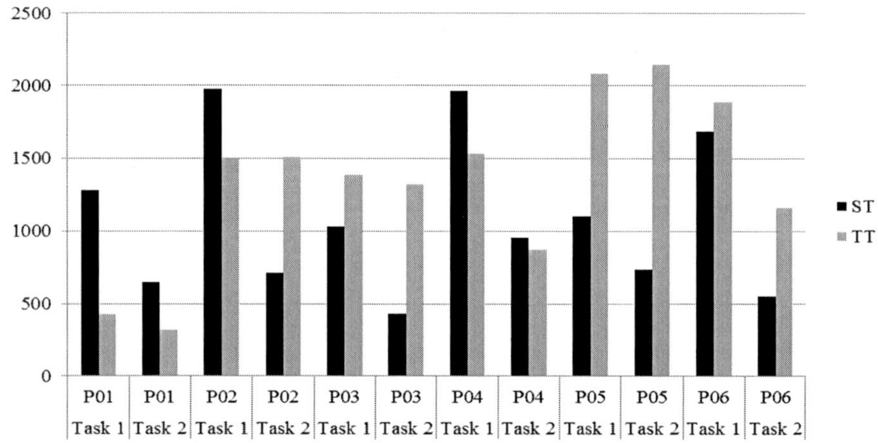

Figure 10-5. Fixation count per participant in source (ST) and target (TT) areas

Moving from fixation count to fixation duration, studies of word fixations have shown that fixation durations are typically 200 to 250 ms (Rayner 1998) and that duration varies according to a vast array of parameters. In these data, average fixation durations are not very different despite the difference in task times and number of fixations, but they are always shorter in post-editing tasks. The average fixation duration in the source text area was 291.36 ms (range 233.5 - 331.3 ms by-translator average) for translation and 266.47 ms (range 205.08 - 312.43) for post-editing. In the case of the target text area, the average fixation duration was 301.50 ms (range 223.47 - 356.61) in translation and 256.19 ms (range 190.32 - 351.41) in post-editing.

Text complexity does not seem to affect fixation duration in these data. These results are in line with other studies showing a lack of differentiation in fixation duration in different tasks. For example, Jakobsen and Jensen (2008) also did not observe differences in fixation duration between tasks in their study. O'Brien (2010) found no significant difference in fixation duration for texts that had been edited using controlled language rules and versions that were uncontrolled. Similarly, Doherty et al. (2010) found no significant differences when observing the average fixation duration in an experiment where participants were instructed to evaluate both good and poor quality MT outputs.

Gaze time

By comparing task time and gaze time, we were able to calculate how much of the total task time participants looked at the screen during the two tasks.

The average gaze time on the source text area across participants was 35.20% (range 25.34% - 44.75%) while translating and 29.92% (range 11.88% - 77.29%) while post-editing. In the case of the target text area these global percentages were 38.85% (range 10.65% - 68.88%) for translation and 46.83% (range 11.59% - 84.39%) for post-editing.

Figures 10-6 and 10-7 show gaze percentages for both source and target text areas for the participants, for translating (Figure 10-6) and post-editing (Figure 10-7).

In line with previous findings in translation process research (e.g. Jakobsen 2002, Sharmin *et al.* 2008, Alves et al. 2011), most of the translators devoted more gaze time to their own target text than to the source text regardless of the text complexity, except for two of the translators (P01 and P02) who systematically devoted more gaze time to the source text while translating the two texts regardless of the text difficulty involved.

Gaze time in the source text area was considerably shorter in the case of post-editing where much of the gaze activity involved in the task took place in the target text area. Only the two participants (P01 and P04) who had to post-edit the most difficult texts (T3 and T4) devoted more time to the source text for both texts in the post-editing task.

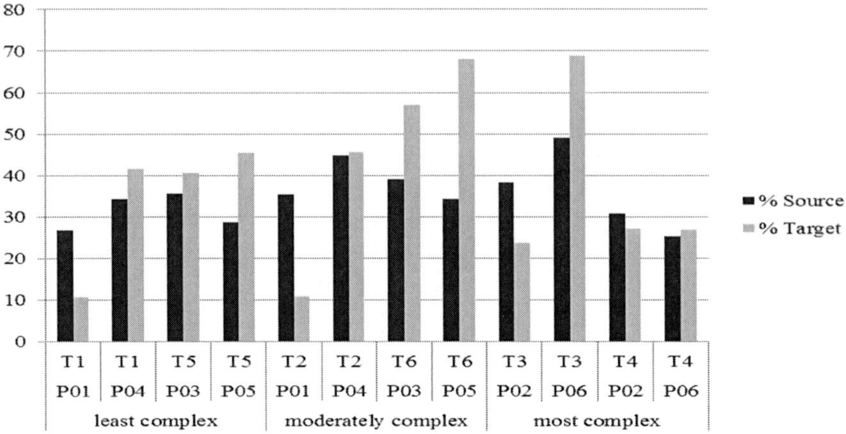

Figure 10-6: Gaze time distribution (%) on source and target areas across participants/texts while translating

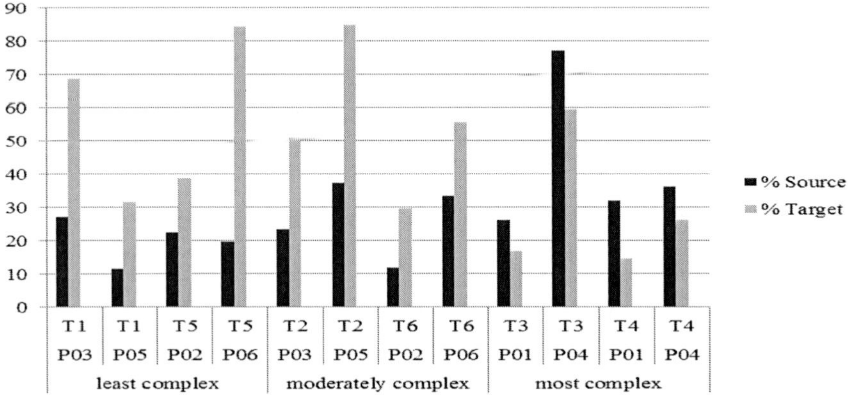

Figure 10-7: Gaze time distribution (%) on source and target areas across participants/texts while post-editing.

Transitions between source and target areas

The data collected reveal important differences between participants with regard to the number of transitions regardless of the text involved. For example, when considering T2 (assessed as a moderately complex text), transitions range from 366 to 834 in translation and from 170 to 1045 in post-editing depending on the translator (see Table 10-3). The differences are probably related to the way human translators differ in the way they manage the reading and alignment process involved in translation from scratch and to what extent they transfer this process when post-editing.

	Task 1: Translation				Task 2: Post-editing			
		Transitions ST/TT		Transitions ST/TT		Transitions ST/TT		Transitions ST/TT
P01	**T1**	449 [3.03]	**T2**	366 [2.59]	**T3**	369 [2.79]	**T4**	509 [5.09]
P02	**T3**	1085 [8.21]	**T4**	969 [9.69]	**T5**	645 [5.28]	**T6**	1698 [14.26]
P03	**T5**	724 [5.93]	**T6**	333[2.79]	**T1**	167 [1.12]	**T2**	170 [1.20]
P04	**T2**	834 [5.91]	**T1**	867 [5.85]	**T4**	721 [7.21]	**T3**	1263 [9.56]
P05	**T6**	1017 [8.54]	**T5**	848 [6.95]	**T2**	1045 [7.41]	**T1**	779 [5.26]
P06	**T4**	283 [2.83]	**T3**	709 [5.37]	**T6**	1427 [12]	**T5**	191 [1.56]

Table 10-3. Number of transitions between source and target text areas per participant [number of transitions per word in brackets].

When considering the number of transitions in relation to text complexity (see Table 10-4 averaging across the different participants), easier texts (T1 and T5) show almost one-fourth more transitions in translation than in post-editing. However, difficult texts (T3 and T4) show a similar number of fixations in both tasks. These findings support the idea that the role of the source text when post-editing poor quality MT and translating from scratch is similar. It does not seem to be the case for post-editing good MT, where the source text receives less attention.

		Task 1: Translation	Task 2: Post-editing
least complex	**T1**	658 [4.44]	473 [3.19]
	T5	786 [6.44]	418 [3.42]
moderately complex	**T2**	600 [4.25]	607 [4.30]
	T6	675 [5.67]	1562 [13.12]
most complex	**T3**	897 [6.79]	816 [6.18]
	T4	626 [6.26]	615 [6.15]

Table 10-4. Average of transitions between source and target text areas per text complexity [number of transitions per word in brackets].

Discussion

In this section the results presented above are further elaborated and it is discussed how the findings add to our knowledge about translators' visual behaviour while translating or post-editing.

The longer task times recorded in the translation tasks may be explained by the requirement to first read the source text—either entirely or in segments—before starting to type the translation. Based on empirical data, differences and similarities in translators' working styles have been modelled by Carl et al. (2011). Three phases emerge for translation from scratch: initial orientation (reading), translation drafting and final revision. Initial orientation generally involves the translator's reading of the source text before starting to produce the translation from scratch. Some translators prefer to systematically read the whole source text before they start translating. Some translators skim the text very briefly, and some translators just read the first couple of phrases or sentences before going straight ahead with target text production. In the case of post-editing, this orientation phase has a very different nature. Krings (2001: 321-360) identifies a source text related process when the post-editor reads the source text with a view to recognizing patterns for reformulation in the target. By contrast, most participants in this study either started reading the target text or just read the first couple of words or sentences in the source text before starting to read the target text in search of errors.

Based on the logical principle that post-editing should aim at being faster than translating from scratch, post-editing can be considered an inherently time pressured task, although no explicit time pressure was imposed here. In line with studies investigating the effect of time pressure in translation (e.g. Jensen 1999, 2000), we see here that most post-editors save time skipping an initial orientation phase. The prototypical initial orientation phase in translation is generally only seen in post-editing oriented towards limited context and not the whole text. Moreover, post-editing in itself being a kind of end revision (of the machine-generated text), post-editors also skip overall final revision after making their changes. Differences in task times can probably be explained by this lack of clear orientation and end revision phases, together with the fact that (in principle) much less typing should be involved in post-editing when compared to translation.

Regarding the fixation counts in this study, translation tasks triggered more fixations in the source text area, presumably due to more careful reading. The intrinsic requirements of translation as a language transfer actvity resulted in a change in participants' gaze behaviour caused by the need to not only comprehend the source text but also to monitor translation progress while typing the translation. The difference in the fixation count for the source-text area amounted to almost 44% more fixations in the source text during translation compared to post-editing. In the translation task, additional fixations on the source text area are necessary not only to feed the brain with input for meaning construction, but also to monitor while typing that the target text conveys the same meaning. The higher number of transitions between the source and target text areas during translation can thus partly be attributed to the need to ensure coordination of comprehension and text production processes. In post-editing tasks, fixations on the source text only exceeded the number of fixations in the target area in the case of complex/difficult texts (T3 and T4). For these texts, the poor quality of the MT output required systematic reading of the source text to enable translators to make sense of the target text provided by the MT engine.

Looking at the data across participants, fixation duration in the target text was always shorter in post-editing tasks. Although the total number of fixations was higher in the target text for post-editing, their duration was shorter when compared to translation tasks. These results may be evidence of the target text evaluation processes described by Krings (2001: 429-471) where the post-editor has to systematically make speedy positive or negative evaluations of the MT output.

Despite the fact that in both tasks translators had to coordinate visual attention between two texts, eye movement behaviour across source and target areas differed between tasks. As a means of illustrating the differences between the reading behaviour in the two tasks, Figures 10-8 and 10-9 show different reading patterns in the form of progression graphs. These two figures show two clear-cut extremes when it comes to reading during translation and reading during post-editing.

Figure 10-8 graphically represents the translation process of participant 05 during translation from scratch. This progression graph shows time in milliseconds on the X-axis, and source text words in the Y-axis (T6 in this study). The diagonal line in the centre of the graph shows typing activity. The symbol × represents fixations on the source text and the symbol + fixations on the target text area. The vertical lines joining these dots are eye movements (saccades) between source and target areas.

The three translation phases described by Carl et al. (2011) can be easily identified in Figure 10-8. An initial orientation phase (reading) with only fixations in the source text area is seen on the left side of the graph. The translation drafting phase is clearly depicted in the centre showing transitions between source and target areas while typing. In the drafting

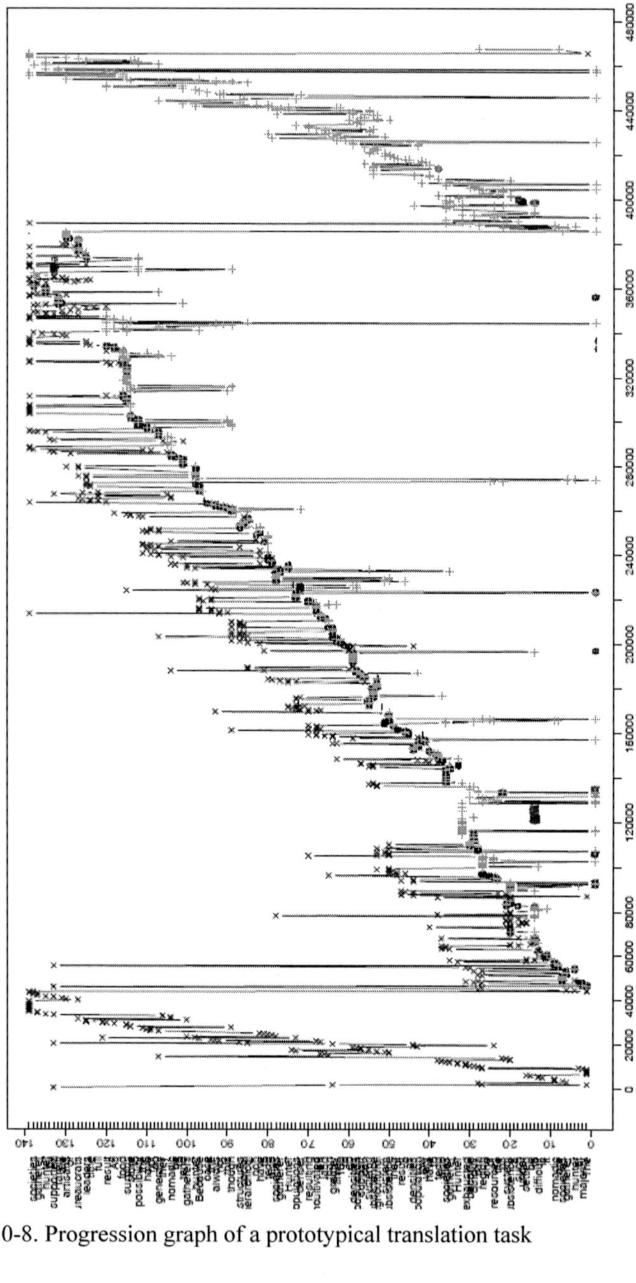

Figure 10-8. Progression graph of a prototypical translation task

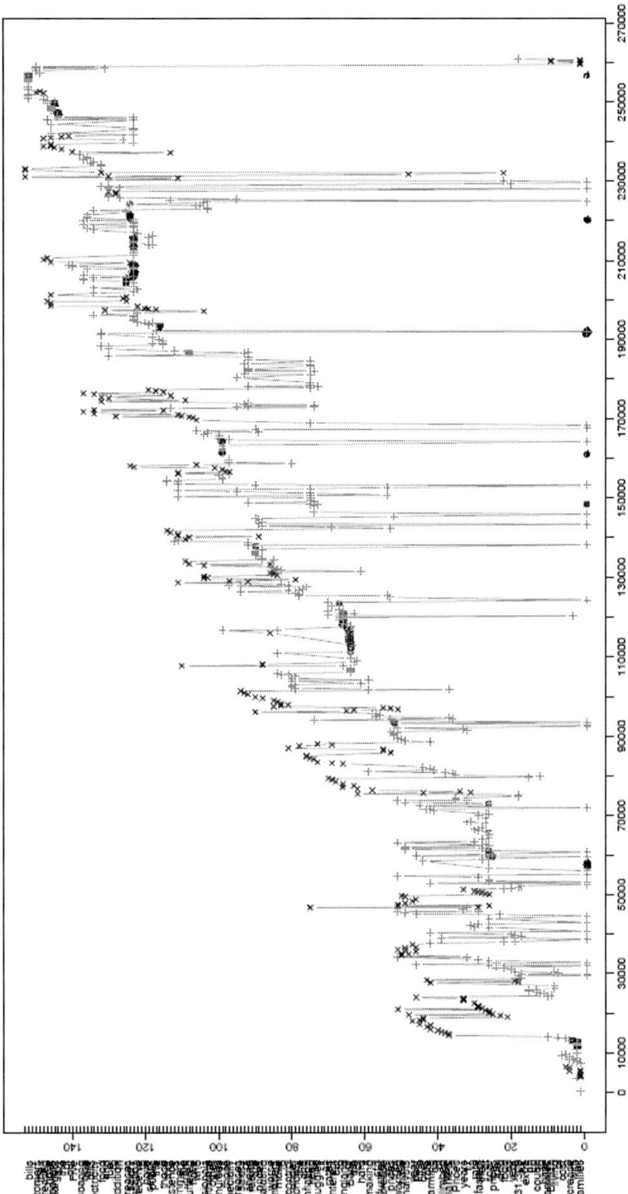

Figure 10-9. Progression graph of a prototypical post-editing task

phase the number of fixations on the source text (symbol ×) are much more frequent than fixations on the target text (symbol +). The final revision phase is seen on the right side of the graph, where the translator focuses on end revision of the target text produced.

An example of prototypical post-editing behaviour among the participants is shown in Figure 10-9. This post-editing progression graph also shows time in milliseconds on the X-axis, and source text words in the Y-axis (T2 in this study). The symbol × again represents fixations on the source text and the symbol + fixations on the target text[7].

Comparing this graph with the one in Figure 10-8 (both representing the processes of participant 05[8] in this study), it is clear that the initial orientation phase and the final revision phase are omitted while post-editing. Much less typing activity is involved in the process and fixations on the target text (represented with the symbol +) are more frequent. Source text fixations (represented with the symbol ×) only appear in parallel with target text fixations and never as a clearly distinct process as is the case during the orientation phase in from-scratch translation. Post-editors generally only refer to the source text after reading the target text and before or after editing the MT output.

The main findings of this exploratory study can be summarized as follows: a) difficult texts took less time to post-edit than to translate from scratch, even though text difficulty was defined in terms of MT quality[9]; b) translators who were slower at translating were not necessarily slower at post-editing; c) overall, post-editing tasks required fewer fixations on source text than translation tasks; d) individually, four out of six participants devoted more gaze time to target than source text across tasks; e) the average fixation duration in source text was longer in translation tasks than in post-editing tasks; f) there were substantial individual differences in the number of transitions from source to target windows.

Conclusion

Overall, these preliminary results support our initial hypothesis that reading patterns differ between translation from scratch and post-editing. Eye movements and gaze time across source and target areas are different when comparing the two tasks. On the one hand, translation from scratch required more time and more fixations in the source text area. On the other hand, post-editing recorded shorter reading times and more fixations in the target text area. With the help of progression graphs, two different styles have also been plotted for translation and post-editing.

Further studies need to be conducted to build new knowledge about the way in which emerging written texts are monitored visually and to discover more about reading patterns in translation and in post-editing. In the future, we anticipate replicating this study with a larger sample in order to be able to generalise our observations to a population as a whole using inferential statistics. As an avenue for future research we also anticipate to use TER/BLEU scores of MT to see whether they correlate with human judgments when classifying texts as difficult/easy to post-edit. Further studies involving different profiles of translators can also reveal new translation and post-editing styles. Previous research has shown that professional translators and novices generally exhibit different translation behaviour (e.g. Jensen 2000, Sharmin et al. 2008, Hvelplund 2011), but there is still a lack of empirical studies about post-editing strategies by different profiles. Building an empirically informed taxonomy of post-editing styles could also inspire the development of advanced translation assistance tools and provide a base for a more successful integration of human machine interaction in post-editing. In particular, gaining knowledge about the role of the source text in post-editing tasks seems a reasonable aim to pursue for the design of specific GUIs for post-editing, since some CAT tools (e.g. SDL Trados Studio, memoQ) already make a distinction between translation and revision modes.

Despite the small number of participants and thus the merely descriptive nature of the results presented here, we hope that this exploratory study will provide further impetus to process-oriented studies, contribute to our better understanding of the nature of translation processes, and motivate us to rise to the challenge of training professional translators for post-editing.

Acknowledgements

The author would like to thank the anonymous peer-reviewers for their insightful and valuable comments on previous versions of this study.

Bibliography

Alves, Fabio, Adriana Pagano, and Igor da Silva. 2009. "New Window on Translators' Cognitive Activity: Methodological Issues in the Combined Use of Eye Tracking, Key Logging and Retrospective Protocols." In *Methodology, Technology and Innovation in Translation Process Research: A Tribute to Arnt Lykke Jakobsen*, edited by Inger M. Mees, Fabio Alves, and Susanne Göpferich, 267-292. Copenhagen: Samfundslitteratur.

Alves, Fabio, Adriana Pagano, and Igor da Silva. 2011. “Towards an Investigation of Reading Modalities in/for Translation: An Exploratory Study Using Eye Tracking Data.” In *Cognitive Explorations of Translation*, edited by Sharon O’ Brien, 175-196. London: Bloomsbury Academic.

Bertram, Raymond, and Jukka Hyönä. 2003. “The length of a complex word modifies the role of morphological structure: evidence from eye movements when reading short and long Finnish compounds.” *Journal of Memory and Language* 48: 615-634.

Carl, Michael. 2012a. “Translog-II: a Program for Recording User Activity Data for Empirical Reading and Writing Research.” In *Proceedings of the Eighth International Conference on Language Resources and Evaluation*, 4108- 4112.

—. 2012b. “The CRITT TPR-DB 1.0: A Database for Empirical Human Translation Process Research.” In *Proceedings of the AMTA 2012 Workshop on Post-Editing Technology and Practice (WPTP 2012)*, edited by Sharon O’Brien, Michel Simard, and Lucia Specia. Stroudsburg, PA: Association for Machine Translation in the Americas, 9-18.

Carl, Michael, and Barbara Dragsted. 2012. “Inside the Monitor Model: Processes of Default and Challenged Translation Production.” *TC3, Translation: Computation, Corpora, Cognition* 2: 127-145.

Carl, Michael, Barbara Dragsted, and Arnt Lykke Jakobsen. 2011. “A Taxonomy of Human Translation Styles.” *Translation Journal* 16.

Carl, Michael, and Martin Kay. 2011. “Gazing and Typing Activities during Translation: A Comparative Study of Translation Units of Professional and Student Translators.” *Meta* 56: 952-975.

Doherty, Stephen, Sharon O'Brien, and Michael Carl. 2010. “Eye Tracking as an MT evaluation technique.” *Machine Translation* 24: 1-13.

Dragsted, Barbara, and Inge Gorm Hansen. 2008. “Comprehension and Production in Translation: A Pilot Study on Segmentation and the Coordination of Reading and Writing Processes.” In *Looking at Eyes. Eye-Tracking Studies of Reading and Translation Processing*, edited by Susanne Göpferich, Arnt Lykke Jakobsen, and Inger M. Mees, 9-29. Copenhagen: Samfundslitteratur.

Frisson, Steven, Keith Rayner and Martin J. Pickering. 1999. “Effects of contextual predictability and transitional probability on eye movements during reading.” *Journal of Experimental Psychology: Learning, Memory and Cognition* 31: 862-877.

Hvelplund, Kristian T. 2011. “Allocation of Cognitive Resources in Translation. An Eye-tracking and Key-logging Study.” PhD diss., Copenhagen Business School.

Hyönä, Jukka, Ralph Radach, and Heiner Deubel, editors. 2003. *The Mind's Eye. Cognitive and Applied Aspects of Eye Movement Research*. Amsterdam: Elsevier.

Jakobsen, Arnt Lykke. 1999. "Logging Target Text Production with Translog." In *Probing the Process in Translation: Methods and Results*, edited by Gyde Hansen, 9-20. Copenhagen: Samfundslitteratur.

Jakobsen, Arnt Lykke. 2002. "Translation Drafting by Professional Translators and by Translation Students." In *Empirical Translation Studies. Process and product*. Edited by Gyde Hansen, 191-204. Copenhagen: Samfundslitteratur.

Jakobsen, Arnt Lykke, and Kristian T. Hvelplund Jensen. 2008. "Eye Movement Behaviour across four Different Types of Reading Tasks." In *Looking at Eyes. Eye-Tracking Studies of Reading and Translation Processing*, edited by Susanne Göpferich, Arnt Lykke Jakobsen, and Inger M. Mees, 103-124. Copenhagen: Samfundslitteratur.

Jensen, Anne. 1999. "Time Pressure in Translation." In *Probing the Process in Translation: Methods and Results*, edited by Gyde Hansen, 103-119. Copenhagen: Samfundslitteratur.

—. 2000. "The Effect of Time on Cognitive Processes and Strategies in Translation." PhD diss., Copenhagen Business School.

Jensen, Christian. 2008. "Assessing Eye-tracking Accuracy in Translation Studies." In *Behind the Mind: Methods, Models and Results in Translation Process Research*, edited by Susanne Göpferich, Arnt Lykke Jakobsen, and Inger M. Mees, 157-174. Copenhagen: Samfundslitteratur.

Jensen, Kristian T. Hvelplund. 2009. "Indicators of Text Complexity." In *Behind the Mind: Methods, Models and Results in Translation Process Research*, edited by Susanne Göpferich, Arnt Lykke Jakobsen, and Inger M. Mees, 61-80. Copenhagen: Samfundslitteratur.

Juhasz, Barbara J., and Keith Rayner. 2003. "Investigating the effects of a set of intercorrelated variables on eye fixation durations in reading." *Journal of Experimental Psychology: Learning, Memory and Cognition* 29: 1312-1318.

Just, Marcel A., and Patricia A. Carpenter. 1980. "A Theory of Reading: from Eye Fixations to Comprehension." *Psychological Review* 87: 329-354.

Kliegl, Reinhold, Ellen Grabner, Martin Rolfs, and Ralf Engbert. 2004. "Length, frequency, and predictability effects of words on eye movements in reading." *European Journal of Cognitive Psychology* 16: 262-284.

Krings, Hans P. 2001. Repairing Texts: Empirical Investigations of Machine Translation Post-Editing Processes, edited by Geoffrey S. Koby. Kent, Ohio: Kent State University Press.

O'Brien, Sharon. 2006. "Eye-Tracking and Translation Memory Matches." *Perspectives: Studies in Translatology* 14: 185-205.

—. 2008. "Processing Fuzzy Matches in Translation Memory Tools–an Eye-tracking Analysis." In *Looking at Eyes. Eye-Tracking Studies of Reading and Translation Processing*, edited by Susanne Göpferich, Arnt Lykke Jakobsen, and Inger M. Mees, 79-102. Copenhagen: Samfundslitteratur.

—. 2010. "Controlled Language and Readability." In *Translation and Cognition*, edited by Gregory M. Shreve and Eric Angelone, 143-168. Amsterdam: John Benjamins.

Pavlović, Natasha, and Kristian T. Hvelplund Jensen. 2009. "Eye Tracking Translation Directionality." In *Translation Research Projects 2*, edited by Anthony Pym and Alexander Perekrestenko, 93-109. Tarragona: Intercultural Studies Group.

Radach, Ralph, Alan Kennedy, and Keith Rayner, editors. 2004. *Eye Movements and Information Processing During Reading*. Hove: Psychology Press.

Rayner, Keith. 1998. "Eye Movements in Reading and Information Processing: 20 Years of Research." *Psychological Bulletin* 124: 372-422.

Rayner, Keith, and Alexander Pollatsek. 1989. *The Psychology of Reading*. Englewood Cliffs, N. J.: Prentice Hall.

Rayner, Keith, and Susana A. Duffy. 1986. "Lexical complexity and fixation times in reading: effects of word frequency, verb complexity, and lexical ambiguity." *Memory and Cognition* 14: 191-201.

Sharmin, Selina, Oleg Špakov, Kari-Jouko Räihä, and Arnt Lykke Jakobsen. 2008. "Where on the Screen do Translation Students Look while Translating, and for How Long?." In *Looking at Eyes. Eye-Tracking Studies of Reading and Translation Processing*, edited by Susanne Göpferich, Arnt Lykke Jakobsen, and Inger M. Mees, 31-51. Copenhagen: Samfundslitteratur.

Vasconcellos, Muriel, and Marjorie León. 1985. "SPANAM and ENGSPAN: Machines Translation at the Pan American Health Organization." *Computational Linguistics* 11: 122-136.

Williams, Rihana, and Robin Morris. 2004. "Eye movements, word familiarity, and vocabulary acquisition." *European Journal of Cognitive Psychology*, 16: 312-339.

Appendix A: Source texts

Text 1- T1 (least complex/difficult to post-edit)

Killer nurse receives four life sentences

Hospital nurse Colin Norris was imprisoned for life today for the killing of four of his patients. 32 year old Norris from Glasgow killed the four women in 2002 by giving them large amounts of sleeping medicine. Yesterday, he was found guilty of four counts of murder following a long trial. He was given four life sentences, one for each of the killings. He will have to serve at least 30 years. Police officer Chris Gregg said that Norris had been acting strangely around the hospital. Only the awareness of other hospital staff put a stop to him and to the killings. The police have learned that the motive for the killings was that Norris disliked working with old people. All of his victims were old weak women with heart problems. All of them could be considered a burden to hospital staff.

Word count: 148. Character count: 671. Sentence count: 10. Words per sentence: 14.8. Characters per word: 4.5

Text 2 - T2 (moderately complex/difficult to post-edit)

Families hit with increase in cost of living

British families have to cough up an extra £31,300 a year as food and fuel prices soar at their fastest rate in 17 years. Prices in supermarkets have climbed at an alarming rate over the past year. Analysts have warned that prices will increase further still, making it hard for the Bank of England to cut interest rates as it struggles to keep inflation and the economy under control. To make matters worse, escalating prices are racing ahead of salary increases, especially those of nurses and other healthcare professionals, who have suffered from the government's insistence that those in the public sector have to receive below-inflation salary increases. In addition to fuel and food, electricity bills are also soaring. Five out of the six largest suppliers have increased their customers' bills.

Word count: 141. Character count: 687. Sentence count: 6. Words per sentence: 23.5. Characters per word: 4.9.

Text 3 - T3 (most complex/difficult to post-edit)

Spielberg shows Beijing red card over Darfur

In a gesture sure to rattle the Chinese Government, Steven Spielberg pulled out of the Beijing Olympics to protest against China's backing for Sudan's policy in Darfur. His withdrawal comes in the wake of fighting flaring up again in Darfur and is set to embarrass China, which has sought to halt the negative fallout from having close ties to the Sudanese government. China, which has extensive investments in the Sudanese oil industry, maintains close links with the Government, which includes one minister charged with crimes against humanity by the International Criminal Court in The Hague. Although emphasizing that Khartoum bears the bulk of the responsibility for these ongoing atrocities, Spielberg maintains that the international community, and particularly China, should do more to end the suffering.

Word count: 132. Character count: 712. Sentence count: 4. Words per sentence: 33. Characters per word: 5.4.

Text 4 - T4 (most complex/difficult to post-edit)

Although developing countries are understandably reluctant to compromise their chances of achieving better standards of living for the poor, action on climate change need not threaten economic development. Incentives must be offered to encourage developing countries to go the extra green mile and implement clean technologies, and could also help minimise emissions from deforestation. Some of the most vulnerable countries of the world have contributed the least to climate change, but are bearing the brunt of it. Developing countries, in particular, need to adapt to the effects of climate change. Adaptation and mitigation efforts must therefore go hand in hand.

Word count: 100. Character count: 558. Sentence count: 5. Words per sentence: 20. Characters per word: 5.6.

Text 5 - T5 (least complex/difficult to post-edit)

Sociology is a relatively new academic discipline. It emerged in the early 19th century in response to the challenges of modernity. Increasing mobility and technological advances resulted in the increasing exposure of people to cultures and societies different from their own. The impact of this exposure was varied, but for some people included the breakdown of traditional norms and customs and warranted a revised understanding of how the world works. Sociologists responded to these changes by trying to understand what holds social groups together and also exploring possible solutions to the breakdown of social solidarity. The term sociology was coined by Auguste Comte (1798-1857) in 1838 from the Latin term socius (companion, associate) and the Greek term logia (study of, speech).

Word count: 122. Character count: 641. Sentence count: 6. Words per sentence: 20.3. Characters per word: 5.3.

Text 6 - T6 (moderately complex/difficult to post-edit)

The majority of hunter-gatherer societies are nomadic. It is difficult to be settled under such a subsistence system as the resources of one region can quickly become exhausted. Hunter-gatherer societies also tend to have very low population densities as a result of their subsistence system. Agricultural subsistence systems can support population densities 60 to 100 times greater than land left uncultivated, resulting in denser populations. Hunter-gatherer societies also tend to have non-hierarchical social structures, though this is not always the case. Because hunter-gatherers tend to be nomadic, they generally do not have the possibility to store surplus food. As a result, full-time leaders, bureaucrats, or artisans are rarely supported by hunter-gatherer societies.

Word count: 119. Character count: 643. Sentence count: 7. Words per sentence: 17. Characters per word: 5.4.

Note: Texts 1, 2 and 3 are borrowed from Hvelplund (2011).

Appendix B: Supplementary tables

	Task 1: Translation				Task 2: Post-editing			
P01	**T1**	12:22 [5.01]	**T2**	10:19 [4.39]	**T3**	06:58 [2.71]	**T4**	04:41 [2.81]
P02	**T3**	14:41 [6.25]	**T4**	10:58 [6.58]	**T5**	07:53 [3.88]	**T6**	08:42 [4.39]
P03	**T5**	08:40 [3.94]	**T6**	07:53 [3.97]	**T1**	06:03 [4.07]	**T2**	04:37 [1.96]
P04	**T2**	10:19 [6.19]	**T1**	11:06 [4.50]	**T4**	05:21 [3.21]	**T3**	03:27 [1.57]
P05	**T6**	09:07 [4.48]	**T5**	11:34 [5.69]	**T2**	06:11 [4.76]	**T1**	10:52 [4.41]
P06	**T4**	17:02 [8.59]	**T3**	11:02 [5.02]	**T6**	05:22 [2.71]	**T5**	05:14 [2.57]

Table i. Task times in minutes per participant and text

	Task 1: Translation				Task 2: Post-editing			
		Fixations ST / TT		Fixations ST / TT		Fixations ST / TT		Fixations ST / TT
P01	**T1**	1184 [8]/388	**T2**	1378 [9.77]/460	**T3**	578 [4.38]/440	**T4**	720 [7.20]/192
P02	**T3**	2298 [17.4]/1600	**T4**	1652 [16.52]/1394	**T5**	826 [6.77]/1668	**T6**	600 [5.04]/1352
P03	**T5**	1016 [8.3]/1288	**T6**	1044 [8.7]/1480	**T1**	424 [2.86]/1684	**T2**	432 [3.06]/956
P04	**T2**	2246 [15.9]/1490	**T1**	1676 [11.3]/1572	**T4**	1182 [11.82]/1080	**T3**	726 [5.50]/658
P05	**T6**	1048 [8.8]/1824	**T5**	1154 [9.4]/2332	**T2**	522 [3.70]/1648	**T1**	956 [6.46]/2642
P06	**T4**	2062 [20.6]/2304	**T3**	1310 [9.9]/1472	**T6**	470 [3.95]/1316	**T5**	640 [5.25]/1004

Table ii. Fixation count per participant in source (ST) and target (TT) areas

Notes

[1] EYE-to-IT - Development of Human-Computer Monitoring and Feedback Systems for the Purposes of Studying Cognition and Translation. Available at http://cordis.europa.eu/fp7/ict/fet-open/portfolio-eyetoit_en.html [accessed 1 March 2013].

[2] The fixation duration threshold was set at a minimum of 100 milliseconds.

[3] In this study, gaze time refers to fixation duration multiplied by fixation count. Although this variable can be predicted from the first two, it is presented as a variable itself in order to make observations on how much time was spent on source text and target text windows overall.

---

[4] Transitions must be understood as gaze shifts between source and target windows in Translog-II.

[5] CRITT Translation Process Research (TPR) Database. Available at http://bridge.cbs.dk/platform/?q=CRITT_TPR-db [accessed 1 March 2013].

[6] The order between the two tasks was not rotated in this exploratory study (translation was always the first task), but such a rotation will certainly have to be introduced in future studies in order to avoid potential order effects.

[7] For more information on how to interpret these progressions graphs, see Carl et al. (2011).

[8] For the purpose of plotting user activity data in a progression graph, participant 05 was selected for being the one with more years of experience both in translation and post-editing.

[9] The author acknowledges that it can be problematic to assume that those texts where the corresponding MT was rated as more difficult to post-edit will also be more difficult to translate from scratch. However, what this result shows is that, even for poor quality MT, post-editing can be faster than translating from scratch. Also, the categorisation in this study overlaps with that of Hvelplund (2011) whose texts were also part of this study.

CHAPTER ELEVEN

PAUSES AND COGNITIVE EFFORT IN POST-EDITING

ISABEL LACRUZ AND GREGORY M. SHREVE

Abstract

A major objective of machine translation programs is to produce output with errors that are few in number and that are easy to correct at the post-editing stage. However, it is difficult to measure how well a program meets this objective for human post-editors. It is challenging to measure directly the cognitive demand imposed on a post-editor by errors in machine translations or the cognitive effort expended by the post-editor in fixing such errors. We discuss the components of cognitive effort and propose readily calculable indicators of cognitive effort in post-editing machine translations. These indicators are based on the identification of short pauses in keystroke log reports and the observation that short pauses are more abundant when post-editors tackle cognitively effortful segments in machine translation output. We identify cognitive effort indirectly by computing the density of complete editing events.

Introduction

In a previous study, Lacruz et al. (2012) introduced the average pause ratio (APR) as a promising metric for distinguishing between machine translation (MT) passages that require higher or lower levels of cognitive effort from the post-editor. The rationale was based on evidence that pauses are well-known indicators of cognitive effort in monolingual and bilingual language processing and in translation (e.g., Schilperoord, 1996; Krings, 2001; Dragsted and Hansen, 2008; Shreve et al., 2011.) In this chapter, we present further evidence for the usefulness of the APR metric in studying cognitive effort in post-editing. We also expand the discussion to introduce related measures that are suggested by a closer examination of the nature of the cognitive effort expended by the post-editor and the cognitive demand imposed by MT.

The MT post-editor must expend a variety of different types of effort. Krings (2001: 531) identified three components: temporal, technical, and cognitive effort. Temporal effort refers to the time spent on the post-edit, and technical effort refers to the amount of keyboard and mouse activity undertaken, while cognitive effort refers to the effort involved in mental processing. Krings proposed that temporal effort is a combination of cognitive and technical effort. While temporal and technical effort can be measured directly through timing and direct observation of activity, cognitive effort can only be measured indirectly.

In general, psychologists define cognitive effort as "the amount of the available processing capacity of the limited-capacity central processor utilized in performing an information-processing task" (Tyler et al., 1979.) In other words, cognitive effort is the total amount of mental resources that must be deployed by an individual to accomplish a given task (Cooper-Martin, 1994.) The total availability of mental resources determines cognitive capacity, which is always limited and will vary considerably from one individual to another. So, cognitive effort will be subject to considerable individual differences (Kellogg, 1987), since any one task will require some individuals to use a greater proportion of their available cognitive resources than others.

The amount of cognitive effort an individual expends while working on a task has typically been assessed using the dual task paradigm (see, for example, Olive, 2003). In dual task experiments, a participant is subjected to a distracting task, which competes for mental resources needed to carry out the primary task. Measurements are made of the increase in time needed to complete the primary task compared with the time needed to complete it when it is performed free from the distraction.

Time measurements relate directly to Krings' concept of temporal effort, which in his view is a combination of technical and cognitive effort. Technical effort is relatively easy to measure, while cognitive effort is more difficult to measure. In post-editing, there is no simple relationship between technical and cognitive effort. For example, one post-edit decision may be easy and quick to make, but the edit action may involve a considerable amount of typing, while another decision may require a great deal of thought, with the actual edit action requiring only a few keystrokes. However, we shall provide evidence below that cognitive effort is related to technical effort, specifically to the patterns of pauses the post-editor makes during the post-editing task. All of this must be accommodated within the expectation of substantial individual differences.

One important source of individual differences is expertise. However, while expertise is likely to influence expenditure of cognitive effort in post-editing, its effects can pull in opposite directions. One characteristic of expertise is a high level of automatic processing, which is associated with a low level of cognitive effort. However, experts are better able to be creative than novices, and creativity is associated with high levels of cognitive effort (see, for example, Kellogg, 1997: 231). In some situations, novices take longer than experts to accomplish a given translation task (see, for example, Göpferich et al., 2011) possibly because they engage in lesser amounts of automatic cognitive processing than experts. This would require them to exert more cognitive effort, and consequently more temporal effort. On the other hand, there are circumstances where expert translators will expend more cognitive effort than novices. For example, Pinto (2004) finds that expert translators engage in more cognitive effort than novices during the orientation and revision phases of translation–phases that may offer more scope for creative thinking. In the context of post-editing, though, little work appears to have been done to understand the roles of automaticity and creativity or to investigate how expertise relates to cognitive effort.

The cognitive effort exerted by post-editors will be driven by an interaction between the internal factors of their available cognitive resources and the extent to which they need to be allocated (which will be influenced by a variety of factors, including expertise), and the external factor of MT quality. This external factor of MT quality imposes cognitive demand on the post-editor. Work is ongoing in an attempt to find good objective measures of cognitive demand in post-editing, and progress has been made in identifying a taxonomy of MT errors on a scale of increasing demand (from typographical as least demanding to word order as most demanding) (Temnikova, 2010; Koponen et al., 2012.) It is apparent, however, that there are individual differences in responses to the same MT errors. For example, some post-editors may expend considerable cognitive effort in struggling to find a solution for a necessary edit to an MT error, such as a mistranslation of an idiomatic expression. For others, however, the translation equivalents of the idiomatic expression may be immediately available, in which case the post-edit could be made with little expenditure of cognitive effort. In other words, the same MT text may, at various points, impose different levels of cognitive demand on different post-editors. The same post-editing task may therefore elicit different levels of cognitive effort from different post-editors.

In addition, individual post-editors can make very different choices about how and what to post-edit when they are presented with the same MT output. Such differences may be related to variation in the cognitive demand placed on the post-editors. In this study, one source text (ST) input and the corresponding MT output were:

ST: Los Mac serán americanos.
MT: The Mac will be Americans.

This elicited different post-editing decisions:

Participant A: The Mac will be American.
Participant C: Macs will be Americans.

Both post-editors recognized the agreement error in the MT segment, but they chose to address it differently. Interestingly, this segment's keystroke log data for Participant C shows a greater density of short pauses than for Participant A. According to the pause metric (APR) proposed as an index of cognitive effort in Lacruz and Shreve (2012) this difference is consistent with Participant C exerting more cognitive effort than Participant A in post-editing this segment. This in turn suggests that the cognitive demand imposed on Participant C by the syntactic error in the MT output was greater than the cognitive demand imposed on Participant A - consistent with the fact that Participant A selected a correct solution, while Participant C's solution is in error.

The effort to identify good objective measures of MT quality is an important one, and such measures will be valuable tools in assessing how demanding a post-editing task might be. However, as we have argued, such measures will not always coincide with a post-editor's subjective assessment of quality–and it is the subjective assessment of quality that will actually co-determine the cognitive demand on that post-editor. This actual cognitive demand determines the degree of the challenge imposed by the post-editing task. Although the cognitive demand will influence the cognitive effort the individual post-editor expends, the cognitive demand will not completely determine the cognitive effort. Cognitive effort corresponds to the amount of cognitive resources the post-editor deploys to carry out the post-editing task, and this may be influenced by many factors other than the cognitive demand. Such factors might include conscientiousness or willingness to do a good job. Accordingly, it is not straightforward to measure how objectively determined quality of a particular MT text relates either to the cognitive demand it places on an individual post-editor or to the cognitive effort exerted by that post-editor.

In the absence of direct measures of the actual cognitive demand that MT imposes on a specific post-editor, Lacruz et al. (2012) focused instead on quantifying the cognitive effort expended by each post-editor. In fact, Lacruz et al. did not carefully track the distinction between cognitive demand and cognitive effort, using the two implicitly related concepts somewhat interchangeably. They quantified the cognitive effort expended through measurements of the only tangible evidence of cognitive effort in the post-editor's end-product–the actual edits made. They worked with the notion of a complete editing event, a "collection of individual editing actions that can be considered to naturally form part of the same overall action." This approach to measuring cognitive effort by (and so, implicitly, cognitive demand on) an individual post-editor has some aspects in common with the Post Editing Action (PEA) approach of Blain et al. (2011.)

The notion of a complete editing event in post-editing is related to the concept of a macro translation unit; in addition, a complete editing event may be composed of several post-editing analogues of micro translation units (Alves and Vale, 2009.) Typically, complete editing events are separated by long pauses (5 seconds or more.) They normally contain short pauses (more than 0.5 seconds, but less than 2 seconds,) and more effortful complete editing events will often include multiple short pauses. Post-editors may make intermediate duration pauses (more than 2 seconds, but less than 5 seconds) during a complete editing event, for instance when they are debating between two options. For example, a post-editor, doubting whether to type "have done' or "did", might begin typing part of "have", but then, after reconsideration, possibly after an intermediate length pause, might delete the initial attempt before typing "did". The false start and the final solution would be considered as part of the same complete editing event. However, although the pause patterns act as a good guide to what constitutes a complete editing event, the determining characteristic is that a complete editing event is a sequence of actions leading to linguistically coherent and complete output.

There are situations where a post-editor will finish a first pass through a segment, with actions comprising several complete editing events, but will then return to a part of the text early in the segment corresponding to a complete editing event that has already been finished. If the post-editor then re-edits that part of the text to change the previous output into another version that is also linguistically coherent and complete, we view that second revision as a further complete editing event.

To provide a concrete example of how post-editing actions are partitioned into complete editing events, consider the following source text (ST) sentence, its corresponding MT output, and the final target text (TT) output after post-editing by one of the participants in this study:

> ST: Con cualquier otra red sería un éxito absoluto tras un año y medio de vida.
> MT: With any other network would be an absolute success after a year and a half old.
> TT: Any other network would be an absolute success a year and a half after its creation.

The Translog log file revealed two complete editing events in the post-editing activity.

After an initial long pause (36.863 sec), the participant made two rapid cursor movements and then made a second long pause (17.051 sec.) The first complete editing event followed. The participant began the complete editing event by rapidly deleting the words "With a", backspacing character by character, made a short pause (0.936 sec,) and then typed "A" to finish the complete editing event.

There was a long pause (23.088 sec) before the initiation of the second complete editing event. This event began with two back to back short pauses (1.451 sec and 1.210 sec) accompanying cursor movements. Then the participant rapidly deleted "old", backspacing character by character, paused for 0.858 sec, and rapidly typed "after its creation". A moderate length pause (2.730 sec) accompanied cursor movement, and then the participant briefly paused (0.718 sec) before finishing the complete editing event by rapidly deleting "after", backspacing character by character.

Each of these two complete editing events could be interpreted as linguistically coherent sequences of actions, which are comparable to Alves and Vale's (2009) macro translation units. They are composed of micro units separated by pauses of various durations.

Lacruz et al. (2012) divided a source text into sentences (or sometimes clauses) to be treated as stand-alone translation units. They referred to these and their MT or post-edited equivalents as segments. After identifying the complete editing events in the target text, they labelled an MT segment as requiring high cognitive effort on the part of the post-editor when a high number of complete editing events could be identified in the corresponding TT segment. Conversely, an MT segment required low cognitive effort from the post-editor when the number of complete editing events was low. The assumption was that each editing event resulted from a coherent expenditure of cognitive effort in post-editing the MT segment. So, the more events there were, the higher the effort would have been. This measure of cognitive effort during the post-editing process is somewhat coarse grained, since it assumes all complete editing events are equal: it assigns the same weight to all complete editing events and does not differentiate between different levels of cognitive effort in response to different types of errors in MT.

Rationale

We do not here attempt to assign weights to different types of complete editing events. However, we do propose other refinements of the measure used in Lacruz et al. (2012). The use of the TT to identify the complete editing events is not ideal. In fact, consistent with comments in Koponen et al. (2012), more information can be captured by identifying complete editing events from the keystroke log report. For example, in some cases participants completed an edit, but then removed or replaced it one or more times at a later stage. Such indecision was likely the result of repeated episodes of cognitive effort made by the post-editor and should not be ignored. Removals and replacements of this sort in post-editing are actions that are analogous to what Alves and Vale (2009) refer to as micro units in the context of from-scratch translation. Once an edit has been made, the working segment has undergone a change, and, with it, the post-editor's perception of that segment has also changed. Consequently, any subsequent change to a change should be viewed as a new complete editing event. Another issue is that the raw count of complete editing events gives no indication of the density of the effort. For example, there is much more concentrated effort when there are five complete editing events in a short segment than when there are five complete editing events in a long segment. For these reasons, our principal index of cognitive effort in post-editing will be the event to word ratio (EWR), where the number of complete editing events is computed from the keystroke log report. EWR is, naturally, an indirect index of cognitive effort. Specifically, for each segment

$$\text{EWR} = \frac{\text{number of complete editing events in key−log report}}{\text{number of words}}.$$

It should be noted that while EWR does succeed in capturing density of effort, it cannot distinguish how the level of cognitive effort varies during the time course of individual complete editing events, or how the overall level varies from one event to another.

The time taken to post-edit a segment should give an indication of the cognitive effort expended, even though such data do not explicitly measure cognitive effort. Very recently, Koponen et al. (2012) investigated post-editing time as a measure of cognitive effort. They cited the work of Koponen (2012) that uncovered discrepancies between Human-targeted Translation Error Rate (HTER) scores and expected time to post-edit. HTER measures the smallest number of single edit actions (such as insertions, deletions, and so on) required to convert an MT product into its final post-edited version (Snover et al. 2006,). Thus, HTER is a measure of technical effort, and so an indirect measure of cognitive effort. Specifically, Koponen found that, in some cases, low HTER scores were unexpectedly associated with high subjective rankings of post-editing effort, and vice versa. Koponen et al. proposed that by focusing on post-editing time it might be possible to measure cognitive effort in post-editing in a simple manner, and they provided evidence to support this view. One of the parameters they considered was the average time it took to process a word in a segment; they used the acronym SPW (seconds per word.) We shall refer to this parameter as the average word time (AWT). Koponen et al. demonstrated a correlation with HTER, namely, as the HTER score increased, the AWT value also increased. In other words, the average post-editing time per word tended to be longer in texts where the required cognitive effort (predicted by HTER scores) was higher. We further investigate this finding, using EWR as our index of cognitive effort.

Our main objective, however, is to gauge cognitive effort through an examination of pause activity in keystroke log reports of post-editing sessions. As we pointed out in the Introduction, pauses during production are well-known indicators of cognitive effort in monolingual and bilingual language processing and in translation (e.g., Schilperoord, 1996; Krings, 2001; Dragsted and Hansen, 2008; Shreve et al., 2011.) We plan to investigate correlations between pause metrics (and associated metrics) and the EWR index of cognitive effort. All of these metrics measure individual patterns of behaviour during the post-editing process–a process where we have previously observed significant individual differences.

Keystroke log reports of post-editing provide a record and a time stamp of the onset of all actions during a session. Actions that are time stamped include keystroking (addition or deletion of characters) and mouse movements, as well as cut, paste, and delete actions. The time taken between time stamps is considered a pause. Most pauses are extremely short (one or two hundred milliseconds) and reflect the physical constraints of the typing task. For example, typing 'word' requires four different keystrokes, and it is physically impossible to make all of those keystrokes without short pauses between strokes. However, the transcripts also show noticeably longer pauses, and a common interpretation of these pauses is that they are associated with the effort of mental processing (O'Brien, 2006.) There is no sharp boundary between pause durations corresponding to technical effort and pause durations corresponding to cognitive effort, and it is likely that there is overlap between the two. Previous authors have generally used a minimum pause duration threshold of one second to study cognitive effort (O'Brien, 2006). Lacruz et al. (2012) chose a threshold of .5 seconds, based on observations that keystroke log reports of post-editing contained many pauses as short as .5 seconds which were not obviously associated with the typing process. However, their patterns of results were not sensitive to this particular choice of threshold, and were in fact replicated at one second and two second thresholds. Here, we again choose to work with a .5 second minimum pause duration threshold.

Unexpectedly, O'Brien (2006) did not find an association between pause ratio (PR), defined by

$$PR = \frac{\text{total pause time in segment}}{\text{total time in segment}},$$

and levels of cognitive effort exerted by the post-editor that she had predicted from differences in negative translatability factors in the source text. In fact, the negative translatability indicators impose cognitive demand on the post-editor. In the same way as we noted above, there is an implicit assumption that the level of cognitive effort expended by an individual post-editor is directly related to the objectively determined cognitive demand imposed by the negative translatability indicators. This objectively determined cognitive demand is not necessarily at the same level as the subjective demand experienced by the individual post-editor, which may explain the lack of the expected effect in O'Brien's study.

However, there are potentially other reasons why O'Brien's pause ratio metric did not correlate with cognitive effort. We had previously observed keystroke log reports for post-edits in response to apparently cognitively demanding MT errors, such as correcting literal translations of idiomatic expressions or word order errors (Lacruz et al. 2012.) Reports of such post-edits frequently exhibited clusters of short pauses (.5 seconds to 2 seconds), sometimes in addition to longer pauses (greater than 5 seconds.) It is possible that such longer pauses correspond to sustained reflection on how to solve the problem posed by the MT output, and some short pauses correspond to some sort of monitoring that accompanies the production of the target text. This may occur more often in situations that are not straightforward and so require high levels of cognitive effort from the post-editor. We had also previously observed keystroke log reports for post-edits that were apparently simpler to execute, such as correcting capitalization errors or incorrect word forms. These frequently exhibited lower densities of short pauses (Lacruz et al. 2012.)

Observations such as these led Lacruz et al. (2012) to propose implicitly that high pause densities during post-editing should be an indicator of high levels of cognitive effort. High densities of short pauses will tend to produce low average pause times during post-editing, but will not necessarily have a major impact on the total pause time. This insight led Lacruz et al. to propose that a modification of pause ratio might give information about the cognitive effort expended during the post-editing of a segment. They defined the average pause ratio (APR) in post-editing an MT segment as

$$\text{APR} = \frac{\text{average time per pause}}{\text{average time per word}};$$

in other words, APR is the average pause time scaled to account for the overall speed of processing.

To highlight the sensitivity of APR to varying densities of short pauses, we consider three examples in which a twenty-word segment is post-edited in a total time of 60 seconds, of which 40 seconds are spent in pauses and 20 seconds are spent in action, such as typing or moving the mouse. Neither the specific thresholds for long and short pauses nor the actual durations of individual pauses are significant for these examples, and they are not used directly in APR calculations. The point of using the short/long pause distinction here is to give concrete examples to build intuition and to help conceptualize how APR is affected by different general types of situations. In each of the cases we use for illustration, the average time per word is the total time in the segment (60 seconds) divided by the number of words in the segment (20). In other words, the average time per word is three seconds.

Let us first examine a case where there is a low density, say 20%, of short pauses. This would occur, for example, if there were one short pause of total duration one second and four long pauses of total duration 39 seconds. In this low density case, there would be five pauses of total duration 40 seconds, and so the average time per pause would be 40/5 = 8 seconds.

The APR, the ratio of average time per pause to average time per word, would be 8/3.

Next, we consider a case where there is a medium density, say 50%, of short pauses. An example might be where there are five short pauses of total duration four seconds and five long pauses of total duration 36 seconds. In this medium density case, there would be ten pauses of total duration 40 seconds, resulting in an average pause time of 40/10 = 4 seconds. The APR would be 4/3.

Finally, we make a computation for a case where there is a high density, say 80%, of short pauses. Such a situation would occur if there were, for example, 16 short pauses of total duration ten seconds and four long pauses of total duration 30 seconds. In this high density case, there would be 20 pauses of total duration 40 seconds, and so an average pause time of 40/20 = 2 seconds. The APR would be 2/3.

These are examples where the total pause time was held constant to make the comparisons simpler. However, the same general patterns can be seen in less artificially controlled situations. In our examples, as the density of short pauses moved from low to medium to high, the APR halved at each stage, moving from 8/3 to 4/3 to 2/3. This progression illustrates a phenomenon that will be important as the discussion develops: post-edited segments where the density of short pauses is high compared with the density of long pauses will have small APRs, while post-edited segments where the density of short pauses is low compared with the density of long pauses will have large APRs. We shall also see that O'Brien's pause ratio metric is relatively insensitive to variations in the density of short pauses.

Lacruz et al. (2012) showed, in a case study, that APR was sensitive to different levels of cognitive demand in an MT segment, when cognitive demand was measured by the number of complete editing events identified in the TT segment. Consistent with the observations of clustering of short pauses during the post-editing of difficult units, Lacruz et al. found that APR was lower in higher cognitive demand segments.

Recall that previous work by O'Brien (2006) showed that the pause ratio metric did not discriminate between MT segments where it was predicted that the post-editor would need to expend higher and lower levels of cognitive effort. Predicted levels of cognitive effort were based on objectively measured properties of the source text (ST). A clue to this apparent lack of discrimination can be found in the three example calculations of APR above. APR was very different for the illustrative segments with high, medium, and low densities of short pauses. However, since both the total time in pause (40 seconds) and the total time in segment (60 seconds) did not change from one scenario to another, PR did not change either. In all cases it was 40/60 = 2/3.

The evidence from prior observations of APR and PR suggests that the pause to word ratio (PWR) for a segment, defined as

$$\text{PWR} = \frac{\text{number of pauses in segment}}{\text{number of words in segment}},$$

might be an even simpler measure of cognitive effort expended in post-editing that takes timing out of the equation: since

$$\frac{\text{average pause time}}{\text{average word time}} = \frac{(\text{total time in pause})/(\text{number of pauses})}{(\text{total time in segment})/(\text{number of words})},$$

an alternative way to express average pause ratio is APR = PR/PWR.

Lacruz et al. found the average pause ratio to be lower in higher cognitive effort segments, while O'Brien found that level of cognitive effort did not influence the pause ratio. Consequently, it should be the case that the pause to word ratio varies with cognitive effort in the opposite direction from average pause ratio. Accordingly, we predict that pause to word ratio will be higher in higher cognitive effort segments, when cognitive effort is indexed by EWR.

Let us illustrate this abstract discussion in the context of the previous concrete examples, where the number of words in a segment was held constant at 20. The pause ratio was always the same in these examples, with a value of 2/3. Recall that in the case where there was a high density of short pauses (which we propose is a marker of high levels of cognitive effort), the APR was 2/3. The total number of pauses was 20, and so the PWR would be 20/20 = 1. At the other end of the spectrum, when there was a low density of short pauses (which we propose is a marker of low levels of cognitive effort), the APR was 8/3, four times as high as before. On the other hand, since the total number of pauses was 5, the PWR would be 5/20, a quarter of the value in the high density example. These examples are in line with our predictions that pause to word ratio will be higher and average pause ratio will be lower in segments where higher cognitive effort (as indexed by EWR) has been measured.

To recap, we propose that an individualized outcome measure, the event to word ratio (EWR) can be used to gauge a post-editor's cognitive effort during the post-editing process. We suggest that higher complete editing event densities, which result in higher EWR values, indicate higher levels of cognitive effort.

We carry out a more extensive observational study than that of Lacruz et al. (2012). Our primary objective is to investigate the correlation between cognitive effort (as indexed by EWR) and various pause metrics measured during the post-editing process. Pause metrics are of interest in the study of cognitive effort in post-editing, since pauses have been shown to indicate cognitive effort in monolingual language contexts and in translation and interpreting (see references above). The pause metrics we focus on are average pause ratio (APR), pause ratio (PR), and pause to word ratio (PWR). Average pause ratio and pause ratio are computed using pause times, while pause to word ratio is computed using pause counts. These three pause metrics are related through the formula

$$APR = PR/PWR.$$

Our predictions are that, for each post-editor,

- APR decreases as EWR increases;
- PR does not change as EWR changes;
- PWR increases as EWR increases.

The first two predictions are motivated by the previous finding of Lacruz et al. (2012) and O'Brien (2006), respectively. The third is consistent with the formula above, provided the previous two predictions are confirmed.

The definition of the average pause ratio, APR, is in terms of the average time per pause in a segment (the average pause time, APT) and the average processing time per word in a segment (the average word time, AWT):

$$APR = APT/AWT.$$

As mentioned previously, Koponen et al. (2012) found a relationship between cognitive effort in post-editing and AWT, namely that AWT increases as cognitive effort increases. As a secondary objective, we investigate correlations between cognitive effort (as indexed by EWR) and the additional metrics of average pause time and average word time. We predict that, consistent with previous findings,

- APT decreases as cognitive effort (EWR) increases;
- AWT increases as cognitive effort (EWR) increases.

These opposite tendencies, if confirmed, would reinforce each other in the formula APR = APT/AWT, unpacking the mechanism for APR to decrease as EWR increases. The correlations of APT and AWT with EWR would, however, necessarily be weaker than that of APR with EWR.

Method

We collected data from four participants. Results from one participant had to be discarded. This participant's pause data were not meaningful in this setting, due to internet use during the post-editing session. Of the remaining three, Participant A was a professional translator with six years of experience, and with L1 English and L2 Spanish. The other two participants were second-year master's students in Spanish translation with some professional experience: participant B with L1 English and L2 Spanish, and participant C with L1 Spanish and L2 English.

There were two source texts, each in versions I and II. The two I texts were part of an article on technology published in a Spanish newspaper. The two II texts were slightly altered versions of the corresponding I texts. (The intent was to compare some results between the two versions of each text. This proved to be impossible, due to the problems with the data from one participant.) All texts were translated into English using Google Translate. The texts were divided into segments roughly corresponding to sentences. Since these were authentic or close to authentic texts, sentence length varied considerably; segment length ranged from 5 to 30 words with a mean of 17.4 words (median 17 words.) Both versions of one text had ten segments and both versions of the other text had 16 segments.

Participants were seated individually in front of a computer in a quiet office, and each was asked to post-edit two MT texts. Participants were instructed to ignore stylistic issues and to concentrate on the meaning. No time limits were set.

The complete source text, divided up into numbered segments, was displayed at the top of the screen. The MT text, divided up into numbered segments matching those of the source text, was displayed at the bottom of the screen. Post-edits were made directly into the presented MT text.

The software program Translog was used to record the keystroke log of the post-editing process. Participants were first given one text to post-edit. When they had completed this task, the researcher saved the file and then presented them with a second text for post-editing.

Results and discussion

The number of pauses, the length of the pauses, and the overall time in segment were extracted from an Excel version of the Translog log files. Other parameters were computed in Excel from these data.

As the participants did not systematically post-edit the same versions of the texts, it was not possible to average meaningfully across participants without losing data from an already restricted set. This problem was compounded by the fact that Participant A made no post-edits in a total of six segments. For these reasons, this investigation was treated as three separate case studies, one for each participant. Apart from baseline checks for consistency with the results from Lacruz et al. (2012), all analyses were correlational.

Since these were correlational case studies of participants carrying out very similar, but not identical assignments, it is not possible to make any claim of generalizability. Nevertheless, it is notable that although the three participants had very different characteristics and there were substantial individual differences in their post-edits, the overall patterns of results were consistent from participant to participant. Consequently, it would be interesting to carry out follow-up studies in a controlled experimental setting.

Replication of the APR effect in Lacruz et al. (2012)

The first analysis was carried out to investigate whether the result from Lacruz et al. (2012) had been replicated in this slightly different setting. In the current setting, the source texts were in Spanish, rather than in English; the segments were presented all at once, rather than sequentially; the data were recorded using Translog, rather than Inputlog. In the previous case study, APR was lower for segments where cognitive effort was higher; cognitive effort in post-editing a segment was measured by the number of complete editing events in the segment. We predicted the same outcome in the current experiment, based on our expectation that segments that required more cognitive effort to post-edit would generally show a greater density of short pauses than segments that required less cognitive effort. Since this was a directional prediction, we used a one-tailed analysis. We also used one-tailed analyses when evaluating other directional predictions later in the chapter.

For each participant, we combined the results for both texts. Just as in Lacruz et al., segments were designated as higher cognitive effort if the number of complete editing events in the TT was four or greater and lower cognitive effort if the number of complete editing events was two or fewer. This was the only feasible cut for a reasonable analysis, but it was not as natural in Lacruz et al., where there were very few segments with three complete editing events.

While there were substantial individual differences in the participants' post-editing output, in all cases the mean APR for higher cognitive effort segments was lower than the mean APR for lower cognitive effort segments. See Figure 11-1. Using the sequential Bonferroni correction in one-tailed *t*-tests (see Abdi, 2010 for a clear explanation), the difference was significant for participant A ($t(12.682) = 2.786$, $p_{\text{Bonferroni}, 1|3} = .024$) and for participant C ($t(11.122) = 2.805$, $p_{\text{Bonferroni}, 2|3} = .018$), while for participant B ($t(17) = 1.473$, $p_{\text{Bonferroni}, 3|3} = .080$) the difference approached significance. The previous result from Lacruz et al. was thus replicated.

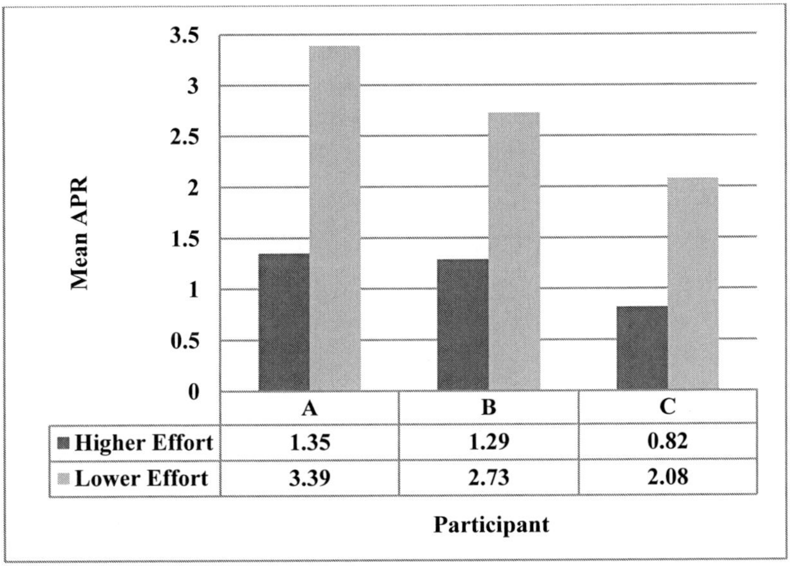

Figure 11-1. Mean average pause ratios for higher and lower cognitive effort segments (effort measured by number of complete editing events).

Interestingly, the APRs decreased in both higher and lower cognitive effort segments as post-editing experience and TT language proficiency decreased. This is consistent with the finding in other contexts that overall cognitive effort is greater for novices than for experts (Göpferich et al., 2011.) See, however, Pinto (2004).

The replication analysis measured cognitive effort using counts of complete editing events. From this point on, we shall use the event to word ratio, EWR, as our indicator of cognitive effort.

APR and the EWR index of cognitive effort

In the replication analysis, in order to contrast the mean APRs for higher and lower cognitive effort segments, it was necessary to create some distance between these categories by discarding some of the data. From this point on, we shall work with the complete data set for each of the participants, studying the correlations between the variables of interest. We shall always combine the data for the two texts post-edited by each participant.

Following standard convention in the behavioral sciences, we use Cohen's (1988) classification of correlation strength: correlation is considered strongly positive if the Pearson correlation coefficient r is at least 0.5, moderately positive if r is between 0.3 and 0.5, and weakly positive if r is between 0.1 and 0.3. On the other hand, correlation is considered strongly negative if r is at most -0.5, moderately negative if r is between -0.3 and -0.5, and weakly negative if r is between -0.1 and -0.3.

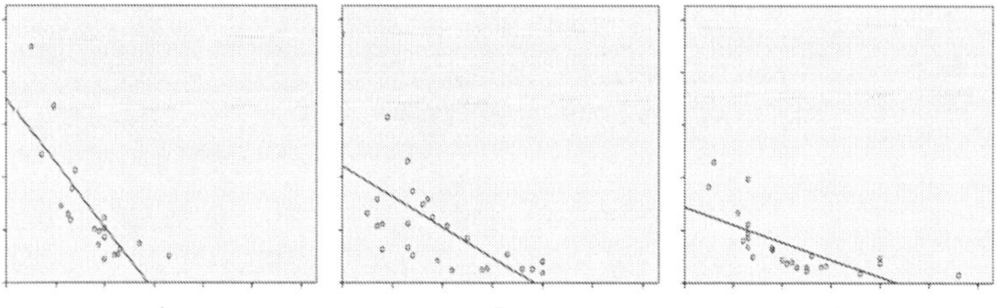

Figure 11-2: Scatterplots with regression lines of APR against EWR, by participant. APR (vertical axis; scale 0 to 10); EWR (horizontal axis, scale 0.0 to 0.6).

Since the previous findings on the relationship between APR and cognitive effort were replicated, we predicted that for our more sensitive index (EWR) of cognitive effort, APR would be lower for segments with higher EWR. The rationale was the same as before: we expected a higher density of short pauses, and so a lower APR, in more cognitively effortful segments. In a one-tailed analysis, there was significant strong negative correlation between APR and cognitive effort (as indexed by EWR) for all three participants, even using the conservative Bonferroni correction. In other words, for each participant there was a strong tendency for APR to decrease as EWR increased. This corresponds to higher cognitive effort when short pause density is higher. For Participant A, $r = -.797$, $N = 20$, $p_{Bonferroni} < .01$; for Participant B, $r = -.650$, $N = 26$, $p_{Bonferroni} < .01$; for Participant C, $r = -.685$, $N = 25$, $p_{Bonferroni} < .01$. Results were also significant in a two-tailed analysis.

Scatterplots, together with regression lines, are shown in Figure 11-2. These scatterplots clearly indicate substantial individual differences.

Pause Ratio

Previous studies had found no relationship between pause ratio (PR) and cognitive effort in post-editing. The present results, where we index cognitive effort by EWR, are more nuanced, but show no consistent pattern from one participant to another.

Since we were not predicting a directional effect, we used a two-tailed analysis. Using the sequential Bonferroni correction (Abdi, 2010), for Participant A, there was weak positive correlation between PR and EWR that was not significant; $r = .164$, $N = 20$, $p_{Bonferroni,\ 3|3} = .480$. For Participant B, there was moderate negative correlation between PR and EWR that was also not significant; $r = -.333$, $N = 26$, $p_{Bonferroni,\ 2|3} = .194$. For Participant C, there was significant strong negative correlation between PR and EWR; $r = -.638$, $N = 25$, $p_{Bonferroni,\ 1|3} < .01$. Thus there is no clear relationship between cognitive effort and the proportion of total post-editing time spent in pauses.

Scatterplots, together with regression lines, are shown in Figure 11-3. These scatterplots clearly indicate substantial individual differences, with no consistent pattern from one participant to another.

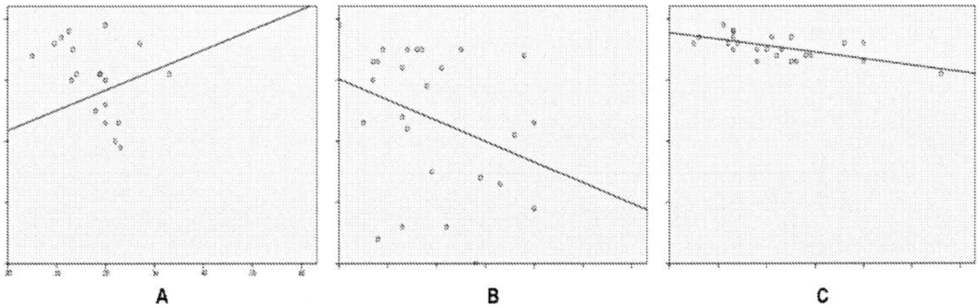

Figure 11-3. Scatterplots with regression lines of PR against EWR, by participant. PR (vertical axis; scale 0.6 to 1.0); EWR (horizontal axis; scale 0.0 to 1.0).

Pause to word ratio

We predicted a positive correlation between pause to word ratio (PWR) and cognitive effort, as indexed by EWR, was based on an interpretation of the formula APR = PR/PWR, together with anticipated negative correlations between APR and EWR and absence of correlations between PR and EWR. Results on APR for all three participants confirmed our expectations. However, there was a range of results on PR, from no significant correlation between PR and EWR for Participants A and B to significant negative correlation between PR and EWR for Participant C. Nevertheless, the current observations on APR and PR are still consistent with our prediction for PWR.

In line with our prediction, even using the conservative Bonferroni correction in a one-tailed analysis, there was a strong positive correlation between the pause to word ratio (PWR) and cognitive effort, indexed by EWR. In other words, for each participant there was a strong tendency for PWR to increase as EWR increased. This is an indication of higher cognitive effort when pause density is higher, even without explicitly distinguishing between long and short pauses. For Participant A, $r = .834$, $N = 20$, $p_{\text{Bonferroni}} < .01$; for Participant B, $r = .818$, $N = 26$, $p_{\text{Bonferroni}} < .01$; for Participant C, $r = .814$, $N = 25$, $p_{\text{Bonferroni}} < .01$. Results were also significant in a two-tailed analysis.

Scatterplots, together with regression lines, are shown in Figure 11-4.

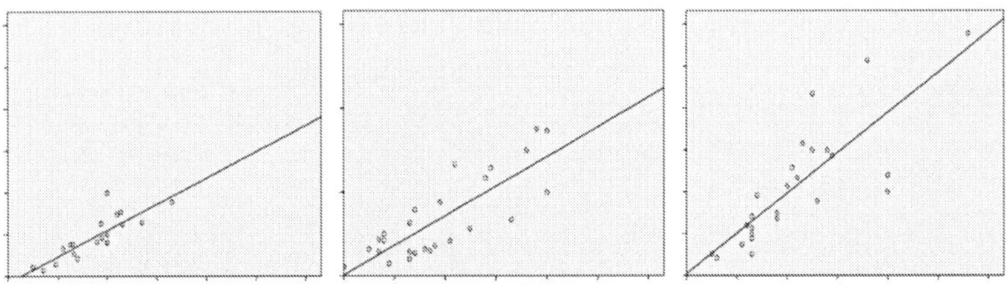

A B C

Figure 11-4. Scatterplots with regression lines of PWR against EWR, by participant. PWR (vertical axis; scale 0 to 3); EWR (horizontal axis; scale 0.0 to 0.6).

Average pause time

We predicted there would be a tendency for average pause time (APT) to decrease as cognitive effort (as indexed by EWR) increased, due to the anticipated higher density of short pauses in more cognitively effortful segments.

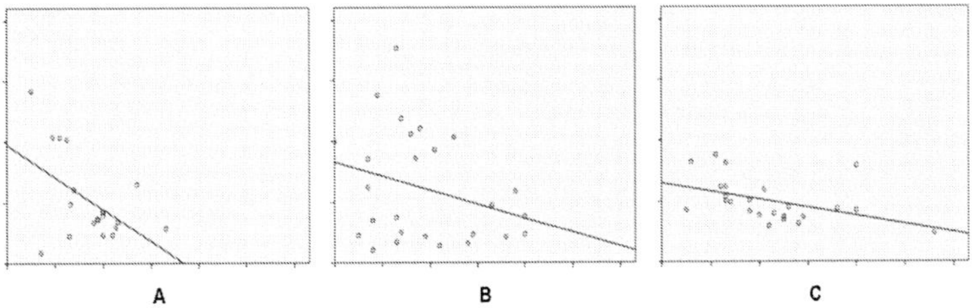

Figure 11-5. Scatterplots with regression lines of APT against EWR, by participant. APT (vertical axis; scale 0 to 24 seconds); EWR (horizontal axis; scale 0.0 to 0.6).

We conducted a one-tailed analysis using the sequential Bonferroni correction. For Participants A and C there was moderate-to-strong negative correlation between APT and EWR. In the case of Participant A, the correlation was significant; r = -.518, N = 20, $p_{\text{Bonferroni, 1|3}}$ = .029. In the case of Participant C, for whom one outlier was dropped from this analysis, the correlation was close to significant; r = -.455, N = 24, $p_{\text{Bonferroni, 2|3}}$ = .084. For Participant B, there was a weak, negative correlation that approached significance; r = -.292, N = 26, $p_{\text{Bonferroni, 3|3}}$ =.074. In other words, there was a clear, if not totally consistent, tendency for average pause time to decrease as cognitive effort (as indexed by EWR) increased. This is consistent with our previous observations that cognitive effort is higher when there is a higher density of short pauses. Scatterplots, together with regression lines, are shown in Figure 11-5.

Average word time

Koponen et al. (2012) recently presented evidence that the time a post-editor spends per word is positively associated with the degree of cognitive demand presented by the text, and so, indirectly, with the cognitive effort expended. Based on Koponen et al.'s finding, we predicted that average word time (AWT) would increase as cognitive effort (as indexed by EWR) increased.

For all three participants there was significant positive correlation between AWT and EWR. The correlation was moderate for Participant A, and strong for Participants B and C. In other words, for each participant there was a strong or moderate tendency for AWT to increase as EWR increased. This corresponds to higher cognitive effort when time spent per word is higher. Using the sequential Bonferroni correction in a one-tailed analysis, for Participant A, $r = .480$, $N = 20$, $p_{\text{Bonferroni, 3|3}} = .016$; for Participant B, $r = .724$, $N = 26$, $p_{\text{Bonferroni, 1|3}} < .01$; for Participant C, $r = .721$, $N = 25$, $p_{\text{Bonferroni, 2|3}} < .01$. Results were also significant in a two-tailed analysis. Scatterplots, together with regression lines, are shown in Figure 11-6.

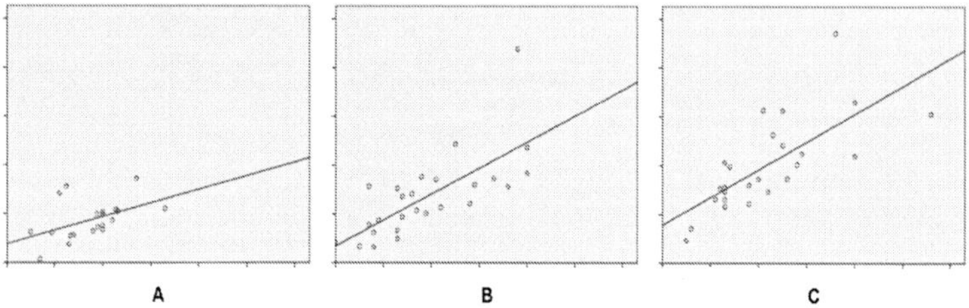

Figure 11-6. Scatterplots with regression lines of AWT against EWR, by participant. AWT (vertical axis; scale 0 to 15 seconds); EWR (horizontal axis, scale 0.0 to 0.6).

Recall that APR = APT/AWT. The strong tendency for APR to decrease as cognitive demand increased can therefore be unpacked into two mutually reinforcing, but not so reliably strong tendencies–the tendencies for average pause time, APT, to decrease and for average word time, AWT, to increase as cognitive effort, as indexed by EWR, increased.

Summary and Future Directions

The primary purpose of the current case studies was to investigate the promise of simple pause metrics as tools for measuring cognitive effort during post-editing.

As reported in Lacruz et al (2102), observations of keystroke log reports during post-editing of MT texts have indicated distinctive distributions of short pauses (lasting between ½ and 2 seconds) and long pauses (lasting at least 5 seconds) at various stages of the post-editing process. The reflective phases of reading, problem recognition, solution proposal, and solution evaluation (Angelone, 2010), all of which presumably require a high level of cognitive effort, tended to be accompanied by clusters of long pauses interspersed with mouse or cursor activity, but exhibited few short pauses. It was common to see a short pause just prior to a post-editing action, such as an insertion or a deletion. Other than a "decision to act" short pause, straightforward post-editing events, such as edits to correct capitalization or word form, were usually carried out with few pauses, long or short. On the other hand, during more cognitively challenging post-editing activities, we often observed clusters of short pauses, sometimes interspersed with longer pauses that interrupted the typing of a word or broke up the typing of a string of words. Examples of such challenging post-editing activities include corrections of mistranslations that affect meaning, including incorrect syntax or mistranslations of idioms.

These observations suggest there will be a higher density and frequency of short pauses during the post-editing of segments that require more cognitive effort from the post-editor.

Since cognitive effort expended during the post-editing of a particular segment is inherently subject to large individual differences, we measured cognitive effort through an analysis of the post-editing process carried out by each individual participant. Our segment level index of expenditure of cognitive effort was the event to word ratio (EWR), the density of complete editing events in keystroke log reports of a post-editor's activity while working on a segment.

We found promising results for three different pause metrics: the average pause ratio (APR), the pause to word ratio (PWR), and the average pause time (APT). For each participant, changes in the values of these pause metrics were associated with changes in EWR. The APR and PWR metrics were more reliable than the APT metric. For all three participants, there was a significant strong correlation between APR and EWR and between PWR and EWR.

- Average pause ratio (APR) decreased for each participant as cognitive effort increased.
- Pause to word ratio (PWR) increased for each participant as cognitive effort increased.

In all three cases, there was a negative correlation between APT and EWR that was either significant or approached significance. The strength of the correlations and their significance varied from one participant to another.

- Average pause time decreased for each participant as cognitive effort increased.

The associations between the three pause metrics and cognitive effort (decrease in average pause ratio, increase in pause density, and decrease in average pause time as cognitive effort increased) were all consistent with higher frequency and density of short pauses during the post-editing of more cognitively effortful segments.

Consistent with results of Koponen et al. (2012), the variation in each individual's processing time from segment to segment was also associated with cognitive effort.

- Average word time increased for each participant as cognitive effort increased.

Correlations were significant for all three participants, but, as with the average pause time, the strength of the correlations was not consistent from participant to participant.

Accordingly, APT and AWT seem to be less promising metrics than APR and PWR for evaluating cognitive effort during post-editing. As we pointed out above, since APR = APT/AWT, the strong tendency for APR to decrease as cognitive demand increased can be unpacked into two mutually reinforcing, but not so reliably strong tendencies–the tendencies for average pause time, APT, to decrease and for average word time, AWT, to increase as cognitive effort, as indexed by EWR, increased.

The limited evidence to date indicates that for each of the participants we have tested, the behavioural metrics of average pause ratio and pause to word ratio appear to be strongly associated with cognitive effort in post-editing machine translations. A potential underlying mechanism may be that short pauses are more abundant when post-editors tackle cognitively demanding errors in MT. However, the data we have acquired is very limited, and it would be premature to make any assertions about generalizability of the results to a wider population, or even to a more extensive body of MT material. Importantly, while it is tempting to speculate that increases in cognitive effort cause the changes we observed in APR and PWR, at this stage we have no basis to infer causality.

Nevertheless, these preliminary data suggest it would be worthwhile testing in an experimental setting the hypotheses that APR decreases and PWR increases as cognitive effort increases. One way to do this, would be to manipulate source texts in a systematic way with several participants so that for critical MT segments some participants would post-edit a version where we expect them to exert a high level of cognitive effort, while others will post-edit a version where we expect them to exert a low level of cognitive effort.

For this endeavour to be successful, it will be essential to identify a reliable indicator of cognitive effort. As we have pointed out, objective indicators of cognitive demand, based for example on a linguistic analysis of a source text, cannot reliably be mapped to the actual level of cognitive effort exerted by an individual post-editor. For example, the correction of a mistranslated idiomatic expression may be highly effortful for one post-editor, but not for another, depending, for instance, on experience with that particular expression and the strength of the association between translation equivalents in memory. A fundamental problem is the difficulty of identifying direct measures of cognitive effort.

In this study, we chose to measure cognitive effort indirectly by computing EWR, the density of complete editing events in a segment. However, the reliability of this measure can be compromised in various ways. First, the judgment of what constitutes a complete editing event in a keystroke log report is to some extent subjective. More seriously, some complete editing events (for example, single keystrokes to correct incorrect capitalizations) will plausibly require less cognitive effort to post-edit than others (for example, serious mistranslations.) We have implicitly assumed that the variability of effort from event to event is consistent for different values of EWR. This is a questionable assumption.

It would be natural to begin to refine the results we have reported by attempting to create categories of complete editing events, to relate those categories to the pause patterns exhibited by different post-editors, and to infer how the categories correspond to the cognitive effort expended by the post-editors. However, this would again circle back to the problems associated with equating supposed cognitive demand with actual cognitive effort. Ultimately, it is necessary to develop a reliable gauge of actual cognitive effort expended. The dual task paradigm seems to be a promising avenue for seeking more accurate measures of the level of cognitive effort expended by post-editors.

For a dual task experiment to give useful information, the distracting secondary task must tap into the same types of mental processes as the primary task, which in this setting would be post-editing. Possible secondary tasks might be to require post-editors to verbally translate words they hear at random intervals; or to tap once if a pair of words they hear is a translation pair, but twice if they are not a translation pair. The objective of the secondary task is to increase the cognitive load on the participant, and so to make it more difficult to accomplish the primary task. If APR and PWR are reliable indicators of cognitive effort, their values should be different in comparable segments that were or were not disrupted by the secondary task. Large samples would be needed to draw reliable generalizable conclusions, but it would be feasible to carry out such an experiment on a large enough scale, since close hands-on analysis of keystroke logs would no longer be needed to identify complete editing events: instead, the necessary data could be extracted automatically using macros.

Another approach to calibrating actual cognitive effort would be to triangulate eye-tracking data, including known indicators of cognitive effort, such as pupil dilation measurements, with keystroke log reports. A drawback to this approach is that it would be very labour intensive, which would limit the feasibility of acquiring a large enough data set to be able to draw reliable conclusions.

We have focused on the question of whether the behavioural metrics of APR and PWR are associated with cognitive effort in post-editing. The ultimate goal would be to establish a causal functional relationship that would allow us to predict levels of cognitive effort in post-editing from the APR or PWR metrics. Developers of MT programs have a vested interest in optimizing their products to make the post-editing process as quick and easy as possible. Post-editors are also motivated to develop their skills in such a way that the post-editing process will be a quick as easy as possible. Accordingly, if APR and PWR prove to be reliable predictors of cognitive effort in post-editing, there would be useful applications in empirically based evaluation of the utility of MT programs that would assist developers as they work to optimize the programs. There would also be implications for the design of training programs to help translators to become more effective post-editors.

Bibliography

Abdi, Hervé. 2010. "Holm's Sequential Bonferroni Procedure." In *Encyclopedia of Research Design*, edited by Neil Salkind, 573-577. Thousand Oaks, CA: Sage.

Alves, Fabio and Daniel Couto Vale. 2009. "Probing the Unit of Translation in Time: Aspects of the Design and Development of a Web Application for Storing, Annotating, and Querying Translation Process Data." *Across Languages and Culture* 10 (2): 251-273.

Angelone, Erik. 2010. "Uncertainty, Uncertainty Management, and Metacognitive Problem Solving in the Translation Task." In *Translation and Cognition*, edited by Gregory M. Shreve and Erik Angelone, 17-40. Amsterdam/Philadelphia: John Benjamins.

Blain, Frédéric, Jean Senellart, Holger Schwenk, Mirko Plitt, and Johann Roturier. 2011. "Qualitative analysis of post-editing for high quality machine translation." *MT Summit XIII: the Thirteenth Machine Translation Summit [organized by the] Asia-Pacific Association for Machine Translation (AAMT)*. 164-171.

Cohen, Jacob. 1988. *Statistical Power Analysis for the Behavioral Sciences* (2nd Ed.). Hillsdale, NJ: Lawrence Erlbaum Associates.

Cooper-Martin, Elizabeth. 1994. "Measures of Cognitive Effort." *Marketing Letters* 5: 43-56.

Dragsted, Barbara, and Inge Gorm Hansen. 2008. "Comprehension and Production in Translation: a Pilot Study on Segmentation and the Coordination of Reading and Writing Processes." In *Looking at Eyes,* edited by Susanne Göpferich, Arnt Lykke Jakobsen, and Inger M. Mees, 9–30. Copenhagen Studies in Language 36. Copenhagen: Samsfundslitteratur.

Göpferich, Susanne, Gerrit Bayer-Hohenwarter, Friederike Prassl, and Johanna Stadlober. 2011. "Exploring Translation Competence Acquisition: Criteria of Analysis Put to the Test." In *Cognitive Explorations of Translation,* edited by Sharon O'Brien, 57-86. Continuum Studies in Translation. London: Continuum.

Kellogg, Ronald T. 1987. "Effects of Topic Knowledge on the Allocation of Processing Time and Cognitive Effort to Writing Processes." *Memory and Cognition* 15: 256-266.

—. 1997. *Cognitive Psychology.* London: SAGE Publications.

Koponen, Maarit. 2012. "Comparing Human Perceptions of Post-Editing Effort with Post-Editing Operations." In *Proceedings of the Seventh Workshop on Statistical Machine Translation.* 181-190. Association for Computational Linguistics.

Koponen, Maarit, Wilker Aziz, Luciana Ramos, and Lucia Specia. 2012. "Post-Editing Time as a Measure of Cognitive Effort." In *AMTA 2012 Workshop on Post-Editing Technology and Practice (WPTP 2012).* 11-20.

Krings, Hans P. 2001. *Repairing Texts: Empirical Investigations of Machine Translation Post-Editing Processes*, edited by Geoffrey S. Koby. Kent, Ohio: Kent State University Press.

Lacruz, Isabel, Gregory M. Shreve, and Erik Angelone. 2012. "Average Pause Ratio as an Indicator of Cognitive Effort in Post-Editing: A Case Study." In *AMTA 2012 Workshop on Post-Editing Technology and Practice (WPTP 2012).* 21-30.

O'Brien, Sharon. 2006. "Pauses as Indicators of Cognitive Effort in Post-editing Machine Translation Output." *Across Languages and Cultures* 7: 1-21.

Olive, Thierry. 2003. "Working Memory in Writing: Empirical Evidence from the Dual-task Technique." *European Psychologist* 9: 32-42.

Pinto, Péricles de Souza. 2004. "Professional vs Novice Translators: A Study of Effort and Experience in Translation." MA Diss., Federal University of Minas Gerais and Federal University of Santa Caterina.

Schilperoord, Joost. 1996. *It's About Time: Temporal Aspects of Cognitive Processes in Text Production*. Amsterdam: Rodopi.

Shreve, Gregory M., Isabel Lacruz, and Erik Angelone. 2011. "Sight Translation and Speech Disfluency: Performance Analysis as a Window to Cognitive Translation Processes." In *Methods and Strategies of Process Research*, edited by Cecilia Alvstad, Adelina Hild, and Elisabet Tiselius, 121-146. Amsterdam/Philadelphia: John Benjamins.

Snover, Matthew, Bonnie Dorr, Richard Schwartz, Linnea Micciulla, and John Makhoul. 2006. "A Study of Translation Edit Rate with Targeted Human Annotation" In *Proceedings of the 7th Conference of the Association of Machine Translators of the Americas*. 223-231.

Temnikova, Irina. 2010. "A Cognitive Evaluation Approach for a Controlled Language Post-Editing Experiment." In *Proceedings of the International Conference "Language Resources and Evaluation" (LREC2010)*, 3485-3490. Valletta, Malta. 3485-3490.

Tyler, Sherman W., Paula T. Hertel, Marvin C. McCallum, and Henry C. Ellis. 1979. "Cognitive Effort and Memory." *Journal of Experimental Psychology, Human Learning and Memory* 5: 607-617.

PART III:

GUIDELINES AND EVALUATION

CHAPTER TWELVE

ASSESSMENT OF POST-EDITING VIA STRUCTURED TRANSLATION SPECIFICATIONS

ALAN K. MELBY, PAUL J. FIELDS AND JASON HOUSLEY

Abstract

Machine translation often has need of post-editing, but there is no common standard of quality for post-editing. Different projects require different specifications; yet a static approach to apply one set of specifications to all situations has dominated commercial translation quality assessment for many years. Every approach to measuring post-editing effort requires a definition of translation quality and a reliable method of determining whether post-editing has achieved the desired result. There is a need for a common framework that applies to all post-editing of machine translation. We propose a framework that includes a universal definition of translation quality, structured translation specifications connected with the definition, and a rubric or analytic error-category approach, based on specifications. Translation quality should focus on the degree of accuracy and fluency required for the audience, purpose, consideration for end-user needs, and all other negotiated specifications. The analytical error-category approach in this framework uses the Multidimensional Quality Metrics (MQM) system. The proposed framework is hoped to be widely adopted to facilitate the evaluation and comparison of various methods of measuring post-editing effort.

Introduction

The last ten years have seen a substantial increase in research exploring post-editing of machine translation (MT). Most previous studies have focused on the effort required to post-edit raw machine translation output. The post-editing effort may be defined in a number of ways; most notably the work of Krings (2001) divides post-editing effort into three categories: *temporal*, *technical*, and *cognitive*. Temporal effort measures how long it takes the post-editor to finish editing the target text, whereas technical effort measures the changes made to the MT-generated text during the post-editing process. The cognitive load is difficult to measure because techniques designed to measure the thought processes of translators/post-editors often make the task of translating more difficult (O'Brien 2005). Specia has developed a system of measuring expected post-editing effort so that companies can estimate whether a particular machine translated text is worth sending to post-editors (Specia and Farzindar 2010). All three categories of post-editing effort rely on some method of assessing the adequacy of the post-editing effort. However, it may not always be clear what constitutes an acceptable result.

Measuring the temporal effort—or the time it takes to post-edit raw machine translation—assumes that the post-edited target text is of acceptable quality. However, acceptability is a not an intrinsic property of a text. The same post-edited text may be useless for one type of project while being suitable for another. The time necessary to successfully post-edit a text will change dramatically when project requirements are different, even if the source, raw MT text, and human post-editor are the same. Likewise, the technical effort—measured in number of changes made—required for a useable result will change depending on the instructions to the post-editor and how well those instructions are followed. The instructions to the post-editor must be derived from the project specifications. It is also the case that the cognitive load on the post-editor depends on the instructions being followed. Indeed, all aspects of post-editing, including assessment of whether a post-editing task was successfully accomplished, must be based on project specifications.

Consider two extremes in project specifications for a technical repair manual and a translation of a company's annual report distributed to potential investors in the company.

In the case of the technical repair manual, perhaps the only thing that counts toward a useable result is whether a technician can use the post-edited translation to repair a machine, regardless of any grammatical/spelling errors or awkwardness that do not impact the technician's ability to complete the repair job. Obviously, any such errors that fundamentally change the meaning or render the text unintelligible would impact usability and would need to be fixed, but more minor errors may leave the text usable for the intended purpose, albeit "ugly." These specifications could be called "technician" specifications. A post-editor working to these specifications would be requested to leave some issues uncorrected unless they impact the ability of the technician to utilize the text. For example, the stilted and ungrammatical verbal forms in "One must pushes the release lever to the full off position" should not be corrected by the post-editor because they do not impede usability. In the case of "One must collapse the lever of release to the full off position," however, the word *collapse* (a mistranslation where *lower* would be appropriate) and phrase *lever of release* (a potentially confusing phrase instead of *release lever*) would be likely to impact usability and would be corrected.

In the case of the annual report,[1] the post-edited translation must be indistinguishable from a translation by a professional human translator who is instructed to make the target text not only accurate but also highly readable, as if it had been authored by a skilled technical writer who is a native of the target language. These second specifications could be called "beauty" specifications. In this case even minor errors in grammar, spelling, and discourse flow that do not impact the readers' ability to understand the text would need to be corrected because the functional requirements for the text include demands that would be impacted by even small problems that would not matter in the case of the technical manual.

In both cases, quality consists in fulfilling project specifications rather than in meeting one abstract notion of an ideal, perfect translation. Instead, quality is determined in a dynamic fashion, based on the purpose, audience, text type, etc. This dynamic approach to quality contrasts with the static approach in which one set of specifications is applied to all situations. The static approach has dominated commercial translation quality assessment for many years.

Suppose that it takes 10 minutes with a dozen changes to post-edit a raw machine translation according to *technician* specifications and 30 minutes with two dozen changes, some of which are re-translations of entire sentences, to post-edit the same raw machine translation to *beauty* specifications. It would obviously be unfair to conclude that the second post-editor did a worse job than the first, simply because more time was required, or that the first post-editor failed to do his job because some obvious errors were left in the text. Likewise, post-editing time cannot be used as a measure of raw machine-translation quality, unless the specifications are taken into account. Measures of post-editing effort should be embedded in a dynamic definition of translation quality and a system for defining various sets of specifications within a single framework that facilitates comparison of specifications and assures fairness in assessing the work of post-editors using well-defined metrics. For an assessment to be fair, it must be reliable. This means the work of a post-editor will be judged similarly, regardless of who uses the metric.

Metrics are an essential component of any satisfactory quality framework; however, at present, there is no generally accepted method of constructing metrics for translation quality assessment.

A metric is a standard of measurement or evaluation. To take a very simple example, a researcher could say, "I want to assess a person's height, so the metric is vertical distance from the bottom of the foot to the top of the head when a person is standing upright on a solid surface, without wearing shoes, and the distance is measured in meters with a precision of one centimeter." This metric assumes that height is well defined. If height were not well defined, or seriously misunderstood through mispronunciation, one person might measure height as "heat" by using a thermometer attached to a person's ear. A "height" of 37 (37 degrees Celsius is a typical body temperature) would be meaningless if interpreted as height in centimeters.

The example about height may seem unrelated to post-editing, but the same principle is applicable. Measuring the effort to accomplish a task such as post-editing is meaningless unless the task is well-defined. To take another extreme example that is a bit closer to translation, suppose the task at hand is to clean a living room. Unless the task is well-defined, measuring the time spent in accomplishing it is meaningless. Does the cleaning task include vacuuming the carpet? Does it include dusting the walls? What about washing the windows? And how about removing the covers from all the couch cushions and hand removing dog hair and then washing and drying them? Likewise, unless a post-editing task is well defined, it is meaningless to measure the effort required to accomplish it. Otherwise, one post-editor could be checking the target text, segment by segment against the source text, checking every term against a bilingual glossary, and bringing the target text into compliance with the details of a style guide, while another post-editor may only be speed reading the target text for unusually long and convoluted sentences and then running it through a spell checker.

Metrics are part of a quality framework that includes a definition of quality. Within the field of translation, we have so far argued that the definition of quality, in order to be valid, must take into account specifications. Metrics must be checked for reliability, and the entire framework must be refined until it is achieved. In other words, principled, specifications-based, reliable assessment of translation quality is needed.

An examination of the proceedings of the 2012 AMTA workshop on post-editing (WPTP 2012) shows the lack of a common quality framework. The foreword to the workshop proceedings invites discussion of how to "properly and objectively assess post-editing effectiveness". The paper by Tatsumi et al. ("How Good is Crowd Post-Editing?…" in WPTP 2012) states that it is focused on "the quality we can expect from crowd members" but does not define translation quality. It contains guidelines for crowd post-editors ([1] "avoid over-editing", [2] "ignore stylistic differences", and [3] "start from scratch when needed") that should ideally be derived from project specifications. In fact the first two of these guidelines, *avoid over-editing* and *ignore stylistic differences*, will almost certainly rely on covert assumptions about what is important: over-editing can only be defined with respect to an ideal output that is *not* over-edited, but which will vary depending on the quality expectations; *which* stylistic differences will require attention also depends on expectations. The paper by Poulis and Kolavratnik ("To Post-Edit or Not to Post-Edit" in WPTP 2012) discusses post-editing at the European Parliament. It mentions some particular specifications that must be followed, such as the obligation "to re-use the exact same translations that have been produced in other documents which are being referred to in the current source document." This requirement to leverage existing translations, presumably by using translation memory or copy-pasting from existing translations, should be expressible within a quality framework. The paper by Valotkaite and Asadullah ("Error Detection for Post-Editing Rule-Based Machine Translation" in WPTP 2012) includes an error classification that is used in the assessment of machine translation, but that error classification is not part of a general framework used in other projects. The paper by Zhechev ("Machine Translation Infrastructure and Post-Editing Performance at Autodesk," in WPTP 2013) discusses assessment of post-editing performance. Each of these papers is important, but it is difficult to compare conclusions from multiple studies because they did not use specifications derived from a common framework and they are not based on a common definition of translation quality.

The definition of post-editing proposed by the Centre for Next Generation for Localisation (CNGL) and Translation Automation User Society (TAUS) in January 2011 (http://www.cngl.ie/tauscngl-machine-translation-post-editing-guidelines-published/)—"Post-editing is the correction of machine-generated translation output to ensure it meets a level of quality negotiated in advance between client and post-editor"—also implies the need for a common framework for negotiating the specifications in advance.

This chapter addresses the need for a common framework for quality that includes a basis for assessment of whether a post-editing task has been successfully accomplished. The proposed framework consists of a new and universal definition of translation quality, a recently published systematic way to construct the translation specifications that are crucial to this definition, and two types of translation-quality metrics based on this definition and specification system: a rubric approach to assessing the result of a post-editing task, and an error-category approach to assessment of translation quality, whether it be human, machine, or post-edited translation. The error-category approach described herein is part of an on-going European project called QT LaunchPad.

The overarching claim of this chapter is that every approach to measuring post-editing effort requires a definition of translation quality and a reliable method of determining whether post-editing has achieved the desired result. The hope of the authors is that the proposed quality framework will be widely adopted and will facilitate the evaluation and comparison of various methods of measuring post-editing effort.

The remainder of this chapter expands on key points of the proposed quality framework and is broken down into five parts: (1) translation quality, where translation quality will be defined on the basis of specifications; (2) Structured Translation Specifications, which describes the proposed system for constructing translation specifications; (3) a rubric approach (describing a type of metric based on structured translation specifications); (4) an analytic error-category approach that is also based on structured translation specifications (introducing the approach being developed within QT LaunchPad); and (5) a conclusion.

Translation Quality

A clear and sufficiently encompassing definition of *translation quality* is required before one can make a reasonable attempt at comparing the quality of various translations. We suggest the following universal definition of translation quality:

> A quality translation demonstrates required **accuracy** and **fluency** for the **audience** and **purpose** and complies with all other negotiated **specifications**, taking into account **end-user needs**.

This new definition, which is the evolution of dynamic definitions dating back more than two decades (Melby 1990; Melby et al. 2007; Hague et al.

2011), addresses, in its current incarnation, the three major aspects of quality that apply across multiple industries: *transcendent* quality, *manufacturing* quality, and *user* quality (Garvin 1984). Hague et al. (2011) provided considerable detail on the close connection between the specifications approach used in this definition and Functionalism in translation studies, but did not yet bring in the work of Garvin in quality assessment. The work of Garvin and others has had a major impact on a number of industries but for some reason has been ignored in the translation/localization industry until now.

(Note that the term "translation quality" is carefully chosen here to argue that traditional, transcendent notions of quality are inadequate within a Functionalist approach. Quality, in this context, is not simply something inherent in the text—source or target—itself or the translation process alone, but must be understood with respect to specifications. Thus the exact same text might be judged to be of poor quality or exceptional quality, depending on requirements, and a translation process considered to be of poor quality in one environment might be high quality for another set of specifications. This notion, however, is not one of radical relativism: texts can be compared to one another and ranked by an abstract notion of quality, but statements about quality *always* refer to a set of specifications, either implicit or explicit, even in the case of an absolute notion of "perfect" translation.)

We will now discuss Garvin's three aspects of quality in more detail. *Transcendent quality* is the aspect of which most translators are already aware, namely the idea that a quality translation is one that obtains the maximum degree of accuracy between source and target texts while maintaining a high level of fluency, that is, readability and naturalness in the target language. An extreme perspective, relying on the transcendent aspect, argues that in order for a translation to be high quality the target text must have complete accuracy and fluency, being indistinguishable from a document authored in the target language by a skilled writer and producing exactly the same effect on the reader of the translation as is produced on a reader of the source text. However, such a perspective quickly becomes untenable when one recognizes that in different cases, different degrees of accuracy and fluency are necessary. For instance, it is not always the case that the target must be undetectable as a translation and instead the translator may render some portions closer to the source language in order to educate the reader about the source culture or for some other purpose. Likewise, if the audience of the translation is not interested in every minute detail of the language content but instead intends to glean only a particular set of necessary information—such as is often the case when deciding whether a document is relevant or in summary translations—then full accuracy is not necessary. Sometimes complete accuracy and full fluency are at odds with each other. In other words, real-world translation projects vary in the degree of accuracy and fluency necessary for a translation, depending on the audience and purpose of the translation. The transcendent perspective on quality is not sufficient.

Manufacturing quality is most important when the project is a business transaction, i.e., when one party requests translation services from another party. Manufacturing quality addresses various concerns that the parties may have regarding the target text itself, the steps taken to generate the target text, and other circumstances related to the translation. For example, in order to ensure quality one party may need to follow certain quality-assurance procedures, or another party may be required to use particular software in generating the translation. *A translation that does not meet negotiated specifications cannot be accepted as a quality translation even if it would otherwise satisfy expectations of accuracy and fluency.* (For example, if a translation must be made in a secure corporate facility but the translator smuggles the text home and works on it using an unsecured laptop, thereby raising the spectre of industrial espionage, the translation is a bad one from a manufacturing perspective, even if it is a perfect one from a transcendent perspective.) The specifications that need to be met are the ones negotiated by the parties involved; implicit expectations about the translation should be avoided because they may not be shared by all of the parties. Similar to other industries, the translation industry has standards that help to define and suggest the types of specifications that may apply to various translation projects, e.g., ISO/TS 11669 (General Guidance – Translation Projects).

User quality addresses the needs of the people who use the translation. This is not the same as manufacturing quality, because the end-user is, more often than not, someone other than the parties involved in producing the translation. For example, suppose a tourism pamphlet/map for exploring Nara Japan's famous monuments needs to be translated from Japanese to English in order to accommodate international visitors. The parties involved in producing the translation may be the Nara Tourism Bureau and a freelance translator, but the end-user is ultimately the individual tourist who has to navigate by relying on the translation. Even if the target text corresponds well with the Japanese original and reads naturally in the target language, and even if the translation met all other specifications put in place by the translator and the Nara Tourism Bureau, if the foreign tourist attempting to use the translated pamphlet is confused or frustrated then the translation cannot be said to have achieved quality.

Such a result may occur because there is information that is known to Japanese tourists but unknown to foreign tourists that would need to be added to the English version (e.g., the location of a landmark, well-known to Japanese but not to foreigners, that is not shown on the map but referred to in the text) in order for the translation to provide the same benefit to end-users as the Japanese original. In other words, simply meeting specifications, including necessary accuracy and fluency, does not entail that the translation will successfully achieve its purpose for its intended audience. Specifications can be explicit yet defective. The needs of the end-user should be carefully taken into account when determining project specifications.

Another facet of user quality is that a translation should not result in harm to the end-users or to society. If the translator is aware of a potential danger to end-users that may not be clear in even a highly accurate rendering of the source text, it would not be quality work to omit that detail. This is particularly important when translating documentation for complex machinery that many people rely on such as an elevator or an aircraft. If the target text does not sufficiently draw the attention of technicians to potential dangers, it is woefully lacking in quality, especially if implied information generally associated with the source text successfully protects people using the text in the original language but the implication does not survive the translation. This means that taking into account end-user needs goes beyond simply those needs that the end-users are aware of and includes the translation professional's moral obligation to try to ensure that his or her work does not result in harm to society.

The three aspects of translation quality (transcendent, manufacturing, and user) relate directly to post-editing. Quality post-editing can be taken as a subset of quality translation where particular specifications are consistently applied. Machine translation is used to generate an initial target text and then a post-editor revises this text according to the specifications. Quality is assessed relative to the specifications, regardless of whether the initial translation was done by a human or by a machine.

Structured Translation Specifications

Although the notion of translation specifications (also called a *translation brief* in Translation Studies literature) is well established, until now such specifications have varied widely in content, format, and level of detail. While even unstructured specifications provide a real benefit for the translation process, their diversity makes comparison a challenge. In addition, lack of standardization can lead to ambiguity that makes it difficult for translators to consistently apply specifications.

In order for specifications to be compared, they must be derived from a common framework. We developed a machine-readable format for translation specifications we named "formalized structured translation specifications" (FSTS). The basic components of the format are derived directly from the 2012 ISO document ISO/TS 11669 (General Guidance – Translation Projects) and the status descriptors in the Linport STS format (Linport 2012; Melby et al. 2011). Using FSTS allowed us to write software applications to manage specifications (Ruqual Specifications Writer) and generate a rubric (Ruqual Rubric Viewer) for assessing post-editing (see code.google.com/p/ruqual/ for source code and latest version downloads). Since it uses a rubric to assess quality, the name of the software is Ruqual, a blend of "rubric" and "quality."

As shown in Table 12-1, the main categories in the FSTS format are as follows:

- **Linguistic[2] product** (divided into **Source** Content Information and **Target** Content Requirements)
- **Production** tasks to be performed during the project, that is, process
- **Environment** requirements for the translation project
- **Relationships** between parties involved in the translation project, namely the requester (sometimes called the client, although "client" is ambiguous) and the translation service provider.

It should be noted that these divisions constitute a translation-specific instantiation of the well-known division among product, process, and project that is found in many areas of industry:

- The linguistic parameters provide information about the *product* (translated text) itself, as well as the source text. Both source and target parameters must be specified since, in many cases, they will differ. While in most cases the text type of a source text will be the same as the text type for its translation, this is not always the case. For example, the source text might be an ancient religious text, but its translation will be presented as a chapter in a text book for college students in a history of world religions class, augmented with explanatory notes, cross-references, and other features not found in the source.

- Production tasks correspond to *process* requirements. They define the tasks that must be carried out in the translation process. These tasks vary from project to project: in one instance a service provider may be asked to research terminology, edit the target text, and format it nicely; in another only translation may be requested.
- Finally, the Environment and Stakeholder Relationships sections provide *project* requirements. Project requirements focus primarily on how the translation is carried out as a project: were workplace requirements met, were deadlines met, relevant information presented, payment received as expected, and were all parties satisfied?

A. Linguistic *product* parameters [1–13]

Source-content information [1–5]

[1] textual characteristics
- a) source language
- b) text type
- c) audience
- d) purpose

[2] specialized language
- a) subject field
- b) terminology

[3] volume

[4] complexity

[5] origin

Target content requirements [6–13]

[6] target language requirements
- a) target language
- b) target terminology

[7] audience

[8] purpose

[9] content correspondence

[10] register

[11] file format

[12] style
- a) style guide
- b) style relevance

[13] layout

B. Production *process* tasks [14–15]

- [14] typical production tasks
  - a) preparation
  - b) initial translation
  - c) in-process quality assurance
- [15] additional tasks

C. *Project* Environment [16–18]

- [16] technology
- [17] reference materials
- [18] workplace requirements

D. *Project* Stakeholder Relationships [19–21]

- [19] permissions
  - a) copyright
  - b) recognition
  - c) restrictions
- [20] submissions
  - a) qualifications
  - b) deliverables
  - c) delivery deadline
- [21] expectations
  - a) compensation
  - b) communication

Table 12-1. Translation Parameters for Product, Process, and Project

The five FSTS categories (Source, Target, Production, Environment, and Relationships) arrange the 21 translation parameters into logical groups. Translation parameters are numbered with braces ("[…]") in Table 12-1. A parameter is a heading for requirements that pertain to a translation project. A specification is a value for a particular parameter. The specifications for a translation project are the parameter values that represent the translation project's requirements. Some parameters have attributes (numbered alphabetically) that help to further subdivide their content. Additionally, all parameters have two attributes that assist in determining their importance for a particular project: Status and Priority. The priority of a parameter is expressed as an integer. The value of the status attribute can be one of four options: Incomplete, Not Specified, Proposed, and Approved.

An incomplete status means that the person initially writing the specification has not finished completing the specification. The default for a specification is "incomplete." In order to maximize the effectiveness of structured translation specifications, no parameters in an FSTS should have the status of "incomplete" at the time the translator or post-editor begins working on the target text. If a specification is to be left blank, meaning that it is not relevant to the current project, the status should be changed to "not specified." If a specification contains some information but not necessarily all the information relevant to that particular parameter, or if a specification requires the input or approval of another party, the specification should have a status of "proposed". Once a specification has been approved, or if changing the specification is no longer an option (such as if compensation is non-negotiable), the status should be set to "approved." The status attribute is important because it indicates whether a specification has been sufficiently determined to proceed with the project. One cannot expect full compliance with specifications that are not approved.

One of the key components of the FSTS approach to specifications is the use of directives to break down arbitrary prose descriptions into instructions that can be evaluated by a grader. Several parameters and attributes in an FSTS may take a list of directives as their value. A directive is a single injunction to some member of the translation workflow in regards to the translation project. Directives were designed with the intention of being used as instructions for the post-editor or a reviser. A directive has two attributes: Request and Priority. The priority indicates how important it is that the request be fulfilled. The priority of parameters that contain directives is calculated from the priority of the contained directives. The request consists of natural language content describing the post-editor's task. For example, a request could be that the target text should not break long Japanese sentences into smaller English sentences even if this results in a somewhat awkward sentence.

The rubric software for assessing post-editing automatically converts some specifications into implied directives. For example, providing an Audience specification implies a directive that the post-editor or translator must make sure the target text is appropriate for the audience provided. Exactly what is appropriate for a particular audience is a theoretical question beyond the scope of this discussion. In any case, the assumption behind the implied directive is that the person receiving the instructions will understand what is and is not appropriate for the audience specified.

It is possible to implement the FSTS format described here via a number of different technologies. We have tried to remain implementation agnostic in the above description, but in actual practice the FSTS format was implemented in Java via the YAML data serialization language (Ben-Kiki et al. 2005). This allowed for the linking and merging of specifications from specification libraries. JSON (www.json.org) or XML could have been used instead of YAML.

More details on various aspects of FSTS can be found in Housley (2012). Detailed descriptions of the parameters used in FSTS can be found in ISO/TS 11669 and at the translation parameter website (www.ttt.org/specs).

Rubrics and Error Analysis

In assessing translation, two primary approaches to metrics are common. Currently the most common approach is an *error-count* or *error-category* approach, sometimes called an analytic approach, in which errors in the translation (e.g., spelling errors, mistranslations, omissions, etc.) are identified and counted. Based on the number of errors found, a score is assigned, often as a percentage (where a translation with a 100% represents a hypothetical perfect translation). While many error-category approaches have an implied transcendent basis, they can be adapted to suit a variety of specifications.

The second approach is known as a *rubric* approach (see Colina 2008 for a discussion of rubric-based assessment of translations in a functionalist framework). In a rubric-based assessment, reviewers are asked to rate translated texts on a scalar measurement system (e.g., on a scale from 1 to 5, with 1 indicating that the text fails to meet expectations and 5 indicating that it fully meets them, per category). Rubric approaches do not identify particular segments of text and have the advantage of being easy to implement and use, but they do not provide a way to identify and address an issue in a specific segment of text. Rubrics fill the gap between holistic and analytical approaches. The more categories of assessment in a rubric approach, the closer it is to an analytical assessment.

An Analytical Error-Category Approach

One error-category approach that has incorporated an explicitly Functionalist notion of quality is found in the Multidimensional Quality Metrics (MQM) system currently under development by the European Union-funded Quality Translation Launchpad (QTLaunchPad) project (see http://www.qt21.eu/launchpad/). The project description states that

> QTLaunchPad is launching a new free and open system for translation quality assessment. Using standards-based "dimensions" to describe translation requirements, it enables users to create custom metrics suitable for specific projects, while including support for existing methods. It clearly distinguishes between source and target quality problems and recognizes improvements made by translators. It integrates methods for assessing human and machine translation.

MQM provides a common framework for developing metrics for translation quality focused on the translation *product*. *Process* (such as who performed which tasks when) and *full-project* assessment (such as whether the translation was delivered and compensated for in a timely manner) can easily be added to product assessment, but are out of scope for MQM itself. MQM is already closely tied to the framework in this chapter. It builds on the same definition of translation quality found in this chapter, thus basing its dimensions on the same system of structured specifications used herein, with a focus on product (that is target text) specifications. Its hierarchy of possible source-text and target-text issues relate directly to structured specifications. The detailed hierarchy of issues types in MQM is thus a largely conformant subset of the translation parameters enumerated in ISO/TS 11669 that focuses on textual and formatting characteristics, setting aside those parameters that relate primarily to project and manufacturing process aspects of quality.

For most purposes, MQM recommends that users select issue types from the following list of "core" types (note that every item, including ones like *Accuracy* or *Content,* counts as an issue type):

- Accuracy
    - Terminology
    - Mistranslation
    - Omission
    - Addition
    - Untranslated
- Fluency
    - (Content)
        - Register
        - Style
        - Inconsistency
    - (Mechanical)
        - Spelling
        - Typography
        - Grammar

        - Locale violation
    - Unintelligible
- Verity
    - Completeness
    - Legal requirements
    - Locale applicability

For a particular type of translation project, a customized translation quality assessment metric is constructed by selecting relevant elements from the issue-type hierarchy, based on the dimensions, which are in turn derived from the product-related specifications. MQM provides an extensive list of over 120 issue types, arranged in a hierarchy, expanding on the core.

Note that it is not anticipated that MQM users will utilize all of these categories for any particular assessment task, but rather make a selection of contextually relevant issues for a given purpose. For example, a very simple metric for evaluating "gist" translations might only include the categories *Mistranslation, Untranslated,* and *Unintelligible* to provide a "quick and dirty" assessment, while a metric for assessing translation of a legal text might include most of the categories in the core. Additional issues from the larger body of extensions can be added to extend the depth of this hierarchy (e.g., for diagnostic purposes) or to add additional issues not covered (e.g., formatting).

To utilize MQM, users either select from a set of pre-defined assessment metrics or build their own, based on their specifications, covered as a subset of 11 of the 21 TS 11669 categories (plus an additional category, output modality, designed to cover issues with *how* the translated text is to be displayed, e.g., on a screen, as spoken text, etc.). After selecting an appropriate list of issue types and weighting them, MQM users can obtain quality scores relevant to their particular set of project specifications.

Note that the issues covered in MQM are intended to apply equally to human and machine translation, thus helping bridge the historical gap between assessment of human translation (generally based on error-category counts) and machine translation (based on some form of edit-distance or similarity to reference translations).

For more information on MQM and technical details, interested parties are encouraged to review the content at http://www.qt21.eu/launchpad.

A Rubric-Based Approach

In order to compare translation projects, we must first have a methodology for reliably determining the quality of a translation project. Reliability means that a project shown to multiple people will receive effectively the same evaluation from each person. Validity of assessment is determined by whether rubric-based quality assessment matches the opinion of experts. Hypothetically, if one were able to give a particular translation project to every expert translator in the world, along with structured project specifications, and each translator gave the project essentially the same assessment, then we would have a true measure of the quality of the translation project. The same principle can be applied to post-editing as a subset of translation. However, since it is generally impossible to receive an evaluation from every expert translator, and moreover, since using substantial numbers of expert translators would be prohibitively expensive, a methodology for reliably determining the quality of a translation or post-editing project needs to produce results that are valid via inductive reasoning and statistical measures.

The following is a description of an experiment in assessing the work of post-editors that was part of an MA project by one of the co-authors (Housley). One of the research questions was whether non-experts could use a rubric-based assessment to reach the same conclusion reached by experts, as defined below.

We will call the people evaluating translation projects *graders*. In order to be economically feasible, it would be beneficial to use non-experts as graders. Here we define a *non-expert* grader as follows:

(1) non-native speaker of the source language and native speaker of the target language,
(2) having at least some post-secondary schooling,
(3) completely inexperienced in the industry of translation (although the grader may have experience performing translation for course work and should have two or more years of experience studying the source language).

In addition to a pool of graders, we need a means of explaining both the requirements of the translation or post-editing project to the graders and the details of what actually occurred over the course of the project. FSTS give us a way of describing a translation project that fits within a scientific methodology for reliably determining quality. FSTS allow us to organize the requirements of a project in a fashion that should make translation research experiments more replicable.

In addition to specifications, researchers need to provide graders with a *scenario* surrounding the source and target texts or, in the case of post-editing, the source, initial target, and post-edited target texts. The scenario is a prose description of the steps taken in generating the target text. In other words, the grader needs to be given the details of the product, process, and project expectations for the translation project. A scenario does not need to be extensive, but it should be sufficient for a grader to determine whether specifications were met. For example, if the FSTS require that certain software be used in generating a translation, then the grader needs to be made aware via the scenario of whether or not that software was actually used by the translator or post-editor working on the project. It is important that the FSTS and scenario are presented to each grader in an identical fashion in order to minimize the effects the delivery mechanism may have on the graders' perceptions of the project.

Each grader needs to provide an assessment of all aspects of the translation project (including production process, environment, and relationships, not just the translation product) via the same measure. The Ruqual software we created generates rubrics for post-editing assessment, such as the one shown in Figure 12-1.

For each category (Target, Production, Environment, Relationships), check each request that was fulfilled by the post-editor. After reviewing each directive, add the priorities of all of the checked requests and write the number as the category total. Divide that total by the points possible to obtain a score for the category. After reviewing all categories, add the totals from each category and divide by the points possible for the rubric to obtain the overall score for post-editor's work.

Target

Request	Priority	Fulfilled
The target text should be returned in the following format: Microsoft Word 2007 or greater (.docx)	10	☐
The target text should be written in a semi-formal style appropriate for mainstream news media.	5	☐
The target text should not break long Japanese sentences into smaller English sentences even if this results in a somewhat awkward sentence.	5	☐
The target text should match the overall complexity of the source text, which means that the translator should not introduce any technical terms or obscure references.	5	☐
There may be minor alterations in meaning including additions and omissions provided that	10	☐

Request	Priority	Fulfilled
the text still achieves its purpose for the target audience.		
There may be a few minor awkward expressions, but the text should still flow naturally in English.	5	☐
The text is to be adapted to the target language and region so that it does not generally appear to be a translation.	5	☐
The text fulfills the following purpose: To briefly inform people about Apple's products and history.	15	☐
The text is appropriate for the following audience: General Educated Americans.	10	☐
The target text must match terminology found in appleTerms.pdf.	10	☐
The target text is appropriate for readers in the United States.	10	☐
The target text is written in English.	50	☐

Total	Possible	Score
	140	

Production

Request	Priority	Fulfilled
The post-editor must agree to all specifications before beginning post-editing the raw translation.	10	☐
The post-editor must NOT change words or phrases that are sufficiently translated in the raw translation.	15	☐
The post-editor must change words and phrases that violate audience, purpose, or content correspondence requirements.	10	☐

Total	Possible	Score
	35	

Environment

Request	Priority	Fulfilled
The post-editor may not subcontract any portion of the work to a third party.	10	☐
The post-editor must use Microsoft Word 2007 (or greater) to edit the translation.	5	☐
The post-editor must have Adobe Acrobat Reader.	5	☐

Total	Possible	Score
	20	

Relationships

Request	Priority	Fulfilled
The post-editor should confirm receipt of the source materials via email before starting the project.	5	☐
The post-editor should return a copy of the post-edited text with the source text and the raw machine translation.	5	☐
The post-editor must email the deliverables before the deadline of March 25, 2012.	15	☐
The post-editor must delete all copies of the source text, post-edited target text, raw translation, and glossary (appleTerms.pdf when the project is completed.	5	☐

Total	Possible	Score
	30	

Rubric Totals

Total	Possible	Score
	225	

Figure 12-1: Sample Ruqual Rubric

Use of a rubric, such as the one shown in Figure 12-1, helps to facilitate comparable assessments between graders by providing a percentage scale upon which they may assign a definitive score for a particular translation project. In the Ruqual software, a score is determined by taking the sum of the priorities of completed directives, as indicated by the grader, and dividing that by the sum of all directives' priorities. This same metric can be performed for categories of specifications as well as an entire project. However, Ruqual currently only supports post-editing assessment. Similar rubrics could be designed to use specifications for translation of other types of translation projects. (Since MQM uses the ISO/TS-11669 specifications at its heart, it is expected that FSTS can be used as the basis for construction of MQM-compatible metrics as well, providing reviewers the chance to use either a rubric- or error count-based approach to assessment, as appropriate, derived from a single set of specifications. We are currently planning future research to investigate whether error count- and rubric-based scores for the same translated texts converge, which would provide evidence that they are measuring a shared notion of quality.)

In order to test reliability, Intraclass Correlation (ICC) can be used (Shrout & Fleiss 1979). ICC scores can range from 0 to 1 analogous to percentages. There are several advantages obtained from using an ICC, one of which is the ability to measure absolute agreement in addition to consistency. Consistency would mean whether graders' scores rise or fall in tandem to each other, similar to a correlation. The question of reliability in this case is not simply whether graders assign the same relative scores to the post-editors but to what degree they are assigning the *same* absolute scores. In other words, we want to know whether the graders are sufficiently close to assigning the exact same value to a particular project. In order to achieve statistical significance, it is advantageous to have several graders evaluate multiple projects. For example, a pool of 20 graders may be asked to evaluate five projects resulting in 100 data points for comparison. It is important to note that the goal of this methodology is not to determine whether graders can rank projects in the same order but instead it is to determine whether graders agree with each other about the quality of *particular* projects. The appropriate ICC calculation utilizes a two-way random effects model with grader effects and measure effects.

In addition to an ICC, a valid reference point or expert grader is necessary to obtain a means of assessing whether non-expert graders are able to provide valid assessments of post-editing or translation. It is possible that non-expert graders may have a high ICC but not correspond well with an expert grader. We would then have to conclude that although non-experts have a shared concept of what a quality translation project is, the concept does not actually apply to what is recognized as good work in the translation industry. The coefficient of concordance can be used to provide an indicator of how well individual graders match the assessment of an expert grader. Graders that do not correspond well with an expert probably provide invalid assessments, whereas graders that do correspond well with an expert may help to provide a measure of the quality of a given project when they are reliable.

A user study was conducted following the methodology described in this section in order to learn whether non-expert graders could in fact agree on the quality of five translation projects. A detailed description of the results of the study can be found in Melby et al. (2012), but a summary is provided here for the reader's convenience.

In this study, a Japanese source text was translated into English using Google Translate, which is widely used by the public to translate web pages and other content. The text was then edited into five different versions to simulate the efforts of real post-editors with various numbers of violations of specifications introduced into each version. Non-expert evaluators were then asked to rate the quality of the post-editing for each of the texts. The rankings provided by the non-expert evaluators were then compared with the rankings obtained from an expert who evaluated the same samples.

Overall, the study found that, as a group, the non-expert evaluators returned reliable and consistent assessments, with an Interclass Correlation Coefficient (ICC) of 0.927 (an ICC 1.0 would indicate perfect agreement between evaluators). The ICC for individuals, however, averaged 0.426, indicating that any single individual would tend to be relatively unreliable compared to the group.

The assessments tended to be somewhat more favourable than the assessments provided by the expert translator (perhaps because experts are trained to identify issues whereas non-experts are not), but their rankings were quite similar and 12 of 17 non-experts showed at least moderate concordance with the expert in their assessments. Taken individually, the non-experts were not reliable by themselves, but their collective rankings were reliable. They were more reliable in identifying issues related to the translation Environment and Relationships than in identifying production issues or linguistic issues in the target text, where more variability was found (and indeed, these areas are ones where our experience indicates that even experts show more variability in their assessment).

Overall, the results of the user study provide evidence in support of the hypothesis that non-expert graders assess the quality of post-edited translations at a high degree of reliability when taken as a group, although individual scores may be less reliable. This promising result shows that it is possible to obtain agreement about the quality of post-edited texts when using FSTS. Although preliminary and in need of larger-scale confirmation, these results suggest that the quality of translation can be determined when expressed in terms of the proposed universal definition of translation quality. This is an encouraging result because it means that although translation quality is relative, it can be measured.

Future work will need to bear out whether reliability as demonstrated in this study can be regularly obtained. It may turn out that expert graders are needed. The next step in the evolution of this methodology will be to integrate the results of the QTLaunchPad project so that more granular metrics can be used if desired.

Conclusion

As this chapter has discussed, most work on post-editing to this point has been unclear as to assumptions about what constitutes acceptable quality. This underspecification calls into question the results found in post-editing studies since post-editors may have different implicit goals, hindering comparison between individual post-editors and studies. While well-developed written or verbal translation briefs (specifications) can help address this problem within a study, they do not help with problems when comparing results between studies.

This chapter provides preliminary evidence that formalized specifications based on ISO/TS 11669 can address this situation through the use of a well-defined set of specifications in a format that can be shared across projects and studies to help post-editors and quality assessors understand expectations. Furthermore, such specifications can be used to provide a common framework for error-category and rubric quality assessment methodologies. This unified framework can in turn help provide an analytical basis for comparing specific post-editing outcomes to quantifiable issues found in texts, helping post-editing studies move beyond approaches that only look at edit distance or other measures to also bring in specific linguistic features and their impact on post-editing efforts.

As the authors' research has shown, even non-expert graders show reliability when given appropriate specifications. We therefore offer the use of specifications, coupled with appropriate quality metrics as a contribution to improving the infrastructure of post-editing studies.

This chapter furthermore has demonstrated that a unified, functionalist definition of quality provides a way to address the major strands in the literature of quality. By clearly distinguishing product, process, and project aspects, as well as considering user notions of quality, the definition provides a way to reconcile often-contradictory perspectives and to allow scholars to be clear about what facets of quality matter to their studies, as well as fostering industry-academia collaboration within the same quality assessment framework.

The framework proposed in this chapter includes a unified definition of translation quality, a method of developing structured translation specifications, and two approaches to the assessment of translation quality in general and of a post-editing task in particular. The framework allows for assessment of any combination of the three aspects of translation: product, process, and project. Adoption of this framework by the post-editing community, along with refinement of the framework based on implementation experiences, would address the current lack of an explicit foundation for studies in post-editing effort. Much remains to be done on the proposed quality framework, but it provides a needed starting point.

Progress in measuring post-editing effort requires a principled, specifications-based, reliable assessment of translation quality.

Bibliography

Ben-Kiki, Oren, Clark Evans, and Ingy Döt NET. 2005. "YAML Ain't Markup Language Version 1.1." http://yaml.org/spec/1.1/current.html. (Accessed on 4/22, 2012).

Colina, Sonia. 2008."Translation Quality Evaluation: Empirical Evidence for a Functionalist Approach." *The Translator* 14.97-134.

Garvin, David. A. 1984. “What does ‘product quality’ really mean?” *Sloan Management Review*, Fall 1984, pp. 25-43.

Hague, Daryl, Melby, Alan, Zheng, Wang. 2011. "Surveying Translation Quality Assessment: A Specification Approach." *The Interpreter and Translator Trainer* (ITT): Volume 5, Number 2: 243-67

Housley, J.K. 2012. "Ruqual: A System for Assessing Post-editing." Brigham Young University. Department of Linguistics and English Language.

Krings, Hans P. (ed.) 2001. *Repairing Texts: Empirical Investigations of Machine Translation Post-editing Processes*. Kent, OH: Kent State University Press.

Linport. 2013. "Linport: The Language Interoperability Portfolio Project. linport.org." (Accessed on June 20134/23)

Melby, Alan. 1990. "The Mentions of Equivalence in Translation." *Meta*, vol. 35, n° 1, pp. 207-213. (URI http://id.erudit.org/iderudit/003618ar ; DOI: 10.7202/003618ar)

Melby, Alan, Jason Housley, Paul J Fields, and Emily Tuioti. 2012. "Reliably Assessing the Quality of Post-edited Translation Based on Formalized Structured Translation Specifications". *Proceedings of the*

AMTA 2012 Workshop on Post-editing Technology and Practice. 2012. (http://amta2012.amtaweb.org/AMTA2012Files/html/15/15_paper.pdf - accessed March 2013)

Melby, Alan K., Arle Lommel, Nathan Rasmussen & Jason Housley. 2011. "The Container Project." *First International Conference on Terminology, Languages, and Content Resources*, Seoul, South Korea.

Melby, Alan K, Alan D. Manning and Leticia Klemetz. 2007. Quality in Translation: A Lesson for the Study of Meaning. *Linguistics and the Human Sciences* 1.403-46.

O'Brien, Sharon. 2005. "Methodologies for Measuring the Correlations between Post-Editing Effort and Machine Translatability." *Machine Translation* 19.37-58.

Shrout, Patrick E., and Joseph L. Fleiss. 1979. "Intraclass Correlations: Uses in Assessing Rater Reliability." *Psychological Bulletin* 86.420-28.

Specia, Lucia, and Atefeh Farzindar. 2010. "Estimating Machine Translation Post-Editing Effort with HTER." *AMTA-2010 Workshop Bringing MT to the USER: MT Research and the Translation Industry*, Denver, Colorado.

WPTP. 2012. Proceedings of the AMTA 2012 Workshop on Post-editing Technology and Practice (http://amta2012.amtaweb.org/AMTA2012Files/html [accessed March 2013]), edited by Sharon O'Brien, Michel Simard, and Lucia Specia.

Notes

[1] It must be acknowledged that an annual report would generally be translated by a skilled financial translator rather than using machine translation and post-editing, but this example is illustrative only.

[2] Reviewers pointed out that "textual" would be a better label for this category. Nevertheless, the 2012 version of ISO/TS 11669 uses the label "linguistic" here and this article maintains that usage. Even conceding "textual" would be a better label, we nevertheless maintain that the parameters have specifically linguistic implications and correlates.

CHAPTER THIRTEEN

DEFINING LANGUAGE DEPENDENT POST-EDITING GUIDELINES: THE CASE OF THE LANGUAGE PAIR ENGLISH-SPANISH

CELIA RICO AND MARTÍN ARIANO

Abstract

This chapter reports part of the work carried out in the context of EDI-TA (Rico and Díez Orzas 2013a, 2013b), a research project focusing on the study of the different aspects of machine translation (MT) post-editing (PE) as an essential element in the translation workflow. More specifically, it focuses on the methodology used in the project for defining language dependent post-editing guidelines for the English-Spanish (EN-ES) pair.

After a detailed introduction to the project's objectives and main outcomes, the chapter goes on to describe the formal framework employed for designing PE guidelines. This is followed by a comprehensive account of how language dependent guidelines are defined and implemented, resulting in a whole set for the EN-ES combination, illustrated with actual examples. The chapter closes with a discussion of the value of this contribution to the field of MT post-editing as, so far, the specific definition of PE guidelines for the language pair concerned has been overlooked in the relevant literature, with a few exceptions (Guzmán 2007, 2008; Guerberof 2012).

Post-editing as an essential element in the translation workflow: the case of EDI-TA

While waiting for the advent of the "universal translator", one that is able to translate any type of text in any setting and language combination, Language Service Providers (LSP) have come to realize that it is worth making room for MT in the translation workflow. Numerous surveys and studies report on the successful implementation of MT as a business driver in the language industry (Binger et al 2012; DePalma 2009; Houlian 2009; Hurst 2008; van der Meer 2013, among others), which makes us look at post-editing (PE) as a practice gaining momentum. No matter what routes one follows in the identification of the different phases in the translation workflow (Dunne 2011:171; Gouadec 2007:12-26; Lewis *et al* 2007; Rico 2002; Zouncourides-Lull 2011:77; to name but a few), if one is to consider the use of MT, one might as well examine the effects of introducing PE in the process. How do you go about implementing Post-editing (PE) in your company as an LSP? How does PE differ from reviewing TM fuzzy matches? What is the post-editor's role and how can it fit in the company's workflow? How is quality to be assessed? How about productivity? Is it true that PE contributes to reducing costs? These are just a few of the many questions that might typically arise when contemplating the implementation of PE in a real setting.

In order to come up with adequate answers, the project EDI-TA[1] was launched in March 2012 with the following objectives:

- Contributing to defining metadata suitable for post-editing purposes and testing to what extent the PE process can be, thus, improved.
- Defining a practical methodology for post-editing, including the definition of PE guidelines for each language pair.
- Suggesting improvements to the MT system so as to optimize the output for post-editing specific purposes.
- Showing the feasibility and cost reduction of implementing post-editing in a real scenario.
- Identifying functions for improving post-editing tools.
- Defining a methodology for training post-editors.

These are certainly ambitious objectives set out with the purpose of comprehensively analysing the different aspects usually involved in a PE project. This chapter will only focus on the description of one of them, namely, the definition of PE guidelines for the EN-ES language pair. What follows here is an account of EDI-TA's workplan and outcomes so that the project's framework is adequately set out. Other findings have been reported in Rico and Díez Orzas (2013a, 2013b) and are duly referred to when necessary.

As a business-oriented R&D project, EDI-TA adopted a practical outlook. Accordingly, it used *Linguaserve*'s resources and translation workflow for setting up an experimental scenario along the following lines:

- MT output was produced by a rule-based system (Lucy Software).
- The language pairs involved in the project were EN-ES, ES-EN, ES-EU and ES-FR.
- The number of words per language pair was 50,000.
- The text typology referred to the following areas: information on cultural events, administrative directions to the citizens, online customer information from a department store, website content from a mobile company, and advertising material from an oil company.
- A translation memory system (Star Transit) was used as a tool for PE.
- The PE team consisted of four junior translators, one senior translator, and one project manager.

EDI-TA laid its groundwork following Allen's proposals (2003) and TAUS/CNGL guidelines (2012), defining PE as "the correction of machine-generated translation output to ensure it meets a level of quality negotiated in advance between client and post-editor". The project lasted 7 months, from March 2012 to September 2012, and work was organized into three phases, as summarized in Figure 1 below.

Phase 0 (*Initial training*) was set up with the aim of reaching a balance among team members' knowledge and expertise on PE tasks. This involved a series of practical sessions for learning the tools to be used, together with training on how to understand PE and apply guidelines. Most team members had never been faced with PE, which turned out to be an advantage for gathering valuable information on task perception and defining post-editors competences. The main findings on this can be found in Rico and Torrejón (2012), where the PE competences are defined according the tasks and processes involved (following Krings and Koby, 2001): source text-related processes, machine translation-related processes, target text production, target text evaluation, reference work-related processes, physical writing processes, global task-related processes.

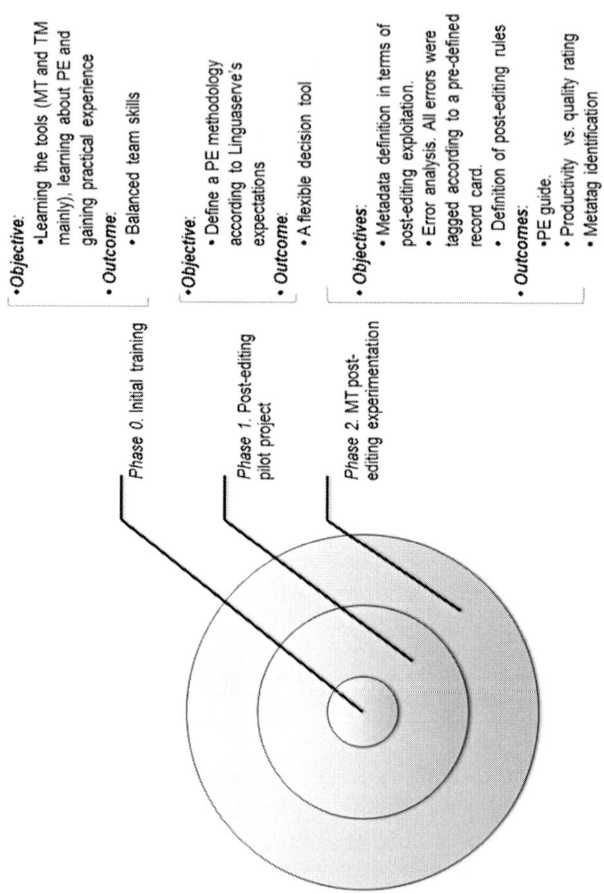

Figure 1: EDI-TA's phases

Phase 1 (*Post-editing pilot project*) focused on defining a post-editing methodology to respond to LSP's needs and expectations. *Linguaserve*'s working scenario was taken as the basis for setting up a pilot test that would serve as a reference in subsequent phases of the project. Core tasks in this phase included the following:

- **Web content selection**. A first set of web content was selected for this pilot test. Language pairs included EN-ES, ES-EN, ES-EU, ES-FR, and domains referred to online customer information in mobile technology, and administrative information for citizens.

- **Text analysis for post-editing**. This involved the identification of PE problems as well as the registration of MT output errors to be reported back to MT engine developers. The MT output was evaluated so as to detect possible errors (lexical, syntactic, and terminological). These were identified and handed over to MT developers for codification. This task is relevant because error detection contributes both to the evaluation of output quality and, thus, PE effort estimation (Guerberof 2009, O'Brien 2011, Plitt and Masselot 2010, Roturier 2004, Specia 2011, Specia *et al* 2009, Specia and Farzindar 2010, Thicke 2011), and to registering errors that later contribute to improving MT performance. As Thicke (2013a:16) puts it, "feeding back the corrections into the engine is the critical step in our MT process, where corrections from the post-editing phase are fed back into the system to improve the output. The ideal is to do this in as close to real time as possible in order to achieve maximum benefits from the post-editing process".
- **Metadata definition in terms of post-editing exploitation**. A first approach to metadata was made in this first part of the project. The extended metadata identification was undertaken in phase 2, following the Online MT System ITS 2.0 demonstration[2].

The main outcome of this pilot test was a *flexible decision tool* for implementing PE guidelines (Rico 2012) which allows for the definition of translation project specifications, including audience and purpose, among others. This tool was to be put to use in the remainder of the experiment, and specifies different text characteristics to be taken into account when establishing PE guidelines. As we will see later in this chapter, it also plays an essential role for the definition of guidelines to be applied. Other major outcomes of this phase were the acknowledgement that terminology management plays a key role in smoothing out the PE process, and that MT output analysis should be performed prior to PE.

Phase two (*MT Post-editing experimentation*), the last part of the project, focused on conducting a PE experiment on the basis of previous findings. The following tasks were undertaken:

- **Selecting a new set of web content**. This set amounted to a total of 50,000 words per language pair and made up the major corpus of the project. Text domains included online customer information from a department store, website content from a mobile company, and advertising material from an oil company.

- **Text analysis and experimentation for post-editing purposes.** Work conducted at this stage was similar to that of the previous phase: identification of PE problems, registration of MT output errors, reporting to MT engine developers.
- **Definition of post-editing guidelines.** PE guidelines were specified with the help of the flexible decision tool, as mentioned above. These included explicit reference on what to expect from the MT output in terms of quality and how to proceed in each case. The specific details of this process constitute the core of the present chapter.
- **Analysis of metadata contribution to improving PE processes.** An exhaustive analysis of metadata was carried out, following directions from The MultilingualWeb-LT (Language Technologies) Working Group. Each of them was evaluated towards determining its possible effect on a PE project, whether it would contribute to a better quality in the PE output. The list of meta tags identified as relevant for PE purposes were [translate], [localization note], [language information], [domain], [provenance], [localization quality][3].

The formal framework for specifying PE guidelines

A significant part of the project was devoted to the design of a suitable methodology that could be implemented in different contexts and which gave an answer to translators' requests and expectations when involved in PE (Guerberof 2013; Rico and Torrejón 2012; Thicke 2013b). The PE methodology implemented in EDI-TA involved three major steps: 1) preliminary analysis of MT output and other associated aspects; 2) defining PE guidelines, and 3) error reporting and quality control.

Preliminary analysis

The main objective of this preliminary analysis was to analyse MT output quality with a view to:

- Establishing PE patterns for each language combination in the project.
- Reporting on recurrent MT errors that could be fixed prior to starting the PE process.
- Reporting new terms to be included in project glossaries.

This analysis was assigned to the PE team manager who supervised the correct implementation of PE guidelines, and worked with the following tools and materials:

- Access to a representative sample of MT output in the project languages so that all necessary tests could be adequately conducted.
- Access to the MT engine with its complete functionalities.
- Availability to client's glossary for controlling term consistency.
- PE guidelines specification, including explicit reference on what to expect from the MT output in terms of quality and how to proceed in each case.

This preliminary step involved, then, the sequence of operations as shown in Figure 2. First, a sample text from the MT output was chosen with a view to conducting the different analyses which would later contribute to defining adequate PE guidelines. Next, term consistency was examined, revising term use according to project/client's glossaries and eventually reporting any deficiencies to the terminology management team. Recurrent MT errors were also identified and reported to the development team for system adjustment when necessary (and possible). With all these relevant facts at hand, the post-editor was now ready to take an informed decision in specifying PE guidelines.

Post-editing guidelines specification

The specification of PE guidelines involves gathering in a single source all aspects influencing the post-editor's decision so that PE directions can be easily drawn, adequately supported with actual examples and, more importantly, shared and replicated along different PE projects. In the case of EDI-TA, a *flexible decision tool* was designed (Rico, 2012), as mentioned above, so that all aspects involved in the PE project could be considered before taking a decision. This tool is used as a guide for taking PE decisions and it implies following a series of steps: 1) collecting data from project information; 2) collecting data from text profile; 3) deciding which language independent PE guidelines to activate; 4) determining language dependent guidelines to be used; 5) providing example cards for each of the guidelines.

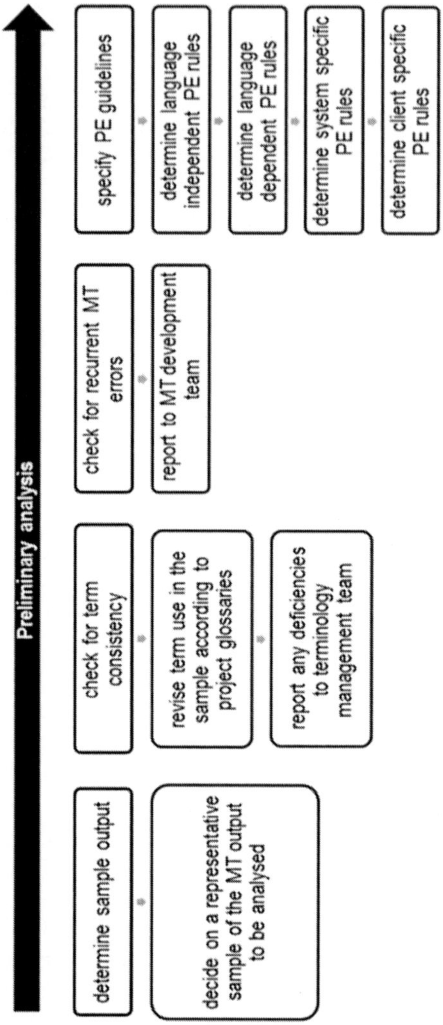

Figure 2: preliminary analysis

The first two steps result in two data sets providing practical information on the PE project and serving the PE team manager both to keep track of its most practical aspects and to gather broad knowledge on the task at hand. This information refers to client identification and description, text identification and description (including subject area), glossary availability and its quality, MT engine used in the process (with a reference to any specific guidelines activated, glossaries used, training data or interaction with translation memories, if any), MT output quality, communication channel, functionality of the translated content, the speed at which the PE output is to be handed, and the importance of impact on brand image (Rico, 2012:55-62). With this information, the post-editor determines PE guidelines with clear indications on how to proceed. These are, then, divided into two sets: language independent and language specific.

The set of language independent (LI) guidelines used in EDI-TA follow those laid out in Torrejón and Rico (2002) and refer to the following:

- *LI Guideline 01*. Fix any wrong term in the text, either technical or non-technical. Correct also any inconsistent use of the same term.
- *LI Guideline 02*. Fix any syntactic error which consists of wrong part of speech, incorrect phrase structure, wrong linear order of words and phrases.
- *LI Guideline 03*. Fix any morphological error which consists of wrong morphological form (number, gender, case, person, tense, mood, voice, aspect).
- *LI Guideline 04*. Fix any missing text (paragraph, sentence, phrase, word) as long as the omission interferes with the message being transferred.
- *LI Guideline 05*. Fix any misspelling.
- *LI Guideline 06*. Fix incorrect punctuation as long as it interferes with the message.
- *LI Guideline 07*. Do not fix stylistic problems, unless they interfere with the message.
- *LI Guideline 08*. Fix any offensive, inappropriate or culturally unacceptable information.

In the context of EDI-TA, these guidelines were illustrated with a set of post-editing example cards for each of the project's language combination. The aim was to use them, first, as training material and, later, as reference for further support. A comprehensive description of these and their implementation can be found in Rico and Torrejón (2012). The detail of language dependent guidelines is given later in the sections that follow.

Error reporting and quality control

The last step in the PE process is to report feedback to allow for MT improvement and/or source content optimization, which can help solve repetitive mistakes in the MT output. This involves: (a) conducting quality control according to on-demand client specifications and expectations; and (b) collecting samples of different post-editing issues in order to facilitate training of other fellow post-editors in the team. During this phase, post-editors would typically work in close collaboration with the PE team manager. They provide project feedback which would be used for improving MT performance, updating project glossaries and revising PE guidelines, following the process shown in Figure 3.

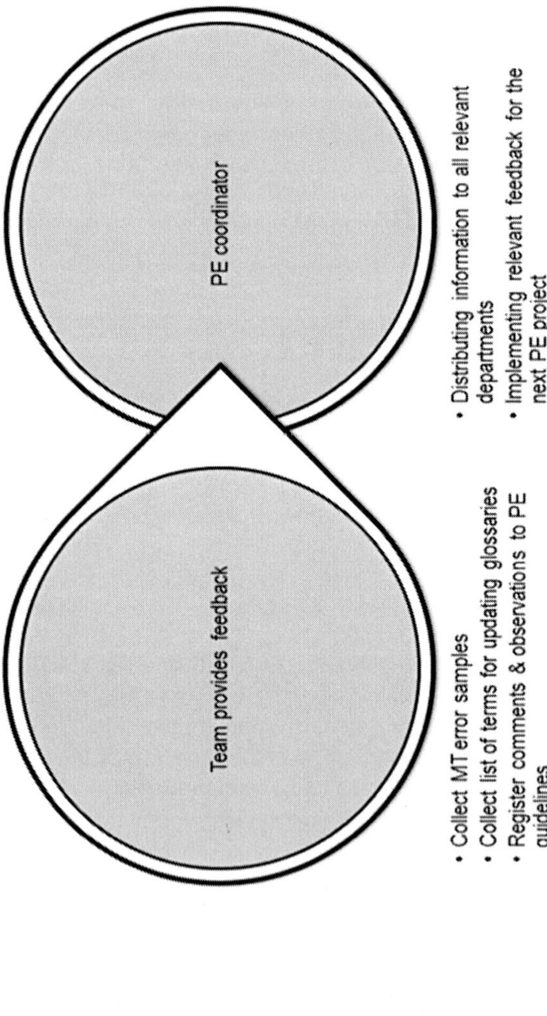

Figure 3: error reporting and quality control

PE guidelines for the combination EN-ES

This section will focus on a comprehensive account of how *language dependent guidelines* are defined and implemented, resulting in a whole set for the combination EN-ES, illustrated with actual examples. Together with the general PE guidelines referred to above, there might be some language specific ones that also need to be taken into consideration. These are, for instance, the use of a particular language locale, lexical collocations or specific sentence structures, how product names should be dealt with (whether there is an equivalent available or the source language name should be used), to name but a few. In the EN-ES language combination, guidelines would typically include instructions on how to deal with the translation of sentences using the infinitive tense, how to PE third person singular, or an indication of when to delete unnecessary uses of definitive article, among others.

In this connection, it is worth mentioning here the work of Guzmán (2007 and 2008) and Guerberof (2012) as, so far, they represent two of the major efforts in dealing with PE issues in the EN-ES language pair. The former presents a list of PE guidelines with a view to automating the process by using regular expressions so that "the most complex and repetitive linguistic errors can be identified and replaced with the right text in the MT output" (2007:49). In his two experiments, Guzmán analyses the MT system behaviour and identifies a series of linguistic patterns which are typically found when post-edited Spanish output is generated by a rule-based engine. These refer to the following:

- Misspellings in the use of accents
- Misspellings in the use of the Spanish coordinating conjunction "y" (*and*)
- Incorrect use of punctuation
- Incorrect use of the article before trademarks
- Grammatical agreement
- Wrong word order produced by *that* relative clause in the source
- The use of the Spanish reflexive pronoun "se"
- Style conventions: "usted" vs. impersonal construction
- Redundancies
- Mistranslations of *–ing* words
- Mistranslations of subordinate relative clauses
- Mistranslations of subordinate conditional clauses
- Mistranslations of verbs with several meanings

As for the work of Guerberof, she conducts an experiment with a view to analysing the correlation between machine-translated segments and fuzzy matches in terms of PE productivity, using Moses statistical MT engine. This has a bearing on this chapter because the languages involved in the study are English and Spanish and because this among the instructions given to translators and reviewers, those that refer to linguistic aspects are also valid for PE purposes (Guerberof, 2012: appendix C):

- Compliance with Spanish language grammar and spelling rules
- Imperative in English will be translated as infinitive in Spanish
- Infinitive in English will be translated as infinitive in Spanish
- Gerund in English will be translated with a noun in Spanish or an equivalent expression in the Spanish language
- All software options will be translated in Upper Case as in the source English text

In EDI-TA, language specific (LS) PE guidelines were defined after a thorough analysis of MT output and error identification and categorization. The resulting specifications are as follows:

- *LS EN-ES PE Guideline 01.* Replace upper-case letters for low-case letters, when applicable.
- *LS EN-ES PE Guideline 02.* Time format.
- *LS EN-ES PE Guideline 03.* Date format.
- *LS EN-ES PE Guideline 04.* Change order of figures when used as adjectives.
- *LS EN-ES PE Guideline 05.* Correct –ING adjectives by translating them as adjectives or relative clauses.
- *LS EN-ES PE Guideline 06.* Translate –ING forms as infinitive forms, when used as subject.
- *LS EN-ES PE Guideline 07.* Translate the infinitive phrase ‘to be + infinitive’ with a future tense.
- *LS EN-ES PE Guideline 08.* Translate the present continuous with a future tense, when used to refer to a future event with a future tense.
- *LS EN-ES PE Guideline 09.* Correct translation for verbs ‘estar/ser’.
- *LS EN-ES PE Guideline 10.* Replace the “de” preposition if appearing excessively in the text.

- *LS EN-ES PE Guideline 11.* Insert articles when necessary to convey the meaning.
- *LS EN-ES PE Guideline 12.* Translate 'for' as *para/por* as the case may be.

The example cards below illustrate how each of the guidelines are to be applied.

LS Example card 01. EN-ES PE Guideline 01: Replace upper-case letters for low-case letters, when applicable

EN > ES PE guideline 01: Replace upper-case letters for low-case letters, when applicable	
MT input: EN	The *Mayor* insisted it was a wonderful thing for the capital of Catalonia to give official recognition to the bold man that he was.
MT output: ES	El *Alcalde* insistió que fue una cosa maravillosa que la capital de Cataluña le diera reconocimiento oficial al hombre atrevido que fue.
PE output: ES	El *alcalde* insistió que fue una cosa maravillosa que la capital de Cataluña le diera reconocimiento oficial al hombre atrevido que fue.
Comments	It is a very well-known fact that English makes a much more abundant use of capital letters than Spanish does. MT systems will typically reproduce the use of capital letters as they appear in the input text in the output text. Incorrect capitalization is considered an orthographic mistake by the Real Academia Española [4], the authoritative institution which issues recommendations and guidelines regarding Spanish usage. In the example above, understanding of the text is not impeded; however, if the client asks for better quality, it might be necessary to correct the excessive use of capital letters.

LS Example card 02. EN-ES PE Guideline 02: Time format

EN > ES PE guideline 02: Time format	
MT input: EN	Numbers will cease to be distributed after *3 pm*.
MT output: ES	Los números se pararán de distribuir después de *3 p.m.*
PE output: ES	Los números se pararán de distribuir después de las *15:00 h.*
Comments	English and Spanish differ in the way they handle time formats. Whereas the English language uses a 12-hour-clock in which the 24 hours of the day are divided in two periods (*a.m* and *p.m.*), Spanish uses the military time consisting of a 24-hour-clock. Adjustments will have to be made during the post-editing of the text if the MT system has not been fed with the appropriate time conversion rules.

LS Example card 03. EN-ES PE Guideline 03: Date format

EN > ES PE guideline 03: Date format	
MT input: EN	If you want to discover the residences where bourgeoises and intellectuals from Barcelona lived in the 18th century.
MT output: ES	Si quieres descubrir las residencias donde los burgueses e intelectuales de Barcelona vivieron en el *18º Siglo*.
PE output: ES	Si quieres descubrir las residencias donde los burgueses e intelectuales de Barcelona vivieron en el *siglo XVIII*
Comments	The date format also poses a problem for MT since both languages have a different notation. The example above shows that while English uses ordinal numbers to write centuries, Spanish uses Roman numerals. Also, date notation for days, months and years differs between both languages. Whereas a format such as January 25th, 2013 may not cause problems, the same date written only with numbers (25-01-2013) will create a translation issue since the MT system will most likely not recognize the string of numbers as a date and, therefore, no conversion will be done.

LS Example card 04. EN-ES PE Guideline 04: Change order of figures when used as adjectives

EN > ES PE guideline 04: Change order of figures when used as adjectives	
MT input: EN	The building is expected to open during the *2013-2014* school year.
MT output: ES	Se espera que el edificio se abra durante el *2013-2014* año escolar.
PE output: ES	Se espera que el edificio se abra durante el año escolar *2013-2014.*
Comments	In English, figures can fulfil an adjectival function by putting them before a noun, whereas in Spanish this is not possible. MT systems will typically treat all numbers as placeables, that is, non-translatable information. It will be the post-editor's task to put the figure after the noun, when applicable.

LS Example card 05. EN-ES PE Guideline 05: Correct –ING adjectives by translating them as adjectives or relative clauses

EN > ES PE guideline 05: Correct –ING adjectives by translating them as adjectives or relative clauses	
MT input: EN	The *participating* schools this year are:
MT output: ES	El *participar* escolariza este año son:
PE output: ES	Las escuelas *participantes* este año son:
Comments	-ING words are extremely versatile and can fill many different grammatical roles. So much so that experts on controlled English advise against its use (Kohl (2013). This is certainly the case of Spanish, where the gerund form exists but it is not as productive as in English. In the example, it has an adjectival function modifying a noun, and the post-editor will have to translate it as either an adjective or a relative clause in Spanish. The MT output wrongly interpreted the gerund as a verb and therefore translated it as an infinitive.

LS Example card 06. EN-ES PE Guideline 06: Translate –ING forms as infinitive forms, when used as subject

EN > ES PE guideline 06: Translate –ING forms as infinitive forms, when used as subject	
MT input: EN	*Creating* a favourable ecosystem for the ICT sector will promote the creation of new businesses.
MT output: ES	*Creando* un ecosistema favorable para el sector de ICT promoverá la creación de nuevos negocios.
PE output: ES	*Crear* un ecosistema favorable para el sector de ICT promoverá la creación de nuevos negocios.
Comments	As explained in the previous guideline, gerunds can cause problems for machine-translation software. In this case, the –ING form should have been translated as an infinitive but the MT system misinterpreted it as an adjectival form. Again, the post-editor will have to make the necessary adjustments as the meaning is radically changed in the output version.

LS Example card 07. EN-ES PE Guideline 07: Translate the infinitive phrase 'to be + infinitive' with a future tense

EN > ES PE guideline 07: Translate the infinitive phrase 'to be + infinitive' with a future tense	
MT input: EN	The Council *is to cover* all requests for food grants.
MT output: ES	El Ayuntamiento *es cubrir* todas las peticiones de becas de comida.
PE output: ES	El Ayuntamiento *cubrirá* todas las peticiones de becas de comida
Comments	This type of infinitive phrase is used to refer to future events. It expresses near certainty that what is forecast will happen. In Spanish, though, there is no future tense which expresses that same degree of certainty. Nevertheless, that English structure is usually translated with a simple future tense in Spanish, which to some extent conveys the same meaning (see PE output above).

LS Example card 08. EN-ES PE Guideline 08: Translate the present continuous with a future tense, when used to refer to a future event with a future tense

EN > ES PE guideline 08: Translate the present continuous with a future tense, when used to refer to a future event	
MT input: EN	More than 6,000 families *will be receiving* individual school dinner grants.
MT output: ES	Más de 6.000 familias *estarán recibiendo* becas de comida de escuela individuales.
PE output: ES	Más de 6.000 familias *recibirán* becas de comida de escuela.
Comments	The present continuous (-ING form) can also be used in English to talk about formal arrangements in the future. A literal translation of this structure in Spanish would sound awkward and very colloquial. Given that the example sentence above consists of a piece of news from the City Council, a future gerund (*estarán recibiendo*) will have to be replaced in Spanish with a simple future (*recibirán*) to make the translation suitable for this given context.

LS Example card 09. EN-ES PE Guideline 09: Correct translation for verbs 'estar/ser'

EN > ES PE guideline 09: Correct translation for verbs 'estar/ser'	
MT input: EN	This first competition *is open* to all shops
MT output: ES	Esta primera competición *es|está* abierta a todas las tiendas
PE output: ES	Esta primera competición *está* abierta a todas las tiendas
Comments	The verb 'to be' in English can be translated as either *ser* or *estar* in Spanish, although in a few cases they could be used interchangeably. Being aware of this difference, the MT system developers have created an algorithm that presents the user with both verbs so the post-editor can choose which one applies depending on the context.

LS Example card 10. EN-ES PE Guideline 10: Replace the "de" preposition if appearing excessively in the text

EN > ES PE guideline 10: Replace the "de" preposition if appearing excessively in the text	
MT input: EN	This is a pledge from the Council, which will be earmarking 2.5 million euros in the coming days, to cover the requests for *dinner grants from families* on the waiting list (...)
MT output: ES	Esto es una promesa del Consejo, que estará destinando 2,5 millones de euros en los próximos días, para cubrir las peticiones de *becas de comida de familias* en la lista de espera (...)
PE output: ES	Esto es una promesa del Consejo, que estará destinando 2,5 millones de euros en los próximos días, para cubrir las peticiones de *becas de comida de parte de familias* en la lista de espera (...)
Comments	Prepositional phrases in Spanish present some difficulties for the MT system, especially when it comes to using the preposition 'de', which is the main connecting device used in this language. The 22nd edition of the Diccionario de la Real Academia lists 27 different uses and meanings for this preposition (such as possession, precedence, content, material, subject, cause, etc.). MT systems will most likely not differentiate all these nuances and will typically translate noun clusters into prepositional phrases connected with 'de'. For the sake of clarity, it is advisable for the post-editor to critically analyse the MT output and try to spot any possible ambiguity. In the example above, by replacing a simple 'de' with the phrase 'de parte de' the meaning of precedence is more clearly and univocally conveyed[5].

LS Example card 11. EN-ES PE Guideline 11: Insert articles when necessary to convey the meaning

EN > ES PE guideline 11: Insert articles when necessary to convey the meaning	
MT input: EN	A pianist with a passion for *taxidermy*, one of the leaders of the "outraged" people's movement, a legendary Galician singer, the last representative of hippy *culture* and a couple of "squatters".
MT output: ES	Un pianista con una pasión por *taxidermia*, uno de los líderes del movimiento de la gente "escandalizada", un cantante de gallego legendario, el último representante de *cultura* hippie y un par de "ocupantes ilegales".
PE output: ES	Un pianista con una pasión por *la taxidermia*, uno de los líderes del movimiento de la gente "escandalizada", un cantante de gallego legendario, el último representante de *la cultura* hippie y un par de "ocupantes ilegales".
Comments	English tends to make a lesser use of definite articles than Spanish. Again, although the meaning is correctly conveyed in the MT output, the absence of definite articles for the specific nouns 'taxidermia' and 'cultura' will strike the reader as extremely odd, since the syntactic rules of Spanish call for the insertion of definite articles in such cases.

LS Example card 12. EN-ES PE Guideline 12: Translate 'for' as *para/por* as the case may be

EN > ES PE guideline 12: Translate 'for' as *para/por* as the case may be	
MT input: EN	To create a favourable environment *for* businesses and entrepreneurs in the ICT sector.
MT output: ES	Crear un ambiente favorable *para|por* negocios y empresarios en el sector de ICT
PE output: ES	Crear un ambiente favorable *para* negocios y empresarios en el sector de ICT.
Comments	Like the 'to be' and 'ser/estar' situation, the preposition 'for' has two equivalents in Spanish: 'por' and 'para'.

Conclusion

We have presented here part of the work conducted in EDI-TA, a comprehensive project involving practical aspects of PE, specifically focusing on the definition of language dependent PE guidelines. These have been illustrated for the language pair English-Spanish with a series of example cards with the aim of offering an exhaustive description of how guidelines are to be implemented. In this sense, we believe that ours is a valuable contribution since we provide, so to speak, off-the-shelf instructions which can be readily put to use in scenarios comparable to the one described here. Guidelines have been developed following the methodology laid out in the decision tool, also designed in the context of EDI-TA (Rico 2012), which takes into account different project specifications. Accordingly, PE guidelines would need to be adapted for different contexts. In this respect, we understand that further assessment of their applicability would be desirable. All in all, the work reported here represents an attempt at conducting an in-depth exam on the errors resulting from using a rule-based MT engine for translating from English into Spanish, a combination widely used in the translation industry. We realize that some guidelines are more critical than others since not all mistakes made by MT software impede understanding. However, it is the accumulation of all these minor mistakes what may lead to some misunderstanding of the text on the part of the reader. Likewise, the level of PE will also depend on the client's specifications and expectations as well as on the purpose of the text.

In any case, it is important to bear in mind that this chapter is not meant to be the ultimate guide on EN>ES post-editing and is limited in scope. Translation is a multifaceted activity where many factors come into play and the same holds true for post-editing. For instance, the number of PE guidelines could be easily extended and is largely dependent on the type of MT software used. As stated above, all findings draw on the experiment carried out with an RBMT software. Undoubtedly, we would encounter other issues if we used a statistical MT engine. Moreover, the MT system we worked with had not been previously customized and results could change significantly if we fine-tuned the software.

Bibliography

Allen, Jeff. 2003. "Post-editing." *Computers and Translation: A Translators Guide*, edited by Harold L. Somers, Benjamins Translation Library, 35, 297-317. Amsterdam: John Benjamins.

Binger, Gregory and Dion Wiggins. 2012. "The Evolution of Translation." *Asia Online*. Accessed January 11, 2014, http://www.asiaonline.net/Webinars.aspx.

DePalma, Don. 2009. "The Business Case for Machine Translation." *Common Sense Advisory*. Accessed January 11, 2014, http://www.mt-archive.info/MTS-2009-DePalma-ppt.pdf.

Dunne, Keiran J. 2011. "From Vicious to Virtuous Cycle. Customer-focused Quality Management using ISO and Agile." *Translation and Localization Project Management*, ATA Series XVI, 153-187. Amsterdam/Philadelphia: John Benjamins.

Gouadec, Daniel. 2007. *Translation as a Profession*. Amsterdam/Philadelphia: John Benjamins.

Guerberof, Anna. 2009. "Productivity and Quality in MT Post-editing" *MT Summit 2009 Workshop 3.* Accessed January 11, 2014, http://www.mt-archive.info/ MTS-2009-TOC.htm.

—. 2012. "Productivity and Quality in the Post-editing of Outputs from Translation Memories and Machine Translation." PhD diss., Universitat Rovira y Virgili. Accessed January 11, 2014, http://hdl.handle.net/ 10803/90247.

—. 2013. "What do Professional Translators Think about Post-editing?" *JosTrans* 19:75–95. Accessed January 11, 2014, http://www.jostrans.org/ issue19/issue19_toc.php

Guzmán, Rafael. 2007. "Automating MT Post-editing using Regular Expressions." *Multilingual* 90:49-52.

—. 2008. "Advanced Automatic MT Post-editing." *Multilingual, 95:* 52-57.

Houlihan, David. 2009. *Translating Product Documentation: The Right Balance between Cost and Quality in the Localization Chain.* Accessed January 11, 2014, http://aberdeen.com/Aberdeen-Library/6230/RA-translation-product-documentation.aspx.

Hurst, Sophie. 2008. "Trends in Automated Translation in Today's Global Business." *The Eighth Conference of the Association for Machine Translation in the Americas*, Waikiki, Hawaii, October 21-25. Accessed January 11, 2014, http://www.amtaweb.org/papers/ 4.19_Hurst2008.pdf.

Kohl, John. 2013. *The Global English Style Guide: Writing Clear, Translatable Documentation for a Global Market*. Cary, N.C.: SAS Institute.

Krings, Hans P. and Geoffrey Koby, ed., 2001. *Repairing Texts. Empirical Investigations of Machine Translation Post-Editing Processes*. Kent: The Kent State University Press.

Lewis, David, Stephen Curran, Gavin Doherty, Kevin Feeney, Nikiforos Karamanis, Saturnino Luz, and John Mcauley. 2007. "Supporting Flexibility and Awareness in Localisation Workflows" *Localisation Focus*, 8 (1): 29–38. Accessed January 11, 2014, http://www.localisation.ie/resources/lfresearch/Vol8_1LewisCurranDohertyetAl.pdf.

MultilingualWeb-LT Working Group. Accessed January 11, 2014, http://www.w3.org/International/multilingualweb/lt/

O'Brien, Sharon. 2011. "Towards Predicting Post-editing Productivity." *Machine Translation 25*(3): 197-215.

Plitt, Mirko and Francois Masselot. 2010. "A Productivity Test of Statistical Machine Translation." *The Prague Bulletin of Mathematical Linguistics* 93: 7-16.

Rico, Celia. 2002. "Translation and Project Management." *Translation Journal*, vol. 6, 4. Accessed January 11, 2014, http://www.bokorlang.com/journal/22project.htm,

—. 2012. "A Flexible Decision Tool for Implementing Post-editing Guidelines." *Localisation Focus*, vol. 11, 1: 54-66. Accessed January 11, 2014, http://www.localisation.ie/resources/locfocus/ LocalisationFocusVol11_1Web.pdf_2012.

Rico, Celia, and Pedro Luis Díez Orzas. 2013a. "EDI-TA: Training Methodology for Machine Translation Post-editing." *Multilingualweb-LT Deliverable 4.1.4. Annex II*, public report. Accessed January 11, 2014, http://www.w3.org/International/multilingualweb/lt/wiki/images/d/d4/ D4.1.4.Annex_II_EDI-TA_Training.pdf.

Rico, Celia and Pedro Luis Díez Orzas. 2013b. "EDI-TA: Post-editing Methodology for Machine Translation." *Multilingualweb-LT Deliverable 4.1.4. Annex I*, public report. Accessed January 11, 2014, http://www.w3.org/International/multilingualweb/lt/wiki/images/1/1f/ D4.1.4.Annex_I_EDI-TA_Methology.pdf.

Rico, Celia and Enrique Torrejón. 2012. "Skills and Profile of the New Role of the Translator as MT Post-editor." *Tradumàtica. Post-editing, a paradigm shift?* 10: 166-178. Accessed January 11, 2014, http://revistes.uab.cat/tradumatica/issue/view/3.

Roturier, Johann. 2004. "Assessing a set of Controlled Language rules: Can they Improve the Performance of Commercial Machine Translation Systems?" *Translating and the Computer 26*. London: Aslib.

Ruiz, Remedios. 2003. "A Specification and Validating Parser for Simplified Technical Spanish." M.Sc. Thesis, University of Limerick.

Specia, Lucia. 2011. "Exploiting Objective Annotations for Measuring Translation Post-editing Effort." *Proceedings of the EAMT*. Leuven, Belgium. Accessed January 11, 2014, http://www.ccl.kuleuven.be/EAMT2011/.

Specia, Lucia, Nicola Cancedda, Marc Dymetman, Maroc Turchi, and Nello Cristianini. 2009. "Estimating the Sentence-Level Quality of Machine Translation Systems." *13th Annual Meeting of the European Association for Machine Translation (EAMT-2009)*, 28-35. Barcelona, Spain.

Specia, Lucia, and Atefeh Farzindar. 2010. "Estimating Machine Translation Post-Editing Effort with HTER." *AMTA-2010 Workshop Bringing MT to the User: MT Research and the Translation Industry*. Denver, Colorado. Accessed January 11, 2014, http://transsearch.iro.umontreal.ca/rali/sites/default/files/publis/Specia-Farzindar_AMTA_workshop.pdf.

TAUS/CNGL *Machine Translation Post-editing guidelines*. Accessed January 11, 2014, http://www.cngl.ie/node/2542, 2012.

Thicke, Lori. 2011. "Improving MT Results: A Study" *Multilingual* (February 2011): 37-40.

—. 2013a. "The Industrial Process for Quality Machine Translation" *JosTrans*, 19. Accessed January 11, 2014, http://www.jostrans.org/issue19/issue19_toc.php.

—. 2013b. "Post-editor Shortage and MT" *Multilingual*, Jan/Feb. 2013: 42-44.

Torrejón, Enrique and Celia Rico. 2002. "Controlled Translation: A New Teaching Scenario Tailor-made for the Translation Industry" *6th EAMT Workshop, Teaching Machine Translation*, Nov. 14-15, 2002. European Association for Machine Translation, pp. 107-116.

Van der Meer, Jaap. 2013. *Translation in the 21st Century. Choose Your Own Translation Future.* Accessed January 11, 2014, http://www.translationautomation.com/downloads/finish/57-articles/368-choose-your-own-translation-future.

Zouncourides-Lull, Alexandra. 2011. "Applying PMI Methodology to Translation and Localization Projects." *Translation and Localization Project Management*, ATA Series XVI, Amsterdam/Philadelphia: John Benjamins: 71- 93.

Notes

[1] EDI-TA is a business oriented R&D project conducted by *Linguaserve* and *Universidad Europea de Madrid*, as part of the tasks that *Linguaserve* is developing within *The MultilingualWeb-LT (Language Technologies) Working Group*, which belongs to the W3C Internationalization Activity and the MultilingualWeb community. The MultilingualWeb-LT Working Group receives funding by the European Commission (project name LT-Web) through the Seventh Framework Programme (FP7) Grant Agreement No. 287815.

[2] Identification of metadata relevant for PE purposes is based on http://www.w3.org/TR/2012/WD-its20-20120829/#datacategory-description [accessed January 11 2014]

[3] While it is not the object of this chapter to focus on a full description of meta tags, the complete report can be found at http://www.w3.org/International/multilingualweb/lt/wiki/WP4#WP4:_Online_MT_Systems [accessed January 11 2014]

[4] Real Academia Española: http://www.rae.es/rae.html

[5] For a detailed explanation of the use of "de", see Ruiz (2003, 44-45)